Facts About Oregon

1st Edition

Andrea Jarvela

WestWinds Press™

First edition published 2000

ISBN 1-55868-472-7
ISSN 1529-8949

Key title: The Oregon Almanac

WestWinds Press™
An imprint of Graphic Arts Center Publishing Company
P.O. Box 10306, Portland, Oregon 97296-0306, 503-226-2402; www.gacpc.com

President/Publisher: Charles M. Hopkins
Editorial staff: Douglas A. Pfeiffer, Timothy W. Frew, Ellen Harkins Wheat, Tricia Brown, Jean Andrews, Alicia I. Paulson
Production staff: Richard L. Owsiany, Susan Dupere
Editor: Heath Lynn Silberfeld / Enough Said
Cover and interior designer: Michelle Taverniti
Cover art: Mindy Dwyer
Maps: Gray Mouse Graphics

Printed in the United States of America

Contents

Acknowledgments, 5
Permission, Credits for Photos and Illustrations, 6
Miscellaneous Facts About Oregon, 7
Map of Oregon, 8

Agriculture, 10
Airports, 14
American Indians, 15
Amphibians and Reptiles, 17
Archives, 18
Area Codes, 19
Arts, 19
Astoria, 20
Avalanches, 21

Basin and Range Province, 21
Bend, 21
Birds, 22
Bonneville Power Administration, 24

Caves, 24
Charities, 25
Cities and Towns, 26
Coast, 29
Columbia Plateau, 30
Columbia River and Columbia River Gorge, 31
Congressional Delegation, 32
Constitution, 34
Consular Corps, 34
Counties, 34
Covered Bridges, 40

Dams, 41
Desert, 45
Dunes, 45

Earthquakes, 45
Elected Officials, 46
Endangered Species, 47
Estuaries, 49
Eugene, 50
Explorers, 50

Fairs and Festivals, 52
Fire Lookouts, 56
Fish and Fishing, 57
Fish Hatcheries, 58
Forests, 61
Forest Products Industry, 62
Fossils, 65

Gold, 66
Golf, 67
Government, 68
Governors, 71

Hells Canyon and the Snake River, 73
High Technology, 73
History, 74
Hood River, 82
Hot Springs 82
Hunting, 85

International Trade, 86

Judiciary, 88

Klamath Falls, 90

Lakes and Reservoirs, 91
Laws, 93
Legislature, 93
Lewis and Clark, 97
Libraries, 98
Lighthouses, 102
Lost Treasure, 104

Mammals, 105
Marine Pilots, 106
Medford, 106
Microbreweries, 107
Mileage Chart, 108
Military, 108
Minimum Wage, 110
Mountains, 111
Mount Hood, 112
Museums, 113
Mushrooms, 116

National Forests, 117
National Grassland, 122
National Natural Landmarks, 122
National Parks, Monuments, and Recreation Areas, 123
National Register of Historic Places, 126
National Wildlife Refuges, 128
Newberry Crater, 130
Newspapers and Periodicals, 131

Oregon Trail, 133
Outdoor Recreation, 135

PAC-10, 138
Pendleton, 139
Performing Arts, 139
Petroglyphs and Pictographs, 142
Physical Geography, 143
Plants, 146
Population, 148
Portland, 148
Ports, 150
Prisons, 152

Radio and Television Stations, 154
Railroads, 157
Regional Governments, 159
Rivers, 159
Roads and Highways, 160
Rocks and Gems, 161
Rodeos, 163

Salem, 164
Salmon, 165
Scenic Drives, 166
Seals and Sea Lions, 169
Shipwrecks, 169
Skiing and Snowboarding, 171
Special Service Districts, 172
Speed Limits, 173
Sports Teams, 173
State Parks and Recreation Areas, 175
State Symbols, 180

Taxes, 181
The Dalles, 183
Tides, 183
Transportation, 184
Travel and Tourism, 188

Universities and Colleges, 188

Vehicle Registration and Driver's Licenses, 193
Vital Statistics, 193
Volcanoes and Volcanism, 194
Voting and Elections, 196

Waterfalls, 198
Weather and Climate, 199
Wetlands, 199
Whitewater Kayaking and River Running, 201
Wild and Scenic Rivers, 203
Wild Horses and Burros, 203
Wilderness, 204
Willamette River and Valley, 206
Windsurfing, 206
Wine, 207

Zip Codes, 211
Zoos and Aquariums, 216

News Highlights, 1998-1999, 217
Further Reading, 222
Appendix: Oregon State Constitution Preamble and Declaration of Rights, 226
Index, 233

Acknowledgments

This edition of The Oregon Almanac™ *was compiled from information gleaned from a variety of sources, including publications, information posted on organization websites, and personal interviews with local, state, and federal government agencies, and other organizations and individuals, including (but not limited to) those listed below. In addition, my thanks to Charles Bookman and Elizabeth Brinkley for their valuable contributions to the writing of this book.*

Aviation & Aerospace Almanac
Bonneville Power Administration
The Foundation Center, New York
National Academy of Television Arts & Sciences, Pacific Northwest
National Audubon Society
National Oceanic and Atmospheric Administration (National Weather Service, Western Regional Climate Center, National Marine Fisheries)
National Register of Historic Places
Northwest Weather and Avalanche Center
Oregon Agricultural Statistics Service
Oregon Department of Agriculture
Oregon Department of Corrections
Oregon Department of Fish & Wildlife
Oregon Department of Human Services
Oregon Department of Revenue
Oregon Department of State Police
Oregon Department of Transportation
Oregon Economic & Community Development Department
Oregon Legislative Fiscal Office
Oregon Library Association
Oregon Office of the Secretary of State
Oregon State Legislature
Oregon State Library
Oregon State Parks and Recreation Department
Oregon Tourism Commission
The Oregonian
Pacific 10 Conference
Pacific Northwest Seismograph Network
Portland Trail Blazers
Portland Winterhawks
Professional Golfers Association
The Urban Institute, Washington, DC
U.S. Army
U.S. Army Corps of Engineers
U.S. Bureau of Land Management
U.S. Bureau of the Census (*Statistical Abstracts of the United States*)
U.S. Coast Guard, 13th Coast Guard District
U.S. Department of Agriculture, Forest Service (and individual national forests)
U.S. Department of the Interior; National Parks Service, Bureau of Indian Affairs
U.S. Department of Transportation
U.S. Fish and Wildlife Service
U.S. Geological Survey, Cascades Volcano Observatory

Permissions/Credits for Photos and Illustrations

Page 10, 16, Ray Atkeson. 19, Jennifer Donahoe Photography. 21, Andrea Jarvela. 22, Susan Dupere. 23, Gretchen Daiber. 25, Ray Atkeson. 26, Susan Dupere. 30, 38, 45, Ray Atkeson. 51, Andrea Jarvela. 53, 56, Susan Dupere. 58, Robert M. Reynolds. 61, Andrea Jarvela. 65, Robert M. Reynolds. 66, Andrea Jarvela. 67, Rick Schafer. 72, C. Bruce Forster. 73, Ray Atkeson. 79, Oregon Historical Society. 92, Susan Dupere. 103, Rick Schafer. 107, Loren Nelson. 111, Russ Heinl. 112, Susan Dupere. 115, The Oregon Museum of Science and Industry. 123, Ken Brown. 125, Robert M. Reynolds. 126, Russ Heinl. 129, Ray Atkeson. 130, Lyn Topinka, Cascades Volcano Observatory. 132, The Oregonian. 137, Susan Dupere. 140, Oregon Ballet Theatre. 143, Andrea Jarvela. 146, Susan Dupere. 149, Joel Davis / The Oregonian. 151, Russ Heinl. 160, Susan Dupere. 164, Ray Atkeson. 168, Russ Heinl. 169, Gretchen Daiber. 170, U.S. Coast Guard. 172, Ray Atkeson. 174, Ernie Sapigao. 180, Joyce Bergen. 184, 189, 195, Ray Atkeson. 198, 202, 207, Susan Dupere. 209, Robert M. Reynolds.

See **Suggested Reading** for sources of photos, illustrations, and text excerpts. Every attempt has been made to locate owners of art and photos to obtain permission to reproduce their work.

Miscellaneous Facts About Oregon

Motto: *"She Flies with Her Own Wings."*

Nickname: *The Beaver State.*

State capital: *Salem.*

Organized as a territory: *1848.*

Entered the Union: *1859.*

Governor: *John A. Kitzhaber.*

State population: *3,243,000 (1998).*

Population density: *About 33.8 persons per square mile.*

Largest city in population: *Portland, 509,610.*

Largest city in area: *Portland, 124.7 square miles.*

Largest county in population: *Multnomah County, 641,900.*

Largest county in area: *Harney County, 10,228 square miles.*

Per capita personal income: *$24,393 (1997), 23rd in nation.*

Total land area: *97,073 square miles, 10th largest state.*

Total water area: *1,129 square miles of inland and coastal waters.*

Coastline: *296 miles.*

Highest point: *Mount Hood, 11,235 feet.*

Lowest point: *Sea level, Pacific Ocean.*

Stream miles: *112,640, enough to go all the way around the Earth four and a half times.*

Deepest lake: *Crater Lake, 1,932 feet deep, deepest in the country.*

Longest river completely in state: *Willamette River, 309 miles.*

Shortest river: *"D" River in Lincoln City, shortest in the world.*

Highest temperature: *119° F, at Prineville, July 29, 1898, and at Pendleton, August 10, 1898.*

Lowest temperatures: *-54° F at Ukiah, February 9, 1933, and at Seneca, February 10, 1933.*

Busiest airport: *Portland International Airport.*

Largest newspaper: The Oregonian, *published in Portland.*

Country's largest producer: *Hazelnuts.*

State song: *"Oregon, My Oregon."*

State flower: *Oregon grape.*

State tree: *Douglas fir.*

State nut: *Hazelnut.*

State animal: *American beaver.*

State bird: *Western meadowlark.*

State fish: *Chinook salmon.*

State insect: *Oregon swallowtail butterfly.*

State seashell: *Oregon hairy triton.*

State rock: *Thunderegg.*

State gemstone: *Sunstone.*

Largest natural lake: *Upper Klamath Lake.*

Largest free-standing wooden structure: *Tillimook Naval Air Station Museum.*

Largest miniature-gun collection: *Favell Museum of Western Art and Artifacts.*

Largest wheat-exporting center in the U.S.: *Portland.*

Longest linear park: *OC&E Woods Line State Park, 110.4 miles.*

Largest lake: *Klamath Lake.*

Highest waterfall: *Multnomah Falls, 620 feet high.*

Worst forest fire: *355,000 acres, in 1930, in Tillimook County.*

Least annual rainfall average: *5 inches in the Alvord Desert.*

Tallest sand dunes: *Average 250 feet high; some more than 500 feet.*

Deepest Canyon: *Hells Canyon, 8,430 feet deep.*

Most ponderosa pine harvested in U.S.: *Klamath Falls.*

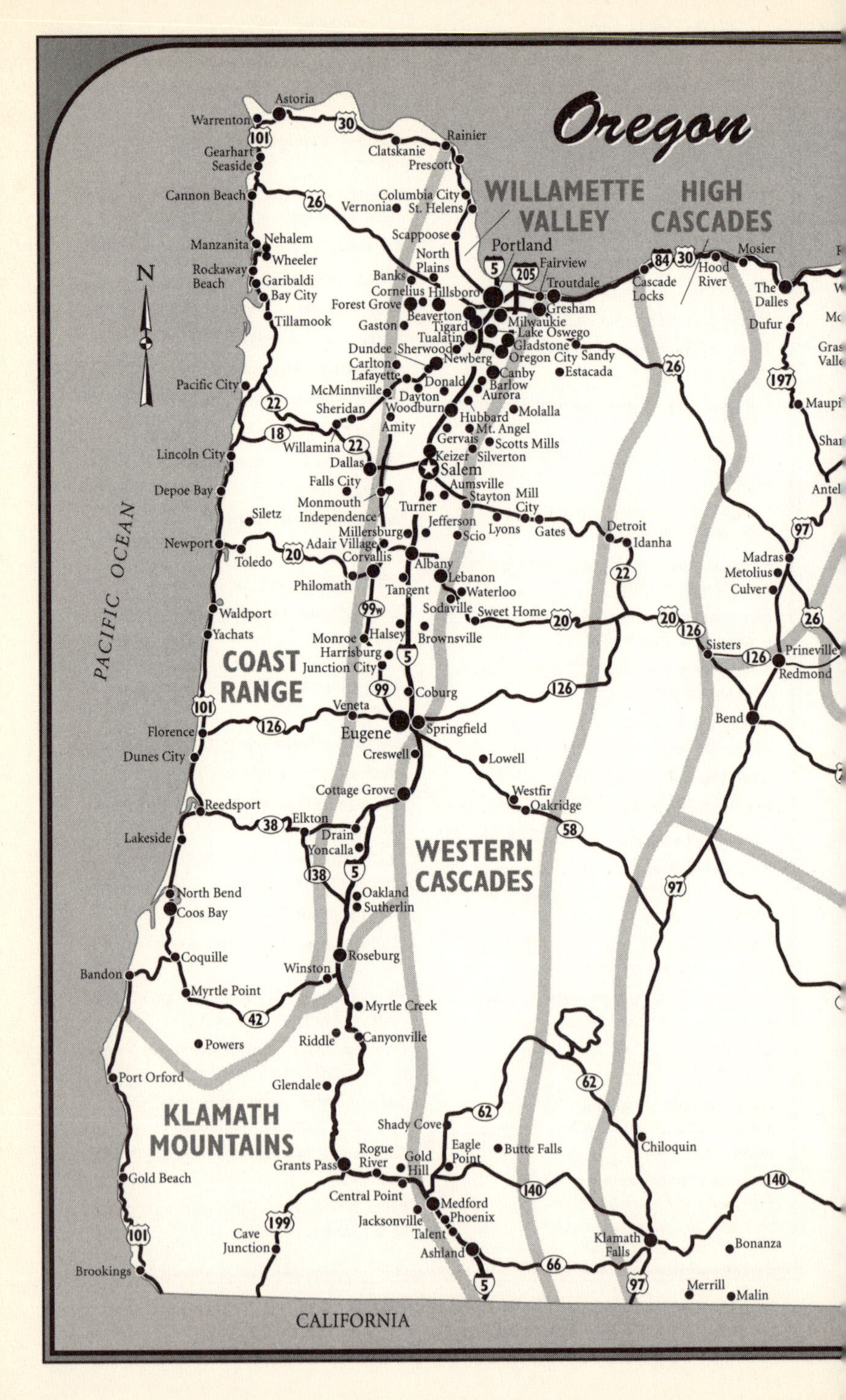
Oregon
WILLAMETTE VALLEY
HIGH CASCADES
COAST RANGE
WESTERN CASCADES
KLAMATH MOUNTAINS
PACIFIC OCEAN
CALIFORNIA
N
Astoria
Warrenton
Gearhart
Seaside
Cannon Beach
Manzanita
Nehalem
Wheeler
Rockaway Beach
Garibaldi
Bay City
Tillamook
Pacific City
Lincoln City
Depoe Bay
Siletz
Newport
Toledo
Waldport
Yachats
Florence
Dunes City
Reedsport
Lakeside
North Bend
Coos Bay
Coquille
Bandon
Myrtle Point
Powers
Port Orford
Gold Beach
Brookings
Rainier
Clatskanie
Prescott
Columbia City
Vernonia
St. Helens
Scappoose
North Plains
Portland
Fairview
Troutdale
Gresham
Banks
Cornelius
Hillsboro
Forest Grove
Beaverton
Tigard
Gaston
Tualatin
Milwaukie
Lake Oswego
Gladstone
Dundee
Sherwood
Newberg
Oregon City
Sandy
Estacada
Carlton
Lafayette
McMinnville
Donald
Canby
Barlow
Aurora
Dayton
Sheridan
Woodburn
Hubbard
Molalla
Amity
Mt. Angel
Gervais
Scotts Mills
Willamina
Dallas
Keizer
Silverton
Salem
Falls City
Aumsville
Stayton
Mill City
Monmouth
Independence
Turner
Jefferson
Lyons
Gates
Detroit
Idanha
Millersburg
Scio
Adair Village
Corvallis
Albany
Philomath
Lebanon
Tangent
Waterloo
Sodaville
Sweet Home
Monroe
Halsey
Brownsville
Harrisburg
Junction City
Coburg
Veneta
Eugene
Springfield
Creswell
Lowell
Cottage Grove
Westfir
Oakridge
Elkton
Drain
Yoncalla
Oakland
Sutherlin
Roseburg
Winston
Myrtle Creek
Riddle
Canyonville
Glendale
Shady Cove
Eagle Point
Butte Falls
Rogue River
Gold Hill
Grants Pass
Central Point
Medford
Jacksonville
Phoenix
Talent
Ashland
Cave Junction
Chiloquin
Klamath Falls
Bonanza
Merrill
Malin
Cascade Locks
Hood River
Mosier
The Dalles
Dufur
Madras
Metolius
Culver
Sisters
Prineville
Redmond
Bend
101
30
26
5
205
84
22
18
20
99W
99
126
38
138
42
58
97
197
62
140
199
66

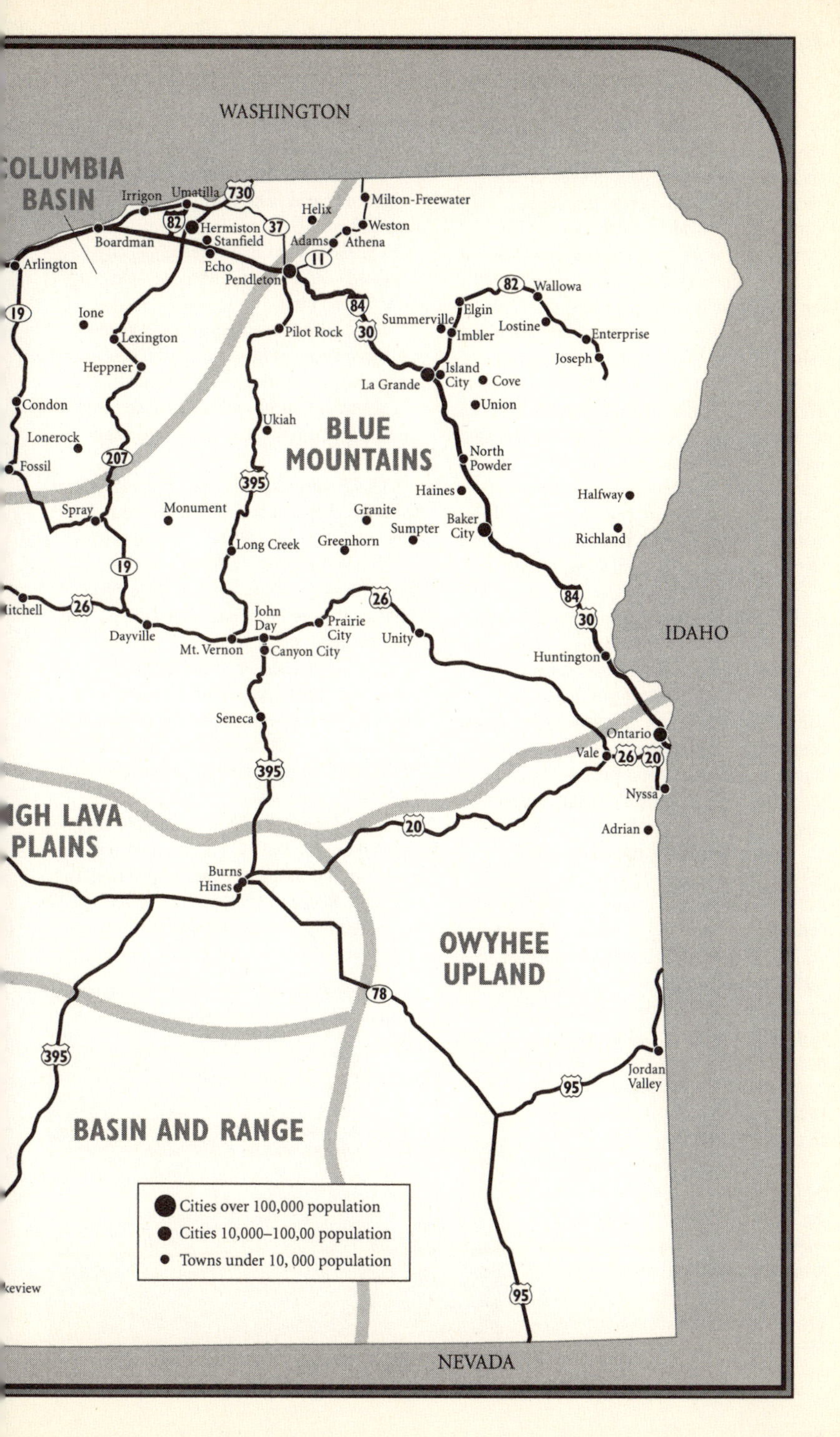
WASHINGTON
COLUMBIA BASIN
Irrigon
Umatilla
730
82
Hermiston
37
Stanfield
Boardman
Echo
Pendleton
Helix
Milton-Freewater
Weston
Adams
Athena
11
Arlington
19
Ione
Lexington
Heppner
Condon
Lonerock
Fossil
207
Spray
19
Monument
Pilot Rock
Ukiah
395
Long Creek
84
30
Summerville
Elgin
Imbler
82
Wallowa
Lostine
Enterprise
Joseph
La Grande
Island City
Cove
Union
BLUE MOUNTAINS
North Powder
Haines
Granite
Sumpter
Greenhorn
Baker City
Halfway
Richland
84
30
IDAHO
Huntington
26
John Day
Prairie City
Unity
Dayville
Mt. Vernon
Canyon City
Seneca
395
Ontario
Vale
26
20
Nyssa
Adrian
HIGH LAVA PLAINS
20
Burns
Hines
OWYHEE UPLAND
78
395
Jordan Valley
95
BASIN AND RANGE
Cities over 100,000 population
Cities 10,000–100,00 population
Towns under 10, 000 population
95
NEVADA

Agriculture

Agriculture is a staple of Oregon's economy. The state is the leading U.S. producer of important crops such as peppermint, ryegrass seed, blackberries, hazelnuts, and Christmas trees and is a leading producer of seed crops, berries, fruits, nuts, vegetables, and horticultural products. About 140,000 Oregonians work in agriculture, with about 60,000 of them employed on about 39,500 farms or ranches. Farm and ranch production from the 1998 season reached a value of $3.44 billion. The agricultural sector purchased about $3.38 billion worth of seed, feed, supplies, and services from local companies. Another $2 billion of value was added through processing of agricultural products. Accounting for transportation, marketing, storage, and other services, nearly 18 percent of Oregon's economy is tied to agriculture.

About 80 percent of Oregon's agricultural production is sold outside the state; about half of this is sold overseas. About 60 percent of the commerce that moves through the Port of Portland are agricultural products. Moreover, the state's most populous county, Multnomah, is the center of Oregon's food processing industry, with more than 5,600 jobs and 104 firms.

Oregon's agricultural base is very diverse—more than 220 commodities are raised in the state. Greenhouse and nursery products are the largest commodity group, with production value of $532 million. Cattle and calves are second, with production value of $365 million. Hay is third in importance, with production value of $343 million. Grass seed ($338 million) and milk ($254 million) round out the top five agricultural commodity groups.

Agricultural exports totaled $2.03 billion in 1998. Major agricultural exports include soft white wheat, frozen French fries, grass seed, hay, and processed corn. The largest international customers for Oregon's agricultural products (1997 data) are Japan ($668 million), Taiwan ($248 million), South Korea ($246 million), the Philippines ($212 million), and Canada ($113 million).

Following are the major agricultural regions of the state:

Central Oregon produces seed crops, peppermint, grains, livestock, and hay.

Harney and Lake Counties produce livestock and hay.

The **Columbia River Basin** has large dry-land wheat farms and some field crops on irrigated land.

The **Hood River Region** and **Wasco County** produce cherries, apples, pears, and some field crops on irrigated lands.

Malheur County produces seed crops, onions, potatoes, sugar beets, and other specialty crops.

The **Pacific Coast** is known for its ocean fisheries, fish farms, dairy farms, and specialty animal products.

The **Willamette Valley** is a horn of plenty for vegetables, berries, wine grape vineyards, hazelnuts, hops, seed crops, and nursery products.

The major issues facing Oregon's farmers include loss of prime agricultural lands in the face of competitive pressures and the aging and eventual retirement of the farming population. Currently, 17.2 million acres are farmed. Seventy percent of the high-value farmlands are in the Willamette Valley—the area with the most rapid urban and suburban growth in the state. Between 1982 and 1992, an estimated 89,000 acres of agricultural land

Wheat field in Umatilla County, northeastern Oregon. From *Oregon III* by Ray Atkeson.

were converted to urban or suburban development. From 1940 to 1970, Portland's population doubled, while the land occupied by the metropolitan area quadrupled. More than 75 percent of farmland is expected to change hands within the next decade. The average age of ranchers and farmers is 54.

Field Crop Production, 1998

Commodity	Production (standard units millions)		Production (metric tons)	Rank Among States	Percentage of U.S. Production
Barley	8.06	bu	175,599	7	3.0
Hay, all	3.37	tons	3.067 MM	20	2.2
Hops	10.2	lbs	4,639	2	17.2
Oats	3.85	bu	55,878	13	2.3
Peppermint	3.3	lbs	1,505	1	34.1
Potatoes, fall	26.2	cwt	1,192,227	6	5.5
Spearmint	.219	lbs	99	3	7.3
Sugar beets	.438	tons	398,182	11	3.0
Wheat, all	57.44	bu	1,566,485	15	3.0

Source: Agricultural Statistics Service

Seed Crops

Commodity	Production (standard units millions)		Production (metric tons)	Rank Among States	Percentage of U.S. Production
Alfalfa seed	6.09	lbs	2,766	5	7.6
Bentgrass seed	6.1	lbs	2,791	1	not available
Fescue seed	132.0	lbs	59,987	1	63.5
Kentucky bluegrass seed	14.9	lbs	6,797	2	26.9
Orchard grass seed	20.5	lbs	9,323	1	99.0
Ryegrass seed	442.0	lbs	200,722	1	99.2

Source: Agricultural Statistics Service

Berries

Commodity	Production (standard units millions)		Production (metric tons)	Rank Among States	Percentage of U.S. Production
Blackberries	38.9	lbs	17,645	1	100.0
Blueberries	23.0	lbs	10,433	3	14.5
Boysenberries and youngberries	6.2	lbs	2,812	1	78.0
Cranberries .	35.0	bu	16,100	4	6.6
Loganberries	.28	lb	127 1		100.0
Raspberries, black	2.6	lbs	1,179	1	100.0
Raspberries, red	14.2	lbs	6,441	2	17.9
Strawberries	50.0	lbs	22,952	3	33.1

Source: Agricultural Statistics Service

Fruits and Nuts

Commodity	Production (standard units tons)	Production (metric tons)	Rank Among States	Percentage of U.S. Production
Apples, all	90,000	81,819	8	1.6
Cherries, sweet	55,000	50,000	2	26.2
Cherries, tart	2,250	2,041	6	1.3
Hazelnuts	15,900	14,000	1	99.4
Peaches	4,000	3,636	20	0.3
Pears, all	245,000	222,727	3	26.5
Prunes and plums	10,500	9,545	1	41.0
Wine grapes	14,700	13,364	7	0.3

Source: Agricultural Statistics Service

Vegetables

Commodity	Production (standard units)	Production (metric tons)	Rank Among States	Percentage of U.S. Production
Carrots, processing	12,370 tons	11,245	8	2.3
Green peas, processing	49,390 tons	44,900	4	10.2
Onions, storage	9.42 cwt	428,182	3	18.8
Snap beans, processing	121,920 tons	110,836	2	17.2
Sweet corn, processing	311,870 tons	283,518	4	10.9

Source: Agricultural Statistics Service

Horticulture

Commodity	Production (standard units)	Rank Among States	Percentage of U.S. Production
Bedding and garden plants	$47,194,000	15	2.6
Christmas trees	8,817,000 trees	1	13.7
Cultivated greens	$6,240,000	3	28.1
Cut flowers	$10,364,000	6	2.5
Potted florist azaleas	$11,839,000	1	28.1
Potted flowering plants	$19,272,000	11	2.8
Potted petunias	$604,000	5	5.6

Source: Agricultural Statistics Service

Animal Products

Commodity	Production (standard units)	Production (metric tons)	Rank Among States	Percentage of U.S. Production
Cattle and calves (1/98 inventory)	1,520,000 head	n/a	24	1.5
Eggs	758,000,000 eggs	n/a	28	1.0
Milk	1,583,000 lbs	718,044	22	1.0
Mink pelts	24630 pelts	n/a	4	9.0
Sheep and lambs (1/99 inventory)	285,000 head	n/a	8	3.6
Trout	$864,000	n/a	14	1.1
Wool production	1,380,000 lbs	626	11	2.8

Source: Agricultural Statistics Service

Organizations of Interest

Oregon Department of Agriculture, 121 SW Salmon St., #240, Portland 97204-2987, (503) 229-6734, www.oda.state.or.us.

Oregon State Grange, 643 Union St. NE, Salem 97301, (503) 316-0106, www.grange.org/oregon1.htm.

Commodities Commissions

Highland Bentgrass Commission, Salem, (503) 364-3346.

Oregon Alfalfa Seed Commission, Ontario, (541) 881-1345.

Oregon Bartlett Pear Commission, Milwaukie, (503) 652-9720.

Oregon Beef Council, Portland, (503) 229-6830.

Oregon Blueberry Commission, Salem, (503) 364-2944.

Oregon Clover Commission, Salem, (503) 370-7019.

Oregon Dairy Products Commission, Portland, (503) 229-5033.

Oregon Dungeness Crab Commission, Coos Bay, (503) 267-5810.

Oregon Fescue Commission, Salem, (503) 585-1157.

Oregon Fryer Commission, Portland, (503) 256-1151.

Oregon Grains Commission, Pendleton, (541) 276-4609.

Oregon Hazelnut Commission, Aurora, (503) 678-6823.

Oregon Hop Commission, Salem, (503) 393-0368.

Oregon Mint Commission, Salem, (503) 364-3346.

Oregon Orchardgrass Commission, Salem, (503) 370-7019.

Oregon Potato Commission, Portland, (503) 731-3300.

Oregon Processed Prune and Plum Commission, Portland, (503) 292-9305.

Oregon Processed Vegetable Commission, Salem, (503) 370-7019.

Oregon Raspberry and Blackberry Commission, Corvallis, (503) 758-4043.

Oregon Ryegrass Growers Seed Commission, Salem, (503) 364-2944.

Oregon Salmon Commission, Lincoln County, (503) 994-2647.

Oregon Sea Urchin Producers Commission, Portland, (503) 229-6734.

Oregon Sheep Commission, Salem, (503) 364-5462.

Oregon Strawberry Commission, Corvallis, (503) 758-4043.

Oregon Sweet Cherry Commission, Salem, (503) 585-7716.

Oregon Tall Fescue Commission, Salem, (503) 585-1157.

Oregon Trawl Commission, Astoria, (503) 325-3384.

Oregon Wheat Commission, Portland, (503) 229-6665.

Oregon Wine Advisory Board, Portland, (503) 228-8336.

Western Oregon Onion Commission, Salem, (503) 378-7349.

Events of Interest

Antique Equipment Show and Threshing Bee, Hildebrand, September, (541) 545-6510.

A Tree Grows in Umpqua

The saga of a tiny seedling's rise from just a sprout in rural Oregon to star status as the state's official nut begins with the first hazelnut tree planted in 1858 in the Umpqua Valley by English sailor Sam Strictland.

The tree grew and thrived.

About 20 years later, a Frenchman, David Gernot, sent to France for seeds of the thin-shell variety. Fifty trees produced from these seeds were planted in the Willamette Valley along a fence row, as was the practice in the Old Country. There they thrived with little attention, providing food for the family and surrounding wildlife.

It was not until around 1885, however, that Felix Gillet, a resolute French horticulturist, introduced the Barcelona variety that is extensively grown today. Today, Oregon produces between 98 and 99 percent of the total U.S. hazelnut crop. . . . Perhaps as a testimony to those tenacious pioneers, that first tree planted in the Umpqua Valley of Oregon is still standing.

—Lucy Gerspacher, *Hazelnuts & More*

Central Oregon Farm Fair, Madras, February, (541) 475-3808.

Clackamas County Fair and Rodeo, Canby, August, (503) 266-1136.

Clatsop County Fair, Astoria, July, (503) 325-4600.

Draft Horse Plowing Exhibition, Washington County, May, (503) 645-5353.

Dufur Threshing Bee, Dufur, August, (541) 467-2349.

Josephine County Fair, Grants Pass, August, (541) 476-3215.

Lane County Fair, Eugene, August, (541) 682-4292.

Malheur County Fair, Ontario, August, (541) 889-3431.

Oregon Ag Fest, Salem, April, (800) 874-7012.

Oregon State Fair, Salem, August, (503) 378-3247.

Polk County Fair, Rickreall, August, (503) 623-3048.

Tillamook County Fair, Tillamook, August, (503) 842-2272.

Tillamook Dairy Festival and Parade, Tillamook, June, (503) 842-7525.

Union County Fair, La Grande, July, (541) 963-2384.

Wallowa County Historic Barn Tour, Enterprise, August, (541) 426-0219.

Wasco County Fair, Tygh Valley, August, (541) 296-5644.

Washington County Fair and Rodeo, Hillsboro, July, (503) 648-1416.

Yamhill County Fair, McMinnville, July, (503) 434-7524.

Airports

(*See also* Transportation) There are 411 public and private airports in Oregon. Of these, eight are commercial airports with scheduled passenger service: Astoria, Eugene, Klamath Falls, Medford, North Bend, Pendleton, Portland International, and Redmond. (*See* map pages 186-187.)

The Oregon Department of Transportation manages 32 Oregon airports, licenses or registers 400 other airports or airfields, registers all pilots and civilian aircraft in the state, and coordinates air rescues.

The state's air transportation hub, Portland International Airport (symbol: PDX) is owned and operated by the Port of Portland. Nearly 13 million passengers passed through the airport in 1998, making it among the 30 busiest in airports the United States. PDX is served by 14 passenger airlines that provide service to 120 cities around the world. Sixteen cargo carriers move over 260,000 tons of cargo through the airport each year. Following are the airlines with the largest passenger market shares:

Alaska	22 percent
United	18 percent
Delta	13.5 percent
Southwest	13 percent
Horizon	12 percent

PDX opened in 1940 and has been remodeled periodically to keep pace with advances in technology and traffic. The most recent modernization occurred beginning in the mid 1990s and is still ongoing. In 1998, PDX handled the following:

13,000,000 total passengers
587,000 total international passengers
20,000 short tons total international cargo
268,000 short tons total cargo
Source: Port of Portland

General Aviation

There are about 9,000 private pilots registered in Oregon. The first plane in Oregon flew at a Portland exhibition on March 5, 1910. In 1912, aviator Silas Christofferson flew his plane from the roof of the Multnomah Hotel in Portland to Vancouver, Washington. This exploit was commemorated with a memorial flight in 1995. Commercial air service to Oregon started in 1919. Airports and air mail emerged in 1926. Scheduled passenger service started in 1928. Charles Lindbergh flew his famous *Spirit of St. Louis* to

Portland on Sept. 14, 1927, to inaugurate the new Portland airport, located at that time on Swan Island in the Willamette River.

Organizations and Events of Interest

Federal Aviation Administration, Northwest Mountain Region, Airports Division, ANM-600, 1601 Lind Ave. SW, #315, Renton, WA 98055-4056, (425) 227-2600, www.faa.gov/arp/anm/anm600.htm.

Oregon Department of Transportation, Aeronautics Section, 3040 25th St. SE, Salem 97310, (503) 378-4880.

Air Fair, Oregon Air and Space Museum, Eugene, July, (541) 345-7224.

Airshow, Hillsboro Airport, Hillsboro, June, (503) 232-3000.

Joseph Airport Fly-In, Joseph, August.

Rogue Valley International Airshow, Medford, August, (541) 773-7773.

American Indians

No one is sure exactly when the first humans arrived in Oregon, but sandals found in Central Oregon's Fort Rock Cave date back 13,000 years.

By the early 19th century, about a hundred bands and tribes were in Oregon, with a total population in the tens of thousands. Virtually all of these people had animistic belief systems, their faiths vested in elements of nature such as mountains, rivers, wolves, crows, and trees. In their view, humans, animals, and matter shared the same spirit.

Plateau tribes in the northeastern part of what is now Oregon, such as the Nez Perce and Cayuse, trained horses and ranged nomadically from the steppes of the Upper Columbia to the alpine valleys of the Wallowas. The region's high, arid southeastern section was sparsely populated, with small bands moving often to find scarce waterfowl and plants. On the western boundary of the dry Great Basin, the Klamath and Modoc tribes caught fish in lakes and waded in marshlands to harvest their staple, the yellow water-lily seed. The tribes of the inland valleys lived on nuts, roots, and game.

The Native cultures of the Pacific Coast and those of the Columbia and lower Willamette Rivers revolved around salmon for both sustenance and trade. The coastal tribes were separated into entirely different societies by thick forest, and some were strict hierarchies, with slaves at the bottom. Inhabitants of the region's northwest corner subsisted on berries, fish, game, and roots and lived in small villages of plank houses. Cedar trees provided material for everything from dugout canoes to clothes made of shredded bark, tule, and grass.

Though all Native American tribes suffered in proportion to Oregon's growth from an unknown, mythical Eden to a territory and finally a state, Native cultures were hit hard by white settlement. Over the past 200 years, the U.S. government has executed treaties, enacted federal laws, and issued executive agreements that established a trust relationship with tribes as sovereign entities. In most of these agreements, the Indians signed away their rights to their traditional homelands in exchange for a single reservation area. Over the course of U.S. history, the federal government—after moving Indians onto reservations—has attempted numerous times to end federal trusteeship of Indian populations. The most recent attempt occurred during the 1950s, when 109 tribes and bands, 62 of them native to Oregon, had their trustee relationships terminated. Since that time, a number of those groups have had their trustee statuses reinstated; others are still working to do so. The current federally recognized tribes are:

Burns Paiute Tribe of the Burns Paiute Indian Colony of Oregon

Confederated Tribes of the Coos, Lower Umpqua, and Siuslaw Indians of Oregon

Confederated Tribes of the Grand Ronde Community of Oregon

Confederated Tribes of the Siletz Reservation, Oregon

Confederated Tribes of the Umatilla Reservation, Oregon

Twenty years before The Dalles Dam was built, Jack Tuckte fished for salmon at Celilo Falls, ancient Indian fishing grounds. From *Oregon, My Oregon* by Ray Atkeson.

Confederated Tribes of the Warm Springs Reservation of Oregon
Coquille Tribe of Oregon
Cow Creek Band of Umpqua Indians of Oregon
Fort McDermitt Paiute and Shoshone Tribes of the Fort McDermitt Indian Reservation, Nevada and Oregon
Klamath Indian Tribe of Oregon

Oregon Indian Reservations

	Population Enrollment	Size (acres)
Grand Ronde	4,155	10,101
Warm Springs	3,814	641,118+
Siletz	3,199	4,345
Umatilla	2,097	158,303
Burns Paiute	282	11,700
Coquille Tribe	n/a	6,512

Source: Bureau of Indian Affairs (U.S. Department of the Interior)

The Dalles

In Klickitat legend, the great Tyhee of all the gods came down from the North Country in a trek that was "difficult even for a god" and settled in a place we now call The Dalles.

We know that people have occupied the The Dalles on the Columbia River for at least 10,000 years. When Lewis and Clark descended the Columbia Gorge in the autumn of 1805, they met the Chinookian people, an expert fishing and gathering people, who lived between the Long Narrows and the Pacific Ocean. The main salmon run and great trading rendezvous of that year was over, yet they found hundreds of tons of baled dried salmon still awaiting storage along the banks of the river.

The Chinooks lived along the only low-elevation trade route through the Cascade Mountains. Each year the salmon run at the narrows initiated a major gathering: dentalia shells and cedar canoes from the coast were exchanged for buffalo robes and horses from the plains; baskets and seeds from California were traded for obsidian from Washington. And while they fished and traded, the Indians held games and gambled with their profits.

At Celilo Falls just east of The Dalles, the ancient Indian fishing grounds were a popular Oregon destination into the 1950s. From platforms built out over the falls, Indian fisherman would scoop up salmon of remarkable size in huge nets on poles.

The falls were submerged by the U.S. Army Corps of Engineers when they built The Dalles Dam in 1957.—Adapted from "Northwest Gateway," by David Kelly, in *Columbia River Gorge*, photography by James Holloway ✣

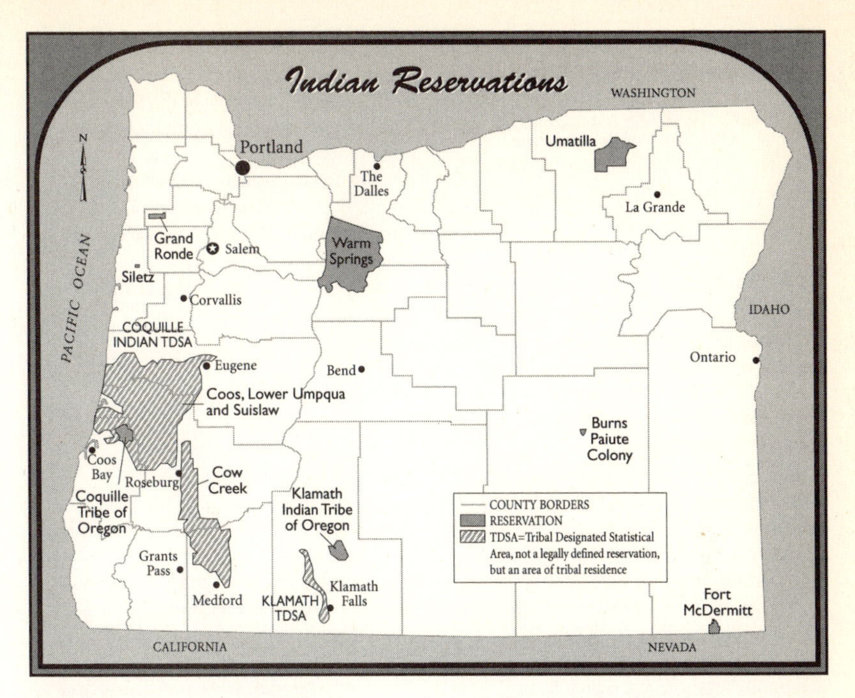

Organizations and Events of Interest

Commission on Indian Services, 167 State Capitol, Salem 97310, (503) 986-1067.

Confederated Tribes of the Grand Ronde Annual Pow Wow, Grande Ronde, (503) 879-5211.

The Museum at Warm Springs, P.O. Box C, Warm Springs 97761, (541) 553-3331, www.tmaws.org/index.html.

Nesika Illahee Pow Wow, Siletz, August, (800) 922-1399.

Pi-Ume-She Treaty Days, Warm Springs, June, (541) 553-2461.

Spring Pow Wow (all tribes), La Grande, May, (541) 962-3741.

Tu-Kwa-Hone' Intertribal Sobriety Pow-Wow, Burns, June, (541) 573-2088.

Wallowa Band Nez Perce Pow Wow, Wallowa, July, (541) 885-8045.

Amphibians and Reptiles

Oregon's wildlife resources include several dozen amphibian and reptile species, including salamanders, frogs, toads, lizards, and snakes. The damp forest environments from the Pacific Coast to the western slopes of the Cascades are home to most of the salamander species, while the drier climate of Eastern Oregon is favored by lizards and the state's only venomous reptile, the western rattlesnake.

Am I Blue!

The theme song of the western fence lizard (Sceloporus occidentalis) might be "Am I Blue!" The large, blue belly patch of each side of its grayish white stomach and, brightest of all, on the throat liven up sagebrush desert in all three Northwest states. For more color, the backs of its limbs are yellowish orange, and blotches and bars give variety to the gray-brown upper part.
—Ann Saling, *The Great Northwest Nature Factbook.*

Three snake species are constrictors: gopher, rubber boa, and king snake. The sharp-tailed snake, *Contia tenuis,* which feeds on slugs, is a protected species. Oregon's largest lizard is the desert collared lizard, which grows to 13 inches long and occurs in southeast Oregon.

Events of Interest

Oregon Museum of Science and Industry (OMSI), Annual Reptile and Amphibian Show, Portland, September, (503) 797-4588.

Archives (*SEE ALSO* LIBRARIES)

In addition to the State Archives, libraries and historical societies throughout the state maintain extensive archives of the state's public and historical documents.

State Archives

Established in 1947, the Archives Division of state government houses the permanent records of Oregon government. The oldest documents at the archives include records of the provisional and territorial governments and the Oregon Constitution. The division also files, codifies, and publishes state agency administrative rules and publishes the *Oregon Blue Book.*

State Archives and Historical Records Advisory Board, 800 Summer St. NE, Salem 97310, (503) 373-0701.

National Archives

The National Archives and Records Services maintains nine regional offices across the country, and the Pacific Northwest collection is held in Seattle. The Seattle Federal Records Center maintains records for Washington, Oregon, and Alaska generated by federal agencies since 1850.

National Archives and Records Administration, Pacific Alaska Region, 6125 Sand Point Way NE, Seattle, WA 98115, (206) 526-6501.

Libraries

(*SEE ALSO* LIBRARIES; UNIVERSITIES AND COLLEGES) The State Library in Salem and public and university libraries designated as "full depository libraries" receive copies of public documents from most state agencies. These libraries make their Oregon documents accessible to the public and retain all depository documents for five years. A number of other community libraries maintain public documents for three years. The State Library is the official archive for publications of the State of Oregon and retains Oregon documents indefinitely.

The full depository libraries are:

Blue Mountain Community College Library
Deschutes County Library
Eastern Oregon State College Library
Hillsboro Public Library
Klamath County Library
Library of Congress
Multnomah County Library
Oregon State Library
Oregon State University Library
Portland State University Library
Southern Oregon State College Library
Southwestern Oregon Community College Library
University of Oregon Library
Western Oregon State College Library

Historical Societies

The state, regional, and county historical societies maintain extensive collections of Oregon historical documents, including local government documents, manuscripts, diaries, maps, photographs, and artifacts. Nearly every county in Oregon has an historical society, and many offer genealogical resources.

The Oregon Historical Society has an extensive archive of personal and family papers; business, professional, cultural, fraternal, and other organizational records; and pictorial materials, such as posters, architectural drawings, and ship and wagon plans. The society also has over 30,000 maps, focusing on western exploration, the Oregon Territory, and the Pacific Northwest; an oral history archive of tapes, discs, and transcripts of more than 1,500 interviews; a film archive; and some 85,000 artifacts of Oregon history.

The research collections may be accessed in person Wednesday through Saturday, from 11:30 A.M. until 5:00 P.M.

Oregon Historical Society, 1200 SW Park Avenue, Portland, OR 97205-2483, (503) 222-1741, fax: (503) 221-2035, orhist@ohs.org. www.ohs.org/homepage.html.

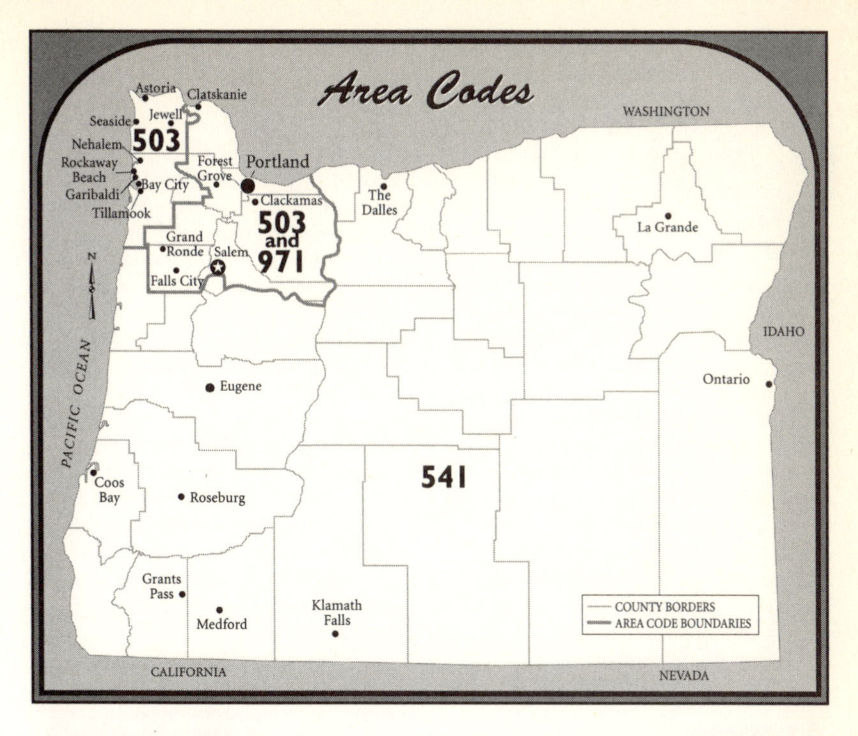

Area Codes Rapid growth in the Portland metropolitan area has resulted in a squeeze on telephone number prefixes. The phone company's fix has been to layer a new area code (971) on top of an old one (503) and require callers in those area codes to use the area code for all calls. The new "ten-digit dialing" requirement was effective Oct. 1, 2000.

Arts (SEE ALSO FAIRS AND FESTIVALS; MUSEUMS; PERFORMING ARTS) Oregon has several major arts agencies that fund both organizations and individuals. Established in 1967, the Oregon Arts Commission (OAC) became part of the Oregon Economic Development Department in 1993. In 1998 the OAC awarded $966,928 across the state, from experimental theater and dance in Portland and the major cluster of arts organizations in Eugene to the Oregon Shakespeare Festival in Ashland and the Peter Britt Music Festival in Medford. East of the Cascade Mountains, money went to the Cascade Festival of

Ashland hosts the Oregon Shakespeare Festival every summer. Photo courtesy Jennifer Donahoe Photography.

Music Association in Bend, the Oregon East Symphony in Pendleton, and others.

The OAC's commitment to arts programs as significant contributors to the economy is reflected in the Arts Industry Development Program, which encompasses two-thirds of total gifts. The program contributes to the operating costs of the state's largest nonprofit arts groups.

Artists and patrons of the arts who contribute significantly to Oregon's cultural heritage are recognized annually by the Governor's Awards. The Northwest Booking Conference, which includes the state arts agencies of Washington and Idaho, provides a forum for performing artists and presenters to meet and discuss touring and booking.

Oregon Arts Commission, 775 Summer Street NE, Salem 97310, (503) 986-0088.

Astoria

Astoria's traditional industries, canning and logging, still exist here on a smaller scale, but the real attraction is the city's history. Located at the mouth of the Columbia River, slightly inland from the Pacific shore, this first coastal city was originally an important base for the fur industry. The Columbia River's treacherous bar hampered early explorers until 1792, when Boston sea captain Robert Gray sailed in to find the great river everyone else had dismissed as a myth.

The Lewis and Clark Expedition made camp at Fort Clatsop, a few miles east of Astoria for the winter of 1805-06. The unusually rainy weather, even for this cloudy town, led Clark repeatedly to journal about his days there as "wet, cold, and disagreeable." Food was scarce, and the expedition subsisted on salmon and dogs provided by local Indians.

Four years later, John Jacob Astor, then the richest man in America, sent a ship and an overland team to the mouth of the Columbia to set up a fur trading company. The ship's crew went up the river to Vancouver, where the captain's haughty treatment of the Indians led to battles that killed most of the crew. In a horrible revenge scheme, survivors lured many Indians onto their ship and set it ablaze. The overland team ignored its Indian guides and spent the winter in the mountains, nearly starving to death.

When this party finally reached the coast, it encountered news that the British North West Company was on its way to claim the area, so the party hurried to establish upriver trading posts and settled in Fort Astor. The success was short-lived though because during the War of 1812, a British warship scared the Americans into selling the fort. At the renamed Fort George, North West Company fur traders continued operation even after Astoria was returned to the Americans at the end of the war. A small replica trading post can be found today at the corner of 15th and Exchange Streets.

John Jacob Astor dictated the whole experience to a popular writer of the era, Washington Irving, for the book *Astoria,* a huge best-seller in 1837. Translated into three languages, the book is still in print.

By the turn of the century, sea otter numbers could no longer support the fur industry, and exports of fish and timber grew. Salmon canneries staffed by Chinese laborers lined the Columbia's banks from Astoria to the Cascades. Indians saw their food supplies decimated. Business revived during World War I and World War II, but eventually salmon runs were overfished to the point of extinction, while stands of old-growth trees around Astoria virtually disappeared.

Though the port still hums with oceangoing vessels and fishing boats, tourism has aided the city's survival. Astoria now has more bed-and-breakfasts than any other town on the Oregon Coast, many in elegant, preserved Victorian homes. The Columbia River Maritime Museum displays restored boats, including a rare lightship, the *Columbia.*

The ornate Queen Anne home of Captain George Flavel, a Columbia River bar pilot, has been thoughtfully maintained

The Astoria Column depicts the city's rich history. Photo by Andrea Jarvela.

and now houses a museum. In summer, the Fort Clatsop National Memorial features living history demonstrations, with reenactments of the camp of Lewis and Clark's 33 men and Lewis's Newfoundland dog, minus only the winter weather.

Avalanches

Avalanches are an annual fact of life in Northwest mountains. The Colorado Avalanche Information Center, which maintains world avalanche accidents, reports that during the winters of 1997-98 and 1998-99 there were two fatalities in Oregon, one on Mount Hood and one in the Blue Mountains. Outdoor recreationists who venture into the backcountry during winter can learn to recognize avalanche danger by looking for certain conditions. The snow anywhere may be ready to release when there is a combination of heavy or sticky snow and steep slopes (especially any slope that appears to have experienced a recent slide), or when there is a hollow drumming or *whomp*ing sound beneath the snow. Rime ice on trees is a sign of high winds during a storm that may have overloaded leeward slopes with snow. To learn more about avalanches or to check on avalanche danger in specific areas, contact the **Northwest Avalanche Institute** on-line at www.avalanche.org or check the **Northwest Weather and Avalanche Center** at www.nwac.noaa.gov. For **recorded avalanche information** in backcountry avalanche terrain below 7,000 feet in the Mount Hood area, call (503) 808-2400. You can also monitor Northwest mountain weather on the mountain pass cameras maintained by the **Oregon Department of Transportation,** www.odot.state.or.us/travel.

Basin and Range Province

Eastern Oregon is characterized by a series of solitary north-south–trending mountain blocks separated by basins filled with alluvial material. These landforms, typical of arid high-desert regions, are known as basin and range topography.

The mountains are geological fault blocks. They rise gradually on the west side and drop precipitously on the east side. The western side of Steens Mountain, for example, rises 5,000 feet in 20 miles; the eastern side plummets the same distance in 3 miles. The geological faults in the region allow mineralized hot water to rise to the surface. Mineral springs can be found on both Steens and Hart Mountains, and in other locations in the region.

The Basin and Range Province is quite dry, with alkaline soil. Rainfall at Steens Mountain averages 7 inches per year at the base and 32 inches per year at the top. The alkaline soil in the valleys creates "bad water" lakes that are dry for much of the year but when wet have a very high mineral content. The lakes are important seasonal stops for migrating birds on the Western Flyway.

Bend

(*See also* Skiing and Snowboarding) Set in a dramatic landscape of high desert, lava fields, and mountains,

Deschutes River near Bend. Photo by Susan Dupere.

Bend's location lends itself to tourism, the city's biggest business. Many of its more than 50,000 residents work directly or indirectly for resorts like Sunriver, Mount Bachelor Village, and Inn of the Seventh Mountain, or for skiing, climbing, rafting, camping, and hiking outfitters (*see* Skiing and Snowboarding; Whitewater Kayaking and River Running; Outdoor Recreation). This push toward development began in the 1960s, long after rails were laid to Bend in 1911 to carry ponderosa pine and trails went through the trees to the homes and families of timber workers.

In the early 1920s, Scandinavian loggers began skiing to their destinations, and the sport (along with its 1990s incarnation, snowboarding) has grown in popularity ever since. The Mount Bachelor Ski Area (22 miles southwest of Bend) is the largest ski area in the Pacific Northwest, with seven high-speed lifts and 3,100 vertical feet of groomed slopes. The recently established Newberry National Volcanic Monument encompasses 56,000 acres of the Deschutes National Forest, including Newberry Crater and the mile-long Lava River Cave. Smith Rock State Park to the north attracts some of the best rock climbers in the world.

Residents and visitors enjoy virtually as much sun as Western Oregon cityfolk endure rain. Hot summers and cold winters and cool high-desert nights are the norm, and flash floods can follow drought on the east side of the Cascades. Bordering the city are some of the tallest Cascade peaks, formed 14 to 16 million years ago when the oceanic plate supplanted the North American plate, creating friction. The heat produced lava, which came streaming out of a chain of volcanoes, including Three-Fingered Jack, Mount Washington, the Three Sisters, Broken Top, Mount Bachelor, Mount Thielsen, and Mount McLoughlin.

While dance, music, and theater performances can certainly be found here, Bend's greatest cultural attraction is the High Desert Museum (6 miles south of Bend on U.S. 97), a nonprofit center for natural and regional history. Sophisticated dioramas illustrate Native American times through the 1890s and the story of white settlement. Outside, trails winding past otters and porcupines include replicas of covered wagons, a sawmill, and a pioneer cabin. The museum owns an important collection of Columbia River Plateau Indian artifacts.

Along a section of Bend's main thoroughfare, a preserved historic area still flourishes, offering good restaurants and a microbrewery. The Deschutes Historical Center displays pioneer paraphernalia and exhibits on regional history.

One of the biggest events of the year is the mid-May Pole Pedal Paddle Race. Thousands of participants (both relay teams and individuals) start out skiing downhill runs on Mount Bachelor, change to a cross-country ski circuit, then ride bikes for 22 miles to the Deschutes River for a final, 5-mile kayak or canoe paddle to the finish through Bend's Drake Park.

Birds (*SEE ALSO* ENDANGERED SPECIES)

The Oregon Bird Records Committee lists 467 species of resident and migratory birds that rely on a wide range of feeding, nesting, and resting habitat in the state. A critical part of the Pacific flyway, the state's coastal estuaries, freshwater rivers and lakes, prairies, and mountains are home to marine birds, waterfowl, shorebirds, wading birds, songbirds, and raptors. Among these are endangered and threatened species, such as the northern spotted owl, sandhill crane, bald eagle, and marbled murrelet, which rely on shrinking habitat.

In southeastern Oregon, two large feeding and resting areas for migratory birds are Klamath Lake and the Malheur National Wildlife Refuge. The Malheur refuge hosts, at varying times, flocks of migrating songbirds; wading birds such as black-necked stilts, sandhill cranes, avocets, curlews, and herons; a variety of waterfowl; and raptors, such as golden eagles, prairie falcons, and great horned owls. In the shrub-steppe country of Eastern Oregon and the Great Basin, scrub jays, burrowing owls, such hawks as the ferruginous and Swainson's, and a variety of neotropical migratory birds can be found.

The Pacific coast provides major spring and fall feeding and resting areas for migrating shorebirds and seabirds. Albatrosses, fulmars, shearwaters, storm-petrels, and gulls congregate offshore. Plovers, phalaropes, and sandpipers can be found along the beaches. The landward edge of the coastal region is home to jays and crows and small birds such as chickadees, wrens, and sparrows. The old-growth habitat is home to endangered northern spotted owls and marbled murrelets. The subalpine and alpine areas of the Cascade and Coast Ranges are home to warblers, vireos, buntings, jays, woodpeckers, grouse, and eagles.

Canada goose. From *Going Wild in Washington and Oregon* by Susan Ewing (text) and Gretchen Daiber (illustrations).

Organizations and Events of Interest

Audubon Society, Chapter Service Office, (800) 542-2748, www.audubon.org/chapter/or.

Audubon Society of Corvallis, (541) 929-4041.

Audubon Society of Portland, (503) 292-6855.

Cape Arago Audubon Society, P.O. Box 381, North Bend 97459.

Central Oregon Audubon Society, Bend, (541) 929-4041.

Kalmiopsis Audubon Society, Sixes (Curry County), P.O. Box 1265, Port Orford 97465.

Klamath Basin Audubon Society, P.O. Box 354, Klamath Falls 97601.

> **Meadowlark**
>
> *John James Audubon gave the western meadowlark (*Sturnella neglecta neglecta*) the species name "neglecta" because he felt the bird deserved more attention. Oregon's state bird, its yellow breast marked with a black V with white patches on each side of the short, wide tail, perches on a fence post or roof to sing bubbling, flutelike phrases with seven to ten notes. The female chooses her mate by his call. This bird often nests in depressions in open grassland, weaving the tops of grass blades together for a domed roof. Common in interior valleys and arid uplands among sagebrush and basalt, most fly south or west of the Cascades for winter.*—Ann Saling, *The Great Northwest Nature Factbook*

Lane County Audubon Society, P.O. Box 5086, Eugene 97405.

Rogue Valley Audubon Society, P.O. Box 8597, Medford 97504.

Salem Audubon Society, (503) 588-7340.

Siskiyou Audubon Society, P.O Box 1047, Grants Pass 97526.

Umpqua Valley Audubon Society, P.O. Box 381, Roseburg 97470.

Oregon Field Ornithologists, P.O. Box 10373, Eugene 97440. The complete checklist of Oregon bird species can be found on this group's website at www.cyber-dyne.com/~lb/ofoweb.html.

Christmas Bird Count, December, sponsored by the Audubon Society statewide. Contact any Audubon office for information.

Migratory Bird Festival, April, Burns, (542) 573-2636.

Shorebird Festival, Charleston, September, (541) 269-0215.

Song Bird Celebration, Welches, May, (503) 622-4011.

Bonneville Power Administration

(*SEE ALSO* DAMS) The Bonneville Power Administration (BPA), a division of the U.S. Department of the Interior, is the agency that markets the electrical power produced by federal dams on the Columbia River and its tributaries. BPA's power transmission grid—the "highway system" over which the products of electrical generation flow—provides about three-fourths of the Northwest's power transmission. The agency's 363 substations and 15,012 circuit miles of transmission lines provide service to an area encompassing 300,000 square miles.

BPA supplies, on average, 40 percent of the power sold in the Northwest and controls more than half the region's high-voltage transmission. More than 80 percent of the power BPA sells is hydroelectric, and about 60 percent of the Northwest's electricity comes from hydropower.

BPA sells its power directly to federal agencies, such as the Departments of Energy and the Navy, and to certain nonaluminum industries and utility companies, which in turn sell it to their retail customers. On average, Bonneville markets about 40 percent of its "firm power" (this is calculated as the power that can be produced even under poor water conditions) at cost to public agency customers.

The West Coast power market is quickly becoming a commodities market. New power trading hubs have been established at the California/Oregon border and at Palo Verde, Arizona. Power prices at these hubs are listed daily in the *Wall Street Journal.* BPA power traders sell surplus hydropower on the open market and buy to meet short-term gaps in supply. The agency first offers surplus and excess federal power to buyers in the Northwest. Publicly owned utilities (PUDs) in the Northwest are BPA's largest customer group; traditionally they have accounted for about half of BPA's total revenues.

The federal power system in the Pacific Northwest has conferred significant benefits on the region for more than 50 years, both as a source of inexpensive electricity and for irrigation, flood control, and navigation. In recent years, however, BPA has had to adjust to operating within a much more competitive electricity industry. BPA's power has lost its price advantage due to low natural gas prices, surplus generating capacity on the West Coast, and the opening of the competitive wholesale electricity market, which resulted in lower electricity prices. BPA also had to cope with its high operating costs, which included such items as paying for salmon recovery efforts and payment of its debt to the U.S. government for construction of dam and transmission systems.

BPA is one reason Oregon has enjoyed low-cost electricity. The average residential rate in the Northwest is $.054/kwh, compared to the U.S. average residential rate of $.084/kwh (1995 figures).

Caves

The lava tubes in central and southeastern Oregon comprise the majority of Oregon's caves. Lava tube caves form when thick, basaltic lava moving down a gentle slope begins to slow and cool, forming a crust. Molten lava continues to flow within the crust, either emptying out completely or forming a solid fill at the end of the tube. Limestone and marble caves,

Crescent Beach from a tidal cave. From *Wind on the Waves* by Kim R. Stafford (text) and Ray Atkeson and Rick Schafer (photos).

such as those in the Klamath Mountains, are formed by the dissolving action of acidic groundwater. Ice caves, often quarried by early settlers, are not caves within underground ice but rather well-insulated lava tubes with ice covering the floors and cold air sinking in from high openings.

Arnold Ice Cave. The ice is advancing in this lava tube cave near the Newberry Volcano, making access hazardous without crampons and rope.

Lava River Cave. Emblematic of lava tubes, this cave within Newberry National Volcanic Monument in Central Oregon features frozen lava drips, or "lavacicles," on the smooth, glassy coating of its walls and ceilings.

Malheur Cave (*see* Lakes and Reservoirs). Malheur Lake comes within 1,000 feet of the entrance and completely fills the distant lower end of this 3,000-foot-long lava tube south of Burns. Paiute Indians, who used the cave as a shelter, barricaded themselves inside to survive a long siege by the Bannock Indians in the early 1800s.

Officer's Cave. A maze of a cave 11 miles south of Kimberly in Grant County, Officer's Cave (named for the family who homesteaded the area) is still growing. In 1914, it was measured at 700 feet long; examiners in 1975 recorded its distance at 1,500 feet.

Oregon Caves National Monument (*see* National Parks, Monuments, and Recreation Areas). A single cave high in the Siskiyou Mountains, this is the largest cave on the West Coast formed entirely within marble. Unusually varied formations include stalactites and stalagmites, as well as dripstone and flowstone resembling waterfalls, chandeliers, and grape clusters.

Sea Lion Caves (*see* Seals and Sea Lions). North America's largest natural sea cave extends into a 300-foot headland on the central Oregon Coast. Excavated by waves pounding a vertical wall of volcanic basalt and agglomerate, this is the only known breeding ground of large Steller sea lions. The sea washes constantly through a short natural entrance with enough force to carry the sea lions into a vaulted chamber 125 feet high, with a floor area of 2 acres.

Charities

A number of large charitable foundations supporting a broad range of causes have headquarters in Oregon. According to the Washington, D.C.-based Urban Institute, a national think tank, more than 4,000 charitable organizations are active in the state (that is, they filed a tax statement with the IRS in 1997). The Urban Institute's National Center for Charitable Statistics calculates that Oregon's public charities distribute their largesse in the following way:

Distribution of Charitable Funds

Human Services	41.8 percent
Health	15.0 percent
Arts and Culture	12.0 percent
Education	11.4 percent
Public Benefit	4.7 percent
Religion-related	4.5 percent
Environment and Animals	4.1 percent
International	1.0 percent
Unknown	5.4 percent

Who are the big money organizations? In its "Philanthropy 400" list, the *Chronicle of Philanthropy* included the following Oregon charities among the nation's best fund-raisers:

No. 181. Northwest Medical Teams International, Portland
No. 236. Oregon Community Foundation, Portland
No. 258. Oregon State University, Corvallis
No. 259. University of Oregon, Eugene
No. 273. Oregon Health Sciences Foundation, Portland

The New York-based Foundation Center puts together its "tops" list according to how much charities have in total assets and how much they give away. Oregon charities that made the list in June 1999:

Top 25 Community Foundations by Asset Size—12th, **The Oregon Community Foundation,** with $360,577,539 in assets

Top 25 Community Foundations by Total Giving—17th, **The Oregon Community Foundation,** with $19,987,617 in giving

Cities and Towns

Oregon has 240 incorporated towns and cities. The oldest incorporated city in the state, Oregon City (established in 1844), was also the original territorial capital from 1843 to 1852. However, it was neighboring Portland that grew to be the state's largest metropolitan area and the state's cultural and commercial hub.

A number of Oregon's cities and towns have been honored as great places to live. *Money* magazine rates its "Best Places to Live" in the United States, using 37 "quality of life" factors such as housing cost, cultural opportunities, schools, and crime. For 1998, the magazine ranked cities by region. In the West, the Portland-Vancouver metropolitan area ranked 7th among the large cities; Eugene-Springfield and Salem were ranked 3rd and 8th, respectively, among medium-sized cities; and the best small cities included Medford-Ashland (7th). Portland also made *Fortune* magazine's "Best Places for Business" list, ranking 7th on the list in 1998.

The All-America City Award, sponsored by the National Civic League and Allstate Insurance, recognizes community involvement and problem solving. Over the past years, the following Oregon cities have won this honor:

Albany (1984-85)
Cottage Grove (1968)
Eugene (1969)
Florence (1989)
Grants Pass (1985-86)
Milton-Freewater (1961)
Newport (1989)
Portland (1979-80)
Salem (1960, 1982-83)

Hillsboro teens in Portland's Rose Festival Starlight Parade. Photo by Susan Dupere.

Ten Largest Cities by Population

Portland	509,610
Eugene	133,460
Salem	126,635
Gresham	83,595
Beaverton	68,050
Hillsboro	65,110
Medford	58,895
Springfield	51,700
Corvallis	49,630
Albany	38,925

Ten Smallest Cities by Population

Greenhorn	3
Lonerock	25
Granite	25
Shaniko	30
Prescott	60
Antelope	65
Barlow	125
Unity	145
Adrian	145
Summerville	150

City Populations, 1998

Portland	509,610
Eugene	133,460
Salem	126,635
Gresham	83,595
Beaverton	68,050
Hillsboro	65,110
Medford	58,895
Springfield	51,700
Corvallis	49,630
Albany	38,925
Tigard	37,200
Bend	35,635
Lake Oswego	34,280
Keizer	29,235
McMinnville	24,265
Oregon City	22,560
Tualatin	21,405
West Linn	21,405
Grants Pass	20,590
Milwaukie	20,220
Roseburg	20,215
Ashland	19,220
Klamath Falls	18,940
Newberg	17,355
Pendleton	16,915
Woodburn	16,585
Forest Grove	16,170
Coos Bay	15,615
Troutdale	14,040
La Grande	12,795
Dallas	12,530
Lebanon	12,480
Canby	12,465
Redmond	12,435
Wilsonville	12,290
The Dalles	11,765
Gladstone	11,745
Hermiston	11,595
Central Point	11,255
Ontario	10,680
Newport	10,240
Baker City	10,160
Astoria	10,090
North Bend	9,910
Sherwood	9,600
St. Helens	9,060
Cottage Grove	8,190
Cornelius	8,170
Monmouth	7,980
Sweet Home	7,815
Prineville	6,920
Lincoln City	6,855
Silverton	6,740
Florence	6,715
Sutherlin	6,690
Stayton	6,655
Milton-Freewater	6,500
Seaside	6,170
Fairview	5,910
Independence	5,815
Brookings	5,510
Molalla	5,395
Sheridan	5,330
Sandy	5,135
Hood River	5,130
Talent	5,050
Madras	5,005
Reedsport	4,860
Scappoose	4,855
Winston	4,480
Junction City	4,400
Eagle Point	4,325
Tillamook	4,310
Coquille	4,235
Warrenton	4,175
Phoenix	3,905
Philomath	3,770
Myrtle Creek	3,600
Toledo	3,590
Happy Valley	3,540
Umatilla	3,515
Oakridge	3,260
Creswell	3,150
Nyssa	3,045
Burns	3,015
Mount Angel	3,015
Wood Village	3,005
Veneta	2,950
Aumsville	2,875
Bandon	2,820
Boardman	2,795
Dundee	2,735
Myrtle Point	2,725
Lakeview	2,640
Harrisburg	2,535
Vernonia	2,425
Sublimity	2,400
Jefferson	2,335
Shady Cove	2,315
Hubbard	2,210
Estacada	2,190
Gold Beach	2,150
Lafayette	2,140
King City	2,125
Jacksonville	2,090

City Populations, 1998 *(continued)*

Enterprise	2,050
John Day	2,015
Union	1,990
Rogue River	1,960
Dayton	1,920
Clatskanie	1,870
Waldport	1,845
Stanfield	1,820
Willamina	1,810
Rainier	1,800
Elgin	1,770
North Plains	1,760
Lakeside	1,675
Mill City	1,650
Pilot Rock	1,640
Columbia City	1,635
Durham	1,555
Hines	1,550
Carlton	1,525
Vale	1,505
Heppner	1,500
Brownsville	1,445
Cannon Beach	1,425
Cave Junction	1,425
Gervais	1,370
Canyonville	1,340
Irrigon	1,330
Turner	1,330
Amity	1,315
Dunes City	1,265
Joseph	1,260
Gold Hill	1,240
Rockaway Beach	1,235
Gearhart	1,230
Riddle	1,220
Athena	1,200
Siletz	1,200
Prairie City	1,195
Bay City	1,155
Drain	1,145
Depoe Bay	1,100
Cascade Locks	1,095
Lowell	1,075
Yoncalla	1,065
Lyons	1,060
Port Orford	1,055
Tangent	1,045
Falls City	1,020
Yamhill	975
Garibaldi	970
Island City	920
Oakland	870
Culver	850
Merrill	850
Sisters	850
Banks	845
Condon	830
Chiloquin	795
Manzanita	795
Maywood Park	790
Coburg	790
Glendale	770
Halsey	760
Malin	760
Wallowa	745
Millersburg	730
Canyon City	725
Donald	700
Aurora	695
Metolius	690
Weston	690
Yachats	685
Powers	665
Scio	655
Mount Vernon	650
Echo	640
Cove	625
Johnson City	625
Dufur	620
Gaston	615
Huntington	580
North Powder	580
Adair Village	570
Monroe	555
Gates	535
Arlington	530
Fossil	530
Maupin	490
Haines	470
Butte Falls	425
Wasco	420
Jordan Valley	390
Wheeler	385
Bonanza	380
Detroit	380
Paisley	365
Halfway	350
St. Paul	350
Moro	340
Mosier	335
Imbler	325
Scotts Mills	315
Rufus	310
Lexington	305
Idanha	300
Rivergrove	300
Sodaville	280
Westfir	280
Adams	275
Ione	275
Long Creek	260
Ukiah	245
Waterloo	240
Lostine	230
Nehalem	230
Seneca	230
Mitchell	200
Helix	190
Dayville	185
Grass Valley	185
Elkton	180
Richland	180
Sumpter	175
Monument	165
Spray	165
Summerville	150
Adrian	145
Unity	145
Barlow	125
Antelope	65
Prescott	60
Shaniko	30
Granite	25
Lonerock	25
Greenhorn	3

Source: U.S. Bureau of the Census

The Life and Death of a River Town

If you look for the town of Vanport on a map, you won't find it. The wartime housing project, built in 1942, served 18,700 shipyard workers and their families. Its construction was such a rush job that a Congressional investigating committee criticized not just the buildings themselves but most of its public services. African-Americans, who lived in a segregated area of the project, and women made up a large portion of the workforce. Shifts ran 24 hours a day.

The day before Memorial Day 1948, an engineer inspected the entire dike system around the project and reported that all was well. Unfortunately, part of the dike had been built around a rotting train trestle, filled simply by tossing materials over the side to bury it. Recent heavy rains and melting snow had swelled the Columbia River to record levels, and moisture seeped into the dike.

A siren signal went off on May 30, 1948, just as a 6-foot wall of water crashed into the city. Many people didn't hear the signal, and because previous reports had insisted that warnings would sound well in advance, the response was slow. Some tried to help neighbors and collect belongings before they realized, in the words of one store owner, that "life, not property, was the question." Within minutes, the break widened to 600 feet, and in two hours up to 20 feet of debris-filled water covered the town.

Witnesses saw floating cars crushed by buildings, men in small boats breaking into upper-floor windows, and frightened residents evacuated by police at gunpoint. Rescue workers picked people off roofs. Hundreds fled on foot around traffic jammed at the few exit routes. Drivers of cars aimed for higher ground took on as many people as they could.

In the following days, families were reunited at a Red Cross center in Vancouver, Washington, that provided 10,000 cots and blankets. A family friend drove one 5-year-old girl and her brother to the center. Years later she said, "We lost everything but had nothing, really." Today you can look at a map of the Portland area, find West Delta Park, and know what is underneath. ✭

Organizations of Interest

League of Oregon Cities, 1201 Court St. NE, Salem 97301-1474, (503) 588-6550, www.orlocalgov.org.

Coast

(*See also* Dunes; Lighthouses; Seals and Sea Lions) Oregon's Pacific coast is one of the most beautiful, unspoiled, and least developed coastlines in the contiguous 48 states. Along the 362-mile length of coast, one can see dramatic headlands and capes; rocky shores that expose tidepools filled with marine life at low tide; wind-sculpted sand beaches, some of black sand scattered with agates, garnets, and jade pebbles; river estuaries; freshwater lakes trapped behind sand dams; weather-carved sea caves, arches, and sea stacks; and mountains rising directly from the sea.

The Pacific Coast Highway (U.S. 101), which runs the length of the Pacific coast from Washington through Oregon and California, is one of the state's most scenic drives. From the highway, one can access bicycle trails and state parks (recreational areas and state parks are spaced roughly 5 miles apart). In 1913, Governor Oswald West declared the beaches public highways, and Oregon law now requires public access to beaches at least every 3 miles.

Bays and Estuaries. The most important bays for coastal shipping are Tillamook Bay, Yaquina Bay, and Coos Bay, the leading ocean harbor for freighters on the Oregon Coast; smaller bays include Alsea Bay, Netarts Bay, and Salmon Inlet. The river inlets include those for the Columbia, Necanicum, Nehalem, Nestucca, Siletz, Yachats, Siuslaw, Umpqua, Coquille, Rogue, Sixes, Elk, Pistol, Chetco, and Winchuck Rivers.

Beaches. Beaches fringed with low dunes line much of the coast. The best known dune formation is the 40-mile-long Oregon Dunes National Recreation Area (*see* National Parks, Monuments, and

Tillamook Bay. From *Wind on the Waves* by Kim R. Stafford (text) and Ray Atkeson and Rick Schafer (photos).

Dangerous Beauty

The Oregon Coast has a justly deserved, worldwide reputation for its spectacular scenery. However, the processes that contribute to its beauty are also the source of hazards that can put people and property at risk. Waves, currents, tides, and storms cause erosion, landslides, and flooding. Piled-up driftwood, which may look like an inviting playground to children, can shift, causing logs to roll. Unexpectedly large waves can sneak up on an unsuspecting beachwalker. In March 1999, a 6-year-old boy drowned when a "sneaker" wave swept over him and pulled him seaward. A year earlier, a wave caused a large log to roll over two children, killing one of them. Coast Guard and emergency-response personnel urge visitors to Oregon's beaches to remember simple safety rules:

Never turn your back on the ocean.
Watch out for waves.
Stay off logs.
Be aware of the tides.

Recreation Areas) between Coos Bay and Florence. It stretches more than a hundred miles and extends 3 miles inland, with dunes up to 600 feet tall. Nowhere else in the world has so much ocean-related sand piled up. Other long, wide (up to about a mile wide), sandy beaches edged with dunes can be found all along the coast. They include Clatsop Spit to Seaside at the north end of the coast, to Bullards Beach and Bandon State Parks outside of Bandon at the southern end. There are also miles of narrower stretches of sandy beach (a few hundred feet wide) in between. Many of these, such as Seaside, Cannon Beach, Manzanita, Rockaway, Lincoln City, and Newport, have become popular beach vacation destinations.

Capes and Headlands. Rugged cliffs and headlands that jut into the sea provide dramatic relief along the Oregon Coast. From Seaside, Oregon, to the California border, a number of such features stand out. They are (from north to south):

Tillamook Head
Cape Falcon
Cape Lookout, Cape Meares, and Cape Kiwanda (all accessible from the Three Capes scenic route off U.S. 101)
Cascade Head
Cape Foulweather
Yaquina Head
Cape Perpetua
Heceta Head
Cape Arago
Cape Blanco
Cape Sebastian
Cape Ferrelo

Columbia Plateau

The Columbia Plateau is one of the world's most spectacular volcanic regions. It covers most of northeastern Oregon, eastern Washington and western Idaho. The Columbia River forms the northwestern-most border of the Columbia Plateau. The area is actually a basin between the Rockies and the Cascades that was covered by hundreds of lava flows more than 4 million years ago. In some areas, these lava flows are thousands of feet deep.

Columbia River and Columbia River Gorge

Columbia River and Columbia River Gorge The Columbia River is the major river of western North America and forms much of the boundary between the states of Washington and Oregon before emptying into the Pacific Ocean. The Native Americans called it the "Ouragon," meaning "River of the West." After explorer Robert Gray traversed the mouth of the Columbia in 1792, naming the river after his ship, so many people still called it by its native name that "Ouragon" soon denoted the entire region. Lewis and Clark explored the Lower Columbia from 1805-06, followed in 1811 by Canadian David Thompson, who in 1811 followed the river from its source to its mouth.

Large oceangoing ships can navigate the lower Columbia River as far as Vancouver, Washington, and with the aid of locks, smaller marine vessels can travel 186 miles farther upstream to The Dalles. Barges and other shallow-draft boats can navigate 137 miles farther. A series of dams provides flood control and navigation.

The Columbia's great salmon population supported a booming canning industry until fish stocks were severely depleted in the 1900s as a result of dam construction and pollution. In 1994 the Northwest Power Planning Council began efforts to revive the salmon population by increasing water flow through the dams and developing habitat-protection standards.

The Columbia River ends at one of the world's most hazardous river mouths and sandbars. Wildly variable currents and winds up to 60 miles an hour have caused more than 2,000 shipwrecks and 1,500 deaths, earning the river mouth and bar the nickname "Graveyard of the Pacific."

The Columbia River Gorge, the only sea-level route through the Cascades, is 80 miles long and up to 4,000 feet deep. On Nov. 17, 1986, President Ronald Reagan signed into law an act creating the 292,500-acre Columbia River Gorge National Scenic Area. The designation is not the same as that of a national park or wilderness. It allows for existing rural and scenic characteristics while encouraging compatible growth and development within urban areas. The Columbia River Gorge National Scenic Area is jointly managed by the U.S. Forest Service, Oregon, Washington, and the Columbia River Gorge Commission with 12 voting members appointed by the states and 1 non-voting member appointed by the U.S. Secretary of Agriculture. The visitor center at Multnomah Falls, accessible from I-84 as well as from the Historic Columbia River Highway, offers information about the Columbia River Gorge. You can also obtain Trail Park Passes, which are required to park at certain trailheads within national forests.

Organizations of Interest

Columbia Gorge Discovery Center and Wasco County Historical Museum, 5000 Discovery Dr., The Dalles 97058, (541) 296-8600. This 50-acre interpretive center features the geological history of the Gorge region, 10,000 years of Native American life, and the stories of explorers who paved the way for white settlement. A 33-foot-long water model of the Columbia River shows the power of Celilo Falls before the

> ### Legendary Falls
>
> *The Columbia River, still one of the Northwest's most spectacular natural wonders, was once a free-flowing river with falls and cataracts in numerous places. Considered obstacles to navigation by early pioneers, the river's waterfalls fell victim to the ambitious dam construction programs that began in the 1930s. Among the most celebrated of these was Celilo Falls, just northeast of The Dalles. Indian fishermen once speared migrating salmon here and passed on prized fishing stands from generation to generation. The beginning of the end of Celilo Falls was the 1908 construction of a lock and dam to make the river more navigable. In 1956-57, with completion of The Dalles Dam, the falls were obliterated completely.*

construction of dams. Child-friendly exhibits include a ride on a windsurfing simulator, a chance to create your own canning label, and the opportunity to dress in period clothing.

Columbia River Gorge Commission, P.O. Box 730, White Salmon 98672, (509) 493-3323.

U.S. Forest Service Columbia River Gorge National Scenic Area Headquarters, 902 Wasco Ave., #200, Hood River 97031, (541) 386-2333, Portland: (503) 668-1440, www.fs.fed.us/r6/columbia.

Congressional Delegation

Oregon's U.S. congressional delegation consists of two senators and five members of the House of Representatives.

Composition of Oregon Congressional Delegation by Political Party

	House	Senate
101st Congress (1989-90)	3D, 2R	2R
102nd Congress (1991-92)	4D, 1R	2R
103rd Congress(1993-94)	4D, 1R	2R
104th Congress (1995-96)	4D, 1R	1D, 1R
105th Congress (1997-98)	4D, 1R	1D, 1R
106th Congress (1999-00)	4D, 1R	1D, 1R

106th Congress on the Internet: www.senate.gov and www.house.gov.

U.S. Senate

Gordon H. Smith (Rep.)

First Elected: 1996

Term expires: 2003

Committees: Budget; Energy and Natural Resources; Foreign Relations; Year 2000 Problem Committees; chair, Water and Power Subcommittee; chair, Subcommittee on European Affairs; member, Forests and Public Land Management; member, Energy Research, Development, Production and Regulation Subcommittees; member, Subcommittees on East Asian and Pacific Affairs, Near Eastern and South Asian Affairs, and International Operations

Washington, D.C. Office: SD B-359, Washington, D.C. 20510, (202) 224-3753, senate.gov/~gsmith.

District Offices:

Central Oregon—Jamison Bldg., 131 NW Hawthorne Ave., No. 208, Bend 97701, (541) 318-1298.

Eastern Oregon—Jager Bldg., 116 S Main St., No. 3, Pendleton 97801, (541) 278-1129.

Portland—One World Trade Center, 121 SW Salmon St., No. 1250, Portland 97204, (503) 326-3386.

Southern Oregon—Security Plaza; 1175 E Main, No. 2D, Medford 97504, (541) 608-9102.

Western Oregon—Federal Bldg., 211 E 7th Ave., Suite 202, Eugene 97401, (541) 465-6750.

Ron Wyden (Dem.)

First Elected: 1996 (previously served in the U.S. House of Representatives)

Term expires: 2005

Committees: Member, Budget Committee; Commerce, Science & Transportation Committee; Energy & Natural Resources Committee; Environment & Public Works Committee; Special Committee on Aging; bipartisan Senate Reform Task Force

Washington, D.C. Office: 259 Russell Senate Office Bldg., Washington, D.C. 20510, (202) 224-5244, www.wyden.senate.gov/~mail.htm.

District Offices:

Bend—The Jamison Bldg., 131 NW Hawthorne Ave., No. 107, Bend 97701, (541) 330-9142.

Eugene—The Center Court Bldg., 151 W 7th Ave., No. 435, Eugene 97401, (541) 431-0229.

La Grande—Sac Annex Bldg., 105 Fir St., No. 210, La Grande 97850, (541) 962-7691.

Medford—The Federal Courthouse, 310 W 6th St., Room 118, Medford 97501, (541) 858-5122.

Portland—500 NE Multnomah St., No. 320, Portland 97232, (503) 326-7525.

Salem—707 13th St. SE, No. 110, Salem 97301, (503) 589-4555.

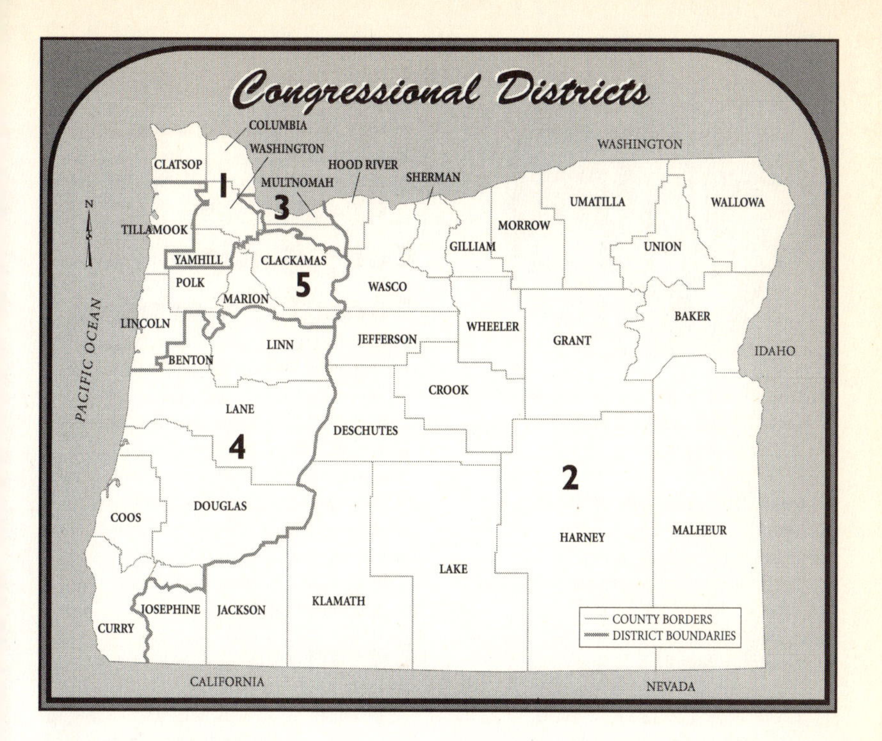

U.S. House of Representatives

First District: David Wu (Dem.)

Counties: Clatsop, Columbia, Washington, Yamhill, and small parts of southwestern Multnomah and northwestern Clackamas

First Elected: 1998

Committees: Member, Education and Workforce Committee; Early Childhood Education; Employer-Employee Relations Subcommittees

Washington, D.C. Office: 510 Cannon Office Bldg., Washington, D.C. 20515, (202) 225-0855, fax: (202) 225-9497.

District Office: 620 SW Main St., No. 606, Portland 97205, (503) 326-2901, (800) 422-4003.

Second District: Greg Walden (Rep.)

Counties: All counties east of the Cascades, all of Jackson and most of Josephine

First Elected: 1998

Term expires: 2001

Committees: Member, Agriculture; Government Reform; and Resources Committees

Washington, D.C. Office: 1404 Longworth House Office Bldg., Washington, D.C. 20515, (202) 225-6730, greg.walden@mail.house.gov.

District Office:

Medford—843 E Main St., No. 400, Medford 97504, (541) 776-4646.

Third District: Earl Blumenauer (Dem.)

Counties: Most of Multnomah and northern part of Clackamas

Committees: Member, Transportation and Infrastructure Committee; Ground and Water Subcommittees

First Elected: 1996

Washington, D.C. Office: 1406 Longworth House Office Bldg., Washington, D.C. 20515, (202) 225-4811, write.earl@ mail. house.gov, www.house.gov/ blumenauer.

District Office: 516 SE Morrison St., No. 250, Portland 97214, (503) 231-2300.

Fourth District: Peter DeFazio (Dem.)
Counties: Coos, Curry, Douglas, Lane, Linn, northern part of Josephine, and most of Benton
First Elected: 1986
Committees: Member, House Transportation and Infrastructure Committees; House Resources Committee; Aviation and Surface Transportation Subcommittees; ranking Democrat on Water and Power Subcommittee
Washington, D.C. Office: 2134 Rayburn House Office Bldg., Washington, D.C. 20515, (202) 225-6416, fax: (202) 225-0032, peter.defazio@mail.house.gov, www.house.gov/defazio/index.htm.
District Offices:
Coos Bay—125 Central, No. 350, Coos Bay 97420, (541) 269-2609.
Eugene—151 W 7th Ave., No. 400, Eugene 97401, (541) 465-6732, (800) 944-9603.
Roseburg—P.O. Box 2460, Roseburg 97470, (541) 440-3523.

Fifth District: Darlene Hooley (Dem.)
Counties: Lincoln, Marion, Polk, Tillamook, northern Benton, most of Clackamas
First Elected: 1996
Committees: Member, House Budget Committee, Banking and Financial Services Committee
Washington, D.C. Office: 1419 Longworth House Office Bldg., Washington, D.C. 20515, (202) 225-5711, fax: (202) 225-5699, www.house.gov/hooley.
District Office:
Salem—315 Mission St. SE, No. 101, Salem 97302, (503) 588-9100.

Constitution (*See* Laws)

Consular Corps

The thirteen foreign nations that maintain consulates in Oregon are Belgium, Czech Republic, Finland, France, Germany, Guatemala, Italy, Korea, Mexico, The Netherlands, Norway, Sweden, and Thailand. The consuls are their countries' official representatives. Their duties include assisting their countries' citizens and businesses operating in this country. Most of the foreign consulates in Oregon are located in Portland.

Counties

Oregon's first counties were four districts established in 1843 by the Provisional Government of the Oregon Country: Yamhill, Clackamas, Tuality (renamed Washington County), and Champoeg (now Marion County). Those original four have been divided and redrawn into the 36 counties that exist today.

The land area and population of Oregon's counties vary widely. Harney County, the largest in land area, is 10,228 square miles and is also the most sparsely populated at less than one person per square mile. The smallest physically, Multnomah, with less than 465 square miles, has the most population and is the most densely populated. The fastest-growing county during the 1990s was Deschutes County, which had a whopping 39.9 percent increase in population. The least growth during that same time was in Sherman County, which saw a drop in population of -0.9 percent.

Oregon's county governments have the highest degree of local discretionary authority of any state in the country. This was not always the case. Prior to 1958, when the state authorized county "home rule," county government activities were authorized or mandated by state law. Two-thirds of Oregon's counties are run now by a board of three to five commissioners, and the rest are governed by a county judge and two commissioners who comprise a "county court."

Largest Counties by Area

Harney	10,228 square miles
Malheur	9,926 square miles
Lake	8,359 square miles
Klamath	6,135 square miles
Douglas	5,071 square miles

Smallest Counties by Area

Multnomah	465 square miles
Hood River	533 square miles
Benton	679 square miles
Columbia	687 square miles
Yamhill	718 square miles

Most Populated Counties

Multnomah	641,900
Washington	397,600
Clackamas	323,600
Lane	313,000
Marion	271,900

Least Populated Counties

Wheeler	1,600
Sherman	1,900
Gilliam	2,100
Wallowa	7,200
Lake	7,400

County Profiles

Baker County, 1995 3rd St., Baker City 97814, (541) 523-8200. Population: 16,700. Area: 3,089 square miles. Year established: 1862. Baker County was formed from part of Wasco County and named after Col. Edward D. Baker, a U.S. senator from Oregon. The deepest gorge in the United States—Hells Canyon—is located in Baker County. Before 1861, the pioneers of the Oregon Trail only passed through Baker County on their way west. Then gold was discovered and the county became one of the Northwest's largest gold producers.

Benton County, 408 SW Monroe Ave., No. 111, Corvallis 97333, (541) 757-6800, www.peak.org/benton-county. Population: 76,600. Area: 679 square miles. Year established: 1847. Benton County was created from Polk County and named after Senator Thomas Hart Benton of Missouri, an advocate of developing the Oregon Territory. Oregon State University, agriculture, and lumber and wood-products manufacturing form the basis of Benton County's economy.

Clackamas County, 906 Main St., Oregon City 97045, (503) 655-8581, www.co.clackamas.or.us. Population: 323,600. Area: 1,879 square miles. Year established: 1843. Clackamas was one of Oregon's four original counties, created in 1843. Named for the Clackamas Indians, its dominant feature is elegant Mount Hood. Oregon City, the county seat, was the first capital of the Oregon Territory and is now home to the End of the Oregon Trail Interpretive Center, a living history museum of the state's pioneer past.

Clatsop County, 749 Commercial, Astoria 97103, (503) 325-1000, clatsop.county@co.clatsop.or.us, www.co.clatsop.or.us. Population: 34,700. Area: 843 square miles. Year established: 1844. Clatsop County, named for the Clatsop Indians, is where the Lewis and Clark Expedition wintered over in the Pacific Northwest before returning east. It is also home to the state's oldest city, Astoria, which was established as a fur trading post in 1811.

Columbia County, Courthouse, St. Helens 97051-0010, (503) 397-4322, www.columbia-center.org/home. Population: 42,300. Area: 687 square miles. Year established: 1854. American Capt. Robert Gray, commanding the ship *Columbia*, for which the river and the county are named, landed on this county's shoreline in 1792. The county has 62 miles of Columbia riverfront and contains deepwater ports. By 1997 population figures, this is the fastest-growing county in Oregon.

Coos County, 250 N Baxter, Coquille 97423, (541) 396-3121, www.iceinternet.

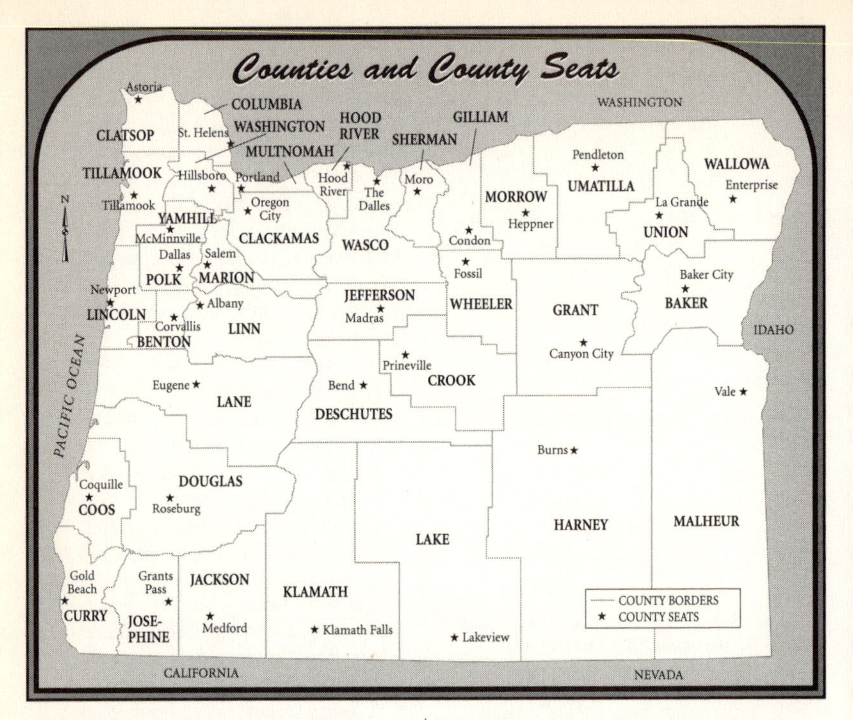

com/~coosdp. Population: 61,400. Area: 1,629 square miles. Year established: 1853. Coos County was created from parts of Umpqua and Jackson Counties and originally included Curry County. The name "Coos" is from a native Indian word for "lake" or "place of pines." The Port of Coos Bay is the world's largest forest-products shipping port. Oregon Dunes National Recreation Area is located in the county.

Crook County, 300 E 3rd, Prineville 97754, (541) 447-6555. Population: 16,650. Area: 2,991 square miles. Year established: 1882. Crook County was formed from Wasco County in 1882 and named for Maj. Gen. George Crook of the U.S. Army. Crook County, Oregon's geographic center, has only one incorporated population center, the city of Prineville, founded in 1868. The county is prime rockhounding country.

Curry County, 29821 Ellensburg Ave., Gold Beach 97444, (541) 247-7011. Population: 22,000. Area: 1,648 square miles. Year established: 1855. The county, named after Territorial Governor George L. Curry, features some of Oregon's spectacular coastal scenery. The county has valuable standing timber, including myrtle wood, along with recreational clamming, crabbing, and fishing (freshwater and saltwater).

Deschutes County, 1130 NW Harriman, Bend 97701, (541) 388-6570, www.deschutes.org. Population: 104,900. Area: 3,055 square miles. Year established: 1916. French-Canadian fur trappers named the river for which Deschutes County is named the "Rivière des Chutes," or "River of the Falls." The county boundaries were carved from part of Crook County. An outdoor recreation mecca, the county features Mount Bachelor ski area, Lava River Caves State Park, and the Three Sisters Wilderness.

Douglas County, 1036 SE Douglas, No. 217, Roseburg 97470, (541) 672-3311. Population: 100,300. Area: 5,071 square miles. Year established: 1852. Douglas County, named for U.S. Senator Stephen A. Douglas, an ardent advocate for Oregon settlement, extends from the Cascade Mountains to the Pacific Ocean. The county's resources include nearly 2.8 million acres of commercial forest and the world's largest stand of old-growth timber.

Gilliam County, 221 S Oregon St., Condon 97823-0427, (541) 384-6351. Population: 2,100. Area: 1,223 square miles. Year established: 1885. Gilliam County, in the heart of the Columbia Basin wheat country, was created from a part of Wasco County and named after Army Col. Cornelius Gilliam. The county features two of the state's major rivers, the John Day and the Columbia.

Grant County, 200 S Canyon Blvd., Canyon City 97820, (541) 575-1675. Population: 8,000. Area: 4,528 square miles. Year established: 1864. Grant County was created from Wasco and Umatilla Counties and was named for Gen. Ulysses S. Grant. The John Day Fossil Beds and the headwaters of the John Day River are located in Grant County, in the north-central part of the state.

Harney County, 450 N Buena Vista, Burns 97720, (541) 573-6356. Population: 7,600. Area: 10,228 square miles. Year established: 1889. Harney, the largest county in Oregon, is also its most sparsely populated. In fact, it has more cattle than people—its large cattle ranches support more than 100,000 head. Among the county's natural wonders are Steens Mountain, the Alvord Desert, and the Malheur National Wildlife Refuge, well-known for its rich and varied bird life.

Hood River County, 309 State St., Hood River 97031-2093, (541) 386-3970. Population: 19,500. Area: 533 square miles. Year established: 1908. Hood River County was created in 1908 from Wasco County and is famous today for fruit and windsurfing. The county has more than 14,000 acres of commercial fruit orchards and is the world's leading producer of Anjou pears. The Columbia River Gorge, which forms the county's northern border, has become a world mecca for windsurfers attracted by the steady winds.

Jackson County, 10 S Oakdale, Medford 97501, (541) 776-7248. Population: 172,800. Area: 2,801 square miles. Year established: 1852. Named for President Andrew Jackson, this county was formed from Lane County and the unorganized area south of Douglas and Umpqua Counties. This southern county is home to Oregon's best known theater venue, Ashland's Shakespeare Festival.

Jefferson County, 75 SE "C" St., Madras 97741, (541) 475-2449. Population: 17,400. Area: 1,791 square miles. Year established: 1914. Jefferson County was established from a portion of Crook County and named for Mount Jefferson. A rich agricultural area, the county is also a popular outdoor recreation area that boasts 300 days of sunshine per year.

Josephine County, 500 NW 6th St., Grants Pass 97526, (541) 474-5100, www.magick.net/~jocogov. Population: 73,000. Area: 1,641 square miles. Year established: 1856. Josephine County has a rich Old West history. Named for Virginia "Josephine" Rollins, the first white woman to settle there, the county was the site of a gold rush and the Rogue River Indian War. Major natural attractions include Oregon Caves National Monument, Hellgate Canyon-Rogue River, and the Kalmiopsis Wilderness.

Klamath County, 305 Main St., Klamath Falls 97601, (541) 883-5100. Population: 62,000. Area: 6,135 square miles. Year established: 1882. Klamath County is best known for Crater Lake National Park and Klamath Lake, the state's largest lake. Natural geothermal hot wells provide heat for many homes, businesses, and the Klamath Falls campus of the Oregon Institute of Technology.

Lake County, 513 Center St., Lakeview 97630, (541) 947-6003. Population: 7,400. Area: 8,359 square miles, Year established: 1874. Lake County, created from Jackson and Wasco Counties, is noted for a number of natural areas—Hart Mountain National Antelope Refuge, Fort Rock, Abert Lake and Abert Rim, among them—and sunstones, the state gemstone. Lakeview, the county seat, is a popular hang-gliding area.

Lane County, 125 E 8th, Eugene 97401, (541) 682-4203, www.co.lane.or.us.

The Rogue River Bridge, at Gold Beach in Curry County, not long after it was completed in 1932. From *Oregon, My Oregon* by Ray Atkeson.

Population: 313,000. Area: 4,620 square miles. Year established: 1851. Lane County was named for the first territorial governor and frontier hero Gen. Joseph Lane. The county extends from the Willamette Valley to the Pacific Coast. It is the home of the University of Oregon and the famous Sea Lion Caves.

Lincoln County, 225 W Olive St., Newport 97365, (541) 265-6611, www.co.lincoln.or.us. Population: 43,200. Area: 992 square miles. Year established: 1893. Named for President Abraham Lincoln, this coastal county features miles of scenic coastline. Agate Beach, the OSU Hatfield Marine Science Center, the Oregon Coast Aquarium, and Yaquina Head Lighthouse are all located in Lincoln County.

Linn County, 300 4th Ave. SW, Albany 97321, (541) 967-3825, www.co.linn.or.us. Population: 102,200. Area: 2,297 square miles. Year established: 1847. Linn County, in the center of the Willamette Valley, is named for U.S. Senator Lewis F. Linn of Missouri, author of the Donation Land Act, which provided free land to settlers in the West. The county's economic base includes agriculture, forest products, rare metals, manufacturing, and recreation.

Malheur County, 251 B St. W, Vale 97918, (541) 473-5124, (541) 473-5151, kharrod@malheurco.org, ddelong@ malheurco.org, www.malheurco.org. Population: 29,200. Area: 9,926 square miles. Year established: 1887. Malheur County, created from Baker County, gets its name from the Malheur River, which was named by French trappers. They called it the "Rivière au Malheur" or "Unfortunate River" because their property and furs were stolen as they camped there. The county is 94 percent rangeland.

Marion County, 100 High St. NE, Salem 97301-3670, (503) 588-5212, commissioners@open.org, www.open. org/marion. Population: 271,900. Area:

1,194 square miles. Year established: 1843. Marion County, in the heart of the Willamette Valley, is the site of Salem, the state's capital. Salem is one of the oldest cities in the Willamette Valley, as well as the county seat.

Morrow County, 100 Court St., Heppner 97836, (541) 676-9061, mcjudge@centuryinter.net. Population: 9,400. Area: 2,049 square miles. Year established: 1885. Morrow County, created from Umatilla County, was named for citizen J. L. Morrow. Located in north-central Oregon, the county's growth was spurred by the development of center-pivot irrigation technology. The Columbia River and the Blue Mountains are among its major natural features.

Multnomah County, 1021 SW 4th, Portland 97204, (503) 248-3511, www.multnomah.lib.or.us. Population: 641,900. Area: 465 square miles. Year established: 1854. Multnomah County is dominated by the city of Portland, the state's largest urban area. It is the state's smallest and most densely populated county. It is also the state's transportation hub, home to its largest port, the Port of Portland, and its largest airport, Portland International Airport.

Polk County, 850 Main St., Dallas 97338, (503) 623-8173. Population: 59,500. Area: 745 square miles. Year established: 1845. Polk County, named for President James Knox Polk, was the primary destination of early wagon trains that took the southern route across the Cascades in Oregon. The county's rural attractions include covered bridges and vineyards and wineries.

Sherman County, P.O. Box 365, Moro 97039, (541) 565-3416. Population: 1,900. Area: 831 square miles. Year established: 1889. Sherman County, located along the Columbia River in north-central Oregon, was named for Civil War Union Army Gen. William Tecumseh Sherman. The county's wide-open spaces support wheat and cattle ranches.

Tillamook County, 201 Laurel Ave., Tillamook 97141, (503) 842-3403, (800) 488-8280, ssapp@co.tillamook.or.us, www.co.tillamook.or.us. Population: 24,000. Area: 1,125 square miles. Year established: 1853. Tillamook County was named for the Tillamook Indians. This coastal county is known for its dairy farms—and famous cheese—and for the state's worst forest fire, which occurred in the 1930s. It laid waste to over 300,000 acres of forest, an area that came to be known as the Tillamook Burn and is today the focus of activities to turn it into a state park.

Umatilla County, 216 SE 4th St., Pendleton 97801, (541) 276-7111, www.pendleton-oregon.org/county.html. Population: 67,100. Area: 3,231 square miles. Year established: 1862. Umatilla County is home to one of the country's greatest rodeos, the Pendleton Round-Up. This wide-open area of amber waves of grain was settled by cattle ranchers, but it was the development of dryland wheat farming, and later irrigation, that spurred growth.

Union County, 1106 K Ave., La Grande 97850, (541) 963-1001, www.union-county.org. Population: 24,400. Area: 2,038 square miles. Year established: 1864. Union County's defining feature is the Grande Ronde Valley, an agriculturally rich area that boasts of never having had a general crop failure. Union County's boundaries encompass parts of the rugged Wallowa Mountains and the Blue Mountains.

Wallowa County, 101 S River St., Enterprise 97828, (541) 426-4543. Population: 7,200. Area: 3,153 square miles. Year established: 1887. This remote area of Oregon was the hunting and fishing grounds and ancestral homeland of Chief Joseph's band of the Nez Perce Indians. Its name, "Wallowa," is from the Nez Perce word *wallowa,* which describes a tripod of poles used to support fishnets. The county's natural features include parts of the Wallowa Mountains, the Eagle Cap Wilderness, and Hells Canyon National Recreation Area.

Wasco County, 511 Washington St., The Dalles 97058, (541) 296-6159. Population: 22,600. Area: 2,396 square miles. Year established: 1854. Wasco County features the Columbia and

Deschutes Rivers, Pulpit Rock, The Dalles Dam, the Warm Springs Indian Reservation, and part of Mount Hood. Its county seat is the trading hub of north-central Oregon. The Dalles is near a site along the Columbia River where Indian tribes once gathered to trade and fish.

Washington County, 155 N 1st Ave., Hillsboro 97124-3072, (503) 648-8611, www.co.washington.or.us. Population: 397,600. Area: 727 square miles. Year established: 1843. Washington County was originally called Tuality County and was one of the four original counties created by the Provisional Government of Oregon. The name was changed to honor President George Washington. The county's Tualatin Valley is one of the fastest developing areas in the state.

Wheeler County, 701 Adams St., P.O. Box 327, Fossil 97830, (541) 763-2400. Population: 1,600. Area: 1,713 square miles. Year established: 1899. Wheeler County's claim to fame is one of North America's best-known fossil areas, the John Day Fossil Beds National Monument. The county's terrain varies from sagebrush, juniper, and rimrock to pine and fir forest. Forest lands cover nearly one-third of the county.

Yamhill County, 535 NE 5th St., McMinnville 97128, (503) 434-7501, www.co.yamhill.or.us. Population: 81,900. Area: 718 square miles. Year established: 1843. Yamhill County was one of the state's original four districts. It was named after the Yamhelas or Yamhill Indians of the Kalapooian family, who lived along the Yamhill River. This is the heart of Oregon's wine industry, with nineteen wineries.

Organizations of Interest

Association of Oregon Counties, 1201 Court Street NE, P.O. Box 12729, Salem 97309, (503) 585-8351, www.orlocalgov.org.

Covered Bridges

Though the rustic appeal of old wooden-truss bridges in Oregon inspired committed preservation efforts, only 45 remain of the 450 that existed in the early 1900s. In 1851 engineers began to cover some wooden bridges in Oregon, thereby extending their life expectancy from 10 to 30 or more years. Even so, floods, decay, and the cost of preservation all contributed to the disappearance of these historic landmarks. The oldest remaining housed wooden-truss bridge is the Fisher School Bridge (also called the Five Rivers Bridge) built in 1919 in Lincoln County. The 38 covered bridges listed below are on the National Register of Historic Places.

Benton County: Harris Bridge west of Wren; Hayden Bridge, west of Alsea.

Coos County: Sandy Creek Bridge on Sandy Creek Rd., remote.

Deschutes County: Rock o' the Range Bridge north of Bend.

Douglas County: Milo Academy Bridge southeast of Days Creek.

Jackson County: Lost Creek Bridge southeast of Lakecreek; McKee Bridge south of Ruch.

Josephine County: Grave Creek Bridge in Sunny Valley north of Grants Pass.

Lane County: Belknap Bridge off Oregon 126, Rainbow; Chambers Bridge south of River Rd., Cottage Grove; Coyote Creek Bridge southeast of Crow; Currin Bridge east of Cottage Grove; Deadwood Creek Bridge northeast of Swisshome; Dorena Bridge northwest of Dorena; Ernest Bridge northeast of Marcola; Goodpasture Bridge west of Vida; Lake Creek Bridge west of Greenleaf; Lowell Bridge at Dexter Reservoir; Mosby Creek Bridge east of Cottage Grove; Office Bridge crossing North Fork of the Middle Fork Willamette River, Westfir; Parvin Bridge south of Dexter off Lost Creek Rd.; Pengra Bridge southeast of Jasper; Stewart Bridge southeast of Walden; Unity Bridge north of Lowell; Wendling Bridge northeast of Marcola; Wildcat Creek Bridge west of Eugene, Walton.

Lincoln County: Chitwood Bridge off Oregon 20 Chitwood; Fisher School Bridge on Five Rivers Rd., Fisher; North Fork of the Yachats Bridge northeast of Yachats.

Linn County: Crabtree Creek, Hungry Hill Dr., 1.8 mi. north of Crabtree; Crawfordsville Bridge on Oregon 228, Crawfordsville; Hannah Bridge on Burmester Creek Rd., Scio; Larwood Bridge east of Crabtree; Short Bridge on High Deck Rd., Cascadia; Thomas Creek, Goar Rd., 3 mi. north of Crabtree; Thomas Creek, Richardson Gap Rd., 2 mi. east of Scio.

Marion County: Gallon House Bridge northwest of Silverton.

Polk County: Ritner Creek Bridge south of Pedee.

Organizations of Interest

The Oregon Covered Bridge Advisory Committee, 329 Transportation Building, Salem, 97310, (503) 986-4200.

Dams

There are 1,200 large dams in Oregon and thousands more small ones. These dams serve a variety of purposes: to generate hydropower; to provide water for irrigation, for flood control, for recreation; and to hold water supplies or aid in maintaining water quality.

Dams are owned by governments, by private companies, and by individuals. Both private and public utility companies operate large hydroelectric projects. Among nonfederal power projects in Oregon are those owned by large utility companies, including Portland General Electric Co., Pacificorp, Puget Power & Light, and Idaho Power, and the cities of Portland, Eugene, and Ashland.

The big hydroelectricity-generating dams are all located on the Columbia River and its tributaries. While the Northwest's dams were originally heralded as public works projects that benefited the state and its people, in recent years there has been much focus on their lethal impact on native salmon runs (*see* Endangered Species, salmon). Dams block the way for fish returning upstream to spawn. For salmon fry headed downstream toward the ocean, passing through a dam at certain times was akin to swimming through a Cuisinart. The mortality rate could range from 15 percent to 35 percent per dam, depending on the rate of river flow. Solutions such as trucking salmon fry around the dams or spilling more water over them may help somewhat, but the salmon runs have been seriously depleted. A more drastic approach—taking out dams—has been proposed and may actually come to pass where the dams have outlived their original purpose. Dams that are essential to the local or regional economies, such as those on the Columbia, are less likely to come tumbling down anytime soon.

The Bonneville Dam spans the Columbia River east of Portland. From *Portland from the Air* by Sallie Tisdale (essay) and Russ Heinl (photos).

Major Hydroelectricity-generating Dams

Columbia and Willamette Rivers System

Stream	Project	Capacity (megawatts)	Owner
Brunswick Canyon Creek	Brunswick Creek	0.0	R.L. Horning
Bull Run River (offstream)	Ground Water Pumping Station	4.5	City of Portland
Bull Run River	Bull Run No. 1	23.8	City of Portland
Bull Run River	Bull Run No. 2	11.9	City of Portland
Bull Run River	Wolf Creek	0.1	Wolf Creek Hwy.Water District
Calapooia River	Thompson's Mills	0.1	Boston Power Co. Inc
Canyon Creek	Canyon Creek	0.1	Douglas Water Power Company
Clackamas River	Faraday	34.5	Portland General Electric Co.
Clackamas River	North Fork	38.4	Portland General Electric Co.
Clackamas River	River Mill	19.1	Portland General Electric Co.
Clackamas River, Oak Grove Fork	Oak Grove	51.0	Portland General Electric Co.
Clackamas River, Oak Grove Fork	Stone Creek	12.0	Puget Sound Power & Light Co.
Clear Branch	Middle Fork Irrigation Dist. 3	2.1	Middle Fork Irrigation District
Columbia River	John Day	2160.0	U.S. Army Corps of Engineers
Columbia River	McNary	980.0	U.S. Army Corps of Engineers
Columbia River	The Dalles	1807.0	U.S. Army Corps of Engineers
Crooked River	Opal Springs	4.3	Deschutes Valley Wtr. Dist.
Deschutes River	Bend Power	1.1	PacifiCorp
Deschutes River	Cline Falls	21.7	PacifiCorp
Deschutes River	Pelton	97.2	Portland General Electric Co.
Deschutes River	Pelton Reregulation Dam	15.0	Warm Springs Tribal Council
Deschutes River	Round Butte	247.1	Portland General Electric Co.
Falls Creek	Falls Creek	4.0	Frontier Technology Inc.
Farmers' Ditch	Farmers' Irrigation Dist. 2	3.0	Farmers' Irrigation District
Hood River	Powerdale	6.0	PacifiCorp
Irrigation Conduit	Middle Fork Irrigation Dist.	20.6	Middle Fork Irrigation District
Lacomb Irrigation Canal	Lacomb	1.0	Lacomb Irrigation District
Low Line Ditch	Farmers Irrigation Dist.	31.8	Farmers' Irrigation District

Major Hydroelectricity-generating Dams *(continued)*

Columbia and Willamette Rivers System *(continued)*

Stream	Project	Capacity (megawatts)	Owner
McKenzie River	Carmen-Smith	114.5	City of Eugene (Eugene Water and Electric Board)
McKenzie River	Cougar	25.0	U.S. Army Corps of Engineers
McKenzie River	Leaburg Dam	15.0	City of Eugene (Eugene Water and Electric Board)
McKenzie River	Trail Bridge	10.0	City of Eugene (Eugene Water and Electric Board)
McKenzie River	Walterville	8.0	City of Eugene (Eugene Water and Electric Board)
Mill Creek	Mill Creek	0.6	City of Cove
Mitchell Butte Lateral	Mitchell Butte	1.9	Owyhee Project Irrigation District
Mount Tabor Reservoir No. 5	Mount Tabor	0.2	City of Portland
Odell Creek	Odell Creek	0.2	F. L. Plog
Oswego Creek	Lake Oswego	0.5	Lake Oswego Corp.
Owyhee Lake	Owyhee Tunnel No. 1	8.0	Owyhee Project Irrigation District
Owyhee River	Owyhee Dam	4.3	Owyhee Project Irrigation District
Rock Creek	Rock Creek	0.8	Oregon Trail Electric Consumers Co-op
Santiam River, Middle Fork	Green Peter	80.0	U.S. Army Corps of Engineers
Santiam River, North Fork	Big Cliff	18.0	U.S. Army Corps of Engineers
Santiam River, North Fork	Detroit	100.0	U.S. Army Corps of Engineers
Santiam River, South Fork	Foster	20.0	U.S. Army Corps of Engineers
Santiam River, South Fork	City of Albany	0.5	City of Albany
Sandy River	Bull Run	21.0	Portland General Electric Co.
Snake River	Hells Canyon	391.5	Idaho Power Co.
Snake River	Oxbow	190.0	Idaho Power Co.
Stayton Power	Canal Water Street	0.2	Santiam Water Control District
Umatilla River	Jim Boyd	1.2	J. & J. Boyd
W. Evans Creek	Middle Fork Irrigation District	10.6	Middle Fork Irrigation District
Wallowa Creek, East Fork	Wallowa Falls	1.1	PacifiCorp
Wallowa Valley Imp. Dist. Cnl.	Canal Creek	1.1	Joseph Hydro Association, Ltd.
Wallowa Valley Imp. Dist. Cnl.	Ferguson Ridge	1.9	Joseph Hydro Association, Ltd.

(continued on page 44)

Major Hydroelectricity-generating Dams *(continued)*

Columbia and Willamette Rivers System *(continued)*

Stream	Project	Capacity (megawatts)	Owner
Wallowa Valley Imp. Dist. Cnl.	Upper Little Sheep Creek	4.3	Joseph Hydro Association, Ltd.
Willamette River	Dexter	15.0	U.S. Army Corps of Engineers
Willamette River	Hills Creek	30.0	U.S. Army Corps of Engineers
Willamette River	Lookout Point	120.0	U.S. Army Corps of Engineers
Willamette River	Oregon City	1.5	Smurfit Newsprint Corp.
Willamette River	T.W. Sullivan	15.4	Portland General Electric Co.
Willamette River	West Linn	3.6	Simpson Paper Co.
Willamette River, Middle Fork	Black Canyon	8.0	U.S. Bureau of Reclamation

Klamath and Coast Range Rivers and Creeks

Stream	Project	Capacity (megawatts)	Owner
Ashland Creek	Reeder Gulch	0.7	City of Ashland
Clearwater River	Clearwater 1	15.0	PacifiCorp
Clearwater River	Clearwater 2	26.0	PacifiCorp
Cow Creek	Galesville	1.7	Douglas County
Denny Creek	Denny Creek	0.1	C.A. & D.E. Curtiss
Euchre Creek	Skyview Ranch Power	0.0	W. J. Krieger
Fish Creek	Fish Creek	11.0	PacifiCorp
Keene Creek	Green Springs	16.0	U.S. Bureau of Reclamation
Klamath River	East Side	3.2	PacifiCorp
Klamath River	John C. Boyle	80.0	PacifiCorp
Klamath River	West Side	0.6	PacifiCorp
Lake Creek	Lake Creek No 1	0.1	Mountain Energy Co.
Little Butte Creek, N. Fork	Little Butte Ranch	0.0	M. Coe
Little Butte Creek.	Eagle Point	2.8	PacifiCorp
N. Umpqua River	Lemolo 1	29.0	PacifiCorp
N. Umpqua River	Lemolo 2	33.0	PacifiCorp
N. Umpqua River	Slide Creek	18.0	PacifiCorp
N. Umpqua River	Soda Springs	11.0	PacifiCorp
N. Umpqua River	Toketee	42.6	PacifiCorp
Nichols Branch, Tributary	Nichols Gap	0.9	G. B. & P. P. Ryan
Rogue River	Diversion	1.3	U.S. Bureau of Reclamation
Rogue River	Lost Creek	49.0	U.S. Army Corps of Engineers
Rogue River	Prospect 2	32.0	PacifiCorp
Rogue River (off-stream)	Prospect	13.8	PacifiCorp
Rogue River (off-stream)	Prospect 4	1.0	PacifiCorp
Rogue River, South Fork	Prospect 3	7.2	PacifiCorp
Sprague River, North Fork	N. Fork Sprague	1.2	HDI Assoc. & V. & F. D. Ehlers

Source: Northwest Power Planning Council

Desert

Oregon's vast southeastern corner is largely desert. Southeast of Bend, straddling the high lava plain and the Basin and Range region is the area known as the High Desert, and in the basin east of Steens Mountain lies the Alvord Desert. Desert elevation averages over 4,000 feet and receives only about 10 inches or less of rain in the High Desert and a scant 5 inches in the Alvord Desert, the lowest rainfall level in Oregon. The desert, covered with sagebrush and bunchgrasses, is primarily grazing land for livestock.

The Alvord Desert is named for Brig. Gen. Benjamin Alvord, who commanded the Oregon Territory during the U.S. Civil War (1861-1865). Borax was mined from the Alvord Desert early in the 20th century. Mule teams carried the borax 130 miles to the railroad in Winnemucca, Nevada.

Remote, isolated, wide-open, flat, and hard, the Alvord Desert occasionally turns into a mecca for racing enthusiasts. An attempt was made in 1976 to set the world land speed record on the floor of the Alvord Desert. On many weekends, land sailors, cousins to windsurfers, cruise the desert floor on their overgrown skateboards.

The High Desert Museum, south of Bend, has interactive displays and exhibits on the natural history and cultural heritage of the arid regions of the West. This nonprofit center for natural and human history's exhibits include live-animal presentations and paths to otter and porcupine habitats. Other outdoor trails wind through replicas of covered wagons, a sheepherder's camp, an old sawmill, and a settler's cabin. Inside, visitors walk through dioramas from early Indian times through the 1890s. Expansion is still in progress, though two new wings feature Columbia River Plateau Indian artifacts and birds of prey, respectively.

High Desert Museum, 59800 S U.S. 97, Bend 97702, (541) 382-4754.

Dunes

(*See also* National Parks, Monuments, and Recreation Areas) Oregon's coastal dunes are among the tallest and most extensive in the world. At the Oregon Dunes National Recreation Area, south of Florence, the dune system extends inland as much as 4 miles, and the dunes average 250 feet high; some dunes surpass 500 feet in height.

Oregon Dunes National Recreation Area lies south of Florence. From *Oregon III* by Ray Atkeson.

Sand dunes are natural geologic features shaped by tides, currents, waves, and wind. The dunes migrate with the prevailing wind—north and northwest in summer, south and southwest in winter. Ripples on the dunes' surfaces indicate that they are actively migrating. The constant shifting and movement are inhospitable to vegetation. In fact, in some areas the migrating dunes have buried coastal forests—stumps may be seen poking up through sand-covered regions.

The coastal dunes are popular destinations for dune-buggy enthusiasts. The sport is a great deal of fun, but care must be taken to operate safely—and with respect for the environment.

The 40-mile-long Oregon Dunes National Recreation Area between Coos Bay and Florence is accessible from U.S. 101.

Earthquakes

(*See also* Volcanoes and Volcanism) Earthquakes occur because pressure builds where sections of the earth's crust, called plates, eventually drift together and slide or grind against each other. In Oregon, the small Juan de Fuca plate off the coasts of Washington, Oregon, and northern California is slowly moving eastward and being forced down beneath the much larger North American continent plate. While scientists cannot predict precisely where, when, or how large the next destructive earthquake in Oregon will be, the best possibility is along the Cascadia fault of the Juan de Fuca plate and North American plate. Similar subduction zones off Alaska and Chile have produced the largest earthquakes on record. Such huge, tsunami-producing quakes occur about once every 400 years, plus or minus 200 years. The last one near Oregon—an estimated 9.0—is thought to have struck the coast in January 1700. According to the Oregon Department of Geology and Mineral Industries, an earthquake of that magnitude would cause an estimated $11.8 billion in economic losses, destroy or extensively damage 54,000 buildings, and leave 12,400 people homeless.

In another study, scientists located active earthquake faults running parallel to the Willamette River directly beneath Portland. The East Bank fault underlies the University of Portland, the Oregon Convention Center, and the Lloyd Center area; the Portland Hills fault runs along the foot of the West Hills from the northern edge of Forest Park, beneath Portland State University, and under the Willamette River southeast to Milwaukie.

In 1993, Oregon experienced its two largest earthquakes in recent years. The March 25,1993, Scotts Mills earthquake, magnitude 5.6, was soon surpassed by the Klamath Falls earthquake of Sept. 20 that same year, with twin shocks of 6.0 and 5.9. The March earthquake cracked the rotunda of the Oregon capitol in Salem and caused minor injuries. In Molalla, two walls at the high school partially collapsed, and bricks and a chimney fell from the school.

Earthquake damage is primarily caused by ground shaking, which displaces and distorts nonstructural features of buildings, such as windows, doorways, ceiling tiles, and partitions. Other hazards from earthquakes include ground liquefaction, landslides on slopes and bluffs, and flooding in coastal areas, the result of tsunamis, which are large waves produced by undersea earthquakes and landslides. The Oregon Coast is particularly vulnerable to overflooding from a tsunami, even one originating far off in the Pacific Ocean.

The Oregon Department of Geology and Mineral Industries maintains earthquake preparedness information on its website at sarvis.dogami.state.or.us/eq/eqprog.htm.

The Pacific Northwest Seismograph Network, based at the University of Washington in Seattle, operates seismograph stations and locates earthquakes in Washington and Oregon. On its website, you can check the latest seismograph data and read more about earthquake preparedness (Pacific Northwest Seismograph Network, www.geophys.washington.edu/SEIS).

Elected Officials

Oregonians elect six statewide officials to manage the executive branch of government. These officials are the governor, secretary of state, state treasurer, attorney general, commissioner of labor and industries, and superintendent of public instruction.

Governor: John A. Kitzhaber (Dem.) (*see* Governors); elected 1994, 1998; term expires 2002. 254 State Capitol, Salem 97310, (503) 378-3111, fax (503) 378-4863, www.governor.state.or.us. The governor is the chief executive of Oregon. The governor is elected to a four-year term and is limited to two terms in office. Before taking office, the governor must be a U.S. citizen, at least 30 years old, and an Oregon resident for at least three years.

Secretary of State: Phil Keisling (Dem.); elected 1992, 1996; term expires January 2001; 136 State Capitol, Salem 97310-0722, (503) 986-1523, executive-office@sosinet.sos.state.or.us, www.sos.state.or.us. The Office of Secretary of State evaluates and reports on the financial condition and operations of state government, interprets and applies state election laws, is filing officer for state elections, publishes and distributes the "Voters' Pamphlet" for all elections, investigates election-law violations, is public records administrator, supervises the state archivist, publishes the administrative rules for state agencies, and registers domestic and foreign businesses.

State Treasurer: Jim Hill (Dem.); elected 1992, 1996; term expires January 2001; 159 State Capitol, Salem 97310-0804, (503) 378-4329, www.ost.state.or.us. The state treasurer is the state's chief financial and investment officer. The treasurer serves a four-year term and, if reelected, can hold the position for two terms. In 1998, the state treasury had approximately $1.3 billion invested in Oregon.

Attorney General: Hardy Myers (Dem.); elected 1996; term expires January 2001; Justice Building, Salem 97310, (503) 378-6002, www.doj.state.or.us. The attorney general, the chief legal officer of the State of Oregon, heads the Department of Justice and its six operating divisions. The attorney general controls and supervises all court actions and legal proceedings in which the State of Oregon is a party or has an interest.

Commissioner of Labor and Industries: Jack Roberts (Rep.); elected 1994, 1998; term expires January 2003; 800 NE Oregon St., #32, Portland 97232, (503) 731-4070, Jack.R.Roberts@state.or.us, www.boli.state.or.us. The commissioner is chief executive of the Oregon Bureau of Labor and Industries. The commissioner's term is four years with a two-term limitation. The commissioner enforces state laws prohibiting discrimination in employment, housing, public accommodation, and vocational, professional, and trade schools.

Superintendent of Public Instruction: Stan Bunn (Nonpartisan); elected, 1998; term expires January 2003; 255 Capitol St. NE, Salem 97310-0203, (503) 378-3573, www.ode.state.or.us. The superintendent of public instruction is the executive head of the Department of Education. The department carries out educational policies set by the legislature and State Board of Education and assists districts in complying with applicable statutes and rules. The superintendent serves a four-year term.

Endangered Species

The federal Endangered Species Act protects plants and animals that are in danger of extinction throughout all or a significant portion of their range (endangered) or which are likely to become endangered within the foreseeable future (threatened). Oregon also has a state endangered species program. Currently, the following fish and wildlife species are designated as endangered and/or threatened by the State of Oregon (Oregon Department of Fish and Wildlife), the federal government (U.S. Fish and Wildlife Service), or both:

Endangered Animals

(S = State; F = Federal)

Aleutian Canada goose *(Branta canadensis leucopareia)* S
American peregrine falcon *(Falco peregrinus anatum)* S
Arctic peregrine falcon *(Falco peregrinus tundrius)* S
Black right whale *(Balaena glacialis japonica)* S, F
Blue whale *(Balaenoptera musculus)* S, F
Brown pelican *(Pelecanus occidentalis)* S, F
California least tern *(Sterna antillarum browni)* S, F
Borax Lake chub *(Gila boraxobius)* S, F
Columbian white-tailed deer *(Odocoileus virginianus leucurus)* S, F
Fin whale *(Balenoptera phypalus)* S, F
Gray whale *(Eschrichtius robustus)* S
Gray wolf *(Canis lupis)* S, F
Green sea turtle *(Chelonia mydas)* S, F
Humpback whale *(Megaptera novaeangliae)* S, F
Leatherback sea turtle *(Dermochelys coriacca)* S, F
Lost River sucker *(Deltistes luxatus)* S, F
Lower Columbia River coho salmon *(Oncorhynchus kisutch)* S
Oregon chub *(Oregonichthys [=Hybopsis]) crameri)* S

Sei whale *(Balaenoptera borealis)* S, F
Short-tailed albatross *(Diomeda albatrus)* S, F
Shortnose sucker *(Chasmistes brevirostris)* S, F
Snake River sockeye salmon *(Oncorhynchus nerka)* S
Sperm whale *(Physeter macrocephalus)* S, F
Umpqua River cutthroat *(Oncorhynchus clarki clarki)* S, F
Washington ground squirrel *(Spermophilus washingtoni)* S

Threatened Animals

Aleutian Canada goose *(Branta canadensis leucopareia)* F
Bald eagle *(Haliaeetus leucocephalus)* S, F
Bull trout *(Salvelinus confluentus)* S, F
Columbia River chum salmon *(Oncorhynchus keta)* S, F
Fairy shrimp, vernal pool *(Bronchinecta lynchi)* F
Foskett speckled dace *(Rhinichthys osculus spp.)* S, F
Hutton tui chub *(Gila bicolor spp.)* S, F
Kit fox *(Vulpes macrotis)* S
Lahontan cutthroat trout *(Oncorhynchus [=Salmo] clarki henshawi)* S, F
Loggerhead sea turtle *(Caretta caretta)* S, F
Lower Columbia River chinook *(Oncorhynchus tshawytscha)* S, F
Lower Columbia River steelhead *(Oncorhynchus mykiss gairdneri)* S, F
Marbled murrelet *(Brachyramphus marmoratus marmoratus)* S, F
Middle Coumbia River Steelhead *(Oncorhyncus mykiss gairdneri)* S
Northern (Steller) sea lion *(Eumetoias jubatas)* S
Northern spotted owl (*Strix occidentalis caurina)* S, F
Oregon coast and Southern Oregon coho salmon *(Oncorhynchus kisutch)* S, F
Oregon silverspot butterfly *(Speyeria zerene hippolyta)* F
Pacific Ridley sea turtle *(Lepidochelys olivacea)* S, F
Sea otter *(Enhydra lutris)* S, F
Snake River chinook salmon (spring/summer/fall) *(Oncorhynchus tshawytscha)* S, F
Snake River steelhead *(Oncorhynchus mykiss gairdneri)* S, F
Upper Willamette River steelhead *(Oncorhynchus mykiss irideus)* S, F
Upper Willamette River chinook *(Oncorhynchus tshawytscha)* S, F
Warner sucker *(Catostomus warnerensis)* S, F
Western snowy plover *(Charadrius alexandrinus nivosus)* S, F
Wolverine *(Gulo gulo)* S

Endangered Plants

Applegate's milk-vetch *(Astragalus applegatei)* F, S
Big-flowered wooly meadowfoam *(Limnanthes floccosa,* subsp. *grandiflora)* S
Bradshaw's desert-parsley *(Lomatium bradshawii)* F, S
Cook's desert-parsley *(Lomatium cookii)* S
Crinite mariposa-lily *(Calochortus coxii)* S
Cusick's lupine *(Lupinus cusickii)* S
Dalles Mountain buttercup *(Ranunculus reconditus)* S
Gentner's fritillary *(Fritillaria gentneri)* S
Golden paintbrush *(Castilleja levisecta)* S
Grimy ivesia *(Ivesia rhypara,* var. *rhypara)* S
Howell's thelypody *(Thelypodium howellii,* subsp. *spectabilis)* S
MacFarlane's four-o'clock *(Mirabilis macfarlanei)* S
Malheur wire-lettuce *(Stephanomeria malheurensis)* F, S
Marsh sandwort *(Arenaria paludicola)* F
Mulford's milk-vetch *(Astragalus mulfordiae)* S
Northern wormwoood *(Artemisia campestris L.* subsp. *borealis,* var. *wormskioldii)* S
Owyhee clover *(Trifolium owyheense)* S
Peacock larkspur *(Delphinium pavonaceum)* S
Pink sand-verbena *(Abronia umbellata,* subsp. *breviflora)* S
Red-fruited lomatium *(Lomatium erythrocarpum)* S
Rough allocarya *(Plagiobothrys hirtus)* S
Saltmarsh bird's-beak *(Cordylanthus maritimus,* subsp. *palustris)* S
Sexton Mountain mariposa-lily *(Calochortus indecorus)* S
Shiny-fruited allocarya *(Plagiobothrys lamprocarpus)* S
Smooth mentzelia *(Mentzelia mollis)* S
Snake River goldenweed *(Haplopappus radiatus)* S
Spalding's campion *(Silene spaldingii)* S

Umpqua mariposa-lily *(Calochortus umpquaensis)* S
Western lily *(Lilium occidentale)* F, S
White rock larkspur *(Delphinium leucophaeum)* S
Willamette daisy *(Erigeron decumbens)* S

Threatened Plants

Arrow-leaf thelypody *(Thelypodium eucosmum)* S
Boggs Lake hedge-hyssop *(Gratiola heterosepala)* S
Cascade Head catchfly *(Silene douglasii)* S
Coast Range fawn lily *(Erythronium elegans)* S
Colonial luina *(Luina serpentina)* S
Cronquist's stickseed *(Hackelia cronquistii)* S
Crosby's buckwheat *(Eriogonum crosbyae)* S
Davis' peppergrass *(Lepidium davisii)* S
Dwarf meadowfoam *(Limnanthess floccos,* subsp. *pumila)* S
Ertter's senecio *(Senecio ertterae)* S
Golden buckwheat *(Eriogonum chrysops)* S
Golden paintbrush *(Castilleja levisecta)* F
Greenman's desert-parsley *(Lomatium greenmanii)* S
Howell's mariposa-lily *(Calochortus howellii)* S
Howell's microseris *(Microseris howellii)* S
Kincaid's lupine *(Lupinus sulphureus,* subsp. *kincaidii)* S
Large-flowered rush lily *(Hastingsia bracteosa)* S
Lawrence's milk-vetch *(Astragalus collinus,* var. *laurentii)* S
MacFarlane's four-o'clock *(Mirabilis macfarlanei)* F
Malheur Valley fiddleneck *(Amsinckia carinata)* S
Nelson's checker-mallow *(Sidalcea nelsoniana)* F, S
Oregon semaphoregrass *(Pleuropogon oregonus)* S
Packard's mentzelia *(Mentzelia packardiae)* S
Peck's milk-vetch *(Astragalus peckii)* S
Pumice grape-fern *(Botrychium pumicola)* S
Silvery phacelia *(Phacelia argentea)* S
South Fork John Day milk-vetch *(Astragalus diaphanus,* var. *diurnus)* S
Stalked-leaved monkeyflower *(Mimulus patulus)* S
Sterile milk-vetch *(Astragalus sterilis)* s
Tygh Valley milk-vetch *(Astragalus tyghensis)* S
Water howellia *(Howellia aquatilis)* F
Wayside aster *(Aster vialis)* S
White-topped aster *(Aster curtus)* S
Wolf's evening primrose *(Oenothera wolfii)* S

Watery Sanctuary

The South Slough of Coos Bay estuary encompasses 600 acres of tidal marshes, mudflats, and open-water channels leading to the ocean. The first national estuarine sanctuary, established there in 1974, harbors shellfish and small animals.—Ann Saling, The Great Northwest Nature Factbook

Organizations of Interest

Oregon Department of Fish and Wildlife, 2501 SW First Ave., Portland 97207, (503) 872-5263, www.dfw.state.or.us.

U.S. Fish and Wildlife Service, Division of Endangered Species, Eastside Federal Complex, 911 NE 11th Ave., Portland 97232, (503) 231-6121, http://endangered.fws.gov.

Oregon Department of Agriculture, Natural Resources Division—Plant Conservation Biology Program, 635 Capitol St. NE, Salem 97301, (503) 986-4700, www.oda.state.or.us.

Estuaries

(SEE ALSO COAST) An estuary is the tidal portion of a river, where freshwater mixes with salt water. Estuaries are tremendously important for ecological systems because the blending of fresh and salt water creates rich feeding areas and important habitats for marine life. Estuaries are also important for economic reasons—they are ideal locations for commercial ports and also for coastal towns and cities.

Oregon has 17 major estuaries, with a total of 132,000 acres of intertidal and subtidal habitat. The South Slough of Coos Bay became the first estuary in the National Estuarine Research Reserve. This program provides additional environmental protection for the estuary, as well as research on the estuary, and its ecological importance.

Major Estuaries

Alsea Bay Estuary
Chetco River Estuary
Columbia River Estuary
Coos Bay
Coquille River Estuary
Necanicum River Estuary
Nehalem River Estuary
Nestucca River Estuary
Netarts Bay
Rogue River Estuary
Salmon River Estuary
Sand Lake
Siletz River Estuary
Siuslaw River Estuary
Tillamook Bay
Umpqua River Estuary
Yaquina Bay

Eugene

(*See also* Universities and Colleges) Oregon's second-largest city has about 120,000 residents, depending on what quarter it is at the University of Oregon (U of O) and Lane Community College. Unlike some college towns, students and locals mix without much friction, aside from the occasional fraternity party gone mad (*Animal House* was filmed at U of O). This isn't much of a problem since the majority of students disregard the Greek system. A youthful population enjoys the hippie life of tie-dyed shirts, dreadlocks, and henna tattoos while demanding sophisticated arts and culture venues, coffeehouses, and tasty microbrews. Several popular weekend festivals provide a blend of these two dispositions (*see* Fairs and Festivals).

Eugene lies in the I-5 corridor of the Willamette Valley and is split by the flow of the Willamette River. The cooler, more boisterous McKenzie River flows out of its headwaters in the Cascade Mountains and passes Eugene just north of the city. Both rivers inspire kayaking, canoeing, rafting, and fly-fishing (the university offers a class in fly-tying), while nearby Spencer Butte and Skinner Butte offer miles of hiking and mountain-biking trails. Outdoor recreational opportunities attract both new residents and college students from around the nation. Many of the best U of O academic programs connect in some way to the surrounding landscape, such as environmental law and the wilderness program, which teaches survival skills and a range of outdoor sports.

For those who want to stay closer to home, city parks abound. Along the Willamette's banks, Alton Baker Park includes the 4-mile Prefontaine Trail, named for the U of O's Olympic runner, Steve Prefontaine, who died in an auto accident at the peak of his career. Amazon Park, the site of summer outdoor concerts, also has a running circuit. Horticulture overpowers athletics at Hendrick's Park, where paths wind through a 10-acre rhododendron garden. Skinner's Butte Park provides several playgrounds, picnic areas, a well-tended rose garden, and a 12-mile bike and running path.

Arts organizations—some connected to the university, some to the city, and some independents—thrive in Eugene. The Hult Center for the Performing Arts, located downtown, is a world-class concert facility, and Eugene has a number of experimental theater and dance groups. U of O's prominent master of fine arts writing program sponsors readings by celebrated authors from around the nation. With fine arts comes fine dining, and several elegant restaurants have finally come to town, with locales specializing in French, Northwest, Middle Eastern, Caribbean, and Japanese cuisine.

Craft arts are an integral part of Eugene's festival circuit. From April to December, the open-air Saturday Market offers unique pottery, textiles, beadwork, and other crafts sold by the artisans themselves. People move to folk music and snack from the myriad of food carts. Throngs of craftspeople descend on a meandering creekside for July's Oregon Country Fair, reappearing for the Eugene Celebration in late September.

Explorers

(*See also* History; Lewis and Clark) In the 1570s the first ships to see the Oregon Coast simply passed it by, as international competition for other areas of the world took precedence. In 1573 a Portuguese explorer died on his way up the California coast, and his pilot,

Bartolomé Ferrelo, pushed north as far as the mouth of the Rogue River. His legacy is Cape Ferrelo, located between Brookings and Gold Beach. Sir Francis Drake passed the Oregon Coast a few years later, but it would be another 200 years before anyone came closer, while explorers kept busy setting up trade routes in the southern hemisphere.

By 1775, the myth of the Northwest Passage, a possible route from the Atlantic culminating in a great river flowing into the Pacific, as well as an active fur trade in Alaska, focused the attention of several nations on the Pacific Northwest. Even so, in the last decades of the 18th century several explorers saw and ignored, or missed entirely, the great mouth of the "Oregon River," as the Columbia was then known by Native tribes. Spanish explorer Bruno Heceta was the first to note the river's forbidding mouth, and for years after, many attempted in vain to rediscover "Heceta's River." In 1788, John Meares, a Briton working the fur trade independently, added another moniker. Known as a belligerent, imaginative character, he thought he saw the mouth of a great river, then decided he hadn't, and promptly named the mouth of the Columbia "Deception Bay," and the promontory above it "Cape Disappointment."

In 1792, Captain George Vancouver, with his colleague William Broughton, sailed past the mouth. Vancouver also dismissed it as a mere bay, despite the evidence of earthen-colored water and drifting logs. Finally, a Boston trader's desire for fur, which he hoped to trade for Chinese silk, led to the river's discovery. Robert Gray met up with Vancouver's ship near the Strait of Juan de Fuca and argued that the muddy bay could indeed be the mouth of the "Great River of the West." Vancouver would hardly yield to a mere merchant trader, though Broughton was starting to think Gray might be on to something.

Gray turned back south and arrived again at latitude 46 degrees 53 minutes, where the muddy flow raged for four hours before Gray gingerly crossed the bar. He sailed several miles and named the river after his ship, the *Columbia Rediviva.* He traded pelts with local tribes for several days. Doing so, he paved the way for other American fur traders eventually to control the sea otter trade and spend winters in the area, the beginning of a long period of suffering for the original settlers of the area.

A jargon of Chinook, French, and English developed quickly. Though Gray's discovery was the first to establish the U.S. presence on the Pacific Coast, Broughton arrived several months after Gray and sought to go farther. After Vancouver confirmed Gray's find, he allowed Broughton a small wooden boat to explore farther. Broughton spent three weeks on the river, turning back at the mouth of the Columbia Gorge, just east of modern-day Portland. Broughton then claimed the watershed for the British crown.

In the early 1800s President Thomas Jefferson sent Meriwether Lewis and William Clark to explore the lands from the Missouri River to the sea. The explorers led their "Corps of Discovery" on a two-year

Fort Clatsop, where explorers Lowis and Clark spent the winter of 1805-06. Photo by Andrea Jarvela.

odyssey from St. Louis, Missouri, to the mouth of the Columbia River, losing only one man on the entire journey. Their journey brought knowledge of the vast Northwest Territory to U.S. citizens, although the great overland migration would not begin for another 40 years.

Meanwhile, an increasingly sophisticated fur trade flourished, and British-American discord intensified in the Pacific Northwest. Britain's Hudson's Bay Company and North West Company sold over 48,000 sea otter skins to China between 1798 and 1902. American titan John Jacob Astor, for whom present-day Astoria is named, decided to base his own Pacific Fur Company at the mouth of the Columbia River. He intended to trade with the Native tribes and Russian trappers for pelts he would sell overseas. Unfortunately, the ships and an overland party he sent met with continuous disaster. On one ship, the captain was the unpredictable and violent Jonathan Thorn. He was responsible for the loss of eight men at sea. Others among Astor's adventurers decreased their numbers by injury and starvation. One crew of ship clerks suffered by trying to grow a few potatoes they'd brought and then attempting to clear land knotted by magnificent, and sturdy, centuries-old trees, though they were no loggers. An overland contingent became lost near the Snake River and barely survived by eating their moccasins and drinking their own urine.

In the spring of 1911, Thorn reached Vancouver Island. His temper made quick enemies, and when he struck a Native chief across the face with a roll of fur, the Natives massacred Thorn and his crew. To add to the tensions between nations and between the invading nations and Native tribes, the United States declared war on Britain in 1812. To avert British capture, Astor's post sold itself to the Britons, and in 1813 Astoria was renamed Fort George. The few benefits surely didn't exceed the toll of 60 lives Astor's endeavor cost, though a few more American collection stations were established in several areas, including the Willamette Valley, which strengthened the claim laid by Lewis and Clark.

For the next three decades, Britain controlled the region through the Hudson's Bay Company. Fort Vancouver was established in 1825 at the place where the Columbia and Willamette Rivers converged. Fur trade barons built enormous mansions in the then wilderness. The largest belonged to the Chief Factor of the District (Alaska to California), Dr. John McLoughlin, often called the "Father of Oregon." McLoughlin improved white treatment of the Native tribes, putting an end to the practice of feeding them rum to gain better trade deals and gaining a reputation among Native tribes of being a man who kept his word. McLoughlin's main allegiance, though, was to Hudson's Bay Company, his assignment to trap out most of the Northwest to dress London society—and he succeeded.

Britain and America's competing claims by their respective explorers ended with a decision to leave the region open to both countries until 1828, when the issue would be addressed again. McLoughlin's job, however, was to discourage all American settlement. By clearing the fur supplies from the Columbia River area, he had partly succeeded, but settlement already established by the British and French-Canadians encouraged others.

McLoughlin's final action in his position was an altruistic one. French-Canadian trappers had been ordered back to Quebec for mustering out. Starting in 1829, he allowed them to take land parcels in the Willamette Valley, making French-Canadian trappers, not American pioneers, the first official settlers of Oregon. American settlers from the Midwest, though, were not too far behind.

Fairs and Festivals

(*See also* Rodeos; Performing Arts)

Oregon is probably best known for Portland's annual **Rose Festival**, which attracts an estimated two million people each June for 25 days of parades, boat races, jazz, arts, and

A Rose Festival Parade entry. Photo by Susan Dupere.

an airshow. And roses. Lots and lots of roses. The Grand Floral Parade through miles of downtown streets is the single largest spectator event in Oregon with 500,000 people and 50 million television viewers nationwide. In 1999, the U.S. Women's World Cup soccer team played here during the festival month, winning the game and going on to capture the world championship. The whole event brings in more than $79 million annually to the Portland-area economy.

It all started in the late 1800s, when the town pioneers discovered that the climate was perfect for growing roses. E. W. Rowe first championed the idea of a rose festival, and Mayor Harry Lane made it a reality in 1907. While it's now an international attraction, some aspects of the festival still have a small-town flavor. The city elects businesspeople to wear the white suits and straw boaters of Royal Rosarians, and each high school nominates a Rose Princess in the hope she will be crowned the Rose Queen. A Date-a-Sailor hotline aids the men and women of military vessels that line the Willamette River during the event.

Portland Rose Festival Association, 202 NW Second Avenue, Portland 97209, (503) 227-2681, info@rosefestival.org, www.rosefestival.org.

July brings the 31-year-old, three-day **Oregon Country Fair,** staged west of Eugene in Veneta. Craftspeople sell their wares and hippie-styled folk dance to a variety of music. Like the Rose Festival, the fair is organized by a nonprofit board of directors. Through them, endowments are awarded to other organizations that promote "the arts, cultural diversity, and a peaceful, socially-just, and environmentally sound society."

Oregon Country Fair, P.O. Box 2972, Eugene 97402, (541) 343-4298, ocf@efn.org, www.oregoncountryfair.org.

The **Oregon State Fair** has been around even longer than the Rose Festival. While the institution is 140 years old, the two world wars preempted several stagings. (The year 2000 is the 135th.) Its history as an agricultural festival is still apparent, with lots of 4-H and livestock competitions. Prizes also go to bakers, quilters, flower growers, and home-canning experts. Now the fair is one of the few "ag fests" in the nation.

Tens of thousands of people enjoy the late-August/early-September festivities. During the fair's 12 days, people consume 937,000 gallons of soda (enough to fill an Olympic-sized swimming pool 10 times), 250,000 hamburgers, 833,333 hot dogs (78.9 miles of dogs laid end to end), 20,000 ears of corn, 18,000 pounds of onions, and 14,000 pounds of Japanese noodles.

Oregon State Fair and Exposition Center, 2330 17th St. NE, Salem 97303-3201, (503) 378-FAIR, (800) 833-0011, www.fair.state.or.us/fair.html.

The state hosts several well-respected, well-attended music festivals, including Eugene's **Oregon Bach Festival** and the **Peter Britt Festival of Music** in Jacksonville. The Bach Festival was founded by the German organist and conductor Helmuth Rilling, who came to Eugene for a concert in 1970. He and co-founder Royce Saltzman made a group of orchestral performances into a nationally regarded classical music venue drawing 30,000 attendees annually. *(Continued on page 56)*

Calendar of Annual Events

July

Athena—*Caledonian Games, (541) 566-3880*
Bend—*Ruggers Rendezvous (rug hooking), (541) 382-4754*
Brookings—*Southern Oregon Kite Festival, (800) 422-5273*

Coos Bay—*Oregon Coast Music Festival, (541) 267-0932*
Corvallis—*Da Vinci Days, (541) 757-6363*
Eugene—*Oregon Country Fair, (541) 343-4298*
Gladstone—*Gladstone Chautauqua Festival, (503) 656-5225*
Grants Pass—*Fifties Festival, (541) 476-5773*
Gresham—*Mount Hood Festival of Jazz, (503) 231-0161*
Jacksonville—*Britt Festival, (800) 882-7488*
Lane County—*Watermelon Rides (Willamette Valley bike ride), (503) 399-9652*
Lowell—*Blackberry Jam Festival, (541) 937-3487*
Macleay—*All-Oregon Bluegrass Festival, (503) 399-1130*
Ontario—*Japan Nite Obon Festival, (541) 889-8691*
Portland—*Chamber Music Northwest, (503) 223-3202*
Reedsport—*Presbyterian Women's Quilt Show, (541) 271-4783*
Roseburg—*Graffiti Week, (541) 672-1071*
Veneta—*Applegate Trail Days Festival, (541) 935-7304*
Wallowa—*TamKaLiks Celebration, (541) 276-4109*

August

Astoria—*Victorian Homes Tour, (503) 325-2203*
Bend—*Cascade Festival of Music, (541) 382-8381*
Charleston—*Charleston Seafood Festival, (541) 888-8083*
Chiloquin—*Klamath Tribe Restoration Celebration, (800) 524-9787*
Eugene—*Eugene Women in Theater Festival, (541) 485-8041*
Hood River—*Gravenstein Apple Days, (541) 354-2565*
Jacksonville—*Britt Festival, (800) 882-7488*
Junction City—*Scandinavian Festival, (541) 998-9372*
La Grande—*Oregon Trail Days, (541) 963-8588, (800) 848-9969*
Lincoln City—*Sandcastle Contest, (541) 994-2131*
Portland—*Homowo Festival of African Art, (503) 288-3025*
Salem—*Oregon State Fair, (503) 378-FAIR*
St. Helens—*International Dowsers Convention, (503) 774-1129*
Tualatin—*Crawfish Festival, (503) 692-0780*

September

Bandon—*Cranberry Festival, (541) 347-2277*
Beaverton—*Brookhaven Craft and Antique Show, (503) 626-4829*
Corvallis—*Corvallis Fall Festival, (541) 752-9655*
Depoe Bay—*Indian Style Salmon Bake, (541) 883-4208*
Enterprise—*Hells Canyon Mule Days, (541) 577-3247*
Eugene—*Asian Kite Festival, (541) 687-9600*
Florence—*Chowder Blues and Brews, (541) 997-3128*
Independence—*Kermesse Mexican Fiesta, (503) 838-1242*
Jacksonville—*Britt Festival, (800) 882-7488*
Joseph—*Alpenfest at Wallowa Lake, (541) 432-6325*

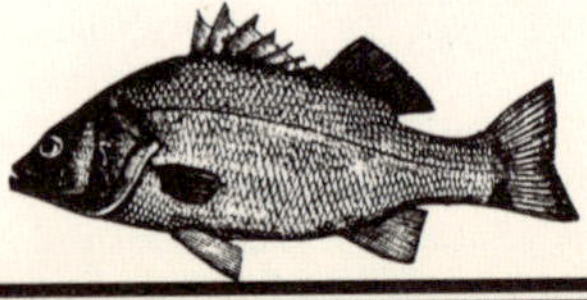

More Calendar of Annual Events

Klamath Falls—*Modoc History Celebration, (541) 883-4208*

Philomath—*Shrewsbury Renaissance Faire, (541) 929-4897*

Sisters—*Sisters Harvest Faire, (541) 549-0251*

Umatilla—*Oregon Governor's Cup Walleye Tournament (fishing), (541) 922-4825*

Vale—*All Horse Parade, (541) 473-2329*

October

Bend—*Bat Day (Oct. 31), (541) 382-4754*

Cottage Grove—*Downtown Celebration and Chili Cookoff, (541) 942-0505*

Eugene—*Eugene Oktoberfest, (541) 689-7391*

Eugene—*Fall Festival and Mushroom Show, (541) 747-3817*

Florence—*Underwater Pumpkin Carving Contest, (800) 789-3486*

Glide—*Art and Craft Sale, (541) 496-0756*

Grants Pass—*Art Fest, (541) 582-2430*

Hood River—*Valley Harvest Fest, (800) 366-3530*

Lebanon—*Flowers! Imagine That, (541) 259-1204*

Lincoln City—*Fall International Kite Festival, (541) 994-7556*

Medford—*Medford Jazz Jubilee, (800) 469-6307*

Newport—*Creatures of the Night, (541) 867-3474*

Portland—*American Sampler Holiday Sale, (503) 645-8109; Fall Home and Garden Show, (503) 246-8291, (800) 343-6973*

Salem—*Stampex (stamps), (503) 371-3831*

Scappoose—*Sauerkraut Festival, (503) 543-6895*

November

Ashland—*Harvest Show of Fine Woodworking, (541) 482-4829*

Eugene—*Festival of Trees, (541) 726-3164*

Eugene—*Holiday Food and Gift Festival, (503) 526-1080, (888) 412-5015*

John Day—*Grape & Grain Festival and Art Auction, (541) 575-0547*

North Bend—*Holiday Craft Fair, (541) 756-2146*

Portland—*Audubon Society's Wild Arts Festival, (503) 292-6855*

Portland—*The Grotto's Festival of Lights, (503) 257-7371*

The Dalles—*St. Peter's Bazaar, (541) 296-2941*

Willamina—*Willamina Coastal Hills Art Tour, (503) 876-5777*

December

Newberg—*Winter Wonderland Bazaar, (503) 538-1564*

Portland—*America's Largest Christmas Bazaar, (503) 282-0974*

January

Gold Beach—*Whale of a Wine Festival, (541) 247-6658, (800) 808-7263*

Sumpter—*Elkhorn Crest Sled Dog Races, (541) 894-2264*

February

Eugene—*Oregon Asian Celebration, (541) 687-9600*

Klamath Falls—*Bald Eagle Conference, (800) 445-6728*

Portland—*Portland International Film Festival, (503) 221-1156*

March

Clackamas—*Country Calico Spring Show, (503) 631-7654*

Coos Bay—*Dixieland Clambake Jazz Festival, (800) 824-8486*

Heppner—*Wee Bit O' Ireland, (541) 676-5536*

April

Canby—*Spring in the Country, (503) 655-2380*

More Calendar of Annual Events

Cannon Beach—*Puffin Kite Festival, (503) 436-2274, (800) 547-6100*
Gleneden Beach—*Easter Pet Parade, (541) 764-2023*
Hood River—*Blossom Festival, (541) 352-1078*
Klamath Falls—*Western Art Show, (541) 882-9996*
Parkdale—*Art Fest, (541) 352-6463*

May

Brookings—*Azalea Festival, (541) 469-3181*
Portland—*Rhododendron Show and Plant Sale, (503) 777-1734*
Scio—*Lamb and Wool Fair, (503) 394-4008*
Sumpter—*Sumpter Valley Country Fair, (541) 894-2264*

June

Brownsville—*Pioneer Picnic, (541) 466-3380*
Cannon Beach—*Annual Sandcastle Day Festival, (503) 436-2623*
Cascade Locks—*Sternwheeler Days, (541) 374-8313*
Eugene—*Oregon Bach Festival, (541) 346-5666*
Jacksonville—*Britt Festival, (800) 882-7488*
Lebanon—*Strawberry Festival, (541) 258-4444*
Lincoln City—*Soap Box Derby, (541) 994-7556*
Portland—*Rose Festival, (503) 227-2681*

Sand sculpture competition at Cannon Beach. Photo by Susan Dupere.

Oregon Bach Festival, 1257 University of Oregon, Eugene 97403, (541) 346-5666, (800) 457-1486. www.bachfest.uoregon.edu.

The relaxed, outdoor Britt Festival, named for Jacksonville's revered pioneer, photographer Peter Britt, runs throughout the summer. Huge crowds sprawl over the grassy hillside, listening to everything from bluegrass to classical.

Britt Festival, P.O. Box 1124, Medford 97501, (800) 882-7488, www.brittfest.org.

The listings on pages 54-56 are a sampling of Oregon fairs and festivals. Contact local visitor centers for more information. For a free events calendar, contact the Oregon Tourism Commission, (800) 547-7842, www.traveloregon.com.

Fire Lookouts In the early 1900s, when the nation's national forests were created, the new Forest Service began erecting the first fire lookouts in the Pacific Northwest. The first of these structures was little more than a crude platform constructed in a tree with a few of its branches removed and a ladder nailed to the tree trunk for access. Gradually, the structures became more permanent and the designs were standardized to make them easier to build and maintain. What they had in common, however, were a mountaintop location and windows all around to accommodate a 360-degree view. For those who really like roughing it, some fire lookouts can today be rented from the U.S. Forest Service. Most of the fire lookouts and cabins are in remote areas and have few to no amenities. Often there is no plumbing or heat, and in most cases you must bring your own cooking utensils, drinking water, bedding, and other supplies. For information, call the **U.S. Forest Service Regional Office,** Nature of the Northwest, 800 NE Oregon St., No. 177, Portland 97232, (503) 872-2750, www. naturenw.org (Cabin/ Lookout Rental Guide).

Fish and Fishing

(*SEE ALSO* SALMON) Oregon's aquatic resources include numerous species of marine and freshwater finfish and shellfish through its ocean and inland marine waters, thousands of miles of rivers and streams, and numerous lakes.

Commercial Fishing

Over 2,800 commercial fishermen were licensed in Oregon in 1998, and 1,783 fishing boats were licensed. Commercial species harvested include groundfish, shrimp, salmon, dungeness crab, trout, and oysters. The major fishing ports are Astoria, Tillamook, Pacific City, Depoe Bay, Newport, Florence, Winchester Bay, Coos Bay, Bandon, Port Orford, Gold Beach, and Brookings. Lincoln County, with the ports of Depoe Bay and Newport, was the state's leading commercial fishing county in 1997, landing 51 percent of the state's total seafood tonnage.

According to the Oregon Agricultural Statistics Service, the 1998 commercial fish landings amounted to 260.9 million pounds, which was valued at $49.6 million. Groundfish, mostly Pacific whiting, had the largest harvest, while crab landings were the lowest since 1991.

Dungeness crab. Dungeness crab harvests have slipped. The estimated ex-vessel value of crab landings in 1998 was $12.5 million, down from $14.7 million in 1997.

Groundfish. About 198 million pounds were landed in 1998, representing 86 percent of the state's total tonnage and 47 percent of the total value of seafood landed. The groundfish catch included rockfish, flatfish, whiting, and lingcod.

Oysters. Oyster production reached a value of $761,810 in 1998, down 43 percent from 1997.

Salmon. Salmon landings have been slipping in recent years. The total ex-vessel value of the 1998 salmon harvest was $2.6 million.

Shrimp. Shrimp landings vary according to natural cycles. The total landings dropped from 19.7 million pounds in 1997 to 6.3 million pounds in 1998, and the ex-vessel price was down to $3.8 million.

Trout. Trout production from private hatcheries was valued at $864,000 in 1998.

Sport Fishing

Oregon has spectacular sport-fishing opportunities on its more than 400 miles of coastline, 62,000 miles of fishing streams, and 1,600 lakes, reservoirs, and ponds. Over 700,000 residents and tourists purchase fishing licenses to catch trout, salmon, steelhead, and warm-water species.

The bays, estuaries, and open coast provide excellent opportunities for salmon trolling and ocean fishing for rockfish, lingcod, and halibut. Every coastal town offers charter boat opportunities.

Oregon's 15 major rivers are ice free in the winter when steelhead fishing is at its peak. The best time of year to catch chinook and coho salmon on the rivers is July through November. Some coastal rivers also sport summer runs of steelhead.

The Columbia River Gorge is fished for salmon and steelhead, as well as for largemouth bass in the sloughs and backwaters below Portland.

The Rogue and Umpqua Rivers are famous for steelhead, salmon, and trout. Farther east, the Deschutes is well-known for winter steelhead runs, spring chinook salmon, and rainbow trout.

Even in the sagebrush eastern portion of

Angling for steelhead in the Umpqua National Forest. See *Oregon's National Forests* by Robert M. Reynolds (photos) and Joan Campf (text).

the state, fishing opportunities are available. The John Day River is hot for smallmouth bass. Sturgeon can be caught on the Snake River below Hells Canyon Dam. The lakes and reservoirs throughout the state abound in warm-water species.

Fishing Licenses and Rules

Fishing license fees range from free to $105, depending on the type of license, species to be fished, and whether the fisher is a state resident or not. The fees are used to fund fish and wildlife programs. Fishing regulations are adjusted annually, to take account of changes in the abundance of species. The annual regulations are distributed free in sporting-goods stores. Information can be obtained directly by mail from **Oregon Department of Fish and Wildlife,** 2501 SW First Ave., P.O. Box 59, Portland 97207-0059, (503) 872-5268, www.dfw.state.or.us.

> **Giants of the Columbia**
>
> *Slow-growing, slow-reproducing, slow-moving (until hooked), the sturgeon probably lives more than a hundred years. The lower Columbia River contains the world's largest and healthiest wild population of white sturgeon, one of the three largest sturgeon species and the biggest freshwater, stream-ascending fish of North American coastal waters.*—Ann Saling, *The Great Northwest Nature Factbook.*

Fish Hatcheries

(*SEE ALSO* FISH AND FISHING; SALMON)

Hatcheries for salmon, steelhead, and trout not only provide most of the commercial and sport-fishing harvest in Oregon; they also are a major tourist attraction, attracting 1.4 million visitors each year from all over the world. The Oregon Department of Fish and Wildlife operates 34 fish hatcheries and 15 satellite rearing facilities, funded by the state and federal governments. Hatchery staff release about 90 million young fish yearly, mostly salmon.

Many hatcheries offer tours, viewing ponds where you can feed fish or see a 6-foot-long sturgeon, and observation areas where you can view spawning. The hatcheries are usually located in watersheds that provide opportunities for camping, hiking, and sport fishing.

State Fish Hatcheries

Alsea Fish Hatchery, 29050 Fish Hatchery Rd., Philomath 97370, (541) 487-7240. Coastal cutthroat trout and winter steelhead. The Alsea River offers good fishing for salmon, steelhead, and cutthroat trout. Several parks with picnic areas are located along the Alsea.

Bandon Fish Hatchery, Rte. 2, Box 418, Bandon 97411, (541) 347-4278. Rainbow trout, salmon, and steelhead. Show pond of large rainbow trout for feeding. Observe salmon spawning October to March. Bird life includes wood ducks that can be seen year-round at intake reservoirs. Swallows are common May to September. Herons and kingfishers are common year-round.

Big Creek Fish Hatchery, Rte. 4, Box 594, Astoria 97103, (503) 458-6512. Chinook, coho, and winter steelhead. Fish rearing pond viewing daily; egg incubation from Sept. 18 through Feb. 15; adult salmon viewing Sept. 1 through Nov. 15; salmon spawning Sept. 18 through Nov. 15; adult steelhead viewing and spawning Dec. 20 through Feb. 15. Big Creek is a popular salmon and steelhead angling stream.

Bonneville Fish Hatchery, Star Route B, Box 12, Cascade Locks 97014, (541) 374-8393. Chinook and coho salmon. Display ponds with large rainbow trout and white sturgeon measuring more than 6 feet long. Viewing area to watch fall spawning.

Butte Falls Fish Hatchery, 580 Fish Lake Rd., Butte Falls 97522, (541) 865-3322. Chinook and coho salmon and rainbow trout. Located in the foothills below Mount McLoughlin with several campgrounds and fishing areas nearby.

Cascade Fish Hatchery, HC 66 Box 750, Cascade Locks 97014, (541) 374-8381. Coho salmon. During the fall, viewing of chinook and coho salmon below the fish rack at the bridge crossing Eagle Creek.

Cedar Creek Fish Hatchery, 33465 Oregon 22, Hebo 97122, (541) 392-3485. Salmon, steelhead, and rainbow trout. Eagles and osprey often seen as well as herons, cormorants, and mergansers.

Clackamas Fish Hatchery, 24500 S Entrance Rd., Estacada 97023, (503) 630-7210. Spring chinook salmon and winter steelhead. McIver State Park, adjacent to the hatchery, offers hiking, camping, picnicking, horse trails, and fishing access.

Cole M. Rivers Fish Hatchery, 200 Cole M. Rivers Dr., Trail 97541, (541) 878-2235. Rainbow trout, coho and chinook salmon, and steelhead. Spawning area and an observation area overlooking collection and holding ponds. There is also a platform for viewing naturally spawning spring chinook at nearby Butte Creek.

Elk River Fish Hatchery, 95163 Elk River Rd., Port Orford 97465, (541) 332-7025. Chinook salmon and steelhead. Cape Blanco State Park (with camping) is 17 miles away.

Fall Creek Fish Hatchery, 2418 E Fall Creek Rd., Alsea 97324, (541) 487-4152. Coho and chinook salmon. The facility has an in-stream habitat display and interpretive kiosk. The area has a good population of black-tailed deer. Tours available for school groups.

Fall River Fish Hatchery, 15055 S Century Dr., Bend 97702, (541) 593-1510. Rainbow and brook trout. The Fall River is just 12 miles long but offers excellent fly-fishing.

Gnat Creek Fish Hatchery, Rte. 2. Box 2198, Clatskanie 97016, (503) 455-2234. Summer and winter steelhead. This is a rearing facility with no adult fish present. A state park and Lewis and Clark National Wildlife Refuge are nearby.

Irrigon Fish Hatchery, Rte. 2, Box 149, Irrigon 97844, (541) 922-5732. Steelhead. Near the Columbia River with a visitor center, wildlife viewing, and a show pond for sturgeon.

Klamath Fish Hatchery, 46161 Oregon 62, Chiloquin 97624, (541) 381-2278. Rainbow, cutthroat, brook, and brown trout, as well as coho salmon. This hatchery raises "desert adapted" trout for the warm, alkali waters of southeast Oregon.

Klaskanine Fish Hatchery, Rte. 1, Box 764, Astoria 97103, (503) 325-3653. Coho salmon and steelhead. The facility is about 22 miles from Fort Stevens State Park south of Astoria. There are many museums and historical sites in the Astoria area. The lower Columbia River estuary offers excellent wildlife viewing.

Leaburg Fish Hatchery, 90700 Fish Hatchery Rd., Leaburg 97489, (541) 896-3294. Rainbow and cutthroat trout and steelhead. Earthen show ponds with Japanese-style landscaping offer year-round viewing of adult sturgeon and trout. Nearby Water Board Park provides picnicking, swimming, and boat access to the McKenzie River. Excellent opportunities to view chinook spawning and osprey.

Lookingglass Fish Hatchery, 76657

Lookingglass Rd., Elgin 97827, (541) 437-9723. Chinook salmon. Small inside display area and viewing window plus information signs on the grounds. The location in the Blue Mountains makes this a good side trip for area visitors.

Marion Forks Fish Hatchery, Star Rte. Box 71, Idanha 97350, (541) 854-3522. Chinook salmon, steelhead, and cutthroat trout. Excellent access to fishing on the North Santiam River. Minto Pond, a satellite facility, is used for steelhead and chinook spawning.

McKenzie Fish Hatchery, 43863 Greer Dr., Oregon 126, Leaburg 97489, (541) 896-3513. Chinook and steelhead. The McKenzie River offers excellent fishing for trout, steelhead, and salmon in a scenic setting. Group tours available.

Nehalem Fish Hatchery, Rte. 1, Box 292, Nehalem 97131, (503) 368-6828. Coho salmon and steelhead. Spawning activity and adult fish viewing. Access to fishing platform for steelhead and salmon angling for those with a wheelchair or blind-angling license. Near Saddle Mountain State Park. Umbrella Falls is 0.25 mile from the hatchery.

Oak Springs Fish Hatchery, Rte. 1, Box 443, Maupin 97037, (541) 395-2546. Rainbow trout and summer and winter steelhead. The hatchery egg-incubation room is accessible for viewing October through March. Group tours are available by appointment to view trout spawning during October and November. This river is a premier trout and steelhead waterway. Good bird-watching opportunities are available during spring and fall migration.

Oxbow Fish Hatchery, HC 66 Box 750, Cascade Locks 97014, (541) 374-8540. Coho salmon hatchery. Fingerlings can be viewed year-round. Though there is no adult fish collection at Oxbow, adult salmon can be seen spawning in Herman Creek (Oxbow's water source) September through November.

Roaring River Fish Hatchery, 42279 Fish Hatchery Dr., Scio 97374, (541) 394-2496. Rainbow trout and steelhead. Rainbow trout weighing up to 15 pounds each are a popular viewing feature. Picnicking and fishing nearby on Roaring River.

Rock Creek Fish Hatchery, P.O. Box 197, Idleyld Park 97447, (541) 496-3484. Coho and spring chinook salmon, steelhead and rainbow trout. A disabled-accessible trail leads to a viewing deck and interpretive signing.

Round Butte Fish Hatchery, P.O. Box 15, Madras 97741, (541) 475-6393. Spring chinook, summer steelhead, and brown trout. Public access by advance arrangements only.

Salmon River Fish Hatchery, 575 N North Bank Rd., Otis 97368, (541) 994-8606. Chinook and coho salmon as well as steelhead. Salmon River and its estuary offer fishing and viewing. Hiking is also popular at nearby Cascade Head.

Sandy River Fish Hatchery, 39800 SE Fish Hatchery Rd., Sandy 97055, (503) 668-4222. Coho salmon. A trail through the grounds offers a good nature hike as well as fishing access to the Sandy River.

South Santiam Fish Hatchery, 43182 N River Dr., Sweet Home 97386, (541) 367-3437. Chinook and summer steelhead. The South Santiam River is one of the top summer steelhead fishing rivers in the state. Foster Reservoir upstream has fishing, boating, picnicking, and camping.

Trask River Fish Hatchery, 15020 Chance Rd., Tillamook 97141, (503) 842-4090. Chinook and coho salmon. Excellent adult salmon viewing in the fall below the hatchery and in Gold Creek. Group tours are available with advance arrangements.

Umatilla Fish Hatchery, Rte. 2, Box 151, Irrigon 97844, (541) 922-5659. Chinook salmon and steelhead. This hatchery rears a portion of its fish in unique ponds called "Michigan ponds," patterned after those used in Michigan.

Wallowa Fish Hatchery, 82119 Fish Hatchery Ln., Enterprise 97828, (541) 426-4467. Rainbow trout and steelhead. The hatchery settling pond has been developed into a small wildlife area. A 0.25-mile trail leads from the hatchery to the pond. This is a good place to see waterfowl, especially nesting geese during spring.

Willamette Fish Hatchery, 76389 Fish

Hatchery Rd., Oakridge 97463, (541) 782-2933. Chinook salmon and rainbow trout. Ponds offer viewing of large trout and white sturgeon. Area for viewing upland game birds.

Wizard Falls Fish Hatchery, P.O. Box 130, Camp Sherman 97330. Trout, kokanee, and Atlantic salmon. A platform for viewing fish in the nearby Metolius River is available. The site is surrounded by the Deschutes National Forest.

National Fish Hatcheries

Eagle Creek National Fish Hatchery, 34288 SE Rainbow Rd., Estacada 97023, (503) 630-6270. Steelhead trout and coho salmon. Salmon and steelhead trout smolts are released from April to early June to begin their downstream migration to the Pacific Ocean. The hatchery is open daily. The best time to visit is during steelhead spawning when all life stages are available for viewing. School and group tours are available upon request.

Warm Springs National Fish Hatchery, P.O. Box 790, Warm Springs 97761, (541) 553-1692. Spring chinook. A natural run of spring chinook salmon is located upriver from the hatchery. Hatchery is open daily from 8:00 A.M. to 4:00 P.M. Environmental education tours are available by reservation.

Forests

(SEE ALSO NATIONAL FORESTS) Nearly half of Oregon's 61.4 million acres are forested (27.5 million acres). Douglas fir and western hemlock predominate between the Cascades and the Pacific Ocean. Ponderosa pine and lodgepole pine are the dominant conifers from the Cascades east. Other species of true fir and larch are also found in Eastern Oregon. The forests in the high country of the central Cascades are noncommercial; the principal species are alpine fir, mountain hemlock, and western juniper.

Oregon's forest lands are owned by the federal government (about 51 percent); the state and Indian tribes (about 6 percent); the forest industry (about 29 percent); and other private, nonindustrial landowners (about 14 percent). Much of the state's forest lands are second- and third-growth timber. Estimates of old-growth timber remaining in the entire Northwest range from about 1.1 million to 4.5 million acres.

Among the most common, and commercially important tree species that make up Oregon's forests are the following:

Bigleaf maple *(Acer macrophyllum).* This tree is well-named—its leaves really are big, up to 12 inches in diameter. Bigleaf maples grow to 100 feet and are up to 4 feet in diameter. They grow on the west side of the Cascades. Bigleaf maple is highly valued for furniture making, paneling, and flooring.

Black cottonwood *(Populus trichocarpa).* This large hardwood grows in wet bottomland. Cottonwood trees grow up to 200 feet and 6 feet in diameter. Their wood is used for making wood pulp.

Douglas fir *(Pseudotsuga menziesii).* King of the forests, the Douglas fir is the most important commercial tree in Oregon. It is prized where large framing pieces are needed, as well as for thousands of other uses. Named for pioneering Scottish botanist David Douglas, who explored Oregon in 1825, the Douglas fir can reach

Oregon's Champion Tree is the world's largest-known Sitka spruce. Photo by Andrea Jarvela.

An Ancient Relic

Beside the Pacific, in the Oregon dunes near the town of Neskowin, off U.S. 101, a forest of old-growth stumps emerged from the surf during the winter of 1998. The stumps, some of which are over 2,000 years old, are relics of an ancient forest. Scientists think a powerful earthquake that occurred about 2,000 years ago in the region dropped the coastline by as much as 7 feet, drowning the coastal forest of Sitka spruce and cedar trees. The stumps emerged as a result of sand movements driven by fierce coastal storms.

250 feet in height. Its cones hang down.

Grand fir *(Abies grandis).* This large (up to 250 feet) conifer is found in moist areas in Western Oregon. The grand fir is used in construction. Young trees are especially popular for Christmas trees.

Lodgepole pine *(Pinus contorta).* Lodgepoles are found in Eastern Oregon and east of the Cascades. They grow up to a hundred feet tall. Their commercial uses include lumber, poles, fiber products, and fencing material.

Ponderosa pine *(Pinus ponderosa).* This is the most important commercial tree in the West and the most common tree east of the Cascades. The ponderosa grows to 180 feet tall and up to 6 feet in diameter. Its bark has an orange tint and a distinctive puzzle pattern. The ponderosa prefers dry mountain slopes. Ponderosa is an ideal general-construction lumber.

Red alder *(Alnus rubra).* Red alder can reach 120 feet in height and 3 feet in diameter. This hardwood tree is found in lowlands below 2,500 feet. Its leaves are large and oval; its bark is gray-white and patchy. Alders play an important role in forest ecology because they add nitrogen to soil; in a natural forest succession, they often pave the way for stands of conifers. Alder is used for making furniture and also pallets.

Sitka spruce *(Picea sitchensis).* Sitka is the largest spruce, growing to 180 feet. It prefers moist, well-drained locales and is found in the Coast Range. Spruce needles are especially short and prickly to the touch. Spruce wood is used in boat and airplane construction, as well as for making musical instruments and newsprint.

Western hemlock *(Tsuga heterophylla).* This large (to 200 feet) conifer is common in western forests. Hemlocks abound in the Coast Range because they prefer deep shade, rain, and fog. Hemlock is used for pulp, plywood, veneer, and general construction.

Western larch *(Larix occidentalis).* The larch is a deciduous conifer; that is, it is a conifer that drops its needles each fall. The larch grows to 180 feet tall. Larch wood is highly resistant to decay and is therefore used for fence posts and mine timbers.

Western red cedar *(Thuja plicata).* Standing up to 200 feet tall, the western red cedar grows in bottomlands near rivers and up adjacent mountain slopes. Its needles are soft to the touch. The wood is even and straight-grained. Red cedar is especially desirable for siding, shakes, and shingles.

Forest Products Industry

The amount of land available for commercial timber harvesting in Oregon has declined over the years. Most of this reduction has occurred on publicly owned lands. Cutting on some private lands has actually increased in recent years. A major reason for the decline in forestry is the need to protect habitat for threatened and endangered species of fish and wildlife. Increased public involvement in public decision making, changing public values, and shifts in forest-products manufacturing capabilities toward using small logs have also been important factors.

Studies have shown that the acreage available for forestry has decreased by more than 24 percent since 1945; however, the forest land base has stabilized in recent years. The reduction in timberlands has resulted in a steady decline in timber harvests. While 9 billion board feet (bf) of timber were harvested in 1971, the harvest in 1997 declined to 4.1 billion board feet. Of that,

- 2.40 billion bf were harvested on private, forest industry lands.
- 0.77 billion bf were harvested on other private lands.
- 0.59 billion bf were harvested on U.S. Forest Service lands.
- 0.13 billion bf were harvested on state forest lands.
- 0.09 billion bf were harvested on federal Bureau of Land Management lands.
- 0.08 billion bf were harvested on Indian lands.

Following is the breakdown of harvested timber by species and land ownership in 1995:

Harvested Timber by Species and Land Ownership, 1995

(in thousands of board feet)

Softwood Species	U.S. Forest Service	U.S. Bureau of Land Management	State	Private	Indian	Totals
Cedar	2,694	3,766	597	40,870	8	47,935
Douglas fir	147,238	106,281	80,035	1,539,863	14,558	1,887,975
Hemlock	12,217	6,170	11,039	268,405	61	297,892
Pine	5,467	2,020	21	13,539	0	21,047
Spruce	67	1	711	61,686	9	62,474
True fir	27,018	4,628	638	69,674	0	101,958
Other	0	0	0	126,979	294	127,273
Total Softwood	194,701	122,866	93,041	2,121,016	14,930	2,546,554
Hardwood Species						
Alder	2,210	1,186	7,787	121,838	456	133,477
Madrone	20	42	0	0	0	62
Maple	0	239	32	14,895	0	15,166
Other	50	741	23	62,739	787	64,340
Total Hardwood	2,280	2,208	7,842	199,472	1,243	213,045
Grand Totals	196,981	125,074	100,883	2,320,488	16,173	2,759,599

Source: Oregon Department of Forestry

Acres Harvested by Ownership Group, 1995

Ownership Group	Clear-cut Acres West	Clear-cut Acres East	Partial-cut Acres West	Partial-cut Acres East	Totals
U.S. Forest Service	3,055	4,021	11,686	60,777	79,539
U.S. Bureau of Land Management	3,261	5	2,307	1,437	7,010
State	455	0	4,403	656	5,514
Local Government	332	2,537	676	1,547	5,092
Industry	62,048	8,207	97,334	224,036	391,625
Other Private	18,857	457	72,514	44,755	136,583
Indian	964	1,303	786	1,797	4,850
Totals	88,972	16,530	189,706	335,005	626,121

Source: Oregon Department of Forestry

The Tillamook Burn

Oregon's biggest forest fire started on Aug. 14, 1933. While it wasn't the worst in terms of loss of life, the fire destroyed more of the state's natural resources than any cataclysm before or since. Some felling practices combined with hot, dry weather increased fire risk, and logging became its own worst enemy that day, when a fire lookout on Saddle Mountain noticed a wispy white tail above an area being worked at Gales Creek. Over the next 10 days, several thousand men would fight the 100-mile front in vain as it consumed acres of old-growth Douglas fir—12.5 billion feet of logs. That first fire, and smaller fires that followed, eventually burned some 350,000 acres in an area that came to be called the Tillamook Burn.

Trees up to 500 feet high made enormous torches, creating hurricane winds that roared even louder as uprooted trees crashed to the ground. Ashes floated into Portland homes 50 miles away, blackened splinters fell on the decks of ships at sea, and streams were choked with dead fish. Surprisingly, only one person died in the firestorm, young Frank Palmer of the Civilian Conservation Corps, when a fir uprooted by wind crushed him.

While forest fires kill trees, they don't burn them up completely. Parasites and fungi go to work on the remains, spreading seeds and feeding the soil. By the middle of 1945, new timber had grown up to 15 feet, trout were back in clear water, and birds, deer, and elk had returned.

A second fire over burned land, though, does kill for good, and that's exactly what happened on July 9, 1945. On the Salmonberry River, a watchman saw smoke over a remote bluff. The site's isolation and the early hour (when coolness and moisture usually deter fire) led to the belief that this blaze was sparked by a Japanese incendiary balloon, many of which fell over the Northwest between 1944 and 1945.

Within two hours, a smoke plume towered 4,000 feet. Seeds buried over the last decade in the ground, and any remaining trees with seeds to scatter, were immolated. Again, more than a thousand men couldn't dim the fire that lasted into October, destroying 150,000 acres, almost all of it previously burned. ✷

Big Timber

When the smart operators were laying off the help or limping away to bankruptcy court as recession whipsawed Oregon's timber industry in the early 1980s, Ralph Hull's Hull-Oakes Lumber Company kept its boilers fired. Since the steam-powered head rig bit into its first log in 1939, the mill has never had a shutdown or a plantwide layoff. At the mill, which is wedged in a valley of the Coast Range midway between Corvallis and Eugene, even the lumber is archaic. Big beams, hulking structural timbers of the sort that almost nobody cuts any more, are the company's best-known product. Big, in this case means up to 110 feet in length and 30 inches in thickness. —Mike Thoele, Footprints Across Oregon ✷

The inventory of timber available for harvest on nonfederal land remains stable, that is, harvest rates are roughly in balance with growth rates. On federal land the inventory has begun to increase as the result of cutbacks in harvest rates on federal tracts.

State law requires reforestation of timbered lands. About 80 million seedlings are planted in Oregon each year. Even large burned-over lands have been returned to productive forests. The largest burned area returned to forest is the Tillamook Burn, some 350,000 acres burned by forest fires between 1933 and 1951.

Wood products dominated Oregon's economy for many years. Only within the last decade has high-tech industry surpassed wood products as the state's largest employer. About 61,000 Oregonians now work in the wood-products industry, and that number is declining. However, forestry and wood products remain very important to rural Oregon, accounting for one-third of the state's economy outside the Portland area. Moreover, with growing and cutting now in balance, the state has abundant timber resources for the future. Much of the cutting in the future will be second- and third-growth timber on nonfederal lands. In fact, harvests in the future are estimated to be as much as 40 percent below those that could be sustained if only the amount of timber available was considered. The difference is accounted for by concern for the total ecology of Oregon, including healthy salmon and streams and other factors, including the consequent long-term reductions of harvesting on public lands.

Organizations and Events of Interest

Collier State Park and Logging Museum, U.S. 97, about 30 miles north of Klamath Falls, 46000 U.S. 97, Chiloquin 97624, (541) 783-2471, www.collierlogging museum.org. This large park displays early logging equipment.

A faller sharpens his saw beside a ponderosa pine chosen in a selective cut. From *Oregon's National Forests* by Robert M. Reynolds (photos) and Joan Campf (text).

World Forestry Center, 4033 SW Canyon Rd. (Washington Park), Portland 97221, (503) 228-1367. This museum spotlights the history of logging and Oregon's timber industry. An enormous tiger sculpture carved from a 1,000-year-old tree for the Seoul Olympics is a prominent new acquisition. A 20-foot-tall Douglas fir tells children about its natural growth cycle.

Douglas County Timber Days, Sutherlin, July, (541) 459-9365.

World Championship Timber Carnival, Albany, July, (541) 928-2391.

Fossils (*SEE ALSO* NATIONAL PARKS, MONUMENTS, AND RECREATION AREAS)

Oregon offers an abundance of fossils. The oldest are marine fossils found in eastern Crook County that date from the Paleozoic era, at least 380 million years ago. The most abundant fossils in the state date from the Eocene (45 million years ago) through the Pleistocene. They include tiny relatives of the horse, as well as primitive members of the crocodile family and others. Fossils from 20 million years ago include bearlike animals and ancestors of the dog, weasel, rabbit, elephant, and others. Several species of large mammals disappeared from the scene as recently as 11,000 years ago, about the time that humans first appeared on the North American continent, including species of horses, camels, mammoths, bison, and others.

The plant fossil record is sparser, at least until about 47 million years ago. A number of Eocene, Oligocene, and Miocene fossil beds have yielded plants that are similar in many ways to modern plants. These include tree ferns and gingkoes. The plant fossil record indicates that the climate was somewhat warmer in some epochs.

One of the best places to see fossils is the John Day Fossil Beds, discovered by Dr. Thomas Condon, who later

The Painted Hills of the John Day Fossil Beds. Photo by Andrea Jarvela.

founded the geology department at the University of Oregon. Down-cutting by the John Day River has exposed extensive beds of volcanic tuff. Fossils have been collected from these tuffs since the 1860s.

John Day Fossil Beds National Monument, HCR 82, Box 126, Kimberly 97848, (541) 987-2333, www.nps.gov/joda.

Gold Gold was first discovered in the Northwest in Jacksonville, in southern Oregon Territory. Oregon Trail travelers filled their water buckets off the main trail, intending to take them back to camp, when they found gold nuggets at the bottom of their pails. Though the pioneers were in Indian Territory that was closed to homesteaders, word spread about the "Blue Bucket" route, and California gold-rush fever brought many speculators through Southern Oregon. A modest gold strike in the Rogue Valley in the 1850s attracted thousands more.

Though the rush created buyers for Oregon produce and encouraged some to settle in prime ranching areas throughout Southern Oregon, the influx sparked violence with local tribes, whose salmon runs were being devastated by panning and whose land was being encroached upon. Since securities law barely existed, fraud within the young industry became rampant. Many companies and promoters exaggerated minor finds and conned investors into buying worthless mining stocks. Over the next few decades, more money was spent selling equipment to prospectors and mining rights to investors than ever came from mining gold.

Some companies had genuine success, though their revenue would be modest compared to the production of a modern gold mine. The E & E Mine near Sumpter in Baker County produced an average of 4,200 ounces a year. An important contributor to the local economy, it was mined out over its 12 intermittant years of operation from 1891 to 1922.

Before environmentally protective reclamation laws were in place, mines were often simply abandoned. Camp Carson, 20 miles from La Grande, is one such site. Miners were most active there in 1893 and 1894, dumping major quantities of gravel into Tanner Gulch Creek just below.

The few amazing finds kept the rush going through the turn of the century. An 80-ounce gold nugget rolled into a Blue Mountain placer mine in 1913. Now housed at the U.S. Bank in Baker County, the nugget is valued between $20,000 and $30,000. The Gin Lin Trail near Ruch, 5 miles west of Jacksonville, is named for a Chinese immigrant who dug miles of trenches there in 1881. Lin deposited over a million dollars worth of gold dust in the Jacksonville Bank over that decade. Rumor has it that when he came off the ship he'd taken home to China, Gin Lin was robbed and beaten to death.

By 1930 the excitement was over, though traces of gold can still be found in some Oregon creeks. In 1937, a few solid pieces were found near Vernonia, and farmers in Columbia County reported finding small gold fragments in the stomachs of chickens. Today amateur panning is a popular recreational pursuit.

Gold panning is allowed on most streams and rivers flowing through campgrounds on U.S. Bureau of Land Management and U.S. Forest Service land, but it is forbidden on mining claims on federal lands. The most promising sites are in northeast Oregon, southwest Oregon, and the western Cascades. Oregon beaches owned by the state are also open for recreational gold panning. A gold pan and the right techniques can yield several forms of the metal: small lumps or nuggets, wires, feather-shaped crystals, or flat flecks. The smallest pieces, called "colors," are nearly microscopic. You're free to do what you like with any finds. Jewelry manufacturers or gold buyers may purchase your loot, though the U.S. government no longer buys gold. Larger pieces should receive the higher collector's price, rather than the value of its weight.

Organizations of Interest

Oregon Department of Geology and Mineral Industries, 800 NE Oregon St., No. 965, Portland 97232, (503) 731-4100, www.naturenw.org. Information about recreational gold panning in Oregon can be obtained from this office.

Public Inquiries Office, U.S. Geological Survey (U.S.G.S.), Room 135 U.S. Post Office, West 904 Riverside Avenue, Spokane, WA 99201, (509) 353-2524. U.S.G.S. leaflets ("Gold," "Prospecting for Gold," and "Suggestions for Prospecting") may be obtained singly from this office.

U.S. Geological Survey (U.S.G.S.), **Books and Open-File Reports,** Federal Center Building 41, Box 25424, Denver, CO 80225. Contact this office for maps and information on mine and panning sites.

Golf

It stands to reason that a state that leads in the production of grass seed and turf also has some great golf courses. About 155 golf courses in Oregon are open to the public. The Fred Meyer Classic Challenge, a two-day pro tournament with a $1 million purse, attracts 24 top players each August.

Golf Digest and other publications rank the best courses. Lately, some Oregon favorites have been included:

Broken Top and Crosswater, near Bend. Here are two of the 23 world-class courses that have made Central Oregon a golfer's paradise during certain seasons, similar some say to Palm Springs. Crosswater was selected recently by *Golf Digest* as "America's best new resort course."

Ghost Creek at Pumpkin Ridge, in Cornelius (near Portland). This course was designed to preserve the natural habitat for wildlife. It weaves through forests and past wetlands and creeks.

Sandpines Golf Resort, on the coast in Florence. This Rees Jones-designed course has been compared to Pebble Beach for its coastal challenge and beauty.

A free directory to Oregon golf courses can be obtained from the **Oregon Tourism Commission,** (800) 547-7842.

Events of Interest

Fred Meyer Classic Challenge, Aloha, August, (503) 526-9331.

Oregon Golf Association Tournament of Champions, West Linn, May, (503) 643-2610.

Mount Hood looms over the course at Persimmon Country Club, Gresham. From *Oregon Golf* by Paul Linnman (text) and Rick Schafer (photos).

> ### The Next Great Place
> *Grazing cattle pretty much ignore golfers at the Running Y Ranch Resort near Klamath Falls. But they aren't the only critters that may be encountered there. More than 500 different species of wildlife have been identified in what backers simply refer to as "the next great place. . . ." A member of the Audubon Cooperative Sanctuary System, the Running Y golf course epitomizes designer Arnold Palmer's philosophy of blending the course with the natural environment.*—Paul Linnman, *Oregon Golf*

Pacific Amateur Golf Classic, Bend, October, (800) 800-8334.

Safeway LPGA Championship, Portland, September, (503) 258-8354.

Sagebrush Classic, Bend, July, (541) 923-5191.

Government Governance in Oregon is a complex, multilayered, and multijurisdictional mixture of local, state, and federal governments. Many of the federal agencies with jurisdiction within the state are managers of public lands, such as the U.S. Forest Service, National Park Service, and U.S. Bureau of Land Management (*see* National Forests; National Parks, Monuments, and Recreation Areas). Dams on the Columbia and Snake Rivers and their associated power grids are managed by the U.S. Army Corps of Engineers and the Bonneville Power Administration (*see* Dams; Bonneville Power Administration). The state's neighbors—Idaho and Washington—share management of certain regional resources: Interstate entities include the Pacific Fishery Management Council, Pacific States Marine Fisheries Commission, and Pacific Northwest Electric Power and Conservation Planning Council (formerly the Northwest Power Planning Council).

Local governments include more than 240 municipalities (*see* Cities and Towns), 36 counties (*see* Counties), 30 different types of special-use districts such as irrigation and port districts (*see* Special Service Districts), in-state regional planning councils, and Indian tribal governments (*see* American Indians). Among the regional agencies (*see* Regional Governments) are intergovernmental planning councils, the Idaho-Oregon Planning and Development Association, and the Portland Metropolitan area's Metro, the only elected regional government in the country.

The state government is composed of executive, legislative, and judicial branches (*see* Elected Officials; Judiciary; Legislature). The state's annual budget is close to $30 billion. State government agencies and regulatory bodies are listed by oversight area below.

Oregon State Government Agencies

Government Operations

Office of the Secretary of State
- Elected Head: Secretary of State
- Historical Records Advisory Board

State Treasury
- Elected Head: State Treasurer
- Oregon Municipal Debt Advisory Commission
- Oregon Baccalaureate Bond Program
- Private Activity Bond Committee
- State Land Board and the Prison Industries Board
- Bond Valuation Committee
- Health, Housing, Educational and Cultural Facilities Authority
- Oregon Investment Council

Department of Administrative Services
- Office of Economic Analysis
- Governor's Council of Economic Advisors
- Office for Oregon Health Plan Policy and Research
- Oregon Health Council
- Public Lands Advisory Committee
- Employee Suggestion Awards Commission
- Public Employees Benefit Board
- Board of Tax Service Examiners

Capitol Planning Commission

Department of Revenue
Dispute Resolution Commission
Employment Relations Board
Government Standards and Practices Commission, Oregon
Insurance Pool Governing Board
Lane County Local Government Boundary Commission
Public Employees Retirement System
Tax Supervising and Conservation Commission
State Library

Justice and Human Rights

Oregon Department of Justice
- Elected Head: Attorney General
- Consumer Advisory Council

Commission on Black Affairs
Commission for the Blind
Oregon Disabilities Commission
Commission on Hispanic Affairs
Commission for Women

Education

Department of Education
- Elected Head: Superintendent of Public Instruction
- State Board of Education
- Oregon School for the Blind
- Oregon School for the Deaf
- Fair Dismissal Appeals Board

State Scholarship Commission
Teacher Standards and Practices Commission

Business and Economic Development

Bureau of Labor and Industries
- Elected Head: Labor Commissioner
- Commissioner's Office and Program Services Division
- State Apprenticeship and Training Council
- Oregon Council on Civil and Human Rights
- Advisory Committee on Prevailing Wage Rate Law

Employment Department
- Employment Appeals Board
- Child Care Division
- Commission for Child Care

Economic Development Department
- Oregon Arts Commission
- Oregon Film and Video Office
- Oregon Progress Board
- Oregon Tourism Commission

Department of Agriculture
- Agricultural Commodity Commissions
- State Board of Agriculture
- State Christmas Tree Advisory Committee
- Nursery Research and Regulatory Committee
- Soil and Water Conservation Commission
- Minor Crops Advisory Committee
- State Weed Board

Department of Consumer and Business Services
Travel Information Council
Oregon State Fair and Exposition Center
Oregon Resource and Technology Development Fund
Real Estate Agency
Oregon Racing Commission
State Board of Architect Examiners
Construction Contractors Board
State Landscape Architect Board
State Landscape Contractors Board
State Board of Examiners for Engineering and Land Surveying

Environment and Natural Resources

Department of Environmental Quality
- Environmental Quality Commission
- Air Quality Division
- Waste Management and Cleanup Division
- Water Quality Division

Department of Fish and Wildlife
- State Fish and Wildlife Commission
- Restoration and Enhancement Board
- Access and Habitat Board

State Forestry Department
- State Board of Forestry
- County Forestland Classification Committees
- Emergency Fire Cost Committee
- Forest Resource Trust Advisory Committee
- Forest Trust Land Advisory Committee

State Department of Geology and Mineral Industries
- Geology and Mineral Industries Governing Board
- The Nature of the Northwest Information Center

Department of Land Conservation and Development
- Land Conservation and Development Commission
- Citizen Involvement Advisory Committee
- State Parks and Recreation Department
- State Historic Preservation Office
- Oregon Historic Trails Advisory Council
- Oregon Recreation Trails Advisory Council

Division of State Lands
- Natural Heritage Advisory Council
- South Slough National Estuarine Reserve/South Slough Estuarine Sanctuary Management Commission

Water Resources Department
- Water Resources Commission
- Governor's Watershed Enhancement Board
- Groundwater Advisory Committee
- Klamath River Basin Compact
- Western States Water Council
- Water Development Loan Program

Columbia River Gorge Commission
Land Use Board of Appeals
State Marine Board
Pacific States Marine Fisheries Commission
State Board of Geologist Examiners

Health and Human Services

Housing and Community Services Department
- Manufactured Dwelling Ombudsman Program
- Community Action Directors of Oregon (CADO)
- State Housing Council

Department of Human Resources
- Community Partnership Team
- Governor's Council on Alcohol and Drug Abuse Programs
- Public Welfare Review Commission
- State Office for Services to Children and Families
- Conference of Local Health Officials
- Drinking Water Advisory Committee
- Emergency Medical Services Committee
- Radiation Advisory Committee
- State Trauma Advisory Board
- Athletic Trainer Registration Program
- Board of Barbers and Hairdressers
- Body Piercing Program
- Board of Denture Technology
- Board of Direct Entry Midwifery
- Council for Electrologists, Permanent Color Technicians, and Tattoo Artists
- Advisory Council for Hearing Aid Dealers
- Respiratory Therapist Licensing Board
- Sanitarians Registration Board
- Medicaid Advisory Committee
- Developmental Disabilities Council
- Mental Health Advisory Board
- Eastern Oregon Training and Psychiatric Centers
- Fairview Training Center
- Oregon State Hospital
- State Rehabilitation Council

Department of Veterans' Affairs
- Advisory Committee to the Director of Veterans' Affairs
- Oregon Veterans' Home

State Commission on Children and Families/Juvenile Justice Advisory Committee
Children's Trust Fund
Long Term Care Ombudsman
State Mortuary and Cemetery Board
Oregon Youth Authority
Psychiatric Security Review Board
State Board of Chiropractic Examiners
State Board of Clinical Social Workers
Oregon Board of Licensed Professional Counselors and Therapists
Oregon Board of Dentistry
Board of Examiners of Licensed Dietitians
State Board of Massage Technicians
Board of Medical Examiners for the State of Oregon
Board of Naturopathic Examiners
Oregon State Board of Nursing
Board of Examiners of Nursing Home Administrators
Oregon Board of Optometry

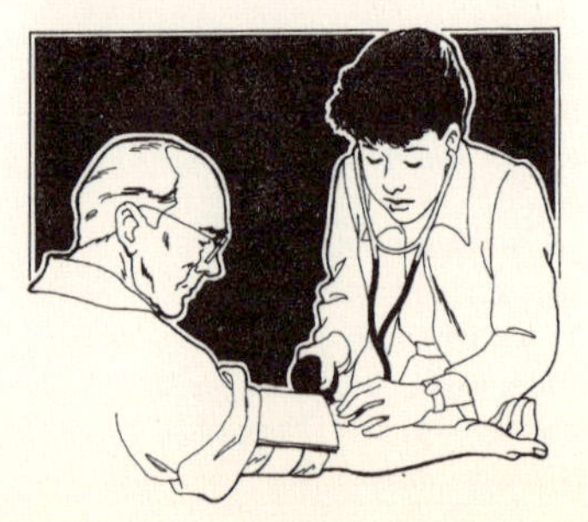

Occupational Therapy Licensing Board
State Board of Pharmacy
Physical Therapist Licensing Board
State Board of Psychologist Examiners
Board of Radiologic Technology
State Board of Examiners for Speech-Language Pathology and Audiology
State Veterinary Medical Examining Board

Public Safety and Corrections

Department of Public Safety Standards and Training
- Board of Public Safety Standards and Training
- Corrections Advisory Committee
- Fire Advisory Committee
- Police Advisory Committee
- Private Security Advisory Committee
- Telecommunications Advisory Committee
- Western Community Policing Center

Department of Corrections
- Oregon Criminal Justice Commission

Department of State Police
State Board of Parole and Post-Prison Supervision

Transportation and Utilities

Department of Transportation
- Oregon Transportation Commission
- Oregon Board of Maritime Pilots
- Aviation Advisory Committee
- Governor's Advisory Committee on DUII
- Governor's Motorcycle Safety Advisory Committee
- Rural Transit Assistance Program Advisory Committee
- Transportation Safety Committee
- Willamette Valley Passenger Rail Advisory Council
- All-terrain Vehicle Account Allocation Committee
- Bicycle and Pedestrian Advisory Committee
- Covered Bridge Advisory Committee
- Historic Columbia River Highway Advisory Committee
- Winter Recreation Advisory Committee

Pacific Northwest Electric Power and Conservation Planning Council
Public Utility Commission of Oregon

Military

Oregon Military Department
- Military Council
- Oregon Air National Guard
- Oregon Army National Guard

Miscellaneous Agencies and Licensing Boards

Oregon Liquor Control Commission
Oregon State Office of the Lottery

State Budget* (millions)

Program	1997-99	1999-2001
Education	$8,528	$9,181
Human Resources	6,478	7,348
Public Safety	1,438	1,772
Economic and Community Development	3,485	3,452
Natural Resources	885	1,064
Transportation	1,600	2,061
Consumer and Business Services	602	631
All Other	3,914	4,062
Total	$26,735	$29,577

Source: Legislative Fiscal Office

*Funding from all sources. Totals may not add up due to rounding.

Governors

(SEE ALSO ELECTED OFFICIALS) Over the past 154 years, 42 people have served as Oregon's governor: one was elected as head of a provisional government, six were appointed by U.S. presidents as territorial governors, and 35 have served as state governors. Four governors died while in office, and three resigned from office. Barbara Roberts was the first—and only—woman to hold that office.

Oregon Provisional Governor

George Abernethy, 1845-1849

Oregon Territorial Governors

Joseph Lane (Democrat), 1849-1850, resigned
Kintzing Prichette (Democrat), 1850, acting governor for two months

John P. Gaines (Whig), 1850-1853
Joseph Lane (Democrat), 1853
George L. Curry (Democrat), 1853 and 1854-1859, acting governor from May to December 1853, presidential appointee in 1854
John W. Davis (Democrat), 1853-1854, resigned

Oregon State Governors

John Whiteaker (Democrat), 1859-1862
A. C. Gibbs (Republican), 1862-1866
George L. Woods (Republican), 1866-1870
LaFayette Grover (Democrat), 1870-1877, resigned
Stephen F. Chadwick (Democrat), 1877-1878
W. W. Thayer (Democrat), 1878-1882
Z. F. Moody (Republican), 1882-1887
Sylvester Pennoyer (Democratic People's Party), 1887-1895
William Paine Lord (Republican), 1895-1899
T. T. Geer (Republican), 1899-1903
George E. Chamberlain (Democrat), 1903-1909, resigned
Frank W. Benson (Republican), 1909-1910, resigned
Jay Bowerman (Republican), 1910-1911
Oswald West (Democrat), 1911-1915
James Withycombe (Republican), 1915-1919, died in office
Ben W. Olcott (Republican), 1919-1923
Walter M. Pierce (Democrat), 1923-1927
I. L. Patterson (Republican), 1927-1929, died in office
A. W. Norblad (Republican), 1929-1931
Julius L. Meier (Independent), 1931-1935
Charles H. Martin (Democrat), 1935-1939
Charles A. Sprague (Republican), 1939-1943
Earl Snell (Republican), 1943-1947, died in office
John H. Hall (Republican), 1947-1949
Douglas McKay (Republican), 1949-1952, resigned
Paul L. Patterson (Republican), 1952-1956, died in office
Elmo Smith (Republican), 1956-1957
Robert D. Holmes (Democrat), 1957-1959
Mark O. Hatfield (Republican), 1959-1967
Tom McCall (Republican), 1967-1975

Gov. John A. Kitzhaber, M.D. Photo by C. Bruce Forster courtesy Governor's office.

Robert W. Straub (Democrat), 1975-1979
Victor G. Atiyeh (Republican), 1979-1987
Neil Goldschmidt (Democrat), 1987-1991
Barbara Roberts (Democrat), 1991-1995
John Kitzhaber (Democrat), 1995-

Tom McCall

Tom McCall, Oregon's champion and its governor from 1967 to [Dec.] 1974, helped establish land-use laws that make the state's development unique by checking urban sprawl and reserving prime farm and forest lands exclusively for those purposes. He introduced the nation's first bottle pollution control and open-space bills, and he founded SOLV, Stop Oregon Litter and Vandalism. But many people believe his greatest legacy was ensuring that Oregon's beaches would forever be held in the public trust.—Magnificent Places: Oregon Coast, text by Jack and Jan McGowan, photographs by Rick Schafer.

Hells Canyon and the Snake River

(*SEE ALSO* NATIONAL PARKS, MONUMENTS, AND RECREATION AREAS; RIVERS) The Hells Canyon of the Snake River is the deepest natural gorge in North America, with a maximum depth of 8,430 feet (the Grand Canyon of the Colorado measures 5,696 feet from top to bottom). Hells Canyon averages 5,500 feet deep for more than 40 miles. The canyon was cut after a large Pleistocene lake was breached. The mighty rush of water cut deep into the Columbia Plateau as it rushed to the sea.

The gorge runs 150 miles and includes 67 miles of untamed, wild river in its natural state. This section of the canyon is protected as the Hells Canyon National Recreation Area, which encompasses 652,488 acres. The recreation area is a mecca for jet boating and river rafting. It also contains over 900 miles of hiking trails. The recreation area is administered by the **Wallowa-Whitman National Forest,** (509) 758-0616.

In 1976, the legendary daredevil Evel Knievel attempted to leap Hells Canyon on a rocket-powered motorcycle. He got about halfway across, then had to descend 6,000 feet by parachute. The canyon remains unjumped.

The Snake River flows 1,038 miles from Jackson Lake, Wyoming, in the Grand Teton Mountains, to join the Columbia River at Pasco, Washington. The Snake River forms the border between Oregon and Idaho. There are 17 dams on the Snake River; 3 of them are on the section that abuts Oregon. Because the dams have decimated native salmon runs, scientists and resource managers are considering whether to breach them to help restore this resource.

Hells Canyon is the deepest canyon on the North American continent. From *Oregon III* by Ray Atkeson.

High Technology

Oregon's high-tech industry has grown into one of the most significant sectors of the state's economy. High-tech products such as electronic instruments, computers, and computer components comprise about half of the state's manufactured exports. The semiconductor industry alone accounts for over one-fifth of the high-tech exports. Just how large the industry is and what its value is to the state economy is difficult to pin down, however. This is because "high tech" is defined differently by different government agencies. The Oregon Employment Department defines the high-tech sector as "office and computing machines industry, electronic equipment, instruments and related products, and the computer and data processing services industry."

The Oregon Economic Development Department divides the industry into three sectors: measuring instruments (test products, timers, etc.); industrial machinery and equipment and computing equipment; and electrical equipment and components. A broader definition of the industry would also include such elements as the biomedical industry, engineering services, research activities of both universities and nonprofit organizations, and Internet and multimedia developers. By whatever definition one uses, however, this sector of the state's economy has grown rapidly during the 1980s and 1990s to rival such long-time major economic sectors as agriculture and forest products.

Eight of the Portland *Business Journal*'s top ten "fastest-growing private companies" for 1998 were engaged in some high-tech endeavor. The first big player in Oregon high-tech was Tektronix, the electronics company that set up shop in the state in 1946. By 1997, the high-tech industry was employing 28 percent of Oregon's manufacturing workforce. While high-tech companies can be found throughout the state, the area from Portland to Eugene contains the greatest concentration of high-tech employment—about 94 percent of all statewide high-tech employment is concentrated here. Southern Oregon and the Bend area are also important high-tech regions. The Oregon Employment Department reported total employment in high-tech (by its limited definition) at about 70,000 in 1998. The electronic equipment industry (which includes semiconductor manufacturers such as the giant chip maker Intel with facilities in Hillsboro) employs 35,500 people, and the software industry counts more than 13,000 employees.

History

13,200 to 10,000 years ago The earliest known Native Americans inhabit such areas as Fort Rock and The Dalles, Mack Canyon on the Rogue River, and Yaquina Head on the Pacific Coast.

1543 Bartolomé Ferrelo, a pilot for Juan Rodrigues Cabrillo, sails north as far as southwest coast of Oregon.

1578 Sir Francis Drake sails north to the southern part of Oregon.

1603 Martin d'Aguilar sails along the Oregon Coast and sights a river where the Columbia is later discovered.

1707 A Spanish galleon sailing from Manila wrecks on the Oregon Coast at the base of Neahkahnie Mountain; its cargo of beeswax will be found for years to come.

1765 British Major Robert Rogers uses the name "Ouragon" in a proposal to explore the country west of the Mississippi, the first known use of the name Oregon.

1774 Spanish explorer Juan José Peréz Hernandez sails along the Oregon Coast and trades with Indians.

1775 Spaniards Bruno de Heceta and Juan de la Bodega y Quadra land near present-day Point Grenville and claim the territory for Spain. They are the first recorded Europeans known to stand on Northwest soil.

1778 Captain James Cook sites the Oregon Coast and names Capes Foulweather, Perpetua, and Flattery. He misses the Columbia River and sails on to Vancouver Island.

1785-87 More British ships sail along the Northwest Coast while trading furs.

1788 Captain Robert Gray, first American landing in Oregon, arrives at Tillamook. Markus Lopius, first black to set foot on Oregon soil, is aboard Robert Gray's sloop *Lady Washington.*

1790 Spain and Britain sign an agreement resolving the dispute over claims along the Northwest Coast in favor of the British.

1792 Captain Robert Gray discovers the great river of the West, naming it the Columbia after his ship, the *Columbia Rediviva.* The same year, British explorer George Vancouver and

Spaniard Bodega y Quadra explore the Northwest coastline.

1794 England and Spain amend their 1790 convention, as Spain withdraws its claims to the Northwest.

1803 President Thomas Jefferson doubles the size of the United States with the Louisiana Purchase.

President Thomas Jefferson

1805 Sent by President Thomas Jefferson, the Lewis and Clark Expedition reaches the Pacific Ocean. This Corps of Discovery spends the winter at Fort Clatsop, near Astoria.

1807 David Thompson, a British fur trader and explorer, begins what will be a four-year journey of travel along the entire length of the Columbia River.

1811 The Pacific Fur Company, financed by American John Jacob Astor, is established near the mouth of the Columbia River, where Astoria now stands. (The post is captured by the British as a prize in the War of 1812 and renamed Fort George.)

1813 The Pacific Fur Company is sold to the British North West Company, which dominates the region's fur trade until 1821.

1814 Jane Barnes, first white woman to land in the Pacific Northwest, arrives at Fort George, and the first livestock in the Northwest arrives by ship from California.

1816 A library is established at the Red River settlement.

1817 William Cullen Bryant uses the name "Oregon" in his poem *Thanatopsis.*

1818 Fort George is returned to American ownership as the United States and England agree on "joint occupancy" for the Oregon Country in the Convention of 1818.

1819 The Adams-Onis Treaty establishes the 42nd parallel as the southern boundary of the Oregon Country.

1821 The Hudson's Bay Company acquires a fur monopoly for all of British North America after merging with the North West Company. It remains the most influential nonnative power in the Northwest for the next 25 years.

1822 Dr. John Floyd urges Congress to look into settling the "Origon" territory, marking the first American use of the name.

1824 Dr. John McLoughlin, Hudson's Bay Company agent, moves the company from Astoria to Fort Vancouver to reinforce British control north of the Columbia River. The United States signs a treaty with Russia to restrict the Russians north of 54 degrees 40 minutes latitude.

1827 Dr. McLoughlin builds the Northwest's first sawmill. The United States and Great Britain renew the terms of the 1818 "joint occupancy" agreement.

1828 Fur trapper Jedediah Smith leads the first party to travel overland from California to Oregon. Fifteen of his 18 men are massacred by Indians on the Umpqua River.

1829 A Hudson's Bay Company post is established at Willamette Falls, the site of present-day Oregon City. Epidemics begin to ravage Indian tribes along the Columbia and Willamette Rivers. American Hall Jackson Kelley organizes the "American Society for Encouraging the Settlement of the Oregon Territory." A French-Canadian farmer begins cultivating land in the Willamette Valley.

1831 Three Nez Perce and one Flathead Indian travel to St. Louis, reportedly seeking missionaries to come to Oregon.

1832 Nathaniel Wyeth leads an American colonizing expedition overland to the Columbia, but the venture fails.

1833 First school in the Pacific Northwest is established at Fort Vancouver. The teacher, John Ball, is a member of the Wyeth party. Timber is shipped from Oregon to China.

1834 Fort Hall, in what is now Idaho, is established by Nathaniel Wyeth on his second expedition. This same year, the Jason Lee party of the first Protestant missionaries to the Oregon Country arrives at Fort Vancouver with Wyeth, and they establish a mission 10 miles north of present-day Salem.

1836 The *Beaver,* the first steamboat on the Pacific Ocean, is brought to Fort Vancouver. Marcus and Narcissa Whitman establish a mission near Walla Walla. Migration of settlers over the Oregon Trail begins.

1837 The Willamette Cattle Company is formed, marking the first cooperative venture among Oregon settlers.

1838 American settler Jason Lee delivers a petition to Congress asking for legislation securing title to lands that settlers occupy and for the extension of the laws of the United States over the Oregon Country. Fathers François Blanchet and Modeste Demers, Catholic missionaries, arrive at Fort Vancouver and hold the first Catholic mass. The first cattle drive of the Northwest arrives from California.

1839 First printing press is brought to the Northwest from Honolulu and used to print a Nez Perce primer, the first book produced in the Pacific Northwest. Father Blanchet establishes a Catholic mission in St. Paul.

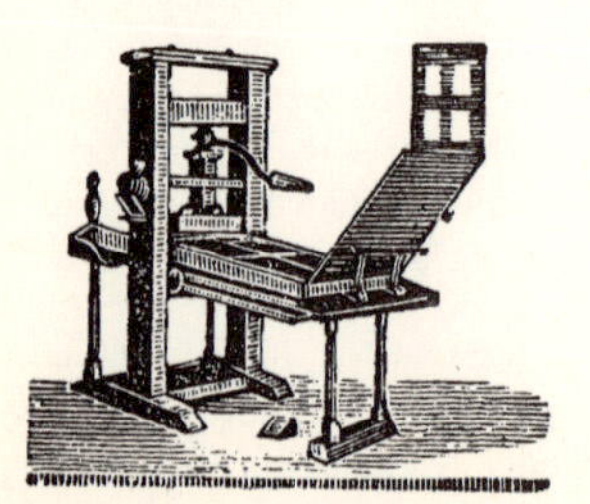

1840 Parties of American settlers from California and Illinois and reinforcements to the Methodist mission arrive in the Willamette Valley. The overland migration of Americans to Oregon has begun in earnest. The population of Americans residing in the Oregon Country is estimated to be 150.

1841 American settlers in the Willamette Valley meet to create a government, but they fail. The *Star of Oregon,* the first ship built by Americans in the Oregon Country, is launched, and Lieut. Charles Wilkes brings the U.S. naval exploring expedition to the region.

1842 Englishman George Simpson begins to consolidate Hudson's Bay Company trade northward. Dr. John McLoughlin begins designing plans for what is now Oregon City. Willamette University is founded, making it the first university west of the Mississippi.

1843 Settlers of the Oregon Territory form a provisional government, which starts a border dispute between England and the United States. "Fifty-four-forty or fight!" becomes a rallying cry. Oregon's first four counties are established: Clackamas, Marion, Yamhill, and Tuality (which will later be renamed Washington County). The first large group of Americans arrives over the Oregon Trail; approximately 900 settlers come to the Willamette Valley. John C. Fremont maps a route south to California from The Dalles east of the Cascades.

1844 Oregon City is selected as the first capital of Oregon Country. Clatsop County is created. Acts to prohibit slavery and to exclude blacks and mulattoes from Oregon are passed. The first American taxes on the Pacific Coast are collected—they are voluntary.

1845 A prison is built in Oregon City. Polk County is established. Oregon's second provisional government is organized, and George Abernethy is elected provisional governor. Settlers residing in the Willamette Valley number 2,000.

1846 The United States and England sign the Oregon Treaty of 1846, defining the

boundary between the United States and Canada at the 49th parallel. The first Oregon newspaper, *Oregon Spectator,* is printed. The Hudson's Bay Company moves its headquarters to Vancouver Island. John McLoughlin resigns from the company and moves to Oregon City. The Applegate Trail is established off the Oregon Trail.

1847 Marcus and Narcissa Whitman and 12 others are killed by Cayuse Indians at the Waiilatpu Mission in the Oregon Territory (present-day Washington). Linn and Benton Counties are established. The first U.S. post office west of the Rockies is established in Astoria.

1848 Oregon Territory is created as a political unit of the United States. The American ship *Honolulu* brings news that gold has been discovered in California seven months earlier.

1849 The territorial government convenes in Oregon City. General Joseph Lane, the first appointed territorial governor, arrives in the territory. Vancouver is designated the military headquarters for the Pacific Northwest.

1850 Congress passes the Donation Land Law, which restricts land claims to 320 acres for a white or half-white male and 320 acres for his wife. Hostilities between Indians and white settlers increase. Mail service between San Francisco and the Columbia River is established. The first Pacific Coast survey is completed between San Francisco and Puget Sound. An unofficial census counts 2,110 people in the territory; the population count includes 110 persons of color but does not include Indians. Indian agents begin signing what will add up to more than 20 treaties with Oregon Indians over the next five years.

1851 Lane County is established. Portland is incorporated.

1852 Douglas and Jackson Counties are established.

1853 Coos and Tillamook Counties are established. The Washington Territory is formed from part of the Oregon Territory. The first labor union in Oregon is formed, the Typographical Society. Willamette University is chartered. A treaty creates the first Indian reservation in the territory. Miners from California begin to flock to a gold strike on the Rogue River. The Rogue River Indian Wars erupt. Seven treaties with Indian tribes signed in 1853-55 extinguish Indian land title in the Willamette Valley.

1854 Columbia, Wasco, and Multnomah Counties are established. Congress authorizes making treaties, whenever necessary, with the Indians in the Oregon Territory.

1855 Curry County is created. The Yakima Indian War begins; it is fought on both sides of the mid-Columbia. A telegraph company begins operating, and the state capitol building, erected only a year earlier, burns.

1856 The Army closes eastern Washington and Oregon to settlers due to Indian war. Josephine County is established. The penitentiary opens in Portland.

1857 A convention is held in Salem to write a state constitution. Voters overwhelmingly ratify it. Climbers reach the summit of Mount Hood for the first time. A lighthouse is built inside the mouth of the Umpqua River.

1859 Congress admits Oregon as the 33rd state on Feb. 14. John Whiteaker becomes the first elected governor. The Ladd and Tilton Bank, first in the state, is founded. Congress ratifies treaties removing all tribes to reservations. Steamboat passenger service is extended along the Columbia River as far as The Dalles.

1860 Daily stagecoach service begins between Portland and Sacramento. The state's population is 12,093.

1861 The village of Champoeg is destroyed by one of the worst floods in Northwest history.

1862 Umatilla and Baker Counties are formed.

1863 The Idaho Territory is created.

1864 Union and Grant Counties are created. Salem becomes the state capital by popular vote. Transcontinental telegraph lines reach Portland via California. A salmon-canning factory is built in Astoria.

1866 A paper mill begins operating in Oregon City.

1868 Corvallis College (now Oregon State University) becomes the first state-supported institution of higher education in Oregon. Railroad construction begins heading south from Portland.

1869 The first public high school in Oregon is established.

1870 The state's population is 54,465.

1871 Abigail Scott Duniway introduces Susan B. Anthony in Oregon to galvanize a women's suffrage crusade.

1873 Oregon Pioneer Association, the state's first historical society, is founded.

1874 Lake County is created from Jackson and Wasco Counties.

1875 The Sisters of Providence found St. Vincent's Hospital in Portland.

1876 University of Oregon opens in Eugene.

1877 The Nez Perce War erupts. The U.S. Army Corps of Engineers begins removing navigation obstacles from the middle and upper Columbia River.

1878 The Bannock Indian War erupts. The telephone is demonstrated in Portland.

1880 The state's population is 90,923. Harness makers in Portland go on strike and win a raise of $1 per day; piece workers get a 20 percent pay raise.

1882 Congress passes anti-Chinese legislation. Schools to train teachers are established at Monmouth and Ashland. Klamath and Crook Counties are formed.

1885 A transplanted New Englander plants the first cranberry bog on the Pacific Coast in Coos County.

1886 Anti-Chinese riots break out throughout the Northwest as whites blame the Chinese for an economic downturn. Mobs led by workers drive Chinese laborers out of small towns. Most displaced Chinese go to Portland's Chinatown where, in part because of the city's close commercial and shipping ties to China, they are not expelled.

1887 A gang of at least four white men rob and murder 31 Chinese miners in the Hells Canyon region of the Snake River. The Dawes Allotment Act allows Indian reservation lands to be divided into 160-acre parcels and assigned to individuals and families. The process is intended to accelerate the conversion of Indians to non-Indian ways. Much land is taken from many reservations, including Colville, Grand Ronde, and Siletz.

1889 Sherman and Harney Counties are created. First transmission of electric power is demonstrated by Willamette Falls Electric, sending electricity over 13 miles from Oregon City to Portland. The Rose Show is held in Portland, and the Portland Rose Society is founded.

1890 Political reform movements begin to make inroads. The coming decade sees a rise in Progressivism. In Oregon, 16 percent of voters vote for the populist People's Party candidate for president. The state's population is 174,768.

1891 Congress passes the Forest Reserve Act, resulting in one-fourth of Oregon's timber resources being protected as national forests by 1908. The Port of Portland is created and empowered to dredge and maintain the river channel.

1892 The Portland Art Association is founded.

1893 Lincoln County is established. A crew from the Willamette Pulp and Paper Company plants tree seedlings on an island in the Willamette River in the first reforestation effort in the state.

1896 Along the Columbia River, fights break out between fishermen from Oregon and fish-trap operators in

Timber workers in Tillamook County, circa 1900. From *The Oregon Story: 1850-2000*, Oregon Historical Society photo.

Washington. The Portland Symphony Orchestra is born.

1899 Wheeler County is established.

1900 The state's population is 317,704.

1902 Oregon passes a law allowing residents to place measures on the ballot and recall existing laws by popular vote. More than 110 forest fires, from Eugene, Oregon, to Bellingham, Washington, burn an estimated 700,000 acres and turn the sky black for hundreds of miles. Crater Lake National Park is created.

1903 Oregonians enact a law giving women workers a 10-hour day. The small town of Heppner is wiped out by a disastrous flash flood.

1905 The Lewis and Clark Centennial Exposition is held in Portland. The Portland Art Museum opens.

1908 Hood River County is created from Wasco County. Oregon voters approve the power to recall elected officials and regulate campaign expenditures.

1909 Oregon Caves National Monument is established. Pendleton holds its first rodeo.

1910 Jantzen Knitting Mills is created (originally called Portland Knitting Company); its familiar red-suited diving girl becomes a familiar trademark. The state's population is 413,536.

1912 Women's suffrage is adopted in Oregon.

1913 The South Jetty at the mouth of the Columbia is completed to facilitate shipping on the Columbia and Willamette Rivers. Oregon's governor designates the ocean beaches as state highways. Workers' compensation laws are passed.

1914 Prohibition is adopted statewide, and capital punishment is abolished (it will later be reversed in 1920, abolished again in 1964, and restored again in 1984). Jefferson County is established from a portion of Crook County.

1916 Deschutes County is created from part of Crook County. Longshoremen strikes spread all along the West Coast. The Columbia River Highway is completed between Portland and Hood River.

1917 As the nation enters World War I, strikes by lumber workers halt 75 percent of the lumber output of Washington, Oregon, and Idaho. The Columbia River is bridged between Portland and Vancouver.

1919 Oregon becomes the first state to institute a gasoline tax. A statewide bond issue provides funds to construct a road the full length of Oregon's coast.

1920 The Oregon League of Women Voters is formed. The state's population is 672,765.

1921 The Ku Klux Klan is organized in Oregon.

1922 A compulsory education law is passed. The state receives its first donation for state park land and its first commercial radio station—KGW—goes on the air.

1923 A state income tax is approved but will be repealed the following year, then reenacted in 1930.

1927 Franchise restrictions for African-Americans and Chinese are repealed.

1927 Charles Lindbergh is on hand to dedicate the state's first municipal airport on Swan Island.

1930 The state's population is 783,389.

1933 One of the nation's worst forest fires wipes out more than 300,000 acres of timber. It comes to be known as the Tillamook Burn. The New Deal's Civilian Conservation Corps (CCC) begins clearing trails, fighting forest fires, and planting trees throughout the state. Construction of Bonneville Dam is authorized.

1934 Congress passes the Indian Reorganization Act, partially reversing the federal government's assimilation policy.

1935 The state capitol, built in 1876, is destroyed by fire. The Oregon Shakespeare Festival first performs.

1936 Nan Wood Honeyman is elected Oregon's first woman representative in Congress.

1937 Timberline Lodge is built on Mount Hood.

1938 Construction is completed on the new capitol building and Bonneville Dam. Voters approve an initiative to create a State Sanitary Authority to clean up the Willamette River and control water pollution.

1940 The state's population is 953,786.

1941 A wartime shipbuilding boom begins in Portland as the first Liberty ship is launched. The legislature passes the Oregon Forest Conservation Act, which requires reforestation on state and private lands.

1942 For the first time, women are called to jury duty in a federal court in Oregon.

1945 Inventor Howard Vollum and businessman Jack Murdock form Tektronix, Inc., which will become the world's leading maker of oscilloscopes.

1946 The state's Rural School Bill is passed to raise standards of rural schools.

1947 Gov. Earl Snell, Secretary of State Robert S. Farrell Jr., and state Senate President Marshall E. Cornett are killed in a private plane crash.

1948 A flood on Memorial Day obliterates the town of Vanport, a Portland suburb of 17,500 built to house wartime workers. The disaster leaves 60,000 people homeless and causes $75 million in property damage. The state legislature passes an Old Age Pension Act.

1949 Portland elects its first woman mayor, Dorothy McCullough Lee.

1950 The state's population is 1,521,341.

1951 Emissions from aluminum reduction plants and pulp and paper mills lead to passage of a state Air Pollution Control Act.

1952 A constitutional amendment is approved, ensuring equal representation in the state legislature.

1953 The state's Fair Employment

Practices Act is enacted. Congress adopts a policy known as "termination," intended "to make the Indians . . . subject to the same laws and entitled to the same privileges and responsibilities as are applicable to other citizens . . . to end their status as wards of the United States." The policy is reversed by the 1960s, but among the 3 percent of all Indians terminated are the Klamath Indians of Southern Oregon and 61 tribes and bands of Western Oregon.

1954 President Dwight Eisenhower dedicates McNary Dam on the Columbia River.

1957 The Dalles Dam closes its gates, flooding out the historic Indian fishing ground at Celilo Falls. Phil Knight meets Bill Bowerman at the University of Oregon; they will cofound the company that will be renamed Nike.

1959 Oregon holds a Centennial Exposition and International Trade Fair.

1960 The state's population is 1,768,687, a whopping 16.3-percent increase from 1950.

1961 I-5 is completed between Salem and Portland.

1962 A devastating storm hits the Northwest on Oct. 12. The "Columbus Day Storm" causes extensive damage as wind gusts reach 96 miles per hour.

1964 Oregon Sen. Wayne Morse speaks out against U.S. involvement in Vietnam; he is one of only two U.S. senators to vote against the Gulf of Tonkin Resolution, authorizing U.S. involvement in Vietnam.

1966 The Astoria Megler Bridge linking Oregon and Washington at the mouth of the Columbia is opened. A ceremony is held to mark the completion of I-5 from Washington to California.

1968 The John Day Dam, the last major dam to be completed on the mid-Columbia River, is dedicated by Vice-President Hubert Humphrey. Robert Kennedy suffers his only presidential primary defeat in Oregon, losing to Eugene McCarthy. The Nike company is established.

1970 The state's population is 1,768,687.

1971 The nation's first Bottle Bill is passed by the Oregon legislature.

1972 South Slough National Estuarine Sanctuary is established as the first estuarine sanctuary in the United States.

1973 Statewide land-use planning is approved. Oregon ratifies the Equal Rights Amendment to the U.S. Constitution (and reaffirms it in 1977).

1974 John Day Fossil Beds National Monument is established.

1977 Oregon bans aerosol sprays. The capitol wings addition is completed. The Confederated Tribes of Siletz win restoration of their tribal trust relationship. The Portland Trail Blazers win the National Basketball Association championship, beating the Philadelphia 76ers.

1978 Congress lists the Oregon Trail as a National Historic Trail.

1980 Mount St. Helens erupts with cataclysmic force in southwestern Washington, triggering destructive mudflows. The busy Columbia River is temporarily closed to deep-draft ships at Portland and Vancouver. The state's population reaches 2,633,156.

1981 Followers of Bhagwan Shree Rajneesh purchase a large ranch near Antelope to found their own utopia.

1982-84 The Cow Creek Band of Upper Umpqua Indians; the Confederated Tribes of Grand Ronde; the Coos; the Lower Umpqua; and the Siuslaw Indians win restoration of their tribal trust relationships.

1985 After 4 years of frustrating local ranchers and townspeople with their antics and political strong-arming, the Rajneesh colony falls apart amid charges of criminal conduct among its leaders.

1986 The Klamath Tribe wins restoration of its tribal trust relationship. MAX (Metropolitan Area Express) light rail begins operation.

1988 The state capitol, now 50 years old, is

officially listed on the National Register of Historic Places. The Grand Ronde Reservation Act reestablishes a 9,811-acre reservation for the Confederated Tribes of the Grand Ronde.

1990 The northern spotted owl is listed as a threatened species. The Oregon Convention Center opens. The state's population is 2,842,32. Voters pass Ballot Measure 5, limiting property taxes that are used to fund schools and government operations.

1991 Barbara Roberts is inaugurated as Oregon's first woman governor.

1992 Portland General Electric closes the Trojan Nuclear Power Plant, stating safety problems. James A. Hill Jr. is the first African-American elected to statewide office. Voters in Springfield approve an anti-gay rights initiative; the next year, the legislature passes a statute preventing anti-gay rights laws at the local level.

1993 The 150th anniversary of the Oregon Trail is celebrated. Oregon holds the nation's first statewide vote-by-mail election. President Bill Clinton and Vice President Al Gore attend the regional Forest Summit, held in Portland to reconcile logging interests with protection of endangered species in Northwest forests.

1996 Oregon conducts the first vote-by-mail election for a federal office. The state conducts its first execution in 34 years at the Oregon State Penitentiary.

1997 The first law in the United States legalizing assisted suicide takes effect in Oregon.

Hood River

Situated alongside the Columbia River just between the dry and wet sides of the state, the climate at Hood River supports the area's two primary industries: windsurfing and fruit production. The city receives enough sun and enough moisture (31 inches annually) to keep orchard trees bearing. The Columbia River Gorge's steep walls funnel winds into ideal, opposite-to-the-current windsurfing conditions. Some windsurfers, or boardheads, settle in town and open equipment stores (there are two dozen applicable local businesses), but most come from all over the world just to ride the waves. The influx of migrant orchard pickers every summer contributes to the high season/low season population swings.

Considered by many as the windsurfing capital of the nation, the sport does permeate nearly every aspect of local life. Wind reports play on every radio station, and many visitors arrive with spectating at the top of their itineraries. Several historic homes have been converted into bed and breakfasts with spectacular views of the river and its riders, while the Columbia Gorge Hotel, built in 1921 by lumber baron Simon Benson, has an exclusive on rooms overlooking Wah-Gwin-Gwin Falls on the Columbia. Two microbreweries, as well as coffee and ice cream vendors and bookstores, do brisk business in the high season.

Visitors also come to hike, fish, climb, and ski on Mount Hood and Mount Adams. Hood River has some of the best mountain-biking trails in the Northwest, and maps are available at the **Hood River Visitors Information Center/Chamber of Commerce,** 405 Portway Dr., Hood River 97301, (541) 386-2000, (800) 366-3530. At least one vineyard in the area offers tours and wine tastings, and several outlets sell local fruit. Hundreds of swimmers take part in an annual swim across the river every Labor Day, despite constant rumors of radioactive leaks from the Hanford Nuclear Reservation 320 kilometers upstream. A recent, highly publicized study did find illegal levels of contamination in riverfront bushes whose roots extend into the water.

Like The Dalles nearby, Hood River has a centuries-long history of Indians living, fishing, and trading along the Columbia. Some of this history is featured in displays of Indian artifacts at the **Hood River County Museum,** Port Marina Park, Hood River 97301, (541) 386-6772.

Locals and visitors enjoy the town's **Blossom Festival,** celebrating the flower-to-fruit transformation, every April.

Hot Springs

Natural hot springs are often associated with active

volcanic regions. In Oregon, the entire state is particularly well-endowed with hot springs found in, among other places, the Cascades, the Coast Range, and the high desert country of the state's southeast corner. The U.S. Geological Survey documents 125 hot springs or pools in Oregon. A few of these may be too small or inaccessible to enjoy—located in volcanic craters, for example—but others are inviting and easily accessible. Some are within easy reach of Oregon's cities and towns. Several have been developed as resorts.

Following is a selection of the most accessible or worthwhile hot springs or pool destinations.

Natural or Primitive Hot Springs

Bigelow Hot Spring (Central Cascades). This small pool in a fern-lined grotto has a trickle of 130°F water rising from the bottom of the hand-dug pool. Drive 9 miles east of McKenzie Bridge on Oregon 126, then turn left onto Deer Creek Rd. (Forest Road 2654). Park just beyond the bridge over the McKenzie River and walk a few feet downstream to the pool.

Borax Lake (Southeastern Oregon). At the edge of the vast Alvord Desert, these springs form a 5-acre pond, which is an excellent birding area. Water is 98°F, with extensive flow. It is necessary to wade out through mud to reach swimming depth. From Denio, Nevada, drive north 20 miles to Fields, Oregon. North of Fields 5 miles, a rough road leads east 2 miles to Borax Lake.

Hart Mountain Hot Spring (Southeastern Oregon). This scenic area lies near the summit of Hart Mountain, in the middle of the antelope refuge, and is adjacent to a primitive camping area. Water is 98°F, with a semi-improved, cemented-over, small pool. About as remote as you can get in a car—beyond the reach of most radio stations! Travel east from Lakeview, north from Adel. Only one signed road crosses the refuge. The hot spring is adjacent to it, near the summit—40 miles from anywhere.

McCredie Hot Springs (Central Cascades). Several springs flow at 140°F, and the water has been directed into a series of shallow pools. Separate pools are located on the north and south banks of Salt Creek. The springs are easily accessible. Clothing is less than optional. To access the north bank, drive east from Oakridge on Oregon 58 about 10 miles. At 0.1 mile past mile marker 45, turn right (south) into a large parking area. Walk about 40 yards to the springs. To access the south bank, drive 0.5 mile farther east on Oregon 58, turn right across the bridge, and stay right on Forest Road 5875. Park at the first curve. Walk down the embankment and downstream 0.5 mile to the springs.

Meditation Pool (Central Cascades). This pool lies in a perfect wooded location on the banks of Wall Creek in the Willamette National Forest. The 104°F water is cooled in the pools to about 96°F. Clothing is optional. In Oakridge, take Rose Street north over the train tracks. Turn east on 1st Street, which becomes Forest Road 24. About 10 miles farther, turn north on Forest Road 1934. Go 0.5 mile and watch for the trailhead on the west side of road. Follow the path about 600 yards to the pools.

Snively Hot Springs (Eastern Oregon). Primitive pools on the edge of the Owyhee River in a scenic canyon. Water with a temperature of about 150°F flows from several springs as well as a concrete standpipe in a remote region that is nonetheless easily accessible. From Owyhee on Oregon 201, go west toward Owyhee State Park. When the road enters Owyhee Canyon, look for the large metal water pipe running up a steep slope on the west side of the road. Proceed 1.4 miles farther and watch on the other side of the road for a low concrete standpipe with steaming water flowing from it.

Terwilliger (Cougar) Hot Spring (Central Cascades). Log and stone pools in a picturesque canyon characterize this spring with an easy walk in. The spring flows at 116°F. Pools get successively cooler as the water flows away from the spring. Take Oregon 126 for 5 miles east of Blue River, then turn south on Forest Road 19 along the west side of Cougar Reservoir. The unmarked trailhead is on the west side of the road, 0.3 mile south of Boone Creek. A parking area lies about 0.1 mile beyond the trailhead.

Umpqua Warm Spring (South-central Oregon). This small pool northwest of Crater Lake in Umpqua National Forest can be found in an attractive rustic shelter on a bluff overlooking a creek. Water of 108°F flows directly from spring to small pool. Drive 60 miles east of Roseburg on Oregon 138 to Toketee Junction. Go north 2.3 miles on Forest Road 34. Turn right on Forest Road 3402 and go 2 miles to the parking area. Walk across the bridge, bear right on the North Umpqua Trail, and climb 0.25 mile east to the hot springs.

Whitehorse Ranch Hot Spring (Southeastern Oregon, Alvord Desert). Water temperature goes up to 114°F in the first pool, in the second up to about 90°F. The location is about as isolated as it can be and still be accessible. From Burns Junction, go 21 miles south on U.S. 95. Turn west and go 21 miles to Whitehorse Ranch. Cross an arroyo, keep going. About 5 miles from the ranch, turn left on the third road. There used to be an orange flag on a power pole. Continue on that road for about 3 miles, curving around a butte. The spring is on the northwest side of the second butte.

Developed Hot Spring Resorts

Bagby Hot Springs (Northwestern Cascades). A burned-out bathhouse has been transformed and is now maintained by a not-for-profit organization. Wooden flumes carry 135°F spring water to two hollowed-out log tubs in a covered atrium in the forest. Contributions are welcome to maintain this facility. Friends of Bagby, P.O. Box 15116, Portland 97215. Drive 32 miles southwest of Estacada on Oregon 224. Take Forest Road 63, then Forest Road 70, then a short trail on the left to the hot springs.

Belknap Hot Springs (Central Cascades, east of Eugene). This rustic riverside resort includes in-room jet-tubs and modern outdoor swimming pools. Springs flow at 196°F, and the temperature is maintained in the pools at 102°F in winter and 93°F in summer. Belknap Hot Springs, P.O. Box 1, McKenzie Bridge 97413, (503) 822-3535. You'll find it on Oregon 126, 6 miles east of McKenzie Bridge.

Breitenbush Hot Springs Retreat and Conference Center (Cascades, east of Salem). An older hot springs resort has been transformed into a holistic conference and educational center. Springs and artesian wells flow at up to 180°F. Outdoor soaking pools are maintained at about 104°F. Full-service accommodations with three vegetarian meals per day, spa treatments, and day use are among the options. Breitenbush Hot Springs Retreat and Conference Center, P.O. Box 578, Detroit 97342, (503) 854-3314. Breitenbush is situated 11 miles east of Detroit.

Cove Swimming Pool (Northeastern Oregon). The water at this public pool and picnic grounds in a small community in the Wallowa Mountains flows at 86°F. Cove Swimming Pool, Rte. 1, Box 36, Cove 97824, (503) 586-4890. From I-84 in La Grande, take the Oregon 82 exit, go east to Oregon 237, then south to the town of Cove.

Crystal Crane Hot Springs (Eastern Oregon). Springs flowing at 185°F support a health spa, private pools, and an 80-foot soaking pond. Mineral water is mixed and cooled in private tubs kept between 95°F and 105°F. Crystal Crane Hot Springs, Rte. 1, Box 50-A, Burns 97720, (503) 493-2312.

Dig Your Own Hot Springs (Central Cascades). Your dig your own hole in lakeshore gravel to trap the underground geothermal flow here. When the lake level is right, the gravel fills with 110°F water. Call for lake levels. Paulina Lake Resort, Box 7, La Pine 97739, (503) 536-2240. From U.S. 97 about 20 miles south of Bend, follow signs east to Paulina Lake. The lake is located in Newberry Crater, a prominent volcanic feature, and access is by a 2.5-mile trail or, in summer, by boat. Dig just below the rock slide on the northeast shore of the lake.

Hot Lake Mineral Springs (Northeastern Oregon). A 186°F spring is piped to a bathhouse at a large RV park at a historic stop on the Oregon Trail. The park offers separate tubs, plus a sauna and swimming pool. Hot Lake Mineral Springs, P.O. Box 1601, La Grande 97850, (503) 963-5587.

Hunter's Hot Spring Resort (South-central Oregon). A dramatic geyser erupts every 2 minutes but, when last visited, this resort was not in operation and the hot spring pools were neither maintained nor readily accessible. Nevertheless, it's worth a detour for the geyser. You'll find it 2 miles north of Lakeview on U.S. 395.

Jackson Hot Springs (Southern Oregon, Siskiyou Mountains). The outdoor swimming pool and indoor tubs are open all winter. The spring flows at 96°F. Jackson Hot Springs, 2253 U.S. 99 North, Ashland 97520, (503) 482-3776, 2 miles north of Ashland.

J Bar Z Guest Ranch (Eastern Oregon). This dude ranch abuts the Strawberry Mountain Wilderness. Several springs flowing at 120°F are piped to an outdoor swimming pool that is kept between 70°F and 90°F, depending on the weather. J Bar Z Guest Ranch, I Z Route, Canyon City 97820, (503) 575-2517. Go south from John Day on U.S. 395. Turn left after 10 miles onto Forest Road 15, and left again to the ranch.

Kah-Nee-Ta Vacation Resort Village (Central Oregon, east of Mount Hood). A full-service gambling resort on the Warm Springs Indian Reservation developed from traditional hot springs. Today you'll find gigantic, family-oriented outdoor pools, plus indoor Roman-style soaking tubs. First-class accommodations and full service, as well as tent and tepee camping, are available. Kah-Nee-Ta Vacation Resort Village, P.O. Box K, Warm Springs 97761, (503) 553-1112. From U.S. 26 in Warm Springs, follow signs 11 miles northeast to the resort.

Lehman Hot Springs (Northeastern Oregon, Blue Mountains). This spring was developed recently into a destination resort. Springs flow at 167°F, then are piped to a series of pools. The resort offers numerous activities for family recreation. Lehman Hot Springs, P.O. Box 247, Ukiah 97880, (503) 427-3015. From Ukiah on Oregon 224, go 18 miles east. Watch for signs.

Summer Lake Hot Springs (South-central Oregon). A small indoor pool with dressing rooms is fed by a spring that flows at 118°F. Water is cooled to a tolerable 102°F. Summer Lake Hot Springs, Summer Lake 97640, (503) 943-3931, is located 6 miles north of Summer Lake on Oregon Route 31.

Hunting

Oregon offers exceptional hunting for big game, small game, and birds, including waterfowl. As in other states, hunters need to be trained in safe hunting practices, obtain a state license, and obey season and bag limits. Over 300,000 people, or about 16 percent of Oregon's adult population, are licensed hunters.

Big Game

Oregon is big-game country, especially for deer, elk, antelope, and bighorn sheep. Deer are the most abundant and popular big-game animals. Black-tailed deer are common in Western Oregon (from the Pacific to the crest of the Cascades). Mule deer predominate in Eastern Oregon. A few white-tailed deer are found in the northeast. Roosevelt elk are native in the coastal mountains. Rocky Mountain elk prefer the more arid, open areas on the eastern flanks of the Cascades and beyond.

The vast deserts of Eastern and Southern Oregon are prime habitat for pronghorn antelope. About 2,000 permits to hunt antelope have been issued annually in recent years, and hunters are scoring about 60 percent success. The largest numbers of antelope are found on the Hart Mountain antelope range in summer and also on Steens Mountain. In cold weather, these ruminant mammals migrate to the Sheldon antelope range, which is at a lower elevation, just across the border in Nevada.

Bighorn sheep were reintroduced to Oregon in the 1950s and have done well. They are found in areas where you find antelope: Hart Mountain, Steens Mountain, and other high-desert ranges. Mountain goats are not native to Oregon, but a few are spotted occasionally, especially in the Wallowa Mountains.

Bears are less abundant in Oregon than in some neighboring states. Yet hunters still take about 1,300 black bears annually from the Coast and Cascade Ranges.

Birds

Ring-necked pheasants, the most popular game birds in America, are not a native species. The first pheasants released in the United States were released in 1881 in Oregon, near Corvallis. The birds were imported from Shanghai, China. In addition to pheasants, Oregon hunters bag turkeys, grouse, ducks, and geese. Bird hunting is excellent throughout the state, especially near agricultural areas for pheasant, turkey, and grouse and near rivers and lakes for waterfowl. Waterfowl hunters bag nearly 600,000 birds each year. The lakes and refuges in the eastern and southern portions of the state are prime locations, as are the various river corridors. Waterfowl hunting is so good because, in part, the Pacific flyway runs through Oregon. Half a million waterfowl may be found in the Klamath Basin during migration seasons.

Accidents

In 1996, 14 hunting accidents occurred in the state. The 10-year average has been 17 accidents and three fatalities.

Hunting Licenses and Rules

Hunting license fees range from $15 to $976, depending on the type of license, species to be hunted, and whether or not the hunter is a state resident. The fees are used to fund wildlife programs. Hunting regulations are adjusted annually to take into account changes in the abundance of species. The annual regulations are distributed free in sporting-goods stores. Information can be obtained directly by mail from the **Oregon Department of Fish and Wildlife,** 2501 SW First Ave., P.O. Box 59, Portland 97207-0059, (503) 872-5268, www.dfw.state.or.us.

International Trade

Trade is an important sector of Oregon's economy, with exports alone valued at over $10 billion. The Port of Portland, the state's largest trade facility, moves over $9.5 billion in goods and services annually. The leading imports at the port include automobiles—Portland is the second-largest auto-handling port on the West Coast in terms of volume—and bulk commodities such as alumina, limestone, cement, and salt.

Not surprisingly, the top trading partners are in Asia, with Japan the largest-volume trading country and Korea, Taiwan, and Singapore rounding out the top 5; Canada is number 2.

Oregon Exports, Millions of U.S. Dollars, 1990-1997

	1990	1991	1992	1993	1994	1995	1996	1997
Total Value	5,120	5,097	5,.639	6,127	7,247	9,.436	9,773	10,069

Top Trade Commodity

	1990	1991	1992	1993	1994	1995	1996	1997
High Technology	246.5	214.4	219.5	265.9	310.5	368.8	373.1	413.5

Top Trading Region

	1990	1991	1992	1993	1994	1995	1996	1997
Asia/ Pacific	2,842.9	2,839.9	2,977.0	3,310.1	3,990.9	5,487.5	5,914.8	5,668.2

Top Trading Partner

	1990	1991	1992	1993	1994	1995	1996	1997
Japan	1,586.1	1,537.9	1,632.1	1,622.0	1,873.3	2,139.2	2,082.8	1,824.5

Major Trading Partners

	1990	1991	1992	1993	1994	1995	1996	1997
Japan	1,586.1	1,537.9	1,632.1	1,622.0	1,873.3	2,139.2	2,082.8	1,824.5
Canada	806.8	735.5	801.4	963.4	1,080.8	1,167.6	1,224.7	1,435.9
Korea	435.7	374.8	335.9	435.5	506.1	839.1	830.5	1,101.6
Taiwan	192.1	173.1	193.7	281.5	376.6	417.3	467.2	586.0
Singapore	102.8	143.5	192.4	246.2	271.1	509.7	683.2	564.5
Philippines	104.9	141.3	162.4	167.3	233.7	256.8	306.4	444.0
Netherlands	70.8	78.1	102.5	103.3	118.5	197.8	213.8	442.5
Germany	192.9	244.3	289.6	364.9	330.9	453.6	438.7	312.1
United Kingdom/ Northern Ireland	263.9	216.6	325.5	274.8	345.1	377.5	334.8	394.9
Pakistan	99.8	75.8	149.2	80.2	134.9	203.2	179.9	274.5

Major Goods and Services Exports

	1990	1991	1992	1993	1994	1995	1996	1997
High Technology	246.5	214.4	219.5	265.9	310.5	368.8	373.1	413.5
Transportation	108.0	79.5	92.3	157.9	234.1	254.0	260.4	355.2
Wood Products	200.1	187.2	212.7	219.1	195.6	173.8	196.8	230.7
Other Manufacturing	55.8	55.3	66.5	82.7	100.0	116.6	119.4	133.7
Agriculture	91.0	91.9	110.4	91.5	88.5	98.7	103.2	113.3
Metals	72.0	63.7	57.4	89.3	98.1	93.8	99.6	107.3
Non-manufacturing	13.3	17.1	16.7	25.3	23.5	26.9	34.2	40.5
Plastics	11.3	16.4	12.8	18.6	20.7	23.4	22.9	25.1
Graphic Communications	3.7	6.7	8.6	7.2	6.5	7.6	9.7	11.6
Fisheries	4.8	2.9	4.1	5.5	2.9	3.6	5.1	4.6

Source: Oregon Economic Development Department, International Division

Judiciary The multilevel judicial system in Oregon includes local courts, state courts, federal courts, and tribal courts.

Local Courts

Local courts include justice courts (also called Justice of the Peace Courts, Municipal Courts, County Courts). Justice court is administered by a justice of the peace, a remnant of territorial days when each precinct of the state was entitled to a justice court. Thirty justice courts currently operate in 19 counties. Justice courts have jurisdiction within their counties concurrent with the circuit court in all criminal prosecutions except felony trials. Justices of the peace also perform weddings.

Municipal courts exist in most incorporated cities. The municipal court has jurisdiction over violations of municipal ordinances and, along with district courts, over criminal cases occurring within city limits or on city property. Municipal courts hear cases involving criminal misdemeanors, traffic crimes and infractions, minor liquor and drug violations, parking violations, and municipal code violations. Most municipal judges are appointed by city councils.

County courts once existed in all of Oregon's counties. In some counties, the chair of the board of county commissioners is called "county judge." Where a county judge's judicial function still exists, it is limited to juvenile and probate matters and occupies only a portion of the judge's time, which is primarily devoted to nonjudicial administrative responsibilities as a member of the county board. The remaining counties that have county judges who retain judicial authority are Gilliam, Sherman, and Wheeler (both juvenile and probate jurisdiction); Grant, Harney, and Malheur (probate only); and Morrow (juvenile only).

State Courts

Oregon's state courts review the actions of the executive and legislative branches of government for compliance with the Oregon Constitution.

Circuit Courts. With the exception of five counties (Gilliam, Grant, Malheur, Sherman, and Wheeler), circuit courts are the state trial courts of general jurisdiction. They exercise jurisdiction in juvenile, probate, adoptions, guardianship, and conservatorship cases. Circuit court judges are elected on a nonpartisan ballot for a six-year term. There are 163 circuit judges who serve 26 judicial districts. The chief justice of the Oregon Supreme Court may assign any circuit judge to sit in any judicial district in the state and appoint members of the Oregon State Bar as temporary circuit judges.

Oregon Tax Court. The Oregon Tax Court has exclusive, statewide jurisdiction in all questions of law or fact arising under state tax laws, that is, income taxes, corporate excise taxes, property taxes, timber taxes, cigarette taxes, local budget law, and property-tax limitations. It consists of a Magistrate Division and a Regular Division; the latter is comparable to a circuit court. The Magistrate Division has one presiding magistrate and one or more sitting magistrates; the judge of the Tax

Cases Filed in Oregon Courts 1992-1997

	1992	1993	1994	1995	1996	1997
Circuit/District Court	621,584	574,032	555,141	561,973	569,424	617,095
Tax Court—Magistrate Division	N/A	N/A	N/A	N/A	N/A	730
Tax Court	578	464	408	370	376	279
Oregon Court of Appeals	5,102	4,410	4,441	4,426	4,321	3,957
Oregon Supreme Court	344	263	409	424	471	448

Source: *Oregon Blue Book*

Court presides over trials in the Regular Division.

Oregon Tax Court, Robertson Bldg., 1241 State St., Salem 97310, (503) 986-5645.

Court of Appeals. The Court of Appeals is composed of 10 judges, elected on a statewide, nonpartisan ballot for six-year terms. The Chief Justice of the Oregon Supreme Court appoints a chief judge from among the judges of the Court of Appeals. The Court of Appeals has jurisdiction over all civil and criminal appeals, except death-penalty cases and appeals from the tax court, and for review of most state administrative-agency actions.

Supreme Court Bldg., 1163 State St., Salem 97310, Records and Case Information, (503) 986-5555, TTY: (503) 986-5561, fax: (503) 986-5560.

Oregon Supreme Court. The Supreme Court of Oregon is composed of seven elected justices who serve six-year terms. The members of the court elect a chief justice to serve a six-year term. The Supreme Court reviews selected decisions of the Court of Appeals. If it decides not to review a case, the decision of the Court of Appeals becomes final. The Supreme Court also hears direct appeals in death-penalty cases and tax-court cases.

Supreme Court Bldg., 1163 State St., Salem 97310, Records and Case Information: (503) 986-5555, TTY: (503) 986-5561, fax: (503) 986-5560.

Federal Courts

The federal court system in Oregon includes the U.S. District Court, the U.S. Court of Appeals, and U.S. Bankruptcy Courts. The federal courts have varying numbers of judges.

District Courts. Most federal cases are initially tried and decided in the U.S. district courts, the federal courts that have general trial jurisdiction. A district may itself be divided into divisions and may have several places where the court hears

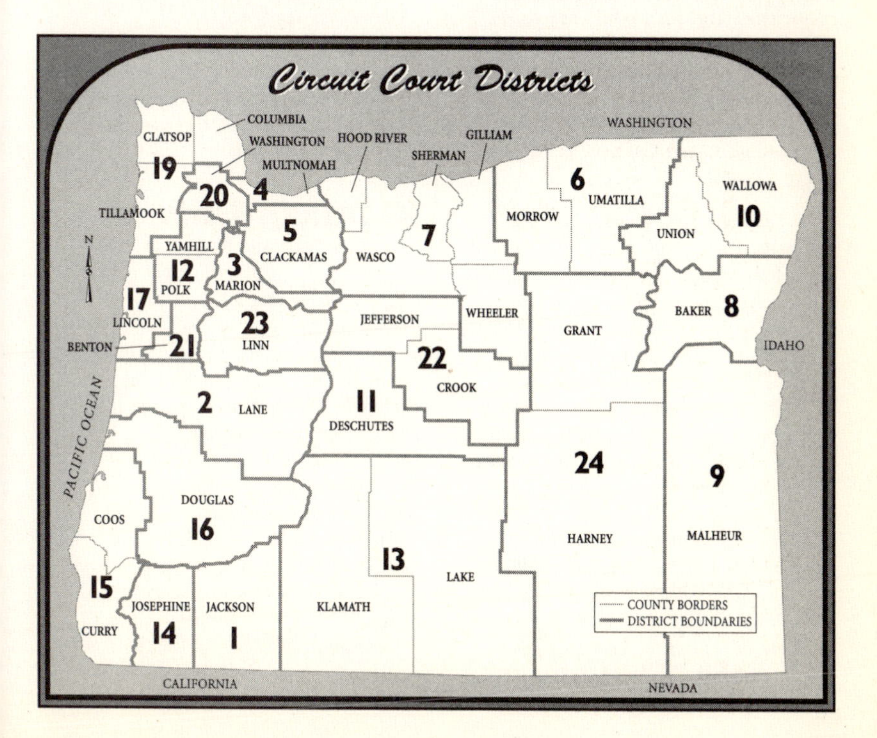

cases. District court judges are appointed for life by the president of the United States with the advice and consent of the U.S. Senate. Congress authorizes judgeships for each district based in large part on caseload. Magistrate judges also handle a variety of matters, including civil consent cases, misdemeanor trials, preliminary hearings, and pretrial motions. The U.S. District Court, Oregon District, has eight district judges and three magistrate judges.

Eugene—100 Federal Bldg./U.S. Courthouse, 211 E 7th Ave., 97401, (541) 465-6423.

Medford—310 W 6th St., 97501, (541) 775-3926.

Portland—620 SW Main, Room 516, 97205, (503) 326-2202.

Bankruptcy Court. Each district court has a bankruptcy unit that hears and decides petitions of individuals and businesses seeking relief from bankruptcy under the federal bankruptcy code. There are four categories of such cases. Bankruptcy judges are appointed by the Court of Appeals for a term of 14 years.

Five judges sit on the U.S. Bankruptcy Court, Oregon District—three in Portland and two in Eugene.

Eugene—151 W 7th, No. 300, 97401.

Portland—1001 SW 5th, 7th Floor, 97204.

U.S. Court of Appeals, Ninth Circuit. The intermediate appellate courts in the federal judicial system are the courts of appeals. They are often referred to as circuit courts. They review matters from the district courts, the U.S. Tax Court, and certain federal administrative agencies. Appeals-court judges are appointed for life by the president of the United States with the advice and consent of the U.S. Senate. Each court of appeals consists of six or more judges, depending on the caseload. Oregon is part of the Ninth Circuit, headquartered in San Francisco, California, which includes Alaska, Arizona, California, Hawaii, Idaho, Montana, Nevada, Oregon, Washington, Guam, and the Northern Mariana Islands. The U.S. Court of Appeals in Oregon has three judges.

Portland—Court of Appeals, Ninth Circuit, 555 SW Yamhill, 97204.

Tribal Courts

Tribal courts have jurisdiction on Indian reservations (*see* American Indians). Each tribe has its own particular set of laws, and tribal courts handle a full array of civil and criminal cases. Non-Indians are often parties to cases, either as plaintiffs or as defendants. Criminal jurisdiction, however, is limited to prosecution of Indians officially enrolled in federally recognized tribes.

Burns Paiute Tribal Court, 100 Pasigo St., Burns 97720, (503) 573-2793.

Confederated Tribes of Grand Ronde Tribal Court, 9615 Grande Ronde Rd., Grande Ronde 97347, (503) 879-2301.

Klamath Judicial Panel, P.O. Box 436, Chiloquin 97624, (503) 783-2218.

Siletz Tribal Court, P.O. Box 549, Siletz 97380, (503) 444-2307.

Umatilla Tribal Court and Appellate Court, P.O Box 1083, Pendleton 97801.

Warm Springs Tribal Court and Court of Appeals, P.O. Box 850, Warm Springs 97761, (503) 553-3454.

Klamath Falls

Isolated from the I-5 corridor by the Cascade Mountains, at the foot of Upper Klamath Lake (Lower Klamath Lake is just across the border in California), Klamath Falls is an isolated bastion of migratory birds, plywood mills, and the Oregon Institute of Technology. So isolated is it, in fact, that residents once tried to secede from Oregon and establish the state of Jefferson. This city of 17,000 now caters to visiting bird-watchers, sport fishermen, and others who like to play outdoors. Klamath County's main industry is lumber; more ponderosa pine is harvested here than anywhere in the nation.

The mills, and many of the city's structures, are powered in part by the geothermal energy found here in abundance. The Oregon Institute of Technology heats all its buildings geothermally.

Surrounding lakes have been diverted for farm production of potatoes, hay, and sugar beets since 1902. So much water was diverted over the years that strict management of the shallow lakes and marshlands became necessary to preserve waterfowl habitat. Upper Klamath Lake, the biggest natural lake in the state, covers only a fraction of its former expanse. Canals and reservoirs are restricted to preserve salmon and sucker fish, and every year, 20,000 acres are flooded to keep the basin's six refuges habitable for thousands of migratory waterbirds.

Another threat to aquatic life comes from an unlikely source. A new-age company grows and harvests a highly touted algal food supplement. Based at a former Ford dealership, the company sells spirulina and related blue-green algaes to health-food chain markets up and down the West Coast. Like natural algae blooms, though, this enterprise consumes a tremendous amount of oxygen, increasing the water's alkalinity and endangering the sucker fish.

White pelicans nest here from March until October. Canadian geese fill the fields every spring and fall. The feature attraction, though, is the hundreds of bald eagles who spend winters in the Klamath Basin, nesting in old-growth trees south of town. At dawn, bird-watchers keep their binoculars pointed to the sky, watching for the first eagle to pass. In a few minutes, the birds fill a wide swath, returning to their nests in the late afternoon.

New tourist services contribute to the recent surge in the Klamath Falls economy. The Running Y Ranch Resort has a 250-room hotel, an Arnold Palmer golf course, and 9,000 nearby acres under development for condominiums. In 1998, the Klamath Indian Tribe opened its Kla-Mo-Ya Casino a few miles north of Klamath Falls International Airport.

The Klamath tribe has a 14,000-year history in the region, having spent winters in "pit" houses, partially built into the ground for warmth, and summers above-ground in willow-branch-framed houses. From the shallow lakes and marshlands the tribe harvested its staple food: water-lily seeds, or "wokas."

In the 1800s, the Klamaths and their more aggressive neighbors, the Modocs, were forced to share a reservation despite a legacy of animosity between the two tribes. Some Modocs retaliated, leaving the reservation to fight for its survival in the 1874 Modoc War.

In 1954, the reservation's 2,000 Klamaths agreed to a federal attempt to break relations between the government and the tribe. The offer was alluring, as the tribe's assets would be divided among individuals, giving each Klamath about $50,000. This was a tremendous sum at the time, not just to members of a culturally devastated, economically poor reservation community. In the years that followed, with Klamath culture and language nearly extinct, a group of Klamaths began working for reinstatement, succeeding in 1991. Now woka gathering, sucker-fish ceremonies, and a spring powwow are annual events.

The Klamath County Museum houses Indian artifacts from all over Oregon, relics from the Modoc War, and a sophisticated display on the region's volcanic geology. On the other side of history's coin stands the impressive Favell Museum of Western Art and Artifacts, displaying 200 works by western artists, an extensive arrowhead collection, and the country's largest miniature-gun collection. Another popular venue here is the Ross Ragland Theater, which presents plays and concerts in an art-deco former movie theater.

Lakes and Reservoirs

Oregon is studded with over 6,000 mountain and desert lakes and coastal dune-block lakes. Over 1,400 are named. Still other lakes in Oregon are human-made, formed behind dams, especially on the Columbia and Willamette river systems.

Goose Lake, an alkaline basin that straddles the Oregon-California border

Deep Blue

At 1,932 feet deep, making it the nation's deepest and the world's seventh deepest lake, Crater Lake has some of the clearest water in the world. Few plants can manufacture food in waters deeper than 200 feet because of limited light, but in Crater Lake a moss species thrives at 400 feet, the greatest known depth of any such moss in the world.—Ann Saling, *The Great Northwest Nature Factbook*

south of Lakeview, is another lake that varies in size depending on the season. Like other shallow alkaline lakes, it can evaporate under dry weather conditions. The largest lake is freshwater Upper Klamath Lake, with 58,922 surface acres. The deepest is Crater Lake, which is also the nation's deepest lake at 1,932 feet and the seventh deepest in the world.

In the high Cascades, glaciers have created tarns and lakes of all sizes. Oregon's highest lake is a tarn at the summit of 10,358-foot South Sister. Most bodies of water in the high Cascades were formed either by glacial movement or by lava flows that dammed up stream valleys. The regions below these mountains depend heavily on Cascades water for irrigation and general water supply. The vast Upper Klamath Lake lies on the eastern edge of the Cascade Range. Other impressive Cascade lakes are Odell Lake and Waldo Lake, located near the crest close to the border of Lane and Klamath Counties.

Some of Oregon's lakes are in collapsed volcanoes. Newberry Crater, for example, a collapsed volcano, is home to Paulina and East Lakes. The largest lake formed in a collapsed volcano is Crater Lake in the summit of collapsed Mount Mazama. The circular lake covers 13,139 acres and is six miles across. Crater Lake has no inlet and no outlet. It receives water from rainfall and drainage from the immediate vicinity of the crater. Water is lost only through evaporation and seepage. One unusual lake is in Malheur Cave, a mile-long lava tube in southeast Oregon.

Several lakes endure in Oregon's high-desert country. Depending on the season, Malheur Lake may have a larger surface area than Upper Klamath Lake. It is the largest freshwater wetlands area in the western United States and a key migration stop for thousands of geese, ducks, swans, and cranes. A thermal spring and regional groundwater feed the lake, while unique species of crustaceans reside at its depths. Silver, Christmas, and Fossil Lakes were all joined during a wetter era. An ancient lake once covered 461 miles of Lake County but has shrunk to Summer Lake and Lake Abert. In the arid Alvord Valley, Borax Lake is fed by a 170°F hot spring that deposits a salty white crust of borax and keeps the temperature of the lake about 97°F. This makes the lake an outstanding destination for birding, especially to see trumpeter swans and plovers. From 1898 to 1907, when shore deposits were at their thickest, Chinese laborers extracted the borax using huge boilers fired by sagebrush.

Wallowa Lake, in the northeast corner of the state, exhibits fine, unique examples

North Lake, Columbia River Gorge. Photo by Susan Dupere.

of glacial moraine. Near the north end of the lake lies the grave of Chief Joseph of the Nez Perce.

Laws

The Oregon Constitution, written in 1859, is the foundation of Oregon state government. New laws are enacted by the state legislature or by passage of citizen initiatives or referendums. Since 1902, the year citizens were given the right to pass laws directly through initiatives and referendums, there have been 288 initiative measures put before the electorate, 99 of which were approved, and 25 out of 61 referendums that were passed. In addition, 206 out of 363 measures referred to the electorate by the legislature became law. To be placed on the ballot for popular vote, a constitutional amendment or statute must be approved for referral by the legislature. To place an initiative or referendum on the ballot, a certain percentage of voters must sign petitions in support of the issue.

Oregon laws are codified in Oregon Revised Statutes, or ORS. The complete text of the ORS can be found on the Internet at landru.leg.state.or.us/ors/orschs-1.html. Directives on how laws are to be administered are found in the Oregon Administrative Rules, or OAR. The complete text of the OAR can be found on the Internet at arcweb.sos.state.or.us/rules/number_index.html. The complete text of the state constitution can be found in the *Oregon Blue Book* and on the Internet at bluebook.state.or.us/constitution/constitutionhome.htm.

The Oregon Law Commission, established in 1997, reviews judicial decisions to identify problems in the law; considers reform proposals from judges, public officials, lawyers, and members of the public; studies the repeal of statutes held unconstitutional by the courts; and prepares legislation needed to implement reforms.

Oregon Law Commission, S-101 State Capitol, Salem 97310, (503) 986-1243.

Legislature

The state legislature consists of the Senate (30 members, currently 13 Democrats and 17 Republicans) and the House of Representatives (60 members, currently 25 Democrats, 34 Republicans, and 1 Independent).

General elections are held in November. Senators are elected to four-year terms, half of them during each even-numbered year. Representatives serve for two years and are elected in even-numbered years from single-member districts. Terms for the state legislature are limited to six years in the House of Representatives and eight years in the Senate, for 12 years total.

The legislature convenes in the State Capitol at Salem the second Monday of each odd-numbered year (most recently, Jan. 11, 1999). Legislative sessions generally last about six months; there is no constitutionally mandated length of time for legislative sessions. To deal with emergencies, special sessions may be called by the governor or by a majority of each house. The session that convened in January 1999 was the 70th Oregon legislature.

Legislative Administration, 140 State Capitol, Salem 97310, (503) 986-1848, www.leg.state.or.us.

To contact a legislator or obtain legislative information call one of these numbers:
Outside Salem: (800) 332-2313.
Within Salem: 986-1187.

State Senate (1999)

Senate Officers

President of the Senate: Brady Adams
Senate Majority Leader: Gene Derfler
Senate Democratic Leader: Kate Brown

Senate Standing Committees

Agriculture and Natural Resources
Business and Consumer Affairs
Education
General Government
Health and Human Services
Information Management and Technology
Judiciary
Public Affairs
Revenue
Rules and Elections
Stream Restoration and Species Recovery (Joint)
Trade and Economic Development
Transportation

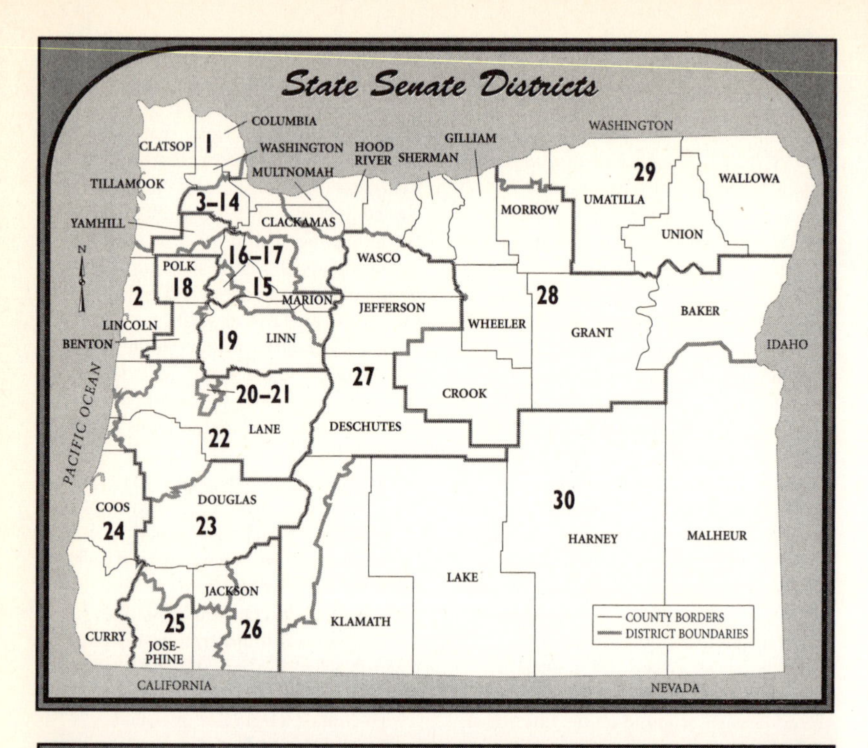
State Senate Districts
COLUMBIA
WASHINGTON
CLATSOP
1
WASHINGTON
HOOD RIVER
SHERMAN
GILLIAM
MULTNOMAH
TILLAMOOK
3–14
YAMHILL
CLACKAMAS
16–17
15
POLK
18
2
MARION
LINCOLN
BENTON
19
LINN
20–21
22
LANE
PACIFIC OCEAN
COOS
24
DOUGLAS
23
JACKSON
25
26
CURRY
JOSE-PHINE
CALIFORNIA
29
WALLOWA
UMATILLA
MORROW
UNION
WASCO
JEFFERSON
28
WHEELER
GRANT
BAKER
IDAHO
27
CROOK
DESCHUTES
30
HARNEY
MALHEUR
LAKE
KLAMATH
COUNTY BORDERS
DISTRICT BOUNDARIES
NEVADA

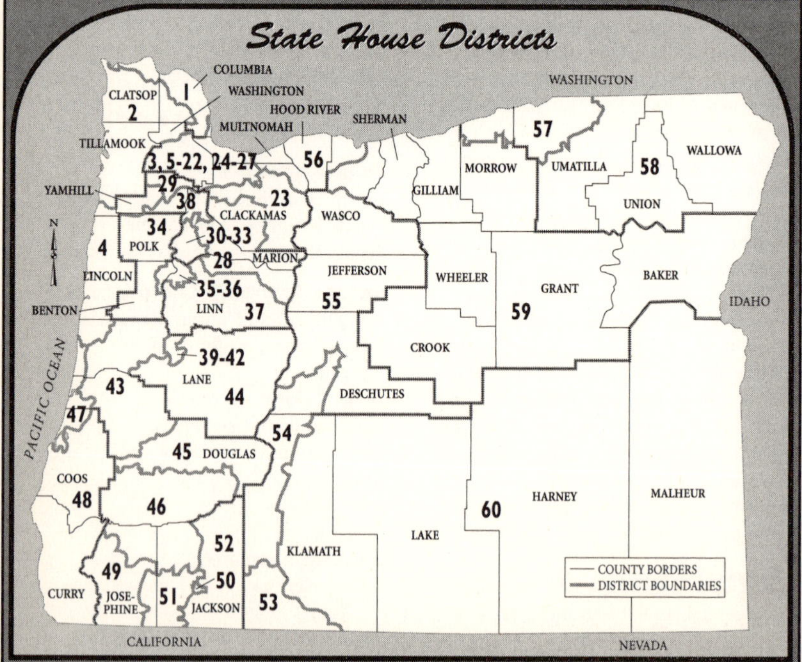
State House Districts
COLUMBIA
WASHINGTON
CLATSOP
1
2
WASHINGTON
HOOD RIVER
MULTNOMAH
SHERMAN
TILLAMOOK
3, 5-22, 24-27
56
29
YAMHILL
38
23
CLACKAMAS
WASCO
34
POLK
30-33
4
28
MARION
LINCOLN
35-36
BENTON
LINN
37
JEFFERSON
55
39-42
LANE
43
44
47
PACIFIC OCEAN
45
DOUGLAS
54
COOS
48
46
52
49
50
CURRY
JOSE-PHINE
51
JACKSON
53
KLAMATH
CALIFORNIA
57
UMATILLA
58
WALLOWA
MORROW
GILLIAM
UNION
WHEELER
GRANT
BAKER
IDAHO
59
CROOK
DESCHUTES
60
HARNEY
MALHEUR
LAKE
COUNTY BORDERS
DISTRICT BOUNDARIES
NEVADA

Water and Land Use
Ways and Means (Joint): Subcommittees on Education; General Government; Human Resources; Natural Resources; Public Safety/Regulation; Transportation and Economic Development

State Senators by District (1999)

1. Joan Dukes (D), S318 State Capitol, Salem 97310-1347, (503) 986-1701.
2. Gary George (R), 15195 NE Ribbon Ridge, Newberg 97132, (503) 538-4122.
3. Tom Hartung (R), 13975 NW Burton St., Portland 97229, (503) 629-8985.
4. Eileen Qutub (R), 11135 SW Partridge Loop, Beaverton 97007, (503) 579-3165.
5. Charles Starr (R), 8330 SW River Rd., Hillsboro 97123, (503) 642-2024.
6. Ginny Burdick (D), 4641 SW Dosch Rd., Portland 97201, (503) 244-1444.
7. Kate Brown (D), P.O. Box 82699, Portland 97282, (503) 777-6274.
8. Thomas Wilde (D), 3826 N Longview Ave., Portland 97227, (503) 281-5940.
9. Frank Shields (D), 10932 SE Salmon, Portland 97216, (503) 252-5956.
10. Avel Gordly (D), 1915 NE 16th, No. 3, Portland 97212, (503) 288-0837.
11. John Lim (R), P.O. Box 1616, Gresham 97030, (503) 239-5200.
12. Verne Duncan (R), 16911 SE River Rd., Milwaukie 97267, (503) 659-8091.
13. Randy Miller (R), P.O. Box 1795, Lake Oswego 97035, (503) 638-2622.
14. Rick Metsger (D), P.O. Box 287, Welches 97067, (503) 622-0127.
15. Marylin Shannon (R), 7955 Portland Rd. NE, Brooks 97305, (503) 463-9624.
16. Gene Derfler (R), 1408 34th Ave., Salem 97304, (503) 399-8013.
17. Peter Courtney (D), 2925 Island View Dr. N, Salem 97303, (503) 585-7449.
18. Cliff Trow (D), 1835 NW Juniper Pl., Corvallis 97330, (541) 752-5395.
19. Mae Yih (D), 34465 Yih Lane, Albany 97321, (541) 327-2666.
20. Susan Castillo (D), P.O. Box 5309 Eugene, OR 97405, (541) 343-1581.
21. Lee Beyer (D), 1439 Lawnridge Ave., Springfield 97477, (541) 726-2533.
22. Tony Corcoran (D), 34475 Kizer Creek Rd., Cottage Grove 97424, (541) 942-1213.
23. Bill Fisher (R), 268 Akin Ln., Roseburg 97470, (541) 672-1908.
24. Veral Tarno (R), P.O. Box 657, Coquille 97423, (541) 396-6965.
25. Brady Adams (R), S203 State Capitol, Salem 97310-1347, (503) 986-1600.
26. Lenn Hannon (R), 240 Scenic Dr., Ashland 97520, (541) 482-5210.
27. Neil Bryant (R), P.O. Box 1151, Bend 97709-1151, (541) 382-4331.
28. Ted Ferrioli (R), 111 Skyline, John Day 97845, (541) 575-2321.
29. David Nelson (R), 1407 NW Horn, Pendleton 97801, (541) 278-1396.
30. Eugene Times (R), 1049 N Ct., Burns 97720, (541) 573-2744.

State House of Representatives (1999)

House of Representatives Officers

Speaker of the House of Representatives: Lynn Snodgrass
Chief Clerk of the House of Representatives: Ramona Kenady
House Majority Leader: Steve Harper
House Minority Leader: Kitty Piercy

House Standing Committees

Agriculture and Forestry
Business and Consumer Affairs
Commerce: Subcommittees on Regulations, Trade and Economic Development
Education
General Government
Human Resources: Subcommittees on Boards and Licenses, Human Services
Judiciary-Civil Law
Judiciary-Criminal Law
Revenue
Rules, Elections, and Public Affairs
State Affairs
Stream Restoration and Species Recovery
Transportation
Water and Environment
Ways and Means (Joint): Subcommittees on Education; General Government; Human Resources; Natural Resources; Public Safety/Regulation; Transportation and Economic Development

State Representatives by District

1. Jackie Taylor (D), 1324 Miller Ln., Astoria 97103, (503) 325-1267.
2. Elaine Hopson (D), P.O. Box 656, Tillamook 97141, (503) 842-5656.
3. Bruce Starr (R), P.O. Box 5875, Aloha 97006, (503) 640-3780.
4. Terry Thompson (D), 215 E Olive St., #2, Newport 97365, (541) 265-6810.
5. Jim Hill (R), 191 NE 33rd Ct., Hillsboro 97124, (503) 693-8915.
6. Ken Strobeck (R), P.O. Box 6690, Beaverton 97007, voice-mail (503) 617-1521.
7. Bill Witt (R), 13197 NW Helen Ln., Portland 97229, (503) 681-8557 x121.
8. Ryan Deckert (D), P.O. Box 2247, Beaverton 97075, (503) 977-1609.
9. Max Williams (R), 12103 SW 135th Ave., Tigard 97223, (503) 524-4275.
10. Lynn Snodgrass (R), 12995 SE Hacienda Dr., Boring 97009, (503) 658-4223.
11. Anitra Rasmussen (D), 3844 SW Jerald Way, Portland 97221, (503) 721-0399.
12. Chris Beck (D), 1207 SW Sixth Ave., Portland 97204, (503) 279-6240.
13. Dan Gardner (D), P.O. Box 82342, Portland 97282-0342, (503) 238-6533.
14. Diane Rosenbaum (D), 2327 SE 41st. Ave., Portland 97214, (503) 238-6298.
15. Randall Edwards (D), 6666 SE Yamhill St., Portland 97215, (503) 257-6592.
16. Jeff Merkley (D), 1351 SE 114th Ave., Portland 97216, (503) 261-7826.
17. Gary Hansen (D), 6971 N Vincent, Portland 97217, (503) 289-3995.
18. Deborah Kafoury (D), 4550 NE 23rd, Portland 97211, (503) 281-3960.
19. Jo Ann Bowman (D), 3145 NE 15th, Portland 97212, (503) 281-1256.
20. Karen Minnis (R), 23765 NE Holladay, Wood Village 97060, (503) 666-7186.
21. Randy Leonard (D), 4530 SE 67th Ave., Portland 97206, (503) 760-9688.
22. Ron Sunseri (R), 4200 SE 26th Place, Gresham 97080, (503) 663-3800.
23. Kurt Schrader (D), 2525 N Baker Dr., Canby 97013, (503) 266-2432.
24. Richard Devlin (D), 10290 SW Anderson Ct., Tualatin, 97062 (503) 691-2026.
25. Jane Lokan (R), 5317 SE El Centro Way, Milwaukie 97267, (503) 654-9691.
26. Kathy Lowe (D), P.O. Box 68256, Milwaukie, 97268, (503) 653-9681.
27. Jerry Krummel (R), 30945 SW Boones Ferry Rd., Wilsonville 97070, (503) 570-8723.
28. Roger Beyer (R), 39486 S Cooper Rd., Molalla 97038, (503) 829-6910.
29. Leslie Lewis (R), P.O. Box 418, Newberg 97132, (503) 537-0879.
30. Larry Wells (R), 3080 Jefferson-Scio Dr. SE, Jefferson 97352, (541) 327-2469.
31. Jackie Winters (R), P.O. Box 126, Salem 97302, (503) 581-9114.
32. Kevin Mannix (R), 2003 State St., Salem 97301, (503) 364-1913.
33. Vic Backlund (R), 1339 Mistwood Dr. NE, Keizer 97303, (503) 393-5927.
34. Lane Shetterly (R), P.O. Box 1025, Dallas 97338, (503) 623-0324.
35. Barbara Ross (D), 4175 Morning St., Corvallis 97330, (541) 752-3605.
36. Betsy L. Close (R), 5220 NW Winn Dr,. Albany 96321, (541) 926-5418.
37. Jeff Kropf (R), P.O. Box 430, Halsey 97348, (541) 369-3555.
38. Juley Gianella (R), 20342 Olmstead Rd. NE, Aurora 97002, (503) 678-5845.
39. Kitty Piercy (D), 1371 W 4th Ave., Eugene 97402, (541) 334-6727.
40. Floyd Prozanski (D), P.O. Box 11511, Eugene 97440, (541) 342-2447.
41. Vicki L. Walker (D), 1425 Ranchwood Dr., Eugene 97401, (541) 344-4545.
42. William E. Morrisette (D), 348 G Street, Springfield 97477, (541) 746-1378.
43. Jim Welsh (R), P.O. Box 580, Elmira 97437, (541) 935-6503.
44. Al King (D), 36890 Edgehill Rd., Springfield 97478, (541) 685-2015.
45. Jeff Kruse (R), 174 Burkhart Rapids Ln., Roseburg 97470, (541) 673-7201.
46. Susan Morgan (R), P.O. Box 2223, Myrtle Creek 97457, (541) 863-6212.
47. Mike Lehman (D), P.O. Box 1476, Coos Bay 97420, (541) 269-5950.
48. Ken Messerle (R), 1740 Coos City-Sumner Rd., Coos Bay 97420, (541) 269-2510.
49. Carl Wilson (R), 560 NE F St., A-502, Grants Pass 97526, (541) 472-8960.
50. Rob Patridge (R), 105 S Grape St.,

No. 405, Medford 97501, (541) 779-8807.
51. Jason Atkinson (R), P.O. Box 1931, Jacksonville 97530, (541) 899-6894.
52. Judith Uherbelau (D), P.O. Box 3189, Ashland 97520, (541) 488-5008.
53. Steve Harper (R), 7121 Sierra Pl., Klamath Falls 97603, (541) 850-9587.
54. Tim Knopp (R), P.O. Box 6145, Bend 97708, (541) 389-7008.
55. Ben Westlund (R), 20590 Arrowhead Dr., Bend 97701, (541) 383-4444.
56. Bob Montgomery (R), P.O. Box 65, Cascade Locks 97014, (541) 374-8690.
57. Bob Jenson (I), 2126 NW 21st St., Pendleton 97801, (541) 276-5821.
58. Mark Simmons (R), P.O. Box 572, Elgin 97827, (541) 437-9060.
59. Lynn Lundquist (R), P.O. Box 8, Powell Butte 97753, (541) 548-1215.
60. R. Tom Butler (R), P.O. Box E, Ontario 97914-0106, (541) 889-7654.

Lewis and Clark In the early 1800s, the 26-year-old United States had a single priority: establishing territorial claims, such as President Thomas Jefferson's deft swap with the French for the Louisiana Purchase in 1803. The new nation's integrity depended on expansion. Jefferson persuaded Congress to fund an overland expedition to the Pacific Northwest and chose his secretary, Meriwether Lewis, to lead the journey. Jefferson chose an old army friend, William Clark, to be Lewis's partner.

The pair had three specific duties. First, the team had to find a land route between the Missouri and Columbia Rivers to facilitate trade and settlement (the tacit charge here being for America to claim land, to become the significant presence in the region). Another duty, besides keeping a meticulous journal including a record of flora and fauna, was to establish good relations with the Native tribes. Again an unspoken assignment was the real priority, as "good relations" with the Native Americans, as far as Jefferson and Congress were concerned, hinged on their "introduction" to the idea of American government in the region.

The explorers left St. Louis in the spring

of 1804. Twenty-nine other men were assigned to the "Corps of Discovery," as the endeavor was called. One of these men, Toussaint Charbonneau, brought his 15-year-old Shoshone wife, Sacagawea, a girl who, by the end of the expedition had proved more useful than her unstable, dissolute husband. Charbonneau had, depending on which legend you believe, won Sacagawea in a game of dice or purchased her from the Hidatsas, who owned her as a slave. Her experience is well-known legend. Along the route she crossed paths with her Shoshone family, whom she had thought she would never see again, and bore a son, Jean-Baptiste, whom she carried on her back on each day's trek. All the while she was a key translator, at one point translating Shoshone into Hidatsa so her husband could turn it into French, with French members of the party delivering the words in English.

When they arrived at the Platte River, Lewis wrote, "We were now about to penetrate a country at least 2,000 miles in width, on which the foot of civilized man has never trodden; the good or evil it had in store for us was for experiment yet to determine." Lewis, more educated, moody, and sensitive than his partner, wrote the finer journal entries, and Clark took up the duty when Lewis was laid down with depression. Among the richness of these journals are indications that they had a difficult time appreciating the Native tribes, though encounters were typically friendly. Lewis recorded his distaste after crossing the Continental Divide: "We were caressed and besmeared with their grease and paint till I was heartily tired of the national hug."

The team ended up having a fairly satisfactory crossing; only one man was lost, to appendicitis, though the lack of variety in their diet nagged them. (At the Columbia River, they finally bought 40 dogs from the Native Americans and roasted them.) They endured sickness, such as colds and dysentery. Also, women's sexual favors were often given by husbands as trade currency. Many of Lewis and Clark's men caught venereal diseases, given to the Native tribes by fur trappers who moved up and down the North American coast. Sexually transmitted diseases weren't the only problem of the Native coast tribes. Capt. Robert Gray had described strong men and "very pretty" women, dressed in deer and otter garments. To Lewis and Clark the Native Americans looked sickly, wearing the tattered castoffs of sailors.

On November 15, 1805, the team beheld the mouth of the Columbia at the Pacific. The journey had taken 19 months, but the most miserable part of it occurred that winter at Fort Clatsop. The expedition members spent four dismal months in a log stockade they built above a bog of tidal creeks. Fleas and rain tormented the party, and they recorded that it rained every day but six. They hunted for game, no longer plentiful, and on Christmas ate "pore Elk, so much Spoiled that we eate it thro mear necessity, Some Spoiled Pounded fish and a fiew roots."

The Corps of Discovery left the Columbia eagerly in March of 1806, and expedition members were greeted in September with the cheers of Americans who had given them up for dead after 19 months. Their work had shown that settlement was possible, and the next great overland journey began four decades later.

Organizations of Interest

Fort Clatsop National Memorial, 92343 Fort Clatsop Rd., Astoria 97103, (503) 861-2471, www.nps.gov/focl.

Lewis and Clark National Historic Trail, 700 Rayovac Dr., #100, Madison, WI 53711, (608) 264-5610.

Libraries

State Libraries

There are 115 libraries and 74 branch libraries in Oregon serving over 3 million residents, of whom half are regular borrowers.

The first library opened in 1842 at Oregon City with 300 volumes. Creation of the Oregon Territorial Library was authorized by Congress in 1848, though the collection went up in smoke with the capitol building in an 1854 fire. In 1996, Sherman County, the last county without service, opened a public library.

Organizations of Interest

Oregon Educational Media Association, P.O. Box 277, Terrebonne 97760, (541) 923-0675, www.teleport.com/noema.

Oregon Library Association, P.O. Box 2042, Salem 97308, ola@olaweb.org.

Library Programs of Interest

Oregon Center for the Book. The Oregon Center for the Book at the state library was created in 1986 as an affiliate of the Center for the Book in the Library of Congress and is one of over 30 state centers. This organization encourages public interest in books, reading, and libraries by sponsoring essay contests, gathering information on challenges to Oregon's libraries, and assisting Partners in Literacy (description follows). Contact the **Oregon Library Association** for information at ola@olaweb.org.

Partners in Literacy: Libraries and the Child Care and Education Community. Partners in Literacy promotes communication between people in the child-care and education communities and Oregon public libraries. The idea is to give children and illiterate adults the best language and literacy development possible. Information provided to teachers and child-care workers covers children's social and emotional development, cognitive development, and physical well-being. For more information contact the **Oregon State Library,** (503) 378-2112 x239, or the **Oregon Department of Education,** (503) 378-5585.

The Oregon Documents Depository Program

Started in 1907, the ODDP arranges for preservation of state documents in public libraries and provides information to the public about finding state documents. Oregon Revised Statute 357.001, which governs the state library, asserts that "It is a basic right of citizens to know about the activities of their government, to benefit from the information developed at public expense and to enjoy access to the information services of state agencies." Documents are accessible free of charge. Contact the **Oregon Library Association** for information at ola@olaweb.org.

Full depository libraries such as these receive all public documents deposited with the state library:

Blue Mountain Community College Library
Deschutes County Library
Eastern Oregon State College Library
Hillsboro Public Library
Klamath County Library
Library of Congress
Multnomah County Library
Oregon State Library
Oregon State University Library
Portland State University Library
Southern Oregon State College Library
Southwestern Oregon Community College Library
University of Oregon Library
Western Oregon State College Library

Core depository libraries receive only public documents identified by the state librarian as those "for which members of the public have the most significant and frequent need." Core documents include Oregon laws, Oregon administrative rules, the *Oregon Blue Book,* the Oregon schools directory, periodicals such as *Oregon Geology,* and specialized reference works such as *Understanding Oregon Taxes* and the state's *Child Abuse Report.* Core depository libraries include:

Albany Public Library
Astoria Public Library
Baker County Library
Beaverton City Library
Douglas County Library
Eugene Public Library
Hood River County Library
Jackson County Library
Josephine County Library
Lake Oswego Public Library
Linfield College Library
Malheur County Library
Salem Public Library
Tillamook County Library
Washington State Library

There are 21 **federal depository libraries** in Oregon, nearly all at state universities and colleges. They include:

Blue Mountain Community College Library, P.O. Box 100, 2411 NW Cardon, Pendleton 97801, (541) 276-1260 x213.

Central Oregon Community College Library/Media Center, Government Documents, 2600 NW College Way, Bend 97701, (541) 383-7560.

Department of Energy Bonneville Power Administration Library, CGIL-P.O. Box 3621, 905 NE 11th Ave., Portland 97232-3621, (503) 230-4171.

Eastern Oregon University Walter M. Pierce Library, 1410 L Ave., La Grande 97850, (541) 962-3540.

Lewis and Clark College Aubrey R. Watzek Library, 0615 SW Palatine Hill Rd., Portland 97219, (503) 768-7285.

Linfield College Libraries, 900 S Baker, McMinnville 97128-6894, (503) 434-2261.

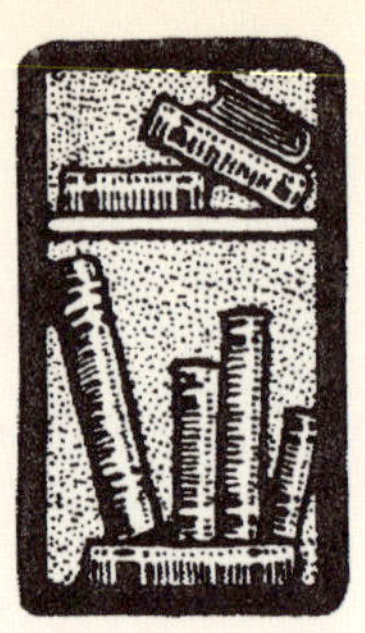

Multnomah County Library Science and Business Section, 801 SW 10th Ave., Portland 97205, (503) 248-5234.

Northwestern School of Law Paul L. Boley Law Library, 10015 SW Terwilliger Blvd., Portland 97219, (503) 768-6688.

Oregon Institute of Technology Library/Documents, 3201 Campus Dr., Klamath Falls 97601-8801, (541) 885-1772.

Oregon State Library, State Library Building, 250 Winter St. NE, Salem 97310-0640, (503) 378-4277.

Oregon State University, The Valley Library, Information Services, Corvallis 97331-4501, (541) 737-2761.

Oregon Supreme Court Law Library, Supreme Court Building, 1163 State St., Salem 97310-0260, (503) 370-6386.

Pacific University Harvey W. Scott Memorial Library, 2043 College Way, Forest Grove 97116, (503) 357-6151 x2292.

Portland State University Branford P. Millar Library, P.O. Box 1151, 934 SW Harrison, Portland 97207, (503) 725-4123.

Reed College Eric V. Houser Library, 3203 SE Woodstock Blvd., Portland 97202-8199, (503) 777-7554.

Southern Oregon University Library/Documents, 1250 Siskiyou Blvd., Ashland 97520-5076, (541) 552-6851.

University of Oregon Knight Library Documents and Microforms Department, Eugene 97403-1299, (541) 346-3070.

University of Oregon Law Library, 1101 Kincaid Ave., Eugene 97403, (541) 346-1657.

Western Oregon University Library, 345 Monmouth Ave., Monmouth 97361-1396, (503) 838-8899.

Willamette University College of Law Library, 245 Winter St. SE, Salem 97301, (503) 370-6386.

Willamette University Mark O. Hatfield Library, 900 State St., Salem 97301-3992, (503) 370-6312.

Public Libraries

Many cities have public libraries (e.g., Joseph City Library in Joseph), and every county does (e.g., Malheur County Library in Ontario). You may also contact library districts individually; there are 17 of these quasi-governmental units in local areas (e.g., Lincoln County Library District in Newport and the Oregon Trail Library District in Boardman).

Academic Libraries

(*SEE ALSO* UNIVERSITIES AND COLLEGES)

Every institution of higher education in the state has some kind of library, while many have more than one library. For example, the University of Oregon encompasses 10 libraries: Knight Library (the central campus library); Architecture and Allied Arts Branch Library; Institute of Marine Biology Library in Charleston; Law Library; Map Library; Mathematics Library; Ocean and Coastal Law Center Library; Pine Mountain Observatory Library in Bend; Science Library; and University Archives.

Specialty state colleges may be helpful to researchers interested in certain areas. If information relating to the field of divinity is needed, there are libraries at the Dove Bible Institute in Medford; Eugene Bible College and Northwest Christian College; both in Eugene; Mount Angel Abbey in Saint Benedict; Multnomah Bible College in Portland; Salem Bible College and Western Baptist College, both in Salem; and others. Libraries focusing on the environment are also numerous. Four legal libraries are found at three institutions: the University of Oregon (2); Lewis and Clark College, and Willamette University. Two college libraries have information on the natural healing arts: the National College of Naturopathic Medicine and the Oregon College of Oriental Medicine, both in Portland.

Special-Interest Libraries

Special-interest libraries are frequently overlooked treasure troves of information, and there are more than 160 of them in Oregon. Some locations make sense, like legal libraries at courthouses, medical information at hospital libraries, and art historical materials at art museums. Some are quasi-educational efforts by certain industries to promote their products, such as the library at the Cowboys Then and Now Museum in Portland, sponsored by the beef industry.

Genealogical information is often available at city and county museums and the museums at county historical societies. Various departments of the government are required to give public access to many documents they produce, and newspapers in major cities have archives. Large companies often have their own libraries.

Some of these museums aren't readily open to the public, so it's a good idea to call ahead for an appointment. The following is a sampling of available resources; contact local visitor centers or the organizations listed at the start of this section for more information.

American Advertising Museum Library, 50 SW 2nd Ave., No. 420, Portland 97204-3528. Access by appointment.

Bonneville Power Administration Library, 905 NE 11th Ave., Portland 97232, (503) 230-4171. Open to the public.

Columbia County Law Library, County Courthouse, St. Helens 97051, (503) 397-3682.

Columbia River Maritime Museum, 1792 Marine Dr., Astoria 97103, (503) 325-2323. Access by appointment.

Crater Lake National Park, Steel Center, Park Headquarters, P.O. Box 7, Crater Lake, 97604, (541) 594-2211. Access by appointment.

Douglas County Museum of History and Natural History, History Research Library, 123 Museum Dr., Roseburg 97470, (541) 957-7007. Open to the public.

Eastern Oregon Psychiatric Center Medical Library, 2600 Westgate, Pendleton 97801, (541) 276-0810.

ESCO Corporation Technical Resource Library, 2141 NW 25th Ave., Portland 97210, (503) 228-2141 ext. 520

Genealogical Forum of Portland Library, 2130 SW 5th Ave., No. 220, Portland 97201-4934, (503) 227-2398. Open to the public, $3 fee per visit, no children.

High Desert Museum, 59800 South U.S. 97, Bend 97702-7963, (541) 382-4754 ext. 367, www.highdesert.org.

Historic Preservation League of Oregon, Oregon Preservation Research Center, 322 NW 5th, Portland 97209, or P.O. Box 40053, Portland 97240, (503) 243-1923.

Intel Corporation Library and Information Services, 5200 NE Elam Young AL4-60, Hillsboro 97124-6497, (503) 264-2982.

Kaiser Center for Health Research Library, 3800 N Kaiser Center Dr., Portland, OR 97227-1098, (503) 335-2442.

Lane, Powell, Spears, Lubersky Legal Library, 520 SW Yamhill St., No. 800, Portland 97204, (503) 226-6151 ext. 2020.

National Railway Historical Society, Pacific Northwest Chapter, Railroad Research Library, 800 NW 6th Ave., No. 1, Union Station, Portland 97209, (503) 226-6747.

Oregon Criminal Justice Commission, Public Service Building, #126, 255 Cottage St. NE, Salem 97310, (503) 378-2053.

Oregon Department of Environmental Quality, 811 SW 6th Ave., Portland 97204, (503) 229-6854, www.deq.state.or.us. Open to the public.

Oregon Historical Society Museum, Oregon History Center, 1200 SW Park Ave., Portland 97205, (503) 222-1741, orhist@ohs.org.

Oregon Jewish Museum, Oregon History Center, 1200 SW Park Ave., Portland 97205. Access by appointment.

Oregon Legislative Library, S-427 State Capitol, Salem 97310, (503) 986-1668. Open to the public.

The Oregon Military Museum, Camp Withycombe, Clackamas 97015, (503) 557-5359.

Oregon Regional Primate Research Center, McDonald Library, 505 NW 185th Ave., Beaverton 97006-3499, (503) 690-5311. Open to the public.

Oregon School for the Blind Library, 700 Church St. NE, Salem 97310, (503) 378-8025. Access by appointment.

Oregon Zoo, 4001 SW Canyon Rd., Portland 97221, (503) 220-5766. Access by appointment.

The Oregonian (newspaper), 1320 SW Broadway, Portland 97201, (503) 221-8131.

Portland Art Museum, Rex Aaragon Library, 1219 SW Park Ave., Portland 97205-2486, (503) 226-2811 ext. 215, www.teleport.com/~library/home.html. Open to the public.

Portland Public Schools, Educational Media Department, P.O. Box 3107, 501 N Dixon, Portland 97208, (503) 916-3382.

Providence Medical Center, Medical Library, 4805 NE Glisan St., Portland 97213, (503) 215-6075. Open to the public.

Southern Oregon Historical Society's History Center, 106 N Central Ave., Medford 97501, (541) 773-6536.

University of Oregon, Computing Center Library, 1225 Kincaid St., Eugene 97403, (541) 346-4406. Open to the public.

University of Oregon Museum of Natural History, 1680 E 15th Ave., Eugene 97403, (541) 346-3024, mnh@oregon.uoregon.edu.

Lighthouses

U.S. 101 could be called the "Lighthouse Trail" because it offers access to some spectacular historical lighthouses. From Cape Disappointment in the north to Cape Blanco in the south, the Oregon Coast is beaded with outstanding lighthouses, each one a beacon to history and also a marvelous vantage point from which to catch the magnificent sweep of the wild coast. The effort to mark the coast with lighthouses began soon after Oregon became a territory in 1848. Lighthouses were important, especially because the settlers depended on maritime trade.

The heart of the lighthouse is its lens. The Fresnel lens was a 19th-century optics marvel, which focused a small light into a powerful beam that could be seen from a great distance. The light for the coastal lighthouses came from oil lamps. Whale oil was used in the earliest days. It was replaced by rock oil, called "kerosene," after it became widely available in the 1860s.

Lighthouses were tended by lightkeepers, dedicated men and their families inured to the isolated life, who were often called upon to rescue unfortunate seafarers in the worst possible weather. Beginning in the 1960s, the lighthouses were automated. Lightkeepers were out of a job, but more important, light stations were electrified. Fresnel lenses were replaced or supplemented with aero beacons and range lights. A large buoy replaced the lightship at the mouth of the Columbia River.

Today, many of the lighthouses are encompassed by state parks. The last lightship to be stationed at the mouth of the Columbia may be viewed at Astoria's Columbia River Maritime Museum.

Cape Arago Lighthouse. Stands on a small island south of the entrance to Coos Bay. The lighthouse can be viewed from a turnout on the south side of Sunset Bay State Park, 12 miles west of U.S. 101.

Cape Blanco Lighthouse. First completed lighthouse in the state, dating from 1870. At the mouth of the Umpqua River. Located 5 miles west of U.S. 101. Follow signs to Cape Blanco State Park from near milepost 297.

Cape Meares Lighthouse. This short tower sits on a sharp headland just south of Tillamook Bay. The lighthouse is located 9 miles west of Tillamook in Cape Meares State Park.

Coquille River Lighthouse. Last lighthouse to be constructed on the coast, built in 1896. Located in Bullards Beach State Park, north of Bandon. Signs mark the park on the west side of U.S. 101, just north of the Coquille River Bridge.

Desdemona Sands Lighthouse. The Desdemona Sands are a large area of shoals inside the Columbia River's mouth and north of the main channel. A lighthouse once marked the area. It stood on piles at the west end of the shoals, 4 miles west of Astoria. All that remain today are broken piles and some riprap stones.

Heceta Head Lighthouse. This light fills a gap between Yaquina Head and the Umpqua River. The last keeper of the light was Oswald Allik, who arrived after serving as the last keeper of the Tillamook Rock Lighthouse. He was the last keeper here, too, retiring after the light was automated in 1963. The light is located in Devil's Elbow State Park, which is west of U.S. 101, near milepost 178.

The Heceta Head Lighthouse was completed in 1894 at a cost of $180,000. From *Magnificent Places: Oregon Coast* by Rick Schafer (photography) and Jack and Jan McGowan (essays).

Point Adams Lighthouse. This lighthouse at the mouth of the Columbia River was the first Oregon light station with a steam fog whistle. Although the Cape Disappointment Lighthouse was built earlier, the Point Adams Lighthouse was actually more important for navigation, as it lay on the south bank of the river entrance and closer to the navigation channel at the mouth of the river. The light station burned down in 1912, and its former site is located within Fort Stevens State Park. Battery Russell, in the park, is near where the lighthouse once stood.

Tillamook Rock Lighthouse. This light sits spectacularly atop a seagirt basalt knob. Tillamook Head was an especially important landfall for mariners approaching the Columbia River from the south. The light was retired in 1957. Since 1980, the Tillamook Rock light has been operated as the eternity light at Sea Columbarium, a mausoleum capable of holding the ashes of 500,000 deceased persons. Access to the light is restricted to those visiting loved ones and making appropriate arrangements. The Tillamook Rock Lighthouse can be seen from Ecola State Park, as well as from the beaches of Cannon Beach and Seaside.

Umpqua River Lighthouse. The present, 100-year-old lighthouse replaced an earlier one that was washed away in a flood. A viewing platform beside the lighthouse offers a spectacular venue for watching the spectacle of wind, wave, and river at the bar at the river's mouth. The lighthouse is located 1 mile west of U.S. 101 in Umpqua Lighthouse State Park, about 6 miles south of Reedsport. The **Umpqua Lighthouse Museum,** 1020 Lighthouse Way, Winchester Bay 97467, (503) 271-4631, has a light that is one of a very few in service that still uses the original lenses that were made in Paris in 1890. The beam is visible from 16 miles at sea. This is a good whale-watching area.

Warrior Rock Lighthouse. Warrior Point and Warrior Rock are at the confluence of the Multnomah Channel of the Willamette River and the Columbia River. Once, this manned light station marked hazards to navigation in the vicinity. Today Warrior Rock is marked by a small white light tower. A half-scale replica of the original light station can be seen behind the Columbia County Historical Society Museum in St. Helens.

Willamette River Lighthouse. A lighthouse and fog signal were constructed in 1895 to mark the confluence of the Willamette and Columbia Rivers. This site has long been abandoned, and today no traces remain.

Yaquina Bay Lighthouse. This light operated only for a few years in the late 1800s. It was replaced by Yaquina Head Lighthouse. The lighthouse is located in Yaquina Bay State Park, at the north end of the Yaquina Bay Bridge.

Yaquina Head Lighthouse. This classic seacoast tower, tallest on the Oregon Coast, stands on a peninsula three miles North of Newport. The lighthouse is in the Yaquina Head Outstanding Natural Area, 3 miles north of Newport on U.S. 101.

Lost Treasure

From Tillamook County in the northwest to Harney County in the southeast, Oregon has its share of lost mines and buried treasure, or at least tales of missed opportunities and broken dreams. The serious treasure hunter, prospector, or historian would be well advised to begin researching at the state museum or library. While much is known about lost troves, including those described below, there is always conflicting information, otherwise lost treasures would have been discovered by now! Following are some of the best destinations for treasure seekers and curiosity hunters.

Blue Bucket Mine. The year was 1845. A wagon train split up at Fort Boise. One group stuck to the established Oregon Trail with their wagons. The other emigrants took an alternative cutoff, which came to be called the Meek Cutoff. The way was difficult, and the settlers got lost in the high, dry country of the Malheur Basin. Somewhere along the trek, a woman died, and a little girl picked yellow nuggets out of a stream and carried them in her blue bucket. Prospectors have been looking for the location of the "Blue Bucket Mine" ever since. Their saying has been "Find me the grave of the woman and I'll show you buckets of gold." Experts have sought to reconstruct the wanderings of the lost party on the Meek Cutoff and to establish exactly which grave of which woman is the landmark, as many graves litter the immigrants' trails. People believe the grave has been found and that it is the grave of S. Chambers, who died Sept. 3, 1845, and was buried on the Winnie Scott ranch in Agency Valley, on the Little North Fork. Two days' travel beyond the grave brings one to the Crane Prairie. The illusory Blue Bucket Mine still awaits the lucky prospector, somewhere out there in the Malheur Country, between Little North Fork and Crane Prairie.

Lost Sheepherder Mine. In 1878, soldiers en route from Harney, Oregon, to Boise, Idaho, unearthed gold-bearing rock at one of their campsites. They were, at the time, three days' ride west and south of the confluence of the Snake and Boise Rivers. The soldiers never made it back to stake their claim. Decades later, in 1912, a young sheepherder lay dying of spotted fever, which he had contracted near Vale. In his delirium, he raved about an 18-inch vein of pure gold that he had discovered. Those attending him did not take him seriously until after he died, when they retrieved his bedroll from the stable. Wrapped in his blanket were samples of pure gold. This story was retold in 1951 in Portland's *Oregon Journal* newspaper. This sparked a mini-gold rush that summer, but the sheepherder's 18-inch vein of pure gold remains to be rediscovered somewhere in upper Owyhee Country, not far from the town of Vale.

Lost Tillamook Mine. The Native Americans of the Tillamook region would commonly pay their bills at the local stores with gold nuggets mined from the hills of the Coast Range. The location of the mine was kept from the settlers until the hegemony of the local Indians was eventually weakened. A farmer on the West Tualatin Plains was told by an old Indian woman, "Where water runs into a lake in a black canyon, you will find it." That was not much to go on, but local farmers searched assiduously and narrowed the location to a six-mile area west of the Tualatin Plains near the summit of the Coast Range. At least one area farmer is said to have found a stream running through a dark canyon into a lake and evidence of Indian camps and diggings in the area, but no claim has ever been patented. The source of the Native Americans' gold remains to be rediscovered, west of the Tualatin Plains, near the summit of the Coast Range.

Neahkanie Mysteries. Neahkanie Mountain rises 1,600 feet on the Oregon Coast, about 30 miles south of the Columbia River. A spit of land formed by the Nehalem River curves around south of the mountain. On this spit, Native Americans found large quantities of beeswax marked with interesting designs. Tales are also told of a ship and men lugging large chests partway up Neahkanie Mountain. Other clues and tales in the region that speak of pirate visits and possibly buried treasure include rocks inscribed with weird hieroglyphics, wrecked hulls of unidentified early 19th-century vessels, historic evidence of an auburn-haired man found among the Indian tribes, Indian heirlooms that include ancient Chinese coins, bronze chest handles blown from beneath a stump, rusty irons leaning on a log, and a treasure map with words in Spanish. Sources for these occurrences include the impeccable diaries of Capt. William Clark and the annals of the first Astor expedition in 1811. It seems clear that a shipwreck occurred very early in the 19th century, if not before, and that there had been occasional unrecorded visits to the area by Spanish adventurers, who had possibly visited China. Whether buried treasure remains to be discovered on Neahkanie Mountain remains an open question. Today, treasure seekers still comb the region with metal detectors and other modern techniques.

Port Orford Meteorite. Dr. John Evans accompanied the Stevens Expedition, which surveyed a railroad route from Minnesota to Puget Sound in 1853. He stayed in the region and became a geologist for the U.S. Department of the Interior. In the summer of 1856, he made an extensive exploring expedition to the Oregon Coast and explored the regions around the Coquille and Umpqua Rivers. During this trip, he discovered and sampled a large and valuable meteorite, close to the summit of a "bald mountain." The meteorite has never been found again, even though many have sought it, and a few claimed to have found it. Part of the problem in rediscovering the meteorite is that mountains that were "bald" in the 1850s may not be bald 150 years later. Serious meteorite hunters are well advised to start with Dr. Evans's journals, which can be viewed at the Lewis and Clark College Library and at the Oregon Historical Society, both in Portland.

Portland Treasure Chart. Judge Everett Smith died in 1933. Found among his possessions was a treasure chart containing names, symbols, and directions. If the chart is to be believed, a man named Sims or Simes buried two caches of stolen lucre on a farm near Portland in 1862. The man was killed in the Civil War, and the treasure chart was passed along and ended up in the judge's possession, probably as the result of probate or civil proceedings. The landmarks on the chart were long gone, even when the judge had the chart, so the unearthing of the Portland treasure must await the luck of someone somewhere who digs a hole at the right place, at the right time.

Mammals (*See also* Endangered Species; Seals and Sea Lions)

There are 146 species of mammals that roam Oregon's diverse habitats, which range from marine waters and islets to arid high desert to alpine forests and meadows (*see* map pages 120-21). The mammals include the smallest fur-bearers, herds of hoofed animals, large carnivores, and sleek marine mammals.

Among the hoofed animals are mule deer, the endangered Columbia white-tailed deer, elk, and pronghorn antelope. Hart Mount National Antelope Refuge in southeastern Oregon is home to one of the largest herds of pronghorn antelope in the Northwest. At the top of the food chain are such carnivores as black bears, cougars, and coyotes. Smaller carnivores include wolverines, fishers, martens, and river otters.

Small fur-bearing animals include rodents such as squirrels and chipmunks, as well as marmots and mountain beavers. Hoary marmots (the largest North

Speed Racer

The Northwest's fastest land animal can outrun the cheetah over distances of more than 1,000 yards. Aided by large heart and lungs, powerful muscles, very strong leg bones, and padded hoofs, the pronghorn antelope (Annlocapra americana) can cruise at 35 miles an hour and reach 70 miles an hour in short bursts.—Ann Saling, The Great Northwest Nature Fact Book

American marmot species) live in the lower elevations of the Cascades. The mountain beaver is not actually a beaver; it is more closely related to voles than beavers. It lives only in the Northwest. One of the rarest mammals in the state is the Washington ground squirrel, which is unique to the Columbia Basin region of Oregon and Washington. In Oregon's coniferous forests, flying squirrels make their homes, and in the coastal alders are rare white-footed voles. Badgers can be found among the sagebrush and grassland prairies of Eastern and Southern Oregon.

Along the marine coast, migrating gray whales feed offshore and sea otters, seals, and sea lions haul out on offshore rocks and islands, as well as on the mainland coast. The state's extensive wilderness areas and wildlife refuges provide ample opportunities for viewing wildlife. In addition to the many wildlife guides available in bookstores, you can find out more about programs to preserve Oregon's biological diversity at the **Oregon Department of Fish and Wildlife,** 2501 SW First Ave, Portland 97207, (503) 872-5263, www.dfw.state.or.us.

Marine Pilots

A pilot is a master mariner with expert local knowledge and superior ship-handling skills. Foreign ships entering Oregon waters, including the Columbia River, are required to take on a state-licensed pilot. Pilots are highly specialized—bar pilots handle the mouth of the Columbia, and river pilots handle the voyage up the waterway, for example. A pilot remains with the vessel until the termination of the voyage. Upon return embarkation, the process is repeated in reverse. For ships in domestic trades, including tugs and barges (except inland towing-industry vessels), the person piloting the vessel must hold a federal first-class pilot's license. State-licensed pilots are overseen by the Oregon Board of Marine Pilots, whose members are appointed by the governor. The following organizations provide state-licensed pilots to foreign vessels and others (foreign vessels navigating the Columbia River bound for Washington take on Washington-licensed pilots):

Organizations of Interest

Columbia River Bar Pilots Association, P.O. Box 87, Foot of 14th St., Astoria 97103, (503) 325-2643.

Columbia River Pilots, 13225 N Lombard, Portland 97203, (503) 289-9925.

Coos Bay Pilots Association, 455 S 4th St., P.O. Box 254, Coos Bay 97420, (541) 267-6555.

Medford

Medford is located near the Oregon-California border, one of a three-city I-5 cluster comprising Medford, Grants Pass, and Ashland.

Medford is a child of the railroads. In the 1880s the Oregon and California Railroad laid tracks between Portland and San Francisco, both stops for transcontinental trains. The gold town of Jacksonville, then the biggest town in Southern Oregon, would have been an obvious place to build a station, but the surrounding hills made it difficult to lay rails. A few miles east, Medford grew around a depot, only existing thanks to its neighbor-of-Jacksonville status.

The early Jacksonville pioneer Peter Britt gave the area two things: his passion for cultivating pear trees and a name now attached to that city's popular Britt Festival of Music. Pears still grow here. Harry and David, the big mail-order fruit provider and gift-basket company, has a retail and discount "outlet" store just south of Medford.

Medford itself is no great beauty. Mobile-home dealers and fast-food restaurants line the main commercial strip. Residents make some money through their inexpensive, serviceable motels, often used by visitors who don't want to pay for pricier accommodations while attending the nearby Ashland Shakespeare Festival or the Britt Festival. One highlight is the Southern Oregon Historical Society Museum downtown, with exhibits on the early pioneers and gold-rush times.

Art and microbrewing commingle at McMenamins Edgefield in Troutdale. Photo by Loren Nelson.

For years now, Medford has been the unwitting center of a major logging controversy around the Bureau of Land Management (BLM) focusing on commodifying, rather than preserving, surrounding forest land. In 1866 a mile-wide swath beside the tracks was granted to the Oregon and California Railroad. The government later repossessed 2.5 million acres, now managed by the BLM. The land is a checkerboard of alternating 640-acre squares (the size of Donation Land Act homestead grants to encourage early settlement) commingling with U.S. Forest Service and private land and is BLM's largest timber holding in the continental United States.

While this layout obstructs adequate ecosystem planning and protection, the BLM continues to assert the land's designation for high-yield, sustainable forestry and leases logging rights to timber companies. Efforts to promote conservation meet with resistance from many residents and town officials, since counties receive 50 percent of logging revenues, enough to keep cities like Medford from settling into depression.

Microbreweries

The United States has more operating breweries than any country in the world, and Oregon is doing its fair share of producing over 400 specialty and craft brews. Microbreweries abound in the state, which is not surprising given that all the ingredients for making beer are grown here. Oregon produces 14 hops varieties (Fuggle, Goldings, Horizon, Liberty, Mount Hood, Nugget, Perle, Santiam, Tettnanger, Willamette, and four others), along with malted barley and brewing yeasts. Hop production in Oregon was more than 10 million pounds, valued at more than $18 million, in 1998. Oregon is second only to neighboring Washington in hop production in the United States. The Oregon Brewers Festival draws up to 85,000 beer lovers to sample some of the approximately half million barrels produced in Oregon. Some of the better-known national microbreweries are listed below. Keep in mind, however, that this is a very fluid business and new microbreweries start up every day while existing ones vanish.

Bandon Brewing Company, Bandon
Bend Brewing Company, Bend
Big Horn Brewing, Salem
Big Horse Brewery & Pub, Hood River
Blue Mountain Brewing Company, La Grande
BridgePort Brewing Company, Portland
Caldera Brewing Company, Ashland
Cascade Lakes Brewing Company, Redmond
Cascade Micro-Brewery, Inc., Salem
Deschutes Brewery & Public House, Bend
Eugene City Brewery, Eugene

Full Sail Brewing Company, Hood River
Golden Valley Brewery & Pub, McMinnville
Hair of the Dog Brewing Company, Portland
McMenamins Pubs & Breweries, Beaverton, Eugene, Gresham, Hillsboro, Lincoln City, McMinnville, Portland, Roseburg, Salem, Tigard, Troutdale
Mount Angel Brewing Company, Mount Angel
Mount Hood Brewing Company, Government Camp
Nor'Wester Beer Company, Lake Oswego
Oregon Trader Brewing Company, Albany
Oregon Trail Brewery, Corvallis
Osprey Ale Brewpub, Medford
Pelican Pub & Brewery, Pacific City
Portland Brewing Company, Portland
Ram Big Horn Brewing, Lake Oswego, Salem
Rock Bottom Brewery, Portland
Rogue Ales, Newport
Saxer Brewing Company, Lake Oswego
Siletz Brewing Company, Siletz
Spencer's Restaurant and Brewhouse, Springfield
Standing Stone Brewing Company, Ashland
Steelhead Brewery & Cafe, Eugene
Umpqua Brewing Company, Roseburg
Widmer Brothers Brewing Company, Portland
Wild Duck Brewery, Eugene
Wild River Brewing Company, Grants Pass
Yamhill Brewing Company, Portland

Organizations and Events of Interest

Oregon Brewers Guild, 510 NW Third Ave., Portland 97209, (530) 295-1862, beer@teleport.com, www.teleport.com/~beer.

Oregon Hop Commission, 152 Chemawa Rd. N, Salem 97303, (503) 393-0368, www.oda.state.or.us/hop.

Harvest Fair Microbrew Festival, Central Point, October, (541) 776-7237.

Hubbard Hop Festival, Hubbard, July, (503) 982-8221.

Mount Angel Oktoberfest, Mount Angel, September, (503) 845-9440.

Oktoberfest Microbrew Festival, Roseburg, September, (541) 672-0452.

Oregon Brewers Festival, Waterfront Park, Portland, July, (503) 778-5917.

Spring Beer Fest, Portland, April, (503) 246-4503.

Mileage Chart

(*see table on facing page*) Mileages reflect the shortest distances between cities over state highways.

Military

While Oregon has no major military bases, it does have U.S. Army Corps of Engineers personnel who manage dams and have environmental oversight of wetlands and estuaries, a U.S. Army chemical weapons depot, and U.S. Coast Guard installations along the coast.

U.S. Army Corps of Engineers, Portland District

The Corps of Engineers has been a part of Oregon's history since 1871. The Corps surveyed rivers, dredged shipping channels, removed snags and rocks, built jetties, and built the large dams on the Columbia River. The organization's district headquarters are in Portland. The Portland District encompasses nearly 97,000 square miles of land and water in Oregon and southwest Washington. The Corps' principal functions are maintaining navigation locks on the 465-mile Columbia-Snake Inland Waterway, dredging navigation channel and harbors, and managing dams. The Corps also has responsibility for environmental protection as the principal permitting agency for any work that affects waterways and wetlands.

U.S. Army Umatilla Chemical Depot, Hermiston

The Umatilla Chemical Depot is one of seven stockpiles of chemical weapons within the continental United States and Johnston

Mileage Table

	Astoria	Bend	Burns	Coos Bay	Eugene	Klamath Falls	Medford	Ontario	Pendle-ton	Portland	Salem	The Dalles
Arlington	228	169	230	347	245	306	381	239	72	136	182	53
Astoria	—	255	385	233	199	364	362	464	300	95	136	175
Baker City	396	247	164	466	356	383	459	72	96	304	350	221
Bend	255	—	130	237	128	137	212	260	241	160	131	131
Brookings	339	295	424	107	216	208	134	555	525	317	272	400
Burns	385	130	—	367	259	235	311	130	198	290	261	260
Clatskanie	35	221	351	256	171	341	334	431	265	61	108	140
Coos Bay	233	237	367	—	116	245	170	498	419	212	177	294
Corvallis	151	127	257	135	40	213	210	388	288	81	35	163
Dallas	129	146	276	164	70	242	236	406	268	60	15	143
Enterprise	409	336	270	528	426	473	548	178	109	317	363	234
Eugene	199	128	259	116	—	173	166	388	318	110	64	193
Florence	184	190	320	48	61	234	190	450	371	164	118	245
Fossil	264	108	172	328	218	245	321	233	123	171	218	89
Gold Beach	311	316	446	78	194	238	162	576	497	290	255	373
Grants Pass	334	241	339	142	138	104	29	470	452	245	199	327
Hermiston	282	219	223	396	297	351	387	195	28	186	232	104
Hood River	154	152	282	273	172	289	335	312	146	62	108	21
Independence	134	143	273	159	63	233	226	404	266	59	12	141
John Day	359	153	70	372	262	290	365	132	127	264	266	190
Junction City	177	130	260	116	14	187	181	391	308	100	54	183
Klamath Falls	364	137	235	245	173	—	76	365	378	279	234	268
La Grande	352	271	205	471	369	408	484	115	52	259	306	177
Lakeview	430	174	139	341	261	96	171	270	337	335	306	305
Lebanon	169	109	239	150	45	214	208	369	288	80	35	163
Lincoln City	110	189	319	123	122	292	266	450	296	88	57	171
Madras	213	42	172	262	151	179	255	278	199	118	155	89
McMinnville	105	158	288	174	86	259	252	411	245	38	26	120
Medford	362	212	311	170	166	76	—	442	454	273	227	343
Milton-Freewater	329	271	227	449	347	408	483	180	29	237	284	155
Newport	135	183	311	98	92	267	240	442	321	114	83	196
North Bend	230	235	364	3	113	248	173	495	416	209	174	291
Ontario	464	260	130	498	388	365	442	—	167	374	392	293
Pendleton	300	241	198	419	318	378	454	167	—	208	254	125
Portland	95	160	290	212	110	279	273	374	208	—	47	83
Prineville	242	35	156	254	144	172	247	250	222	146	148	117
Roseburg	266	192	322	85	71	171	96	453	385	177	132	260
St. Helens	66	189	319	240	139	308	302	399	233	29	76	108
Salem	136	131	261	177	64	234	227	392	254	47	—	129
Springfield	199	124	253	113	4	70	164	384	317	110	64	192
The Dalles	175	131	260	294	193	268	343	293	125	83	129	—
Tillamook	66	206	336	167	130	303	297	448	282	74	74	157

Source: Oregon Department of Transportation

Atoll in the Pacific Ocean. The Umatilla Chemical Depot has been storing chemical weapons at the depot since 1962. The stockpile includes projectiles, rockets, land mines, spray tanks, and bombs containing the nerve agents GB and VX and blister agent HD, commonly known as mustard gas. The U.S. Army is currently constructing a new facility to dispose of the chemical weapons stockpile. Beginning in November 2001, the Umatilla Chemical Agent Disposal Facility, located about 7 miles west of Hermiston, will dispose of 3,717 tons of chemical weapons by October 2003.

U.S. Coast Guard

Coast Guard units in Oregon are part of the 13th Coast Guard District, headquartered in Seattle, Washington. Coast Guard personnel in Oregon engage in search and rescue, enforcement of laws and treaties, aids to navigation (including maintaining lighthouses), and environmental protection.

In addition, the North Bend Air Station frequently responds to calls for assistance in logging and other inland accidents. The resources stationed in the state include five HH65A Dolphin helicopters and three Coast Guard Cutters: the USCGC *Orcas* (WPB 1327), USCGC *Cowslip* (WLB-277), and USCGC *Bluebell* (WLM 313). Aids to navigation teams are located at Astoria, Portland, and Charleston.

Air Station Astoria, arrenton
Air Station North Bend, North Bend
Station Chetco River, Brookings
Station Coos Bay, Charleston
Station Coquille River, Bandon
Station Depoe Bay, Depoe Bay
Station Portland, Portland
Station Rogue River, Gold Beach
Station Siuslaw River, Florence
Station Tillamook Bay, Garibaldi
Station Umpqua River, Winchester Bay
Station Yaquina Bay, Newport

Military Museums and Parks

Battle Rock Park, Port Orford. This site of a fierce battle between Indians and explorers now features a paved upper-level walkway, benches, public restrooms. and a fabulous view. There is also a steep trail to the beach. Port Orford Chamber of Commerce, 502 Jefferson Street in Battle Rock City Park, U.S. 101 S, (541) 332-8055.

The Camp White Military Museum, P.O. Box 2373, White City 97503, (503) 826-2111 x3674. The Veterans Domicilary here was the hospital for Camp White during World War II and displays items from that period.

Fort Stevens, U.S. 101, Hammond, (503) 861-2000, (503) 861-1470. Originally commissioned as a Civil War fortification in 1863, Fort Stevens was deactivated shortly after World War II. It was the target of a Japanese submarine shelling during World War II.

Mount Emily Bombsite Trail, U.S. 101 to County Road 808 (South Bank Rd.) to Forest Road 1205 (Mount Emily Rd.); the trail is located off FR 1205 after spur road 260. During World War II, Japanese planes dropped incendiary bombs here and near Port Orford. Neither bombing did much damage. The trail extends from South Bank Rd., 6 miles on Wheeler Creek Rd. to the east side of Mount Emily. For more information, contact Siskiyou National Forest, Chetco Ranger District, 555 Fifth St., Brookings 97415, (541) 469-2196.

The Oregon Military Museum, Camp Withycombe, Clackamas 97015, (503) 557-5359. Presented here are collections of firearms (some very rare), uniforms, and other artifacts dating back to the 19th century. Vehicles outside the museum are awaiting restoration. An indoor display shows a half-track, an armored car, two jeeps, a late 1930s army motorcycle, and more.

Tillamook Naval Air Station Museum, 4000 Blimp Blvd., Tillamook 97141, (503) 842-1130. One of two original hangars, it is the largest free-span wooden structure in the world. The museum features the Northwest's biggest collection of World War II fighter planes. Located south of town off U.S. 101.

Minimum Wage

The minimum wage for Oregon as of January 1, 1999, is $6.50 per hour. For information about minimum-wage restrictions, contact the Bureau of Labor and Industries. The bureau's Technical Assistance for Employers Program provides information on wage and hour laws, employment of minors, family leave, and civil rights laws, including the state disability law.

Bureau of Labor and Industries, Technical Assistance for Employers Program, 800 NE Oregon, No. 32, Portland 97232, (503) 731-4073.

South Sister, the state's third-highest peak. Photo by Susan Dupere.

Mountains

(*SEE ALSO* MOUNT HOOD; NEWBERRY CRATER; VOLCANOES AND VOLCANISM) Mountains dominate vistas in most areas of Oregon. Mount Hood, the northernmost and highest peak, is part of the most extensive mountain range, the Cascade Range, which extends from British Columbia to California. West of the Cascade Range lies the Coast Range, another elongate north-south range that extends from Alaska to California and abuts at its southern end in Oregon with the Klamath and Siskiyou Mountains before reemerging farther south in California. In Eastern Oregon, the major mountain groups include the Blue and Wallowa Ranges (*see* map pages 144-45).

Aldrich Mountains. This 30-mile-long range extends between Dayville and John Day. Its highest points are Fields Peak (7,360 feet) and Aldrich Mountain (6,988 feet). Geologically, these mountains are layers of ancient ocean deposits that were folded, refolded, and intruded by granitic rocks. Much of the area lies within the Malheur National Forest.

Blue Mountains. The Blue Mountains are broadly defined as the mountains that run from Northeast Oregon into Southeast Washington, but some earth scientists define them more narrowly as the forested mountain range running north and south between Pendleton and La Grande. The highest peak is Rock Creek Butte (9,097 feet).

Calapooya Mountains. This small range is a western extension of the Cascade Mountains. Situated between the Willamette and Umpqua drainages, these were the last major mountains settlers crossed when traveling north into the Willamette Valley on the Applegate Trail.

Cascade Mountains. The Cascade Range, which extends the entire north-south length of Oregon an average of 100 to 150 miles inland from the coast, forms an important climatic barrier, dividing the state's rainier and more densely vegetated western side from its drier eastern portion. Several large river drainages originate in the Cascades, including the state's largest, the Willamette. The state's highest peaks are Cascade volcanoes: Mount Hood, Mount Jefferson, and the Three Sisters.

Coast Range. The Coast Range is a mountain system that runs from Southeast Alaska to Baja California. The system's

Mount Hood. From *Portland from the Air* by Sallie Tisdale (essay) and Russ Heinl (photos).

lowest elevations are found in southern Washington and Oregon. The Coast Range runs the length of Oregon along the western coastline, from the Columbia River in the north to the Klamath Mountains in the south The Oregon Coast Range is marked by ridges running parallel to the coast and narrow valleys between the ridges. The average height of the ridge crests is about 1,800 feet in the north and 3,600 feet in the south. The highest elevation is Mary's Peak (4,097 feet) in Benton County.

Klamath and Siskiyou Mountains. The Klamath Mountains are sometimes lumped together with the abutting Coast Range, but they are actually a geologically distinct mountain group. The Siskiyous of Southern Oregon are part of the Klamath Range, which extends from the southwestern corner of Oregon into California and meets the Cascade Range on its east side. Mount Ashland (7,533 feet) is the highest of these mountains. The Rogue River and Siskiyou National Forests, including the Kalmiopsis Wilderness, cover much of this mountainous area in Oregon.

Ochoco Mountains. The Ochocos, located east of Prineville, have several peaks over 6,000 feet. *Ochoco* is a Paiute word for "willows." Most of these ponderosa pine-covered mountains are located in the Ochoco National Forest.

Wallowa Mountains. The Wallowas of northeastern Oregon are sometimes called the "Switzerland of North America." Outside of the Cascades, the Wallowas are where you will find some of the state's highest peaks: Sacajawea Peak, the Matterhorn, Aneroid Mountain, and Pete's Point. Most of the Wallowas are within the Wallowa-Whitman National Forest.

Ten Highest Peaks

Mount Hood	11,235 feet
Mount Jefferson	10,495 feet
South Sister	10,358 feet
North Sister	10,085 feet
Middle Sister	10,047 feet
Sacajawea Peak	9,839 feet
Matterhorn	9,832 feet
Aneroid Mountain	9,702 feet
Pete's Point	9,675 feet
Mount McLoughlin	9,496 feet

Mount Hood

Snow-clad Mount Hood (elevation 11,235 feet), Oregon's highest peak and fourth highest in the Cascade Range, dominates the skyline from Portland west of the Cascades to the vast wheat fields beyond the mountain's eastern flanks. With its classic conelike shape, it is considered one of the most beautiful of all the Cascade peaks. It erupted repeatedly for hundreds of thousands of years, most recently during two episodes in the past 1,500 years, but there has been no eruptive activity—save for some regular seismic twitchings—since the early 1800s. Twelve glaciers and named snowfields cap the uppermost reaches of the volcanic peak. The mountain was named in 1792 after British Adm. A. A. Hood in 1792 by William Broughton while sailing with Capt. George Vancouver. Next to Mount Fuji in Japan, Mount Hood is the most frequently climbed glacial peak in the world. Skiing is another popular activity and continues well into summer above timberline on Mount Hood's permanent snowfield at Timberline ski area (*see* Mountains; Outdoor Recreation; Skiing and Snowboarding; Volcanoes and Volcanism).

Museums

(*See also* American Indians; Military; Oregon Trail; Railroads) In addition to traditional and specialty museums located around the state (*see* sections cited above), most colleges and universities have museums that are open to the public. The largest museums in the state are listed below.

Art Museums

Coos Art Museum, 235 Anderson, Coos Bay 97420, (541) 267-3901, www.coos.or.us/~cam. The Coos Art Museum, located in the Oregon Coast's largest city, provides many exhibits of big-city quality, while the permanent collection includes Northwest art, prints by nationally known artists, and the Victor West Collection of Historic Maritime Photographs.

Corvallis Arts Center, 700 SW Madison Avenue, Corvallis 97333, (541) 754-1551. The Corvallis Arts Center/Linn-Benton Council for the Arts is housed in a historic church building. The center is known for an exhibition program featuring national, regional, and local artists in a professional setting. Handcrafted items are sold in the Central Park Art Shop gift gallery.

Favell Museum of Western Art and Artifacts, 125 W Main, Klamath Falls 97601, (541) 882-9996, (541) 381-2230. Dedicated to the heritage of the West, the Favell Museum displays over 100,000 Indian artifacts (lots of arrowheads) and works by more than 300 major contemporary Western artists. It also houses the largest miniature-gun collection in the world.

Hoffman Gallery, Oregon School of Arts & Crafts, 8245 SW Barnes Rd., Portland 97225, (503) 297-5544. The Hoffman Gallery features mostly Northwest artists and craftspeople who work in ceramics, glass, metal, wood, fiber arts, or any combination of these. The adjacent sales gallery sells quality fine art and gifts, and each February the gallery exhibits traditional crafts from Third World countries. Unique detailing flatters the variety of buildings on campus.

Marylhurst University Gallery of Art, 17600 Pacific Hwy., Marylhurst 97036, (503) 636-8141. Just south of Portland, Marylhurst is a well-respected venue showcasing the region's established and emerging artists. The adjacent **Art Gym** (a 3,000-square-foot former gymnasium) often mounts major retrospectives, (503) 699-6243.

Portland Art Museum (PAM), 1219 SW Park Ave., Portland 97205, (503) 226-2811. One of the major museums on the West Coast, PAM's permanent collection includes Northwest Coast Indian art, prehistoric Chinese artifacts, tribal art of Cameroon, and modern European and American sculpture and painting. The Gilkey Center for Graphic Arts houses over 22,000 works of art on paper, including prints, drawings, and photographs. PAM oversees the Northwest Film Center, highly respected for its classes and host of the Portland International Film Festival. Movies are presented five times a week.

A bus route along Route 63 (this bus is called "ART") encompasses many of Oregon's cultural attractions, including

PAM. Other stops include the Oregon History Center, the Oregon Museum of Science and Industry, the World Forestry Center, the Oregon Zoo, and the Japanese Gardens. Purchase single-use tickets or all-day or all-month passes at Tri-Met's ticket office downtown at Pioneer Courthouse Square.

Schneider Museum of Art, Southern Oregon University, 1250 Siskiyou Blvd., Ashland 97520, (541) 552-6245. Considered to be Ashland's best art gallery, this museum presents touring exhibitions and selections from its permanent collection, which focuses on 20th-century art.

University of Oregon Museum of Art, University of Oregon, Eugene 97403, (541) 346-3111. This museum presents rotating shows, including particularly strong photography exhibits and selections from its impressive holdings of Orientalia and contemporary Northwest art. A lovely courtyard invites repose. In spring, the museum displays the eclectic work of the U of O's respected graduate students.

Children's Museums

A. C. Gilbert's Discovery Village, 116 Marion St. NE, Salem 97301, (503) 371-3631. Gilbert's is a "kid-designed" outdoor discovery park, with hands-on indoor exhibits.

Children's Museum, 3037 SW 2nd Ave., Portland 97201, (503) 823-2227. A play and learning center for children under 12, many "please touch" exhibits fascinate visitors. Tots can wheel a cart through the child-sized grocery store (mostly canned goods), complete with a checkout line. The basement Clayshop is open Wednesdays. Thursday afternoon family hours are closed to groups, allowing more manageable fun.

History Museums

Almost every county has its own historical museum; contact a visitor center in the area of your interest.

Jacksonville Museum of Southern Oregon History, 206 N 5th St., Jacksonville 97530, (541) 773-6536. Housed in a restored 1883 courthouse, features here include exhibits on collecting American Indian objects and a display of pioneer pottery. The history of the Rogue Valley, from gold-mining camp to bustling trade center, is showcased through artifacts and historical photos and relates the story of the Applegate Trail. The permanent collection includes works by Peter Britt, an early emigrant and the first person to photograph Crater Lake.

Kam Wah Chung & Company Museum, NW Canton/City Park, John Day 97845, (541) 575-0028. This original 1867 building houses artifacts from its history as a general store, the office of a Chinese herbal doctor, and a center for Eastern Oregon's Chinese community until the early 1940s.

Klamath County Museum and the Baldwin Hotel Museum, 1451 Main St., Klamath Falls 97601, (541) 883-4208. Exhibits at these tram-connected sites cover the history, anthropology, geology, and wildlife of the Klamath Basin.

Marion County Historical Society Museum, 260 12th St., Salem 97301, (503) 364-2128. Permanent displays cover Willamette Valley Kalapuyans and pioneer life, while rotating exhibits address black history, historic women, Chinese immigrants, heritage trees, and the history of microbrews.

Oregon Historical Society Museum, Oregon History Center, 1200 SW Park Ave., Portland 97205, (503) 222-1741, orhist@ohs.org. A landmark in the heart of Portland's South Park Blocks (an 18-block, elm-lined isle encompasses several major cultural attractions), the museum's major permanent display showcases Native American dominance of the region, early exploration by Europeans and Americans, white settlement, and the state's political history. Stunning eight-story-high trompe l'oeil murals by Richard Haas depict snippets of Oregon history.

Southern Oregon Historical Society's History Center, 106 N Central Ave., Medford 97501, (541) 773-6536, www.sohs.org. The center displays permanent and changing exhibitions of local and regional history and contains a fine photo archive.

Spray Pioneer Museum, Oregon 19, Spray 97874, (541) 468-2069. A renovated 1912 church houses photographs and stories of early local settlers.

Sumpter Valley Gold Dredge and Railroad Restoration, Greater Sumpter Chamber of Commerce, P.O. Box 250, Sumpter 97877, (541) 894-2290, www.triax.com/sumpter. Sumpter, an historic gold mining town along the Powder River, was mostly destroyed in a 1917 fire, but the gold dredge continued operation until 1954. One can still see the dredge and ride the Sumpter Valley Railroad Restoration train, which also takes visitors up to Phillips Lake. The landscape invites contemplation of the way years of mining can alter geology. An enormous flea market operates one weekend a month during the summer.

Umatilla County Historical Society Museum, 108 SW Frazer, Pendleton 97801, (541) 276-0012. This refurbished 1909 train depot and 1878 one-room schoolhouse display local artifacts, memorabilia, and photographs.

Natural History and Science Museums

Crater Rock Museum, 2002 Scenic Ave., Central Point 97502, (541) 664-6081. Jackson County's natural history is the focus here. The museum also houses the collections of the Roxy Ann Gem and Mineral Society.

Lilah Callen Holden Elephant Museum, Oregon Zoo, 4001 SW Canyon Rd., Portland 97211, (503) 226-1561. This is a one-of-a-kind museum dedicated to the long and rich connection between elephants and people.

Oregon Air and Space Museum (OASM), 90377 Boeing Dr., Eugene 97402, (541) 461-1101. A nonprofit, educational aviation museum, OASM exhibits many historically significant aircraft, including a McDonnell Douglas F-4 Phantom, a Grumman A-6 Intruder, and a Mikoyan/Gurevich MiG 17.

Oregon Museum of Science and Industry, 1945 SE Water Ave., Portland 97214, (503) 797-OMSI, (800) 955-6674. With hundreds of interactive displays, a state of the art OMNIMAX theater, six

The Oregon Museum of Science and Industry is locally known by its acronym. Photo courtesy OMSI.

exhibit halls with live demonstrations and touring shows, and view dining, OMSI attracts more than 600,000 visitors a year. Children and adults enjoy everything from riding disaster simulators to watching chicks hatch. The museum relocated to its current waterfront site in 1992.

University of Oregon Museum of Natural History, 1680 E 15th Ave., Eugene 97403, (541) 346-3024, mnh@oregon.uoregon.edu. This museum is the repository for all anthropological artifacts and specimens found on Oregon state lands (about 500,000 to date), including Thomas Condon's extensive fossil collection and the Fort Rock sagebrush sandals, the latter dated at 13,000 to 9,000 years old. Anthropological and natural science exhibits, from prehistoric to contemporary times, display everything from obsidian tools and cedar baskets to backyard birds and native trees.

Willamette Science and Technology Center (WISTEC), 2300 Leo Harris Pkwy., Eugene 97401, (541) 682-3619. This science museum near Autzen Stadium features hands-on science and mathematics exhibits for children.

Mushrooms

More than 2,000 species of mushrooms grow in the Northwest, dozens of them edible, including the delectable and desirable chanterelles and morels. In fact, the 1999 Oregon legislature voted to make the Pacific golden chanterelle the official state 'shroom. The edible species include the following:

Black picoa, also called Oregon black truffle *(Picoa carthusiana)*

Cauliflower mushroom *(Sparassis crispa)*
Coral tooth mushroom, also called coral hydnum *(Hericium abietis)*
Edible morel *(Morchella esculenta)*
Golden chanterelle and white chanterelle *(Cantharellus cibarius* and *C. subalbidus)*
Horn of plenty *(Craterellus cornucopioides)*
King bolete *(Boletus edulis)*
Matsutake, pine mushroom, or white matsutake *(Tricholoma magnivelare* and *T. ponderosum)*
Oregon white truffle *(Tuber gibbosum Gilkey)*
Shaggy parasol *(Lepiota rachodes)*
Spreading-hedgehog mushroom *(Hydnum repandum)*

Commercial harvesting of wild mushrooms grew dramatically during the 1990s, primarily of *Boletus edulis, Cantharellus cibarius, Morchella esculenta,* and *Tricholoma magnivelare.* Harvesting of the latter—matsutakes—took off in the mid-1990s when pickers discovered that the Winema and Deschutes National Forests were prime hunting grounds for these mushrooms; about 8 percent of the world's matsutake supply comes from these two forests—an annual crop worth millions of dollars to pickers and tens of thousands of dollars in permit fees paid to the national forests. A good day of picking can earn a wild-mushroom harvester hundreds of dollars, which has also resulted in poaching and altercations over harvest areas. Oregon law requires licensing of mushroom buyers and dealers and annual harvest reporting for commercial wild mushrooms. Fall is the biggest season for wild mushrooms. The rains and mild temperatures are perfect for fungi growth.

Few mushroom species are seriously poisonous, but some cases of mushroom poisoning have occurred in the Northwest, especially among recent Asian immigrants who have gathered and eaten deadly *Amanita* species that resemble a species widely consumed in Asia. Another deadly mushroom resembles some *Psilocybe*—"magic mushroom"—species. If you gather wild mushrooms, be sure you correctly identify your mushrooms before you eat them; even cooking does not eliminate the toxins, which can be deadly.

Organizations of Interest

Lincoln County Mycological Society, 6504 SW Inlet Ave, Lincoln City 97367-1140

Mount Mazama Mushroom Association, 417 Garfield St., Medford 97501.

Oregon Coast Mycological Society, P.O. Box 1590, Florence 97439.

Oregon Mycological Society, 1943 SE Locust, Portland 97214, rogersmm@aol.com.

Willamette Valley Mushroom Society, 1454 Manzanita St. NE, Salem 97303.

National Forests

Oregon has six national forests located entirely within its borders and five national forests that share land with neighboring states. The Oregon and Washington national forests comprise the U.S. Forest Service's Region 6, headquartered in Portland. National forest lands encompass more than 15 million acres and 36 wilderness areas. The largest national forest is Wallowa-Whitman in the northeastern part of the state. The largest unbroken area of national forests runs in a continuous chain throughout most of the Cascade Range.

Maps of the national forests can be obtained for a few dollars each at Forest Service offices and at outdoor equipment and information stores and centers. Information about the national forests can be obtained over the Internet at www.fs.fed.us/r6. You may also make reservations for campsites at national forest campgrounds in Oregon on the Internet at reserveusa.com. Cabins and fire lookouts can also be rented. **U.S. Forest Service,** Pacific Northwest Region, 333 SW 1st Ave., Portland, OR 97208.

Deschutes National Forest, 1645 U.S. 20 E, Bend 97701, (541) 388-2715. The 1.6-million-acre Deschutes National Forest encompasses terrain ranging from the Cascade Mountains along its western border to the high desert country of Eastern Oregon. Twenty peaks higher than 7,000 feet, including three of Oregon's 5 highest peaks, are found within the Deschutes. Within this forest are more than 150 lakes and 500 miles of streams, five wilderness areas; six Wild and Scenic Rivers; Newberry National Volcanic Monument; and the Oregon Cascades Recreation Area. The Bend Pine Nursery, which produces between 5 million and 8 million ponderosa and lodgepole pine seedlings each year, is located in the forest, as is the Redmond Air Center, which dispatches smokejumpers, fire crews, retardant planes, and other fire equipment throughout the Northwest and the nation. Both the nursery and the air center provide public tours. Ranger district offices are located in Bend, Crescent, and Sisters.

Fremont National Forest, HC 10 Box 337, Lakeview 97630, (541) 947-2151. The 1.9-million-acre Fremont National Forest is located east of the Cascade Mountains in the high-elevation lava tablelands of south-central Oregon, most of it in sparsely populated Lake County. The forest lies within a semiarid region with distinct climate regimes that support habitats ranging from near-desert to lush coniferous forests. Stands of white fir and drought-tolerant trees such as juniper and ponderosa pine exist here, as well as western white pine, sugar pine, incense cedar, and lodgepole pine. The Fremont's major streams include the Chewaucan, Sycan, and Sprague Rivers. Many of the forest's small lakes and reservoirs are popular fishing and camping areas. More than 300 species of fish and wildlife live here, including such game animals as mule deer, Rocky Mountain elk, and pronghorn antelope. The Gearhart Mountain Wilderness, totalling 22,823 acres, is the forest's only wilderness; its dominant feature is 8,380-foot Gearhart Mountain. Ranger district offices are located in Bly, Lakeview, Paisley, and Silver Lake.

Klamath National Forest, 1312 Fairlane Rd., Yreka, CA 96097, (530) 842-6131. A small area of the Klamath National Forest extends into Oregon just north of the California border. Of the forest's 1.7 million acres, only about 26,000 acres are located in Oregon. No ranger district offices are in Oregon. The nearest ranger station is Happy Camp Ranger District (California 96), P.O. Box 377, Happy Camp, CA 96039, (530) 493-2243.

Malheur National Forest, P.O. Box 909, John Day 97845, (541) 575-3000. The Malheur National Forest covers nearly a million and a half acres in Eastern Oregon's Blue Mountains in Grant, Harney, Baker, and Malheur Counties. The terrain is characterized by juniper and sage flats, rolling forested foothills, and mountain meadows. Elevations range from 4,000 feet to over 9,000 feet at Strawberry Mountain. The Monument Rock and Strawberry Mountain Wildernesses are located within the Malheur. Some of the forest's outstanding features include Arch Rock National Recreation Trail and the John Day Fossil Beds. Ranger district offices are located at John Day, Hines, and Prairie City.

Mount Hood National Forest, 16400 Champion Way, Sandy 97055, (503) 668-1700. The Mount Hood National Forest extends south from the strikingly beautiful Columbia River Gorge across more than 60 miles of forested mountains, lakes, and streams to the slopes of Mount Jefferson. It contains 189,200 acres in five designated wilderness areas: Mount Hood, Badger Creek, Salmon-Huckleberry, Hatfield, and Bull-of-the-Woods. Visitors enjoy fishing, camping, boating, and hiking in the summer, hunting in the fall, and skiing and other snow sports in the winter. Some popular destinations include Timberline Lodge on Mount Hood, Lost Lake, Trillium Lake, Timothy Lake, Rock Creek Reservoir, and portions of the original Oregon Trail, including Barlow Road. Ranger district offices are located in Dufur, Maupin, Estacada, Mount Hood-Parkdale, Zigzag, and Welches.

Ochoco National Forest, 3160 NE 3rd Street, Prineville 97754, (541) 416-6500. Ochoco National Forest comprises over 800,000 acres in the geographic center of Oregon. It was originally part of the old Blue Mountain Forest Reserve, established in 1906 by President Theodore Roosevelt, and divided in 1908 into four smaller units: the Deschutes, Malheur, Whitman, and Umatilla National Forests. The Ochoco was created from parts of the Malheur and Deschutes in 1911. Crooked River National Grassland is administered by Ochoco National Forest staff. Wilderness areas include Black Canyon, Bridge Creek, and Mill Creek. Ranger district offices are located in Prineville, Paulina, Hines, and Madras. The forest lands include popular rockhounding areas.

Rogue River National Forest, Supervisor's Office, 333 West 8th Street, P.O. Box 520, Medford 97501, (541) 858-2200. The 630,000-acre Rogue River National Forest, which includes about 53,800 acres in California, is composed of two separate units of land, each with diverse terrain and vegetation. The variety of environments includes open oak woodlands, dense conifer forests, and rocky ridges. The forest contains the upper reaches of the Rogue River along the slopes of the Cascades. The highest point (9,495 feet) is the top of Mount McLoughlin, one of Oregon's major volcanic peaks. Recreation opportunities include fishing, swimming, hiking, more than 40 developed campgrounds and picnic grounds, and some 400 miles of trails. The Pacific Crest National Scenic Trail (*see* Outdoor Recreation) runs the entire length of the forest. Downhill skiing (at Mount Ashland Ski Area), cross-country skiing, and snowmobiling are popular wintertime activities. Ranger district offices are located in Jacksonville, Ashland, Butte Falls, Prospect, and Central Point.

Siskiyou National Forest, Supervisor's Office, 200 NE Greenfield Rd., P.O. Box 440, Grants Pass 97526, (541) 471-6500. Siskiyou National Forest is located in the Klamath and Coast Ranges, with a small segment extending into northwestern California and the Siskiyous. It encompasses over 1.1 million acres. The Siskiyou contains the most diverse plant life of all the national forests except the Great Smoky Mountains. Of 28 different coniferous species found within the forest, 20 are used commercially. Of the nearly 400 sensitive plants in the region, about

100 are found within the Siskiyou National Forest. Ranger district offices are located in Brookings, Grants Pass, Gold Beach, Cave Junction, and Powers.

Siuslaw National Forest, 4077 Research Way, Corvallis 97333, P.O. Box 1148 (97339), (541) 750-7000. The 630,000-acre Siuslaw National Forest contains some of the most productive tree-growing land in the United States. Tree species that grow here include Douglas fir, western hemlock, western red cedar, Sitka spruce, red alder, and big-leaf maple. The forest and its 30 lakes and 1,200 miles of anadromous streams support 235 species of birds, over 200 species of fish, 60 mammal species, 26 amphibian and reptile species, and numerous sensitive plant species. A number of threatened and endangered species, including bald eagle, Aleutian Canada goose, peregrine falcon, brown pelican, snowy plover, Northern spotted owl, and marbled murrelet, number among the Siuslaw's residents. Ranger district offices are located in Alsea, Hebo, Florence, Waldport, and Yachats. The spectacular Oregon Dunes National Recreation Area is also located within the Siuslaw.

Umatilla National Forest, Supervisor's Office, 2517 SW Hailey Ave., Pendleton 97801, (541) 278-3716. The 1.4-million-acre Umatilla National Forest, located in the Blue Mountains of Southeast Washington and Northeast Oregon, extends across mountains, V-shaped valleys separated by narrow ridges or plateaus, heavily timbered slopes, grassland ridges and benches, and basalt outcroppings. Elevations range from 1,600 to 8,000 feet. Wilderness areas within the Umatilla include the North Fork John Day, North Fork Umatilla, and Wenaha-Tucannon. Ranger district offices are located in Heppner and Ukiah.

Umpqua National Forest, P.O. Box 1008, 2900 NW Stewart Pkwy., Roseburg 97470, (541) 672-6601. The Umpqua National Forest includes nearly a million acres within the western slopes of the Oregon Cascades. Over 50 percent of the Umpqua is classified as old growth. Fishing is popular in the forest's many lakes and rivers, including 3-mile-long Diamond Lake, along with camping, hiking, biking, boating, and whitewater. During the winter, downhill skiers can take Snow-Cats up Mount Bailey. There are 46 campgrounds and 10 picnic areas, as well as boat ramps and historic buildings in the forest. Wilderness areas include the Thielsen, Rogue-Umpqua Divide, and Boulder Creek. Ranger district offices are located in Cottage Grove, Idleyld Park, Glide, and Tiller.

Wallowa-Whitman National Forest, 1550 Dewey Ave., P.O. Box 907, Baker City 97814, (541) 523-6391, TDD (541) 523-1405, www.fs.fed.us/r6/w-w. Wallowa-Whitman National Forest contains 2.3 million acres, nearly evenly divided between Oregon and Idaho. The land ranges in elevation from 875 feet in spectacular Hells Canyon to 9,845 feet in the Eagle Cap Wilderness. The Wallowa-Whitman has 2,653 miles of trails, 58 campgrounds and picnic areas, 268 miles of wild and scenic rivers, and 5,089 acres of lakes and reservoirs. Its wilderness areas are the Hells Canyon, Eagle Cap, North Fork John Day, and Monument. The Hells Canyon National Recreation Area is also located here. Ranger district offices are located in Enterprise, La Grande, Halfway, and Unity. The **Wallowa Mountains visitor center** is located at 88401 Oregon 82, Enterprise 97828, (541) 426-5546.
(Continued on page 122)

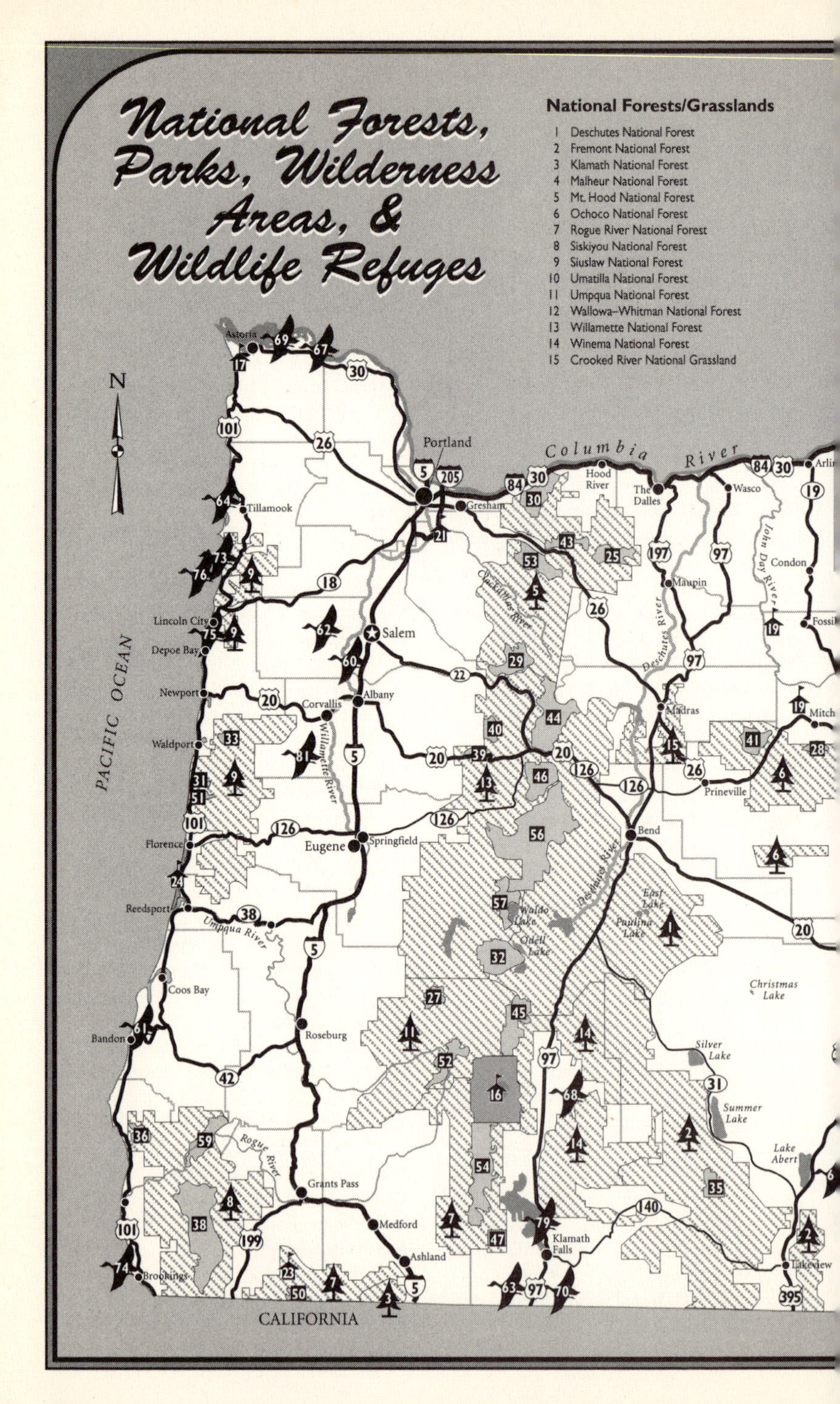
National Forests, Parks, Wilderness Areas, & Wildlife Refuges
National Forests/Grasslands
1 Deschutes National Forest
2 Fremont National Forest
3 Klamath National Forest
4 Malheur National Forest
5 Mt. Hood National Forest
6 Ochoco National Forest
7 Rogue River National Forest
8 Siskiyou National Forest
9 Siuslaw National Forest
10 Umatilla National Forest
11 Umpqua National Forest
12 Wallowa–Whitman National Forest
13 Willamette National Forest
14 Winema National Forest
15 Crooked River National Grassland
N
PACIFIC OCEAN
Columbia River
Astoria
Tillamook
Lincoln City
Depoe Bay
Newport
Waldport
Florence
Reedsport
Coos Bay
Bandon
Brookings
Portland
Gresham
Hood River
The Dalles
Wasco
Condon
Maupin
Salem
Albany
Corvallis
Eugene
Springfield
Madras
Prineville
Bend
Roseburg
Grants Pass
Medford
Ashland
Klamath Falls
Lakeview
Willamette River
Umpqua River
Rogue River
Deschutes River
John Day River
Clackamas River
Waldo Lake
Odell Lake
East Lake
Paulina Lake
Christmas Lake
Silver Lake
Summer Lake
Lake Abert
CALIFORNIA

National Parks, Monuments, Historic Sites/Preserves/ Parks, and Recreation Areas

16 Crater Lake National Park
17 Fort Clatsop National Memorial
18 Hells Canyon National Recreation Area
19 John Day Fossil Beds National Monument
20 Lewis and Clark National Historic Trail
21 McLoughlin House National Historical Site
22 Nez Perce National Historical Park
23 Oregon Caves National Monument
24 Oregon Dunes National Recreation Area

Wilderness Areas

25 Badger Creek
26 Black Canyon
27 Boulder Creek
28 Bridge Creek
29 Bull of the Woods
30 Columbia
31 Cummins Creek
32 Diamond Peak
33 Drift Creek
34 Eagle Cap
35 Gearhart Mountain
36 Grassy Knob
37 Hells Canyon
38 Kalmiopsis
39 Menagerie
40 Middle Santiam
41 Mill Creek
42 Monument Rock
43 Mount Hood
44 Mount Jefferson
45 Mount Thielsen
46 Mount Washington
47 Mountain Lakes
48 North Fork John Day
49 North Fork Umatilla
50 Red Buttes
51 Rock Creek
52 Rogue–Umpqua Divide
53 Salmon–Huckleberry
54 Sky Lakes
55 Strawberry Mountain
56 Three Sisters
57 Waldo Lake
58 Wenaha–Tucannon
59 Wild Rogue

National Wildlife Refuges

60 Ankeny
61 Bandon
62 Baskett Slough
63 Bear Valley
64 Cape Meares
65 Cold Springs
66 Hart Mountain National Antelope Refuge
67 Julia Butler Hanson National Wildlife Refuge for Columbia Whitetail Deer
68 Klamath Marsh
69 Lewis and Clark
70 Lower Klamath
71 Malheur
72 McKay Creek
73 Nestucca Bay
74 Oregon Islands
75 Siletz Bay
76 Three Arch Rocks
77 Tualatin River
78 Umatilla
79 Upper Klamath
80 Wapato Lake
81 William L. Finley

Willamette National Forest, Federal Building, 211 E 7th Ave., Eugene 97401, (541) 465-6521. The 1.6-million-acre Willamette National Forest stretches for 110 miles along the western slopes of the Cascades from the Mount Jefferson area to the Calapooya Mountains. Accessed by four major highways, the forest is within a day's drive from anywhere in Western and Central Oregon. Elevations range from about 1,500 feet above sea level to 10,495 feet at the snowcapped top of Mount Jefferson, Oregon's second-highest peak. The Willamette contains large stands of old-growth Douglas fir, with diameters ranging from 3 to 8 feet. Some 15 other conifer species are also found here, including cedar, pine, hemlock, and several species of fir, along with over 300 species of fish and other wildlife. About 380,805 acres are designated wilderness. Seven major volcanic peaks stand within the forest's boundary, more than within any other national forest in the Northwest: Mount Jefferson, Three-Fingered Jack, Mount Washington, Three Sisters, and Diamond Peak. Two wild and scenic rivers, the McKenzie and the North Fork of the Middle Fork Willamette, are within the forest. Part of the Oregon Cascades Recreation Area is within the Willamette's boundaries.

Winema National Forest, 2819 Dahlia St., Klamath Falls 97601. The 1.1-million-acre Winema National Forest lies on the eastern slopes of the Cascade Range in south-central Oregon. It borders Crater Lake National Park near the crest of the Cascades and stretches eastward into the Klamath River Basin. It includes vast marshes and meadows associated with Upper Klamath Lake and the Williamson River drainage and extensive stands of ponderosa and lodgepole pine on deep pumice and ash that blanketed the area during the eruption of Mount Mazama (now Crater Lake) nearly 7,000 years ago. The newest national forest in Oregon, the Winema was created in 1961.

National Grassland

A national grassland is public land administered by the U.S. Forest Service as part of the national forests system. Unlike the large tracts of land that form the national forests, the national grasslands tend to be made up of dispersed units that are intermingled with state, private, and other federal lands. There are 20 national grasslands nationwide and one in Oregon.

Crooked River National Grassland, 813 SW U.S. 97, Madras 97741, (541) 4756-9272. Of its 174,000 acres, 111,379 are administered as a unit of Ochoco National Forest (*see* National Forests).

This grassland is characterized by sagebrush and juniper, often referred to as high desert, which supports a small herd of antelope, numerous mule deer, quail, and chukars. Picturesque rimrock vantage points, deep canyons, and other unique geologic landforms also characterize the grassland.

National Natural Landmarks

The National Natural Landmarks Program, established in 1962 by the U.S. Secretary of the Interior, identifies and encourages the protection of sites in the United States that contain the best examples of geological and ecological components of the nation's landscape. Sites can be recommended by private citizens or from inventories by outside groups, such as the Oregon Natural Heritage Program administered by the Division of State Lands. Scientists then evaluate recommended areas, using the national significance criteria. If a site fulfills the requirements for landmark status, and if a majority of the private property owners do not object to the designation, the area's nomination is considered by a final advisory board. Once designated, the area is listed on the National Registry of Natural Landmarks.

Crown Point. The Crown Point section of the Columbia River Gorge just east of Portland illustrates gradual stream-valley formation that resulted as downcutting kept pace with the rise of the Cascade Range. At Crown Point the Columbia River Gorge passes from the steeper, more rugged terrain of the western slopes of the Cascade

Range to rolling cultivated plains. The promontory provides a strategic vantage point for observing this classic illustration of riverine processes.

Fort Rock State Monument. This site in Southern Oregon, several miles east of Oregon 31 about halfway between La Pine and Silver Lake, is a striking example of a circular, fortlike volcanic outcrop. Although other volcanic outcrops may exhibit many of the same features, few are as well-shaped and distinct.

Horse Ridge Natural Area. This site 16 miles southeast of Bend is of national significance in providing a characteristic and high-quality example of sandy western juniper *(Juniperus occidentalis)* steppe. Its plants and animals are typical of the Great Basin desert and the transitional area between ponderosa pine *(Pinus ponderosa)* forest and sagebrush *(Artemisia tridentata).*

Lawrence Memorial Grassland Preserve. This site in Eastern Oregon is an excellent example of "biscuit and scabland" topography and pristine grassland and shrubland. It is not accessible to the public.

Newberry Crater. The crater is a young volcano formed within the last million years during the Pleistocene and is the largest Pleistocene volcano east of the Cascade Range just south of Bend. It stands isolated and conspicuous on a broad plateau of lava.

Willamette Floodplain. The site represents the largest remaining native and unplowed example of bottomland interior-valley grasslands in the Northwest.

National Parks, Monuments, and Recreation Areas

The National Park Service administers national parks; national historical parks, sites, and reserves; national monuments; and national recreation areas (*see* map pages 120-21). All units of the park system have equal legal standing.

In Oregon, the national park system includes a spectacular range of natural wonders and an historic pioneer trail. The national recreation areas in the state (Hells Canyon National Recreation Area and Oregon Dunes National Recreation Area) fall within the boundaries of national forests and are thus administered by the U.S. Forest Service (*see* Dunes; Hells Canyon and the Snake River; National Forests).

Crater Lake lies in the caldera of an extinct volcano. Photo by Ken Brown.

Crater Lake National Park, P.O. Box 7, Crater Lake 97604, (541) 594-2211, www.nps.gov/crla. This park, Oregon's only national park, surrounds an extinct volcano, Mount Mazama (*see* Volcanoes and Volcanism), on the crest of the Cascade Range north of Klamath Falls off Oregon 62. Crater Lake, which lies in the caldera of the volcano, is about six miles across, 1,932 feet deep, and known for its beautiful brilliant-blue color. The park features a visitor center on the caldera's south rim; the scenic Rim Drive of 33 miles with more than 20 scenic overlooks; over 50 miles of one-way and loop trails, including 33 miles of the Pacific Crest Trail; numerous campsites; and 71-room Crater Lake Lodge. In winter, there are marked ski trails for cross-country skiing. The park receives heavy snow in winter, and from mid-October until mid-June the north entrance and Rim Drive are closed to the public.

Fort Clatsop National Memorial, 92343 Fort Clatsop Rd., Astoria 97103, (503) 861-2471, www.nps.gov/focl. Fort Clatsop is the site where Lewis and Clark and the Corps of Discovery spent the winter of 1805-1806 near present-day Astoria. A replica of the expedition's tiny 50-by-50-foot fort, an historic canoe landing, and the spring that provided the fort's water supply are the focal points of the 125-acre park. The main site is in an area of coastal forest within the Columbia River estuary. A nearby site commemorates where the expedition made salt from seawater. The Saltworks unit of the park is in Seaside.

Hells Canyon National Recreation Area, 88401 Hwy. 82, Enterprise 97828, (541) 426-4978. The Hells Canyon National Recreation Area extends over 652,488 acres in Oregon and Idaho. In Oregon, it is part of the Wallowa-Whitman National Forest and two others. The Wallowa Mountain Loop Road, a five-hour scenic tour from Baker City to La Grande, provides the easiest access to the rim of Hells Canyon at the Hells Canyon Overlook. The Hells Canyon National Recreation Area has 15 campgrounds on the Oregon side and hundreds of miles of trails. Many trails are located across steep slopes, some immediately adjacent to several-hundred-foot vertical cliffs. Half tunnels have been blasted in rims and stair steps built over rock bluffs. Accessible trails have been constructed at several of the developed recreation sites along the Oregon rim. The area is an access site for rafting and jetboating on the Snake River. There are approximately 100 dispersed river camps; reservations are required to launch float trips from some locations; for reservations, call (509) 758-1957. Self-issue permits are required for powerboaters on all sections of the river.

John Day Fossil Beds National Monument, HCR 82, Box 126, Kimberly 97848, (541) 987-2333, www.nps.gov/joda. The world-renowned John Day Fossil Beds National Monument in Central Oregon is home to a well-preserved fossil record of plants and animals that spans more than 40 million of the 65 million years of the Cenozoic era, or Age of Mammals. The fossil beds, discovered in the 1860s, contain one of the best fossil records of an ancient semitropical forest found on the continent. The national monument contains fossil beds in three widely separated units: the Sheep Rock Unit, the Painted Hills Unit, and the Clarno Unit. The Clarno Unit contains the Clarno Nut Beds, where more than 300 plant species have been found, and the cliffs of the Clarno Palisades, which were formed by volcanic ash mudflows (called lahars) that buried a once lush forest. The Painted Hills Unit contains a series of colorfully striped hills and hummocks created by weathering of the volcanic ash that covered the region. The Sheep Rock Unit has a small museum featuring exhibits of fossils. Among the area's other outstanding characteristics are the narrow, steep-walled gorge of the John Day River and the massive promontory that is Sheep Rock.

Lewis and Clark National Historic Trail (headquarters), 700 Rayovac Dr., #100, Madison, WI 53711, (608) 264-5610, Jan_Lee@nps.gov. The 3,700-mile Lewis and Clark National Historic Trail begins in Illinois and passes through 10 states, ending in Oregon at Fort Clatsop National Monument. Most people follow portions of this trail in a motorized vehicle. Motor routes that follow approximately the route of the historic expedition were marked by state agencies in the 1960s with rectangular signs illustrated with the figures of Lewis and Clark. These highways connect a series of memorials, museums, visitor centers, interpretive exhibits, and historic sites. The Lewis and Clark National Historic Trail is administered by the National Park Service (NPS) in cooperation with federal, state, and local agencies, nonprofit organizations, and private landowners. The NPS publishes a general information brochure and map of the trail.

McLoughlin House National Historic Site, 713 Center St., Oregon City, (503) 656-5156. McLoughlin, head of the Hudson's Bay Company at Fort Vancouver across the Columbia River, came to be known as the "Father of the Oregon

The Wild Sheep Rapids on the Snake River lie within the Wallowa-Whitman National Forest. From *Oregon's National Forests* by Robert M. Reynolds (photos) and Joan Campf (text).

Country." When he retired from the Hudson's Bay Company in 1845, he moved from Vancouver to Oregon City. The elegant home he built there near Willamette Falls, where he lived until his death in 1857, was moved to its present location in 1909 to save it from encroaching development. The house was restored in authentic mid-19th-century style, as it would have been when McLoughlin lived there. Tickets are available at adjacent Barclay House, which was similarly relocated to save it from destruction and today houses the offices and gift shop for the McLoughlin House National Historic Site.

Nez Perce National Historical Park, Rte. 1, Box 100, Spalding, ID 83540-9715, (208) 843-2261, www.nps.gov/nepe. The Nez Perce National Historical Park, devoted to the Nez Perce people, includes 38 individual sites in northern Idaho, Montana, Oregon, and Washington. These sites commemorate the culture and history of the Nez Perce. Some sites are associated with the tribe's 1877 war with the U.S. government, others are associated with settlers, trappers, traders, missionaries, and explorers, including the Lewis and Clark Expedition. The sites located in Oregon are the Old Chief Joseph gravesite in Joseph, the Dug Bar Crossing in Hells Canyon, a summer campsite at Wallowa, and Joseph Canyon Overlook north of Enterprise. The park's visitor center and museum are located in Spalding, Idaho.

Oregon Caves National Monument, 19000 Caves Hwy., Cave Junction 97523, (541) 592-2100, www.nps.gov/orca. Oregon Caves National Monument in the Siskiyou Mountains contains the largest cave on the West Coast formed completely in marble. The cave, formed like all limestone and marble caves from the dissolving action of acidic groundwater, includes five levels with three miles of passages and an underground stream. The largest chamber, the Ghost Room, measures 50 feet wide, 250 feet long, and 40 feet high. These caves contain a variety of dripstone formations, many of which are still growing actively. The guided cave tour lasts about 75 minutes and covers 0.6 mile of passageway, including 550 stairs. An additional 0.3 mile on the surface, partially over steep terrain, completes the loop tour. Above ground, the area is surrounded by old-growth forest, with several nature trails, many of which connect to trails in adjoining Siskiyou National Forest.

Oregon Dunes National Recreation Area, 855 Highway Ave., Reedsport 97467, (541) 271-3611. The Oregon Dunes National Recreation Area extends 40 miles along the Pacific Ocean from the Siuslaw River on the north to the Coos River on the south; it extends inland approximately 2.5 miles at its widest point. The area contains 30 lakes, 14 hiking trails, 13 campgrounds, nine day-use areas, three off-highway riding areas, a dunes overlook, and a visitor center. The dunes were actually formed by eroded sedimentary rock from the Coast Range that was washed to sea by rivers, then carried back onshore by waves and tides. The present shoreline stabilized 6,000 years ago. Tides, wave action, and strong coastal winds moved sand up to 2.5 miles inland over thousands of years. European beach grass, introduced to prevent sand from blocking river channels and roads, has now spread all along the coast and has become a barrier to additional sand movement from the beach. When the sand no longer moves, vegetation easily takes hold. Invading an average of 22 feet of sand a year, plants may entirely cover the dunes within the next 150 years.

National Register of Historic Places

The National Register of Historic Places is the nation's official list of buildings, structures, objects, sites, and districts worthy of preservation for their significance in U.S. history, architecture, archaeology, and culture. National Register listings should not be confused with local historic-property and historic-district designations. Properties and districts listed in the National Register sometimes also receive local designation, but there is no direct correlation between National Register listing and local designation.

There are over 1,500 such places throughout Oregon, including farms and ranches; private residences from mansions to log cabins; public buildings such as courthouses, libraries, schools, and post offices; Forest Service ranger stations and lookouts; industrial sites such as hydroelectric power stations and mills; bridges and railroad stations; and a wide variety of miscellaneous structures such as garages, jails, shipwrecks, and carousels. The entire list can be perused on the Internet at www.nr.nps.gov/nrishome.htm. A sampling from around the state follows:

Agness—**Rogue River Ranch,** east of Agness near confluence of Mule Creek and Rogue River.

Albany—**Albany Custom Mill,** 213 Water St.

Amity—**Briedwell School,** 11935 SW Bellevue Hwy.

Arock—**Sheep Ranch Fortified House,** west of Arock.

Ashland—**Buckhorn Mineral Springs Resort,** 2200 Buckhorn Springs Rd.

Ashland—**Lithia Park,** 59 Winburn Way.

Astoria—**Fort Clatsop National Memorial,** 4.5 miles south of Astoria.

Astoria—**Lightship *Columbia*,** 1792 Maritime Dr.

Astoria—**Svenson Blacksmith Shop,** 1769 Exchange St.

Baker—**Baker Municipal Natatorium,** 2470 Grove St.

Baker—**St. Elizabeth Hospital (Old),** 2365 Fourth St.

Bandon—**Coquille River Life Boat Station,** 390 SW 1st St.

Bend—**Bend Amateur Athletic Club Gymnasium,** northeast of Wall and Idaho Sts.

Bend—**N. P. Smith Pioneer Hardware Store,** 935-937 NW Wall St.

Bonneville—**Bonneville Dam Historic District,** Columbia River between Bradford and Cascade Islands off I-84 in Multnomah County, Oregon, to Washington 14 in Skamania County, Washington.

Brownsville—**Starr and Blakely Drug Store,** 421 N Main St.

Burns—**Pete French Round Barn,** north of Diamond Station.

Butte Falls—**Imnaha Guard Station,** Rogue River National Forest.

Canyon City—**St. Thomas' Episcopal Church,** 135 Washington St.

Cascade Locks—**Cascade Locks Marine Park,** Columbia River.

Central Point—**Central Point Public School,** 450 S 4th St.

Champoeg—**William Case Farm,** southeast of Champoeg off Arbor Grove Rd.

Coburg—**Oregon Railway and Navigation Company Bridge,** southeast of Coburg.

Corvallis—**Pi Beta Phi Sorority House,** 3002 NW Harrison Blvd.

Timberline Lodge was built by expert craftsmen and artisans in the 1930s. From *Portland from the Air* by Sallie Tisdale (essay) and Russ Heinl (photos).

Corvallis—**Willamette Valley and Coast Railroad Depot,** 500 SW 7th St.
Cottage Grove—**Musick Guard Station,** NE of Bohemia Mtn., Umpqua National Forest.
Crown Point—**Vista House,** Historic Columbia River Hwy.
Dallas—**Dallas Tannery,** 505 SW Levens St.
Damascus—**Damascus School,** 14711 SE Anderson Rd.
Danner—**Jean Baptiste Charbonneau Memorial and Inskip Station Ruins,** north of Danner off U.S. 95.
Dayton—**Courthouse Square,** bounded by Third, Fourth, Ferry, and Main Sts.
Dayton—**Opera House,** 318 Ferry St.
Dayville—**James Cant Ranch Historic District,** Oregon 19.
Depoe Bay—**Cruiser *Tradewinds Kingfisher*,** Depoe Bay Boat Basin.
Detroit—**Breitenbush Guard Station,** Willamette National Forest.
Eagle Point—**Snowy Butte Flour Mill,** off Oregon 62.
Eugene—**McDonald Theater Building,** 1004-1044 Willamette St.
Eugene—**Pacific Cooperative Poultry Producers Egg-Taking Station,** 506 Olive St.
Florence—**Heceta Head Lighthouse and Keepers Quarters,** north of Florence on U.S. 101.
Frenchglen—**Frenchglen Hotel,** Oregon 205.
Galice—**Speed's Place on the Rogue,** 11407 Merlin-Galice Rd.
Gold Beach—**Vessel *Mary D. Hume*,** Port of Gold Beach.
Gold Hill—**Gold Hill High School,** 806 6th Ave.
Goshen—**Methodist Episcopal Church of Goshen,** 85896 First St.
Government Camp—**Timberline Lodge,** six miles north of Government Camp, Mount Hood National Forest.
Grants Pass—**Redwoods Hotel,** 310 NW 6th St.
Gresham—**Louise Home Hospital and Residence Hall,** 722 NE 162nd Ave.
Hood River—**Mount Hood Hotel Annex,** 102-108 Oak St.
Hood River—**Oregon-Washington Railroad & Navigation Company Passenger Station,** foot of First St.
Independence—**Parker School,** 8900 Parker Rd.
John Day—**Advent Christian Church,** 261 W Main St.
Jordan Valley—**Birch Creek Ranch Historic Rural Landscape,** Owyhee River, junction with Birch Creek and Gaging Station.
Klamath Falls—**Blackburn Sanitarium,** 1842 Esplanade.
La Pine—**I.O.O.F. Organization Camp,** Paulina Lake, Deschutes National Forest.
Lake Oswego—**Oregon Iron Company Furnace, George Rogers Park,** Oregon 43.
Lakeview—**Post and King Saloon,** N 2nd and E Sts.
Leaburg—**McKenzie Fish Hatchery,** Old 44645 McKenzie Hwy.
Lookingglass—**Wimer, James, Octagonal Barn,** 1191 Coos Bay Wagon Rd.
Medford—**Medford Southern Pacific Railroad Passenger Depot,** 147 N Front St.
Metolius—**Oregon Trunk Passenger and Freight Station,** Washington St. at the foot of Sixth St.
Molalla—**Molalla Union High School,** 413 S Molalla Ave.
Mount Angel—**Queen of Angels Priory,** 840 S Main St.
Mulino—**Howard's Gristmill,** 26401 S Oregon 213.
Newberg—**Minthorn Hall,** North St. on the George Fox University Campus.
Newport—**Old Yaquina Bay Lighthouse,** Yaquina Bay State Park.
Nyssa—**Vinsonhaler Blacksmith Shop,** 122 Good Ave.
Parkdale—**Valley Theater,** 4945 Baseline Rd.
Philomath—**Philomath College,** Main St.
Phoenix—**Glenview Orchard Ensemble,** 1395 Carpenter Hill Rd.
Plush—**Stone Bridge and the Oregon Central Military Wagon Road,** The Narrows south of Plush.
Portland—**Albertina Kerr Nursery,** 424 NE 22nd Ave.
Portland—**Rose City Electric Automobile Garage,** 124 NW 20th Ave.

Portland—**Steam Tug *Portland*,** Willamette River at the foot of SW Pine St.

Portland—**Union Station,** NW 6th Ave.

Powers—**Powers Hotel,** 310 Second Ave.

Prairie City—**Sumpter Valley Railway Passenger Station,** Main and Bridge Sts.

Prineville—**Lamonta Compound-Prineville Supervisor's Warehouse,** Ochoco National Forest.

Rhododendron—**Barlow Road,** roughly north of Salmon and White Rivers from Rhododendron to southwest of Wamic, Mount Hood National Forest.

Roseburg—**U.S. Post Office,** 704 SE Cass Ave.

Salem—**Capitol building,** 900 Court St. NE.

Salem—**Lee Mission Cemetery,** D St.

Salem—**Reed Opera House and McCornack Block Addition,** 189 and 177 Liberty St.

Seaside—**Two-Abreast Carousel,** 300 Broadway.

Shaniko—**Southern Hotel,** 4th and E Sts.

Shedd—**Boston Flour Mill,** east of Shedd on Boston Mill Rd.

Sheridan—**Travelers Home,** 147 NE Yamhill St.

Sisters—**William T. E. Wilson Homestead,** 70300 Camp Polk Rd.

Sixes—**Sixes Hotel,** 93316 Sixes River Rd.

Stayton—**Paris Woolen Mill,** 535 E Florence St.

Sublimity—**Silver Falls State Park Concession Building,** Area 20024, Silver Falls Hwy.

Sumpter—**Sumpter Valley Gold Dredge,** southwest of Sumpter near Cracker Creek.

Talent—**Wagner Creek School,** 8448 Wagner Creek Rd.

Vale—**Vale Hotel and Grand Opera House,** 123 S Main St.

Wemme—**Oregon Trail, Barlow Road Segment,** northwest of Wemme.

West Linn—**Willamette Falls Locks,** west bank of Willamette River.

Whitney—**Antlers Guard Station,** southeast of Whitney, Wallowa-Whitman National Forest.

Winchester—**Winchester Dam,** N Umpqua River at U.S. 99.

Winchester Bay—**U.S. Coast Guard Station, Administration and Equipment Buildings,** Umpqua River.

Wolf Creek—**Wolf Creek Tavern,** about 22 miles north of Grants Pass.

Yachats—**Cape Perpetua Shelter and Parapet,** three miles south of Yachats.

National Wildlife Refuges

Oregon's national wildlife refuges (NWR) are among the largest and most diverse in the country—from desert to rocky ocean islands. They provide important habitat for endangered species, as well as feeding and breeding habitat for migrating birds (*see* map pages 120-21 for a complete listing).

Ankeny NWR, 2301 Wintel Rd., Jefferson 97352, (541) 588-2701. Wintering habitat for dusky Canada geese and other waterfowl. Nearly 200 species of wildlife can be seen here, including herons, hawks, vultures, quail, shorebirds, woodpeckers, songbirds, red fox, and black-tailed deer. The refuge comprises 2,796 acres of Willamette Valley agricultural bottomland. *Directions:* Exit I-5, 10 miles south of Salem at the Ankeny Hill exit. Follow Wintel Rd. west (toward Sidney) about 2 miles.

Bandon Marsh NWR, c/o Western Oregon NWR Complex, 26208 Finley Refuge Rd., Corvallis 97333, (541) 757-7236. Bandon Marsh has 309 acres of undisturbed salt marsh, mudflat, and beachgrass communities. It is a resting and feeding area for shorebirds, wading birds, raptors, and waterfowl. *Directions:* Just north of Bandon between the Coquille River and U.S. 101.

Baskett Slough NWR, 10995 Oregon 22, Dallas 97338, (541) 623-2749. This refuge has 2,492 acres typical of the Willamette Valley's hillsides, knolls, and fields, as well as wetlands at Morgan Lake and Baskett Slough. The area provides wintering habitat for dusky Canada geese. Waterfowl, herons, eagles, hawks, quail, shorebirds, mourning doves, woodpeckers, and songbirds frequent the area. Mammal species include red fox and black-tailed deer. *Directions:* From Rickreall (six miles west of Salem), head west on Oregon 22 about two miles.

Pronghorn antelope are found in the sagelands of Hart Mountain Antelope Refuge in Lake County. From *Oregon III* by Ray Atkeson.

Bear Valley NWR, c/o Klamath Basin NWR, Rte. 1, Box 74, Tulelake, CA 96134, (530) 667-2231. This refuge in the Klamath Basin is a major nighttime roosting site for wintering bald eagles. The Klamath Basin supports the largest wintering concentration of bald eagles (500+) in the Lower 48 states. The refuge has supported as many as 300 eagles in one night. Timbered with pine and fir shrublands and grasslands, the refuge will eventually contain 4,120 acres. The refuge is closed to the public from November through March, but there are viewing areas nearby. *Directions:* 12 miles southwest of Klamath Falls and 1 mile west of Worden and U.S. 97.

Cape Meares NWR, 26208 Finley Refuge Rd., Corvallis 97333, (541) 757-7236. Common murres, tufted puffins, and pelagic cormorants nest along cliffs of this 139-acre coastal area. Band-tailed pigeons and black-tailed deer can be found inland in the forested areas of shore pine and Sitka spruce. *Directions:* About 8 miles west of Tillamook, adjacent to Cape Meares State Park.

Cold Springs NWR, c/o Mid-Columbia River NWR Complex, P.O. Box 700, Umatilla 97882-0700, (541) 922-3232. This refuge is a winter resting and feeding area for ducks and Canada geese. Pheasants, quail, and mule deer are common. There are 3,117 acres of open water, marsh, sagebrush, grasslands, and trees around the lake. *Directions:* Refuge is seven miles east of Hermiston. From Oregon 207 go east on Wall's Rd. one mile, then south on Tabor Rd. to the refuge.

Hart Mountain National Antelope Refuge, P.O. Box 21, Plush 97637, (541) 947-3315. This refuge is part of the Sheldon-Hart Mountain National Wildlife Refuge Complex that has areas in Oregon and Nevada. It includes 241,104 acres of diverse habitats located at elevations between 4,500 and 8,065 feet. The region is characterized by sagebrush, juniper, and native bunchgrasses, along with aspen and pine groves, canyons, and steep, spectacular rock rims. Pronghorn antelope, California bighorn sheep, mule deer, and sage grouse are among the common species found here. The camping facilities are primitive, as is a hot springs. *Directions:* The refuge is 68 miles northeast of Lakeview, off Oregon 140.

Klamath Basin NWR Complex, California and Oregon, c/o Klamath Basin NWR Complex, Hill Rd., Rte. 1, Box 74, Tulelake, CA 96134, (530) 667-2231. Upper Klamath NWR encompasses 14,917 acres of marsh and water at the north end of Upper Klamath Lake. The marshes provide excellent habitat for several species of ducks, as well as white pelicans, herons, egrets, and other colonial nesting birds. *Directions:* The Oregon portion of this refuge is located 25 miles northwest of Klamath Falls along Oregon 140. Access is by boat only. Suggested access points are Rocky Point Resort and Malone Spring.

Oregon Islands NWR, 2127 SE OSU Drive, Newport 97365-5258, (541)

The Klamath Basin

Oregon's Klamath Basin is one of the most heavily used refuge systems on the Pacific Flyway, with five national wildlife refuges hosting one of the world's most spectacular concentrations of waterfowl—nearly a million at peak fall migration—including snow geese, ducks, cormorants, egrets, great blue herons, pelicans, and sandhill cranes. Lower Klamath National Wildlife Refuge, the nation's first refuge for migrating waterfowl (1908), straddles the Oregon-California border, providing small marshes, open water, and grassy uplands.— Ann Saling, *The Great Northwest Nature Factbook*

867-4550. This area is 763 acres of ocean rocks and islands along the Oregon Coast that provide habitat for seabirds and mammals. Most of the refuge is included in the Oregon Islands Wilderness. *Directions:* Inaccessible by land except Coquille Point; contact Oregon Coastal Refuges, (541) 867-4550. Public access on the islands is not permitted.

Three Arch Rocks NWR, 2127 SE OSU Drive, Newport 97365-5258, (541) 867-4550. These 17 acres of rock islands are located entirely in the Oregon Islands Wilderness. They are habitat for nesting common murres. Tufted puffins and Brandt's and pelagic cormorants use the area. Northern and California sea lions and harbor seals are also found here. *Directions:* Located about one mile offshore from Oceanside. The rocks and wildlife can be observed from boats and the mainland, but public access on the islands is not permitted.

William L. Finley NWR, 26208 Finley Refuge Rd., Corvallis 97333, (541) 757-7236. This wildlife refuge comprises 5,325 acres of Oregon oak and maple woodlands, ash thickets, second-growth Douglas fir, bushy hedgerows, marshes, meandering creeks, open meadows, pastures, and cultivated fields. It is important wintering habitat for dusky Canada geese. Wood ducks and hooded mergansers are common summer nesters. Ruffed grouse, ring-necked pheasant, California quail, and black-tailed deer, as well as many other small birds and mammals, are found here. *Directions:* U.S. 99W south of Corvallis about 10 miles to entrance sign, then west about four miles to refuge office.

Newberry Crater

Newberry Crater was once Oregon's highest shield volcano, and it is still the largest of all Northwest volcanoes in volume, covering about 320,000 acres, with its lava flows extending northward tens of miles beyond the volcano. Located about 40 miles east of the crest of the Cascade Range southeast of Bend, Newberry Crater was a 10,000-foot volcano, before its summit collapsed in an eruption. Its highest point is Paulina Peak, elevation 7,985 feet. The flanks of Newberry contain more than 400 cinder cones, some up to 500 feet tall, and fissure vents. The volcano's last major eruption, some 600 years ago, ejected over 170 million cubic yards of obsidian and pumice, producing one of Newberry's many interesting features, called the Big Obsidian

The Big Obsidian Flow, along with Paulina and East Lakes, lies within the Newberry Caldera. Photo by Lyn Topinka, Cascades Volcano Observatory, USGS.

Flow. To protect this fascinating area, the U.S. Congress created the Newberry National Volcanic Monument in 1990.

Lava Lands Visitor Center, 58201 U.S. 97, Bend 97707, (503) 593-2421.

Newberry National Volcanic Monument, Deschutes National Forest, 1645 U.S. 20 E, Bend 97701, (503) 388-2715.

Natural Glass

Obsidian is a natural volcanic glass, black and brittle. Native Americans of the Northwest, with few sources of flint, traveled great distances to find the rock. Because it was easy to fracture, with edges 500 times sharper than a razor blade, they sculpted obsidian into arrowheads. Today scientists use obsidian pieces to date archaeological sites and interpret tribal trading patterns. Glass Buttes, 75 miles east of Bend, is actually a single mountain made entirely of this shiny lava. The most recent obsidian flow, covering a square mile and ending in glassy cliffs 100 feet high, erupted some 600 years ago from the south wall of Newberry Crater. Snowflake obsidian, popular with jewelers and rock collectors, is created when gases under pressure pierce tiny holes in the obsidian, forming the stone's trademark white spots.

Newspapers and Periodicals

Oregon's first newspaper, the *Oregon Spectator,* began publishing in 1846. Today, 19 daily newspapers and a couple hundred weekly and biweekly newspapers, ethnic newspapers, special-interest papers, and periodicals cover business and industry, the arts, law, the environment, and local history. One national news bureau, the Associated Press, maintains a bureau office in Portland. Oregon newspapers and correspondents have garnered national awards for journalism. The prestigious Pulitzer Prize has been awarded to the following:

Oregon Pulitzer Prize Winners

1934—Public Service. *Mail Tribune,* Medford. For campaign against unscrupulous politicians in Jackson County.

1939—Editorial Writing. Ronald G. Callvert, *The Oregonian,* Portland. For distinguished editorial writing during the year as exemplified by the editorial entitled "My Country 'Tis of Thee."

1957—Local Reporting, No Edition Time. Wallace Turner and William Lambert, Portland, *The Oregonian.* For their exposé of vice and corruption in Portland involving municipal officials and officers of the International Brotherhood of Teamsters, Chauffeurs, Warehousemen, and Helpers of America, Western Conference.

Daily Newspapers in Oregon

Albany Democrat-Herald, P.O. Box 130, Albany 97321, (541) 926-2211, www.dhonline.com.

Argus Observer, P.O. Box 130, Ontario 97914, (541) 889-5387, argus@cyberhighway.net.

Ashland Daily Tidings, P.O. Box 7, Ashland 97520, (541) 482-3456.

Baker City Herald, P.O. Box 807, Baker City 97814, (541) 523-3673, bcherald@triax.com.

Corvallis Gazette-Times, P.O. Box 368, Corvallis 97339, (541) 753-2641.

Daily Journal of Commerce, P.O. Box 10127, Portland 97210, (503) 226-1311, www.djc-or.com.

East Oregonian, P.O. Box 1089, Pendleton 97801, (541) 276-2211, (800) 522-0255, www.eastoregonian.com.

Grants Pass Daily Courier, P.O. Box 1468, Grants Pass 97528, (541) 474-3700, (800) 228-0457, courier@cdsnet.net.

Herald and News, P.O. Box 788, Klamath Falls 97601, (541) 885-4410, www.heraldandnews.com

The Bulletin, 1526 NW Hill St., Bend 97701, (541) 382-1811, www.bendbulletin.com.

The Daily Astorian, P.O. Box 210, Astoria 97103, (503) 325-3211, www.dailyastorian.com.

The Dalles Chronicle, P.O. Box 902, The

The Oregonian *looked back at its first 150 years in 2000.* From *The Oregon Story: 1850-2000.*

Dalles 97058, (541) 296-2141, www.eaglenewspapers.com.

Mail Tribune, The, P.O. Box 1108, Medford 97501, (541) 776-4411, www.mailtrib.com.

News-Review, The, P.O. Box 1248, Roseburg 97470, (541) 672-3321, www.oregonnews.com.

Observer, The , P.O. Box 3170, La Grande 97850, (541) 963-3161, www.eoni.com/~observer.

Oregonian, The, 1320 SW Broadway, Portland 97201, (503) 221-8327, www.oregonlive.com.

Register-Guard, The, P.O. Box 10188-2188, Eugene 97440, (541) 485-1234, www.registerguard.com.

Statesman Journal, P.O. Box 13009, Salem 97309, (503) 399-6611, www.statesmanjournal.com.

World, The, P.O. Box 1840, Coos Bay 97420, (541) 269-1222, theworld@ucinet.com.

Selected Periodicals Published in Oregon

Agri-Times, P.O. Box 189, Pendleton 97801, (541) 276-7845.

Backwoods Home Magazine, 29304 Ellensburg Ave., Gold Beach 97444, (541) 247-8900.

Cascade Horseman, P.O. Box 788, Klamath Falls 97601, (541) 883-4000.

Cascades East, 716 NE 4th St., Bend 97701, (541) 382-0127.

Daily Journal of Commerce, P.O. Box 10127, Portland 97210, (503) 226-1311.

Environmental Law, Northwestern School of Law, Lewis and Clark College, 10015 SW Terwilliger Blvd., Portland 97219, (503) 768-6700.

Flyfishing & Tying Journal, P.O. Box 82112, Portland 97282, (503) 653-8108, 800-(541) 9498, fax: (503) 653-2766.

Northwest Labor Press, 1827 NE 44th Ave., #200, P.O. Box 13150, Portland 97213, (503) 288-3311.

Northwest Palate, P.O. Box 10860, Portland 97210, (503) 224-0966.

Northwest Travel, Northwest Regional Magazines, P.O. Box 18000, Florence 97439-0130.

Open Spaces: Views from the Northwest, Open Spaces Publishing, 6327C SW Capitol Hwy., Portland 97201-1937, (503) 227-5764.

Oregon Business Magazine, 610 SW Broadway, #200, Portland 97205-3431, (503) 223-0304.

Oregon Coast, P.O. Box 18000, Florence 97439, (541) 997-8401.

Oregon Geology, 800 NE Oregon St., #965, Portland 97232, (503) 731-4100, fax: (503) 731-4066.

Oregon Grange Bulletin, 643 Union St. NE, Salem 97301, (503) 316-0106.

Oregon Historical Quarterly, Oregon Historical Society, 1200 SW Park Ave., Portland 97205, (503) 222-1741.

Rain City Review, 7215 SW La View Dr., Portland 97219.

Skipping Stones: A Multi-Cultural Children's Quarterly, 1309 Lincoln St., Eugene 97440, (541) 342-4956.

Southern Oregon Heritage, Southern Oregon Historical Society, 106 N Central Ave., Medford 97501-5926, (541) 773-6536.

Willamette Law Review, Willamette University, 245 Winter St. SE, Salem 97301, (503) 370-6186.

Willamette Week, 822 SW 10th, Portland 97205, (503) 243-2122.

Organizations of Interest

The Associated Press, One World Trade Center, 14th Floor, 121 SW Salmon, #1450, Portland, OR 97204, (503) 228-2169.

Eugene Newspaper Guild, 364 East Broadway, #G, Eugene 97401-2769, (541) 343-8625.

Oregon Newspaper Microfilming Project, The, University of Oregon, Eugene 97403, (541) 346-1864.

Oregon Newspaper Publishers Association, 7150 SW Hampton St., #111, Portland 97223-8395, (503) 624-6397.

Pacific Northwest Newspaper Guild, 2900 Eastlake Ave. E, #220, Seattle, WA 98102, (206) 328-1190.

Oregon Trail

(SEE ALSO HISTORY) The Oregon Trail, 2,000 miles long and interrupted by two mountain ranges and several deadly rivers, forced people to suffer for the better life they hoped to find in Oregon. Between 1840 and 1860, over 50,000 settlers braved the trail. In some years, one out of 10 died. The very real hardships of the Trail were shared by the Indians as well, though. Ironically, much of the Trail covered routes first tracked by the Indians who had assisted fur trappers and Lewis and Clark to their destinations, but who spent later decades watching missionaries spread new diseases through their populations—decimating whole tribes—and watching white settlers take over their fishing and hunting areas.

Many of the Indians weren't aware of the losses still to come and remained focused on their often ancient enmities with other tribes. The Elijah White party was the first official one to make the trip, in 1842, after the U.S. government engaged the former missionary doctor as an agent to look after relations between the Native tribes and U.S. citizens. Factions arose among the 112 members of the White party, of which 52 were men over age 18. At one point two men lagging behind to carve their initials on a tree were captured by a band of Sioux, released only when the party's guide, Thomas Fitzpatrick, arranged the sale of weapons to the tribe for their wars against other tribes.

In another instance, several thousand Blackfeet Sioux surrounded the party's wagons and were particularly interested in appraising the women. One man had three lovely daughters, and a young brave stayed at the wagon, bargaining even after the rest of the tribe had retreated, offering 20 horses in exchange for his choice of the girls. The furious father railed through an interpreter, a former fur company clerk, who finally told the young man that it wasn't the custom of white people to sell their women. This irritated the brave, who remarked correctly that white men bought their women all the time.

After four to six months, settlers arrived at Oregon City (later continuing into the Willamette Valley), exhausted, hungry, and with few, if any, cattle or other resources left to start anew. Despite the conflicting pretensions to the region of the British Hudson's Bay Company, John McLoughlin, the company's representative in Oregon, assisted the newcomers. He did so because he believed the area below the Columbia was destined for U.S. hands and that this kept emigrants from settling farther north, where the eventual boundaries were less apparent.

The Other Oregon Trail

The years of travel on the Oregon Trail comprised one of the largest peacetime migrations in history, though many perished along the way. Though most emigrants feared Indian attacks, more died from disease, starvation, accidental shootings, and river crossings. In 1843,

Donation Land Claims

As the British-owned Hudson's Bay Company and U.S. trappers, missionaries, and emigrants vied for control of the Oregon Territory, the U.S. government was eager to promote settlement. In September 1850, Congress enacted the Donation Land Law, which legitimated the claims of arrived settlers while paying for an official survey of the land.

The law induced new settlers with the promise of free acreage. The act stipulated that claimants be males over 18 years of age, "American half-breed included," half-breed indicating a son by a white man and an Indian woman. Each man received 320 acres. If married, the man received 640 acres, half to be held by the wife in her own right. Later amendments gave title to widows who hadn't held their land for the full four years required by law and allowed settlers to patent their claims after two years if they paid $1.25 an acre.

Not surprisingly, tensions with Native tribes, especially those that had not yet been conned by a treaty ceding their land, escalated. Anglo-American relations suffered as Hudson's Bay Company lands were seized (for which individuals later received compensation). Yet another problem with the law arose when the surveyor-general tried to draw boundaries for claims already settled. Some claims were as large as a square mile, and many were awkwardly shaped. Later historians noted that size discrepancies between claims tended to isolate the early settlers, making the growth of towns with diversified goods and services more difficult. ✯

Wagon Prints

I-84 . . . parallels the route of the Oregon Trail from the Snake to the Columbia River. Flagstaff Hill, just outside of Baker City, was a well-known stopover along the trail, and the prairie here still bears the scars of the thousands of covered wagons that passed this way.—Portrait of Oregon, text by Sandra L. Keith, photographs by Rick Schafer ✯

while crossing the then wild Columbia River, brothers Jesse and Lindsay Applegate each lost a son. After settling in the Corvallis area, they vowed to discover a safer, southern route from Idaho to Oregon.

With the help of Levi Scott, the Applegate brothers set out in the summer of 1846, crossing the Cascade Mountains and the deserts of northern Nevada into eastern Idaho. At Fort Hall they recruited emigrants. The first of thousands of wagons to use the trail started west in mid-July (another source says that after the first Applegate party the trail was rarely used until the gold rush). As the emigrants approached the California-Oregon border, the Applegate Party encountered rivers and jagged mountain slopes they hadn't anticipated. Only one of the wagons made it over the mountains without breaking. Rogue River and Clamotte Indians, whose fishing and hunting areas were being taken over by settlers, attacked the group. Frustration mounted until the bitter would-be settlers accused the Applegates of deceiving them about the extent of obstacles on the new trail.

While several people, such as Stephen Meek and Samuel Barlow, established supposedly shorter or safer new routes west, they all proved to be about equally hazardous. In the end, up to 20 people died during that first trip along the Applegate Trail, most from starvation and disease. Still, the Applegate Trail gained popularity when gold was discovered in California in 1850, and again a few years later when Southern Oregon had its own gold strikes.

Organizations and Events of Interest

End of the Oregon Trail Interpretive Center, 1726 Washington St., Oregon City 97045, (503) 657-9336. The buildings shaped like covered wagons house two mixed-media theaters and exhibits, a Willamette Trades and Craft Workshop, and events such as the Oregon Trail Pageant.

National Historic Oregon Trail Interpretive Center, P.O. Box 987, Baker City 97814, (541) 523-1843, (800) 523-1235. Located at Flagstaff Hill on Oregon 86, five miles east of Baker City, the center features exhibits offering audio, video, dioramas, and artifacts that recreate the experiences of Oregon Trail emigrants.

Oregon Trail Advisory Committee, 222 NW Davis, #309, Portland 97209, (503) 228-7245.

Oregon Trail Regional Museum, Campbell & Grove, Baker City 97814, (541) 523-9308. Oregon Trail artifacts and history exhibits housed in a 1920 natatorium.

Oregon Trail Days, La Grande, August, (800) 848-9969.

Outdoor Recreation

(*See also* Skiing and Snowboarding; Whitewater kayaking and River Running; Windsurfing)

Oregon's natural beauty, diverse landscape, and thousands of square miles of public lands make it a popular destination for those who seek their recreation outdoors. Whether your preference is a stroll in the woods or hanging by a thin rope from a sheer rock wall thousands of feet in the air, Oregon has plenty of ways for residents and visitors alike to get their kicks.

Biking

Bicycle touring and mountain biking are popular activities in Oregon. In many Oregon cities, bike lanes and bike racks on buses encourage bicycle commuting. In fact, Oregon has a law (ORS 366.514) that requires the state to expend "reasonable" amounts of state highway funds on bikeways. The Oregon Department of Transportation's Bicycle and Pedestrian Program also offers two free cycling maps for the asking (*Oregon Bicycling Guide* and *Oregon Coast Bike Route Map*) and maintains a list of places to go for more detailed information about mountain biking in specific areas.

In Lane County, Eugene is a major cycling center. City buses are outfitted with bike racks to accommodate riders, and numerous cycling events such as organized tours, races, and clinics occur each year. There are also plenty of cycling clubs. The nearby towns of Oakridge and Cottage Grove also attract mountain bikers.

East of the Cascades, Bend is the mountain-biking mecca. Riders can find plenty of great off-road, single-track mountain-biking areas as well as numerous gravel roads. The Deschutes National Forest, the Metolius-Windigo Trail, the many trails around the town of Sisters, and the McKenzie River National Recreation Trail in Willamette National Forest are all popular mountain-biking destinations along the east slope of the Cascades in the vicinity of Bend.

In the Columbia Gorge, Hood River provides access to some fine single-track mountain biking. From Hood River, you can head up to the east side of Mount Hood to Surveyor's Ridge, which has a 17-mile trail that has great views of Mount Hood's snowfields and glaciers. Mount Hood National Forest is another popular mountain-biking destination, but it is so popular that some trails may be closed from time to time to reduce erosion or to lessen user conflicts. Because the national forests contain so many mountain-biking areas, forest ranger stations are great sources of information. Also, parking passes are generally required to park at trailheads in Oregon and can also be obtained at ranger stations (*see* National Forests).

There are numerous bicycle advocacy groups, touring and racing clubs, bicycle tour guides, and special bicycle events such as the annual Cycle Oregon, a seven-day bicycle tour that each year takes some 2,000 cyclists on a late summer tour through a different part of the state. Two thousand cyclists visit several communities with a full complement of services and amenities along the way. The following sampling of organizations should be enough to get any eager cyclist pointed in the right direction.

Organizations and Events of Interest

Beaverton Bicycle Club, 13939 NW Cornell Rd., Portland 97229, (503) 649-4632.

Bicycle Transportation Alliance (BTA), P.O. Box 9072, Portland 97207-9072, (503) 226-0676, info@bta4bikes.org.

Center for Appropriate Transport, 455 W 1st Ave., Eugene 97401, (541) 344-1197, www.efn.org/~cat.

Club Bump, HC 85 Box 148AF, Myrtle Point 97458, (541) 572-2745, mail.coos.or.us/~dstrain.

Corvallis Mountain Bike Club, 5549 SW Redtop Pl., Corvallis 97333, (541) 754-3752.

Greater Eugene Area Riders, P.O. Box 10244, Eugene 97440, (541) 345-3181.

Klamath Freewheelers, P.O. Box 7485, Klamath Falls 97602, (541) 882-3921.

Knobby by Nature, P.O. Box 5254, Grants Pass, 97527, (541) 476-4037.

Newport MTB Club, 322 NE Eads, Newport 97365, (541) 574-0327.

ODOT Bicycle and Pedestrian Program, 210 Transportation Building, Salem 97310, (503) 986-3555.

ODOT Bicycle Safety Program, 555 13th St. NE, Salem 97310, (503) 986-4196, (800) 922-2022.

Oregon Bicycle Racing Association, P.O. Box 16355, Portland 97292, www.obra.org.

Oregon Cycling Magazine, 455 West 1st Ave., Eugene 97401, (541) 686-9885, www.efn.org/~ocycling.

Rose City Wheelmen, 9205 NW Skyline, Portland 97231, (503) 286-6298.

Salem Bicycle Club, P.O. Box 2224, Salem 97308, (503) 588-8613, www.teleport.com/nonprofit/sbc.

The Siskiyou Velo, P.O. Box 974, Ashland 97520, www.mind.net/siskiyou/velo.

Umpqua Velo Club, 735 SE Flint, Roseburg 97470, (541) 672-1043.

Women's Association of Mountainbikers, P.O. Box 1343, Welches 97067-1343, (503) 829-8487.

Camping and Hiking

Come rain or come shine, camping is extremely popular in the Northwest. For those who like to camp next to their vehicle, or even in it, there are hundreds of campgrounds at state parks and national forests and parks (*see* National Forests; National Parks, Monuments, and Recreation Areas; State Parks and Recreation Areas), as well as at many commercial campgrounds. Campsites range from simple, undeveloped sites with no facilities to campgrounds equipped with RV hookups, tables, sheltered cooking areas, and showers. Due to the popularity of camping, many campgrounds require reservations, especially in the summer months (State Park Campsite Reservations and Information, 800-452-5687; National Forest Campsite Reservations, 800-280-CAMP).

Those who seek the path less traveled, providing they have strong backs and legs, can hike and backpack throughout the state's thousands of square miles of wilderness areas (*see* National Forests; Wilderness). There are so many thousands of miles of trails in the state, the hiking and backcountry guidebooks to these areas could fill a small library. In wilderness areas, permits may be required to hike or camp (the permits are free and usually available at the trailhead), and Trail Park permits are required to park at trailheads in many national forests. The permits can be purchased at most ranger stations and outdoor equipment stores.

A network of existing and proposed long-distance trails called the State Trail Plan links many of Oregon's wild areas. The Pacific Crest Trail and routes east of the Cascades are open to both hikers and equestrians. However, all long-distance trails west of the Cascades summit (except the North Umpqua River Trail) are for hikers only. The components of the State Trail Plan include the following:

40-Mile Loop. This Portland trail connects more than 30 parks around Portland. Over the years, the route has expanded to 140 miles, though the original name is still used.

Clackamas Trail. This route, only partially complete, will eventually link the Portland area to the Pacific Crest Trail near Mount Jefferson.

Columbia Gorge Trail. This trail runs through the Columbia Gorge for 25 miles from Sheppards Dell State Park to Park Viento State Park.

Desert Trail. This route, marked by trail markers and rock cairns, crosses Oregon's high desert, canyons, and sage-brush lands. About 150 miles of the trail are completed from the Oregon/Nevada border and Burns.

Eugene to Pacific Crest Trail. This 74-mile route is about 80 percent complete. The completed portion can be hiked from Lowell to the Pacific Crest Trail near Waldo Lake.

Metolius-Windigo Trail. This trail winds for 45 miles through pine forest. It crosses U.S. 20, five miles northwest of Sisters.

New Oregon Trail. This east-west trail runs from the coast at Cape Blanco to Hells Canyon. It connects the Oregon Coast and Desert Trails and follows part of the Pacific Crest Trail.

North Umpqua Trail. This trail system follows the North Umpqua River for 78 miles from its headwaters at Maidu Lake in the Mount Thielsen Wilderness.

Oregon Coast Trail. Like the Pacific Crest Trail, this north-south trail traverses Oregon from Washington State to California. It crosses beaches, headlands, and forest for 360 miles. The trail is about 80 percent complete.

Pacific Crest Trail. The grand-daddy of western trails, this route runs from Canada to Mexico, with 424 miles of it running along the Oregon Cascades. It is one of two National Scenic Trails included in the 1968 National Trail Systems Act authorized by Congress (the other one is the Appalachian Trail).

Rogue River Trail. There are two separate sections of this trail, the 47-mile Lower Rogue River Trail from Grave Creek to Illahe and the 45-mile Upper Rogue River Trail from Prospect to the northwest corner of Crater Lake National Park.

Timberline Trail. This 38-mile trail circumnavigates Mount Hood, passing through stunning alpine meadows.

For camping reservations, trail permits, and more specific information about recreation opportunities on public lands contact **The Nature of the Northwest Information Center,** Suite 177, 800 NE Oregon Street, # 5, Portland 97232, (503) 872-2750.

Climbing

Oregon's rugged mountains and volcanic rocks provide a wealth of challenging climbs. Mount Hood, the state's highest peak, is the second most climbed snow peak in the world; only Japan's Mount Fuji gets more action. The state's best-known outdoor club, the Mazamas, was organized by 193 climbers who convened on the

Descending Middle Sister. Photo by Susan Dupere.

summit in 1894. Despite the number of people who climb the peak, Mount Hood is no walk in the park. It is a technical climb, with glaciers, treacherous loose rock, and unpredictable weather, and it has one of the highest accident rates of all U.S. mountains. There are over a dozen established routes to the summit, of varying difficulty. The most popular (and the easiest) is the south-side route that begins at Silcox Hut; another commonly used route ascends the east face above the Cooper Spur viewpoint.

Mountaineering and rock-climbing areas are rated by difficulty according to a three-part ranking called the Yosemite Decimal System. This system rates a climbing route's overall difficulty in terms of time required to accomplish the climb (expressed in Roman numerals from I = up to two hours to IV = requires a bivouac) to technical difficulty, the athletic skill required (expressed in Arabic numbers from 1 = hiking to 5 = rope and protection required, with level 5 subdivided even further into more defined categories of difficulty), and climbing aids required (expressed alphanumerically from A1 = solid placements to A5 = marginal protection throughout).

Oregon's premier rock-climbing destination is Smith Rock, which has routes up to level IV-5. Located eight miles north of Redmond in Eastern Oregon, Smith Rock has some 1,000 named routes crisscrossing more than three miles of rock face. The Cascade Mountains offer a number of lesser known but no less challenging rock climbs. In Bull of the Woods Wilderness, Nasty Rock and a nearby unnamed pinnacle to the southwest offer technical rock climbs on untested volcanic crags. Mount Washington has several technical climbs, and just 45 miles east of Albany are two dozen spires of "The Menagerie." The Santiam Pinnacle (near U.S. 20) has four routes of varying difficulty. Shepard Tower, about 14 miles north of Camp Sherman near the Metolius River, has four routes with chimneys and ledges. Within close proximity to Portland at the northern edge of the Cascades, the Columbia Gorge has numerous rock-climbing areas, which include 200-foot Rooster Rock, 700-foot Crown Point, and the 100-foot basalt towers known as the Pillars of Hercules.

In Southern Oregon, the Mount Thielsen area, 72 miles east of Roseburg, has a number of challenging climbs, and just a little farther southeast, in the Boulder Creek Wilderness, is a group of difficult volcanic crags, the largest of which is named Eagle Rock. At the far northeastern corner of the state and just south of Enterprise, the Eagle Cap Wilderness offers the 1,800-foot marble face of the Matterhorn, the highest peak in the Wallowas. In the Mill Creek Wilderness, 20 miles northeast of Prineville, a challenging rock called Steins Pillar has several very difficult climbs, from difficulty III-5.6-A3 to IV-5.7-A4.

Organizations of Interest

Mazamas, 909 NW 19th Ave., Portland 97209, (503) 227-2345.

Oregon Mountaineering Association, 131 NW 4th St., No. 258, Corvallis 97330, (541) 754-6245 ext. 158, www.iworld.net/oma.

Hang Gliding

Two areas provide the type of consistent winds favored by hang-gliding enthusiasts. The tall dunes at Oregon Dunes National Recreation Area south of Florence are considered a great area to practice because the area has good west winds and unobstructed landing sites. Another very popular destination for hang gliding is just 25 miles northeast of Lakeview, where west winds and consistent thermals along the 2,000-foot west scarp of Abert Rim provide perfect conditions for long, sustained flights.

PAC-10

PAC-10 is short for the Pacific-10 Conference, an athletics league of 10 western universities, including Oregon's two largest state institutions. The schools that comprise the PAC-10 are:

Arizona State University, Sun Devils
California State University, Golden Bears
Oregon State University, Beavers

Stanford University, Cardinals
University of Arizona, Wildcats
University of California Los Angeles, Bruins
University of Oregon, Ducks
University of Southern California, Trojans
University of Washington, Huskies
Washington State University, Cougars

The PAC-10 is host to the Rose Bowl and sponsors 10 men's sports and 11 women's sports. In addition to football, the conference schools field teams in basketball, baseball, cross-country, golf, gymnastics, rowing, soccer, softball, swimming, tennis, track and field, volleyball, and wrestling. The PAC-10 also belongs to the Mountain Pacific Sports Federation (MPSF) in five other men's sports and two other women's sports.

Pendleton Pendleton is a nice quiet town in northeastern Oregon until mid-September, when the Pendleton Round-Up sends the place into a frenzy of bulls and horses, cowboys with jangling spurs, and cowgirls in fringed buckskin costumes. When the rodeo isn't bringing in visitors, the town subsists happily on the income from exported grain and the area's flour and woolen mills.

The rodeo has been around since 1910, and several other businesses are nearly as old or older. Hamley's has been selling tack, boots, hats, and custom-made saddles since 1883. Before moving into its brick factory at the southeast edge of town, the Pendleton Woolen Mills had been making blankets since the 1870s for the Indian trade. Now the company offers tours, sells products over the Internet, and offers imperfect wool items at discount prices.

History comes in other guises here, and not just at the festive Hall of Fame Museum below the rodeo grounds. The Pendleton Underground Tour lets tourists view the remains of turn-of-the-century bordellos and opium dens. Chinese railroad workers hand-dug these tunnels, which led back to Chinese businesses, living quarters, and jails where many of them were held. It is believed that many chose to live here because of the maltreatment they received in town society.

Two city landmarks are preserved today as bed-and-breakfast inns. In 1917, L. L. Rogers lived with his family in a 6,000-square-foot mansion. His successful ranch paid for imported Chinese silk wallpaper, a formal ballroom, and a porch overlooking a manicured English garden. Right in the middle of wheat country, Parker House, as it's now called, is one of the most elegant places to stay in Oregon. The Swift Station Inn, which harkens back to a time before automobiles and air travel, sat empty for many years until a Pendleton couple restored it.

In July 1998, residents of the neighboring Umatilla Reservation (many of whom participate in the rodeo) opened the landmark $13 million Tamastslikt Cultural Institute on 640 acres. Ironically, the parcel size derives from an 1850s law that gave away 640 acres of land to any white man who would settle in the Oregon Territory. A moving tribute to Indian history, the institute's exhibits describe the Oregon Trail migration from the point of view of the Indians. White settlement led to the decimation of tribes by disease, the seizure of Indian lands, and the institution of the reservation system.

Performing Arts

Several performing arts venues in Oregon rival those of any city in the country. What makes Oregon different, though, is the way the state's personality is reflected in its events. Several prestigious arts festivals and hundreds of smaller ones take place during those precious days in the Northwest when rain and clouds retreat. In summer, Oregonians and visitors want to spend as

much time as possible outdoors before another nine gray months. The often dramatic expanses of sunnier Eastern Oregon lead potential audiences to dislike the transition from a grand landscape to, say, a dark, stuffy playhouse.

Hence the picnic-on-the-grass ambiance of Jacksonville's Britt Festival, where the hillside setting forms a natural amphitheater surrounded by ponderosa pines and madrones. Through the summer, 50,000 people come to see and hear classical, jazz, folk, bluegrass, country, pop, dance, and music performances. A pioneer of what would later become a gold-rush town, Peter Britt was a horticulturalist and photographer —and the first person to photograph nearby Crater Lake. From late June to early September, his estate hums with celebration.

Fifteen miles south in Ashland, the Oregon Shakespeare Festival overlaps with the Britt. Even though it's probably the best-known arts venue in Oregon, things are casual. A visitor might sleep in a restored pioneer home with a clawfoot tub, ride some rapids in the morning, pick berries in the afternoon, then pull on a clean pair of jeans to see *A Midsummer Night's Dream* under the stars.

The nonprofit Oregon Shakespeare Festival (OSF), which regularly plays to 90-percent capacity, has recently enjoyed a kind of spillover boost from the tremendous popularity of Hollywood movies. *Shakespeare in Love* and *Elizabeth* have been major hits, and the big studios don't look like they're going to fall out of love with the Bard anytime soon.

Established in 1935, OSF's annual attendance tops 350,000, and in 1999 it had its best spring season ever. Eleven plays (five Shakespeare and six classic and contemporary) with readings, lectures, workshops, and tours brought in $90 million during the eight-month season, from a budget of $14.6 million. Plays run from mid-February to October on three stages. The outdoor Elizabethan Theater seats 1,200, the Angus Bowmer 600, and the intimate Black Swan 138. A new theater with 300 seats is due to replace the Black Swan in 2000.

Oregon actually has two major music

The Oregon Ballet Theatre performs under the artistic direction of James Canfield. Photo courtesy OBT, J. David Straub.

festivals, not just the outdoor Britt. The Bach Festival, held annually in Eugene, offers more exclusively classical music, though the atmosphere is still casual. This is Eugene, not Portland, after all. Concerts are held in downtown's Hult Center for the Performing Arts, with one hall seating 2,500 and a smaller theater seating 450. Bach now shares the limelight with other choral-orchestral composers, and a variety of music education workshops and cultural programs are offered.

The program includes a performance of Bach's *St. John Passion* and proceeds from there. World audiences hear portions of the festival on National Public Radio, American Public Radio, Canadian Broadcasting Corporation, and Voice of America. Recordings of works by Bach, Mendelssohn, and Schubert are sold in stores.

In Portland, opening-night opera attendees wear everything from slacks and parkas to evening gowns. Portland benefits from its size, with twelvefold the population of the next largest city, Eugene. International casts perform with the opera, ballet, and symphony, and touring Broadway productions make Portland a regular theater stop. Ballet and symphony companies play here, and the Portland International Film Festival draws huge crowds.

Organizations and Events of Interest

Britt Festival (*see* Fairs and Festivals), Jacksonville, (541) 773-6077, (800) 882-7488, brittfest@aol.com, www.mind.net/britt.

Oregon Ballet Theater, 1120 SW 10th Ave., Portland 97205, (503) 222-5538.

Oregon Shakespeare Festival, P.O. Box 158, Ashland 97520, (541) 482-4331, www.orshakes.org.

Oregon Symphony Association, 921 SW Washington St., No. 200, Portland 97205, (503) 228-4294.

Portland Opera and Portland Opera Presents KeyBank Best of Broadway, 1515 SW Morrison, Portland 97205, (503) 241-1407.

Eastern Oregon

Chamber Music Society of Harney County, P.O. Box 324, Burns 97720, (541) 573-2435.

Crossroads Center for the Creative and Performing Arts, 1901 Main St., Baker City 97814, (541) 523-5369.

Grande Ronde Symphony Orchestra, La Grande 97850, (541) 962-3352.

Grande Ronde Youth Orchestra, La Grande 97850, (541) 962-3855.

Oregon East Symphony, P.O. Box 391, Pendleton 97801, (800) 880-NOTE.

Eugene/Corvallis/Salem

Bijou Art Cinemas, 492 E 13th Ave., Eugene 97401, (541) 686-2458.

Hult Center for the Performing Arts, One Eugene Center, Eugene 97401, (541) 682-5000.

Opera Theater Corvallis, P.O. Box 2266, Corvallis 97339, (541) 758-2478.

Pentacle Theater, 324-52nd Ave. NW, P.O. Box 186, Salem 97308, (503) 364-7121.

Oregon Coast

Astor St. Opry Company, 5115 Birch, Astoria 97103, (503) 325-1604.

Bandon Playhouse, P.O. Box 1047, Bandon 97411.

Coquille Performing Arts Council, P.O. Box 53, Coquille 97423, (541) 396-5131.

Florence Performing Arts Association, P.O. Box 3287, Florence 97439, (541) 997-1994.

Jewel Box Players, Elsie Route, Box 1220, Seaside 97138.

Little Theater on the Bay, P.O. Box 404, 2100 Sherman Ave. (U.S. 101 & Washington), North Bend 97459, (541) 756-4336, www.coos.or.us.

Newport Performing Arts Center (NPAC), 777 W Olive St., Newport 97365, (541) 265-9231.

Northwest Performing Arts, P.O. Box 1135, Seaside 97138, (503) 738-5061.

On Broadway Theater, 226 S Broadway, Coos Bay 97420, (541) 269-2501.

Oregon Coast Music Association, P.O. Box 663, 235 Anderson, Coos Bay 97420, (541) 267-0938.

Oregon Coast Performing Arts Society, P.O. Box 546, Cannon Beach 97110, (503) 436-4580.

Waterfront Players Repertory, Pony Village Mall, North Bend 97459, (541) 756-3222.

Portland

Arlene Schnitzer Concert Hall, 1037 SW Broadway, Portland 97232, (503) 274-6564.

Back Door Theater, 4319 SE Hawthorne Blvd., Portland 97215, (503) 872-8825.

Beaverton Dance Center, 12570 SW Farmington Rd., Beaverton 97005, (503) 644-6116.

Broadway Rose Theater Company, 9000 SW Durham Rd., Tigard 97224, (503) 620-5262.

Brody Theater, 1904 NW 27th Ave., Portland 97210, (503) 224-0688.

Carousel Company Theater for Children, 710 NE Holladay, Portland 97232, (503) 238-0012.

Chamber Music Northwest, 522 SW 5th Ave, No. 725, Portland 97204, (503) 223-3202.

Clinton Street Theater, 2522 SE Clinton St., Portland 97202, (503) 238-8899.

ComedySportz Portland, 3308 E Burnside St., Portland 97214, (503) 236-8888.

Dolores Winningstad Theater, 1111 SW

Broadway, Portland 97205, (503) 248-4335.

Eddie May Murder Mysteries, 1414 SW 6th Ave., Portland 97201, (503) 524-4366.

Hollywood Dance, 4419 NE Sandy Blvd., Portland 97213, (503) 249-0534.

The Jefferson Dancers, 5210 N Kerby, Portland 97217, (503) 916-5180.

Lakewood Center for the Arts, 368 S State St., Lake Oswego 97034, (503) 635-3901.

The LaVoie Actor's Workout, 1336 SW Falcon St., Portland 97219, (503) 244-0801.

Lincoln Performance Hall, 1620 SW Park, Portland 97201, (503) 725-3307.

Metro Police Club, 618 SE Alder St., Portland 97214, (503) 690-5563, 228-9125.

Mission Theater and Pub, 1624 NW Glisan St,, Portland 97209, (503) 223-4031.

Moreland Theater, 6712 SE Milwaukie Ave., Portland 97202, (503) 236-5257.

Mount Hood Jazz Festival, 408 SW 2nd Ave., No. 214, Portland 97204, (503) 219-9833.

Mount Hood Theater, 401 E Powell Blvd., Gresham 97030, (503) 665-0604.

Mount Tabor Theater and Pub, 4811 SE Hawthorne Blvd., Portland 97215, (503) 238-1646.

Musical Theater Company, Eastside Performance Center, 531 SE 14th, Portland 97214, (503) 224-5411.

Newmark Theater, Portland Center for the Performing Arts, 1111 SW Broadway, Portland 97205, (503) 796-9293.

Northwest Children's Theater and School, 1819 NW Everett St., Portland 97209, (503) 222-2190.

Northwest Playwrights Guild, Miracle Theater, 525 SE Stark St., Portland 97214, (503) 236-7253.

Northwest Senior Theater, P.O. Box 25264, Portland 97298, (503) 251-4332.

Oregon Children's Theater, 600 SW 10th Ave., No. 543, Portland 97205, (503) 228-9571.

Oregon Repertory Singers, 1925 Pacific St., Portland 97232, (503) 230-0652.

Pacific Festival Ballet, 4620 SW Beaverton-Hillsdale Hwy., Portland 97221, (503) 977-1753.

The Pan Theater, 419 SE 13th Ave., Portland 97214, (503) 736-9736.

Portland Baroque Orchestra, 1425 SW 20th Ave., No. 150, Portland 97201, (503) 222-6000, www.pbo.org.

Portland Revels, P.O. Box 12108, Portland 97212, (503) 224-7411.

Portland Women's Theater Company, 1728 NE 40th Ave., Portland 97212, (503) 226-8139.

PSU Studio Theater, 1620 SW Park Ave., Portland 97201, (503) 725-4612.

Raindog Theater, 8638 N Lombard St., Portland 97203, (503) 735-1946.

Reed College Theater, 3203 SE Woodstock Blvd., Portland 97202, (503) 777-7284.

Roseway Theater, 7229 NE Sandy Blvd., Portland 97213, (503) 287-8119.

St. Johns Theater, 8704 Lombard St., Portland 97203, (503) 286-1768.

Scottish Rite Theater, 1512 SW Morrison St., Portland 97205, (503) 242-1419.

Sinfonia Concertante Orchestra, 1640 SE Holly St., Portland, 97214, (503) 236-1655.

Stage IV Theater, 527 SE Pine St., Portland 97214, (503) 238-9692.

West Side Players, 2321 26th Ave., Forest Grove 97116, (503) 357-8311.

Southern Oregon

Ginger Rogers Theater, 23 S Central Ave., Medford 97501, (541) 779-3000, www.craterian.org.

Medford Jazz Jubilee, PMB 201, 221 North Central, Medford 97501, (541) 770-6972, (800) 599-0039.

Ross Ragland Theater, 731 Main St., Klamath Falls 97601, (541) 884-0651, www.rrtheater.org.

Southern Oregon Repertory Singers, 1700 Homes Ave., Ashland 97520, (541) 488-2307.

Petroglyphs and Pictographs

Oregon, particularly the Columbia Plateau and Southern Oregon, is rich in Native American rock carvings (petroglyphs) and rock paintings (pictographs). The drawings and carvings, which date from more than 3,000 years ago until the late 1800s record the goings-on of daily life as well as religious ritual, featuring images of humans, animals, and geometric symbols. Petroglyphs were made either by pecking at the base rock with a harder stone or by incising the surface. Petroglyphs are most often found on basalt, a hard, dense volcanic stone. The pigments used for making pictographs were made from minerals in the region, for example crushed iron oxides for reds and yellows, certain clays for white pigments, copper oxides for blue-green, and charcoal and manganese oxide for black. The pigments were applied with fingers, brushes, feathers, or twigs. The mineral pigments have great staying power because they have actually stained the rock surface.

Many pictographs are as old as petroglyphs. Extensive Indian rock art sites along the Columbia River near The Dalles were flooded by construction of The Dalles Dam. Those in Southern Oregon fared better. Among them are those at Petroglyph Lake within Hart Mountain National Antelope Refuge, in Picture Rock Pass (named for its historic images) between Silver and Summer Lakes, at the Greaser Petroglyph archaeological site near Adel, and the Abert Lake Petroglyphs near Lakeview.

Physical Geography

Oregon borders the Pacific Ocean. The ocean brings rain and mild temperatures to the entire western region of the state. Two mountain ranges parallel the ocean and run the length of the state. The Coast Range undulates between 2,000 and 3,000 feet above sea level in the northern portion of the state and between 3,000 and 4,000 feet in the southern portion. The Coast Range forces the maritime weather systems off the Pacific aloft, where they cool and drop their abundant moisture along the range's western slopes, producing some of the heaviest rainfalls anywhere in the world.

Haystack Rock is a familiar landmark on the Oregon Coast. Photo by Andrea Jarvela.

The Cascade Mountains parallel the ocean as well and lie about 75 miles east of the Coast Range, except in the extreme southern region, where the Coast Range and the Cascades merge before entering California. Between the Coast Range and the Cascades in the northern portion of the state lies the Willamette Valley (*see* Willamette River and Valley). The Cascades rise from the valley to an average height of 5,000 feet, with some peaks reaching over 10,000 feet. The highest point is Mount Hood, an active Cascade volcano, at 11,235 feet.

East of the Cascades, stretching all the way across the state through Central and much of Southeastern Oregon are high plateaus and basin-and-range formations. The countryside becomes progressively more arid the farther east one travels. Southeastern Oregon is entirely high desert and lonesome grazing country.

In the far northeast corner of the state lie the Blue Mountains (which include the Wallowa Mountains; *see* Mountains), averaging 5,000 to 6,000 feet with peaks up to 9,000 feet. The Blue Mountains extend southwestward to the valleys of the John Day and Deschutes Rivers in the central portion of the state and northeastward into Washington State.

Steens Mountain is a remarkable topographic feature in the southeast region
(Continued on page 146)

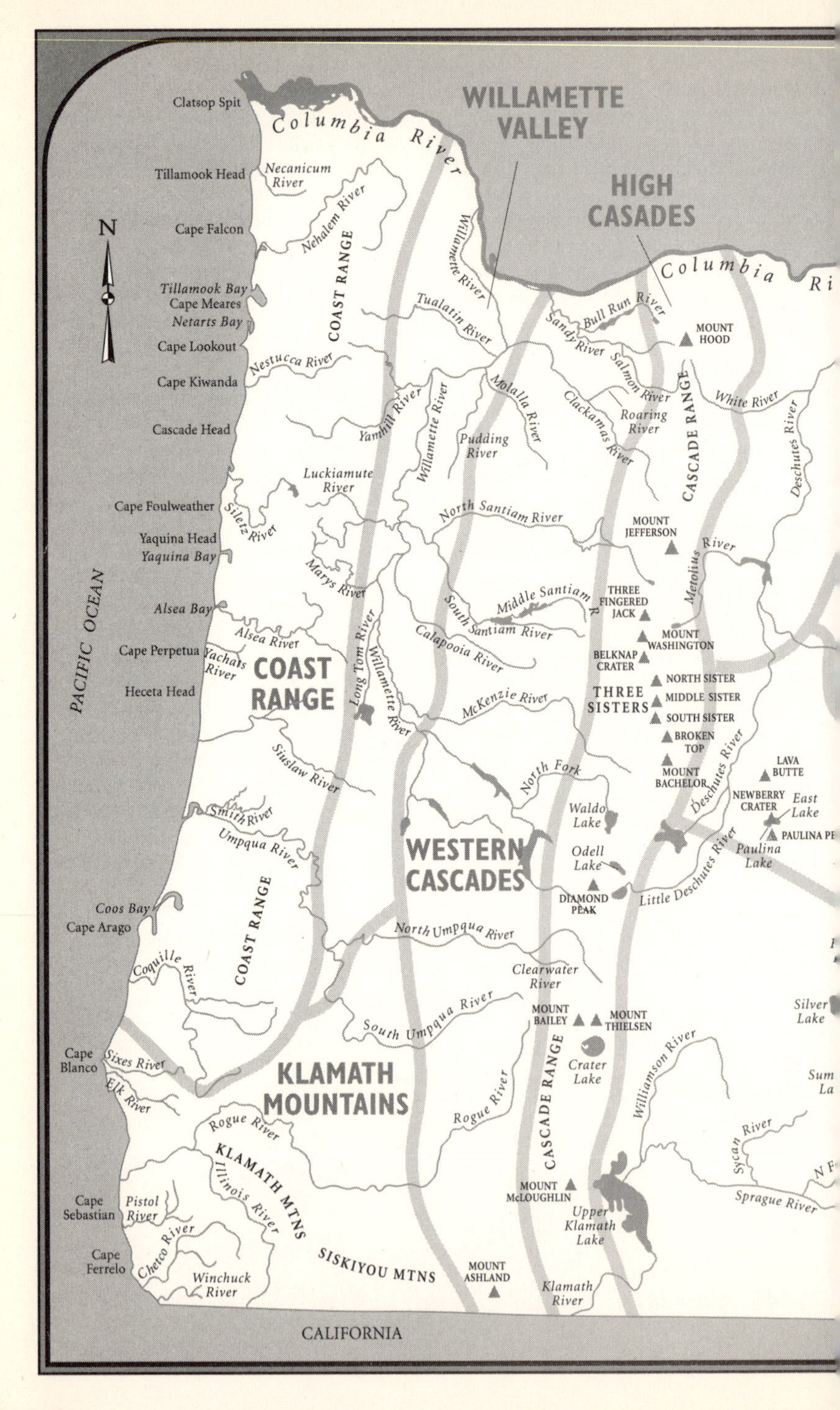

WILLAMETTE VALLEY
HIGH CASADES
Clatsop Spit
Columbia River
Tillamook Head
Necanicum River
Nehalem River
Cape Falcon
N
COAST RANGE
Willamette River
Tillamook Bay
Cape Meares
Netarts Bay
Cape Lookout
Tualatin River
Bull Run River
Sandy River
MOUNT HOOD
Salmon River
Nestucca River
Cape Kiwanda
Yamhill River
Willamette River
Molalla River
Clackamas River
Roaring River
CASCADE RANGE
White River
Cascade Head
Pudding River
Deschutes River
Luckiamute River
Cape Foulweather
Siletz River
North Santiam River
MOUNT JEFFERSON
Yaquina Head
Yaquina Bay
Metolius River
Marys River
PACIFIC OCEAN
Alsea Bay
Middle Santiam R
THREE FINGERED JACK
South Santiam River
MOUNT WASHINGTON
Alsea River
Calapooia River
Cape Perpetua
Yachats River
BELKNAP CRATER
COAST RANGE
Long Tom River
Willamette River
Heceta Head
McKenzie River
THREE SISTERS
NORTH SISTER
MIDDLE SISTER
SOUTH SISTER
BROKEN TOP
MOUNT BACHELOR
Siuslaw River
North Fork
Deschutes River
LAVA BUTTE
NEWBERRY CRATER
East Lake
Waldo Lake
Smith River
Umpqua River
WESTERN CASCADES
Odell Lake
Paulina Lake
Little Deschutes River
DIAMOND PEAK
Coos Bay
Cape Arago
COAST RANGE
North Umpqua River
Coquille River
Clearwater River
South Umpqua River
MOUNT BAILEY
MOUNT THIELSEN
Silver Lake
Cape Blanco
Sixes River
CASCADE RANGE
Crater Lake
KLAMATH MOUNTAINS
Williamson River
Elk River
Rogue River
Rogue River
KLAMATH MTNS
Sycan River
Cape Sebastian
Pistol River
Illinois River
MOUNT McLOUGHLIN
Sprague River
Upper Klamath Lake
Chetco River
Cape Ferrelo
SISKIYOU MTNS
Winchuck River
MOUNT ASHLAND
Klamath River
CALIFORNIA

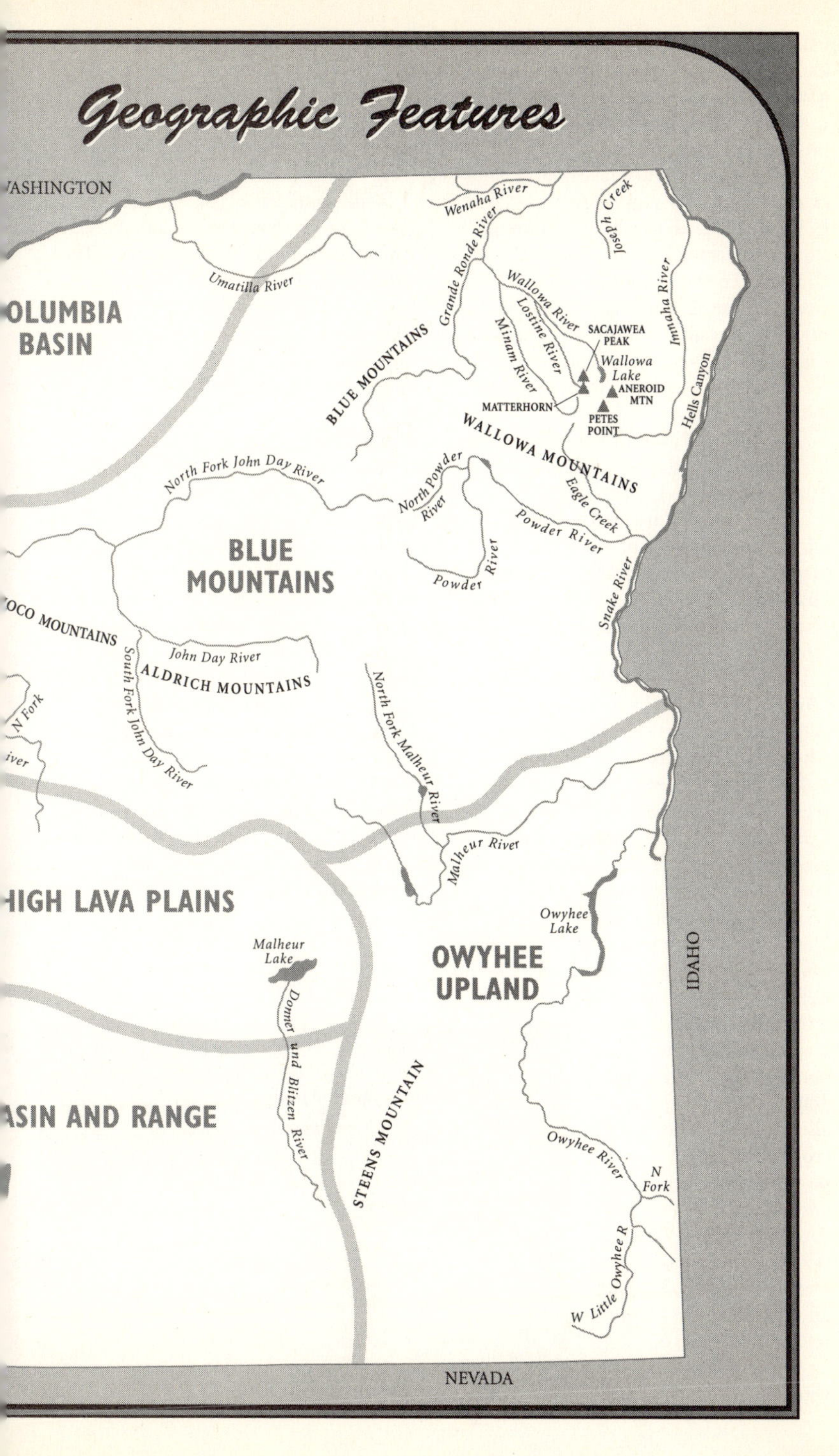
Geographic Features
WASHINGTON
Wenaha River
Joseph Creek
Grande Ronde River
Umatilla River
Wallowa River
Lostine River
Minam River
Imnaha River
SACAJAWEA PEAK
Wallowa Lake
ANEROID MTN
MATTERHORN
PETES POINT
Hells Canyon
COLUMBIA BASIN
BLUE MOUNTAINS
WALLOWA MOUNTAINS
North Fork John Day River
North Powder River
Eagle Creek
Powder River
Powder River
Snake River
BLUE MOUNTAINS
OCHOCO MOUNTAINS
John Day River
ALDRICH MOUNTAINS
South Fork John Day River
N Fork
North Fork Malheur River
Malheur River
HIGH LAVA PLAINS
Owyhee Lake
Malheur Lake
OWYHEE UPLAND
IDAHO
Donner und Blitzen River
STEENS MOUNTAIN
BASIN AND RANGE
Owyhee River
N Fork
W Little Owyhee R
NEVADA

of the state. A classic geological formation known as a graben, Steens Mountain rises gradually from the west to a height of 9,354 feet, then drops off in a dramatic 5,000-foot precipice on its east face.

The Columbia and Snake river systems extend through the region known as the Columbia Plateau, which extends south from Washington into north-central Oregon. The rivers meander through Oregon's ranching and farming country, draining the valleys of many streams that begin high in Oregon's mountains.

Oregon's topography divides the state into six agroclimatic regions:

Coastal and Lower Columbia (Clatsop, Columbia, Coos, Curry, Lincoln, and Tillamook Counties). A maritime climate of moderate temperatures and abundant rainfall produces lush pastures and magnificent forests. Forestry and animal husbandry are major economic activities. Seeds, bulbs, cut flowers, and fruits are also grown.

Columbia Basin (Gilliam, Hood River, Morrow, Sherman, Umatilla, Wasco, and Wheeler Counties). This is the dryland wheat belt, except for the Hood River Valley, which is an important fruit-growing region. Fruit is also grown in Umatilla County; green peas are also grown and processed there. Upper regions of the basin are prime livestock country.

Snake River Basin (Baker, Malheur, Union, and Wallowa Counties). Over five million acres of federal rangeland are found in this high-desert region. Where crops are grown on irrigated land, major crops include wheat, potatoes, barley, oats, and grass seed. Malheur County also produces important crops of sugar beets, onions, peas, tomatoes, berries, sweet corn, and other crops.

South Central Oregon (Crook, Deschutes, Grant, Harney, Jefferson, Klamath, and Lake Counties). This region is the heart of Oregon's livestock industry, with vast grazing ranges.

Southwestern Oregon (Douglas, Jackson, and Josephine Counties). This area is renowned for its Rogue River pear industry. Hay, grain, seed crops, cattle, poultry, and sheep are also grown. Some areas also are used to grow bulbs and hops.

Willamette Valley (Benton, Clackamas, Lane, Linn, Marion, Multnomah, Polk, Washington, and Yamhill Counties). This area is blessed with a mild climate and a long growing season. Fruit and nut farms, truck farming, grape and seed crops are important, as are large poultry and dairy operations and nurseries.

Plants

Oregon's wide variation in climate, terrain, and soil supports an equally wide variety of plant communities—from damp, shady forest to dry, open desert. The Oregon Department of Fish and Wildlife divides the state into 10 distinct biomes based on geological and vegetative patterns: Oregon Coast Range, Klamath Mountains, Western Interior Valleys, West Slope Cascades, East Slope Cascades, Columbia Basin, High Lava Plains, Blue Mountains, Basin and Range, and Owyhee Uplands (*see* map pages 144-45). Within these areas, plant communities include wildflower meadows, thickets of dense underbrush within dense forest, and sparsely vegetated arid rangeland and desert.

Portland's Japanese Garden. Photo by Susan Dupere.

Desert and Rangeland

The shrub-steppe ecosystem of the high desert of southeastern Oregon and the rangelands of the Columbia Plateau are stark contrasts to the dense forested regions. Few trees populate the vast high-desert regions; drought-resistant plants such as sagebrush, greasewood, and bunchgrass prevail. On the rangelands of the Columbia Plateau, shrubs and low grasses predominate. Common plants are sagebrush, rabbit brush, bitterbrush, Idaho fescue, and bluebunch wheatgrass.

Poisonous Plants

There are several dozen types of poisonous plants found in the state that can cause serious illness or severe rash. They include death camas, poison hemlock and water hemlock, mushrooms species, and poison oak and poison ivy.

Trees and Shrubs

Oregon forests contain about 30 different coniferous trees and 37 hardwood species. From the coast to the western slopes of the Cascades, forests abound. The lush western forests are characterized by conifers—spruce, hemlock, fir, pine—and dense undergrowth. The drier eastern Cascade slopes and the Blue Mountains are dominated by ponderosa and lodgepole pine and sparse undergrowth. In river valleys and lowlands, deciduous trees such as alder, ash, maple, and white oak are fairly common. In Eastern Oregon, deciduous species include cottonwood, aspen, and birch.

Among the undergrowth in Oregon's evergreen forests are sword ferns *(Polystichum munitum);* Oregon grape *(Berberis nervosa),* a common evergreen low shrub with hollylike leaves; kinnickinnick *(Arctoaphylos uva-ursi),* another low, berried shrub; red flowering currant *(Ribes sanguineum),* a tall shrub with bright red flowers and black berries; and lichens such as old man's beard *(Usnea* spp.*),* a gray-green lichen that grows on tree bark or branches.

Wildflowers

Wildflowers abound throughout all parts of Oregon, from alpine meadows to river

valleys and rocky cliffs. Members of the lily family, such as Lobb's mariposa tulip *(Calochortus subalpinus),* mission bells *(Fritillaria lanceolata,* also called checker lily or chocolate lily*),* and Oregon fawn lily or trout lily *(Erythronium oregonum)* are found in both dry meadows and forest meadows. Species of paintbrush *(Castilleja* spp.*),* such as common paintbrush *(Castilleja miniata),* grow in dry meadows and rock outcrops. Rocky cliffs and outcrops are also home to penstemons, chickweed monkeyflower, and Oregon stonecrop (*Sedum oregonium),* a common succulent.

Alpine meadows are home to the rough wallflower or prairie rocket *(Erysimum asperum),* beargrass *(Xerophyllum tenax),* another member of the lily family, red mountain heather *(Phyllodoce empetriformis),* elephant's head *(Pedicularis groenlandica),* and coneflowers *(Rudbeckia occidentalis).* Forest wildflowers include orange honeysuckle *(Lonicera ciliosa),* twinflower *(Linnaea borealis),* spring queen *(Synthyris reniformis),* wintergreen *(Pyrola secunda),* western trillium *(Trillium ovatum),* woodland phlox *(Phlox adsurgens),* and lupines (*Lupinus* spp.). In bogs and marshes, irises (*Iris* spp.) and shooting stars *(Dodecatheon jeffreyi)* are common.

Some popular wildflower viewing areas include Lawrence Memorial Grassland Preserve and Tom McCall Preserve in Central Oregon, the Eagle Cap Wilderness and Hells Canyon Dam in northeastern Oregon, and Table Rock in southwestern Oregon.

Organizations and Events of Interest

Oregon Native Plant Society (NPSO), 2584 NW Savier St., Portland 97210-2412, (503) 248-9242, www.NPSOregon.org.

Wildflower Show (April), Box 332, Glide 97443.

Population

The U.S. Census Bureau numbered Oregon's residents at 3,243,000, in *Statistical Abstracts U.S.—1998.* Oregon is the 29th most populous state and among the 10 fastest-growing states, with a 14.1 percent net change in population—that means an additional 401,000 residents—from 1990 to 1997. Population per square mile of land area in the state is 33.8 persons. The state's population change for this time period includes 309,000 births, 197,000 deaths, 49,000 immigrants from foreign countries, and 244,000 residents who moved from elsewhere in the United States. In addition, an estimated 33,000 undocumented immigrants live in the state. The racial makeup of the state includes 58,000 African-Americans; 44,000 American Indians, Eskimos, and Aleuts; and 101,000 Asians and Pacific Islanders. Persons who claim Hispanic origin number 190,000.

Population growth for 1998-99 was projected at 1.5 percent. Most of the recent growth (79 percent) occurred in four urban areas—Salem, Eugene, Portland, and Medford. That reflects a growing imbalance of urban over rural population, as the four urban areas now have 71 percent of the population, and the upper Willamette Valley has 54 percent. While the urban areas were growing, 11 counties either lost population or stayed the same: Benton, Coos, Curry, Josephine, Lake, Malheur, Sherman, Union, Wallowa, Wasco, and Wheeler.

The Urbanization of Oregon

In the 12 months ending in July 1998, 50,500 more people became Oregonians, most of them in the Portland area. Hillsboro was the fastest-growing city, growing at a rate of 11.5 percent to 65,110. The state total included 34,050 newcomers from outside the state and about 16,450 more births than deaths, an overall gain of about 1.6 percent.

Portland

Portland's celebrated aesthetic beauty is, to a great extent, a natural result of its pragmatic location. In 1843, Portland's first settlers noted the accessible boat routes: The Willamette River flowed south into the valley named after it, and the Columbia rolled a hundred miles west to its Pacific Coast mouth. The water was calm enough and deep enough for the new town to become a port.

To the east, Mount Hood rises to 11,235 feet, the tallest point in the state. Also nearby to the north is Mount St. Helens, which erupted on May 18, 1980, producing a trail of ash that nearly circumnavigated the globe and dumping several feet on much of the Northwest.

More than 0.5 million people live in the Portland metropolitan area, far more than the next largest city, Eugene. Residents have a clear commitment to balancing growth and preservation, and city planners seem to understand that most, if not all, of the time. Downtown buildings are kept relatively low; a rapid and clean light-rail system (MAX) extends into the suburbs; a freeway over the Willamette's west-bank riverfront has been replaced by Tom McCall Waterfront Park; and a park is taking shape on the east-bank riverfront.

The city is known for its extensive urban greenspaces, none more beautiful than Northwest Portland's Forest Park, nearly 4,700 acres bordered by densely populated areas, 7.5 miles long and 1.5 miles wide. The mostly second-growth forest grows freely without any of the manicured greenery, playgrounds, or performing arts stages typical in parks. Trails give walkers and joggers opportunity to encounter deer,

Portlandia, *sculpted by Raymond Kaskey, arrived in Portland in October 1985.* From *The Oregon Story: 1850-2000*, written by the staff of *The Oregonian*. Photo by Joel Davis/*The Oregonian*.

coyotes, and warblers, as well as a variety of other wildlife.

Landscaped gardens do have their advantages, though. The Washington Park Rose Garden in Southwest Portland is a horticultural treasure, with 400 varieties of *rosa*. The city's affection for roses started in 1907 with the first Rose Festival, a tradition that's been going strong ever since. Up the hill from the Rose Garden are the serene Japanese gardens; a mile west of those sits the Oregon Zoo, the Vietnam Veterans' Living Memorial, and the 175-acre Hoyt Arboretum, with its impressive collection of native and exotic flora and well-maintained trails.

The downtown core is built cozily around red-brick and purple-tiled Pioneer Courthouse Square, often referred to as "the city's living room," where festivals, concerts, and speakers can be found nearly every summer afternoon and weekend. It is also the site of one of historic preservation's biggest losses, the genteel Portland Hotel. The original Pioneer Courthouse still stands, though today it serves as a U.S. post office. Tri-Met has an office and ticket outlet at the square, and visitor guides and public transportation can be found here.

A few blocks southwest of the square lie the arts-filled South Park Blocks, all 25 of them (though a few managed to turn residential). This elm-lined strip encompasses the Portland Art Museum, the Oregon Historical Society, the Performing Arts Center, and other attractions. Each block has its own sculpture or fountain.

Portland's great respect for public art is evident everywhere. Elaborate fountains include the waterfront Salmon Street Springs, timed to spout the highest in the city's busy summer months. In Old Town, the bronze Skidmore Fountain shows four women lifting a water-filled basin above their heads. Built in 1888 for "men, horses, and dogs," the fountain is an example of the many bronzes around the city featuring historical figures and events.

Old Town Portland, around the Burnside Bridge, bustles with nightlife, brewpubs, coffee bars, galleries, and unusual draws like Darcelle's drag shows and the Church of Elvis. Neighborhood character is intact, with cast-iron facades still on the old brick buildings. The city's popular Saturday Market is held under the Burnside Bridge on Saturdays and Sundays, March through December. Next to Old Town is Portland's Chinatown, designated a National Historic District in 1989, the oldest and largest historic district in Oregon.

One area where gentrification meant a purge of historic elements is ghostly Portland Center, south of SW 3rd and Market, where unremarkable condos and office buildings replaced ethnic neighborhoods in a 1960s "urban renaissance." North of Burnside and west of downtown, Northwest Portland is today an interesting collection of renovated residences and a bustling commercial district in what used to be called Nob Hill. The Pearl District, a triangular-shaped neighborhood closer to downtown, was formerly devoted to commercial use but today is full of apartments, condos, lofts, and galleries converted from warehouse space or built on formerly vacant land close to Union Station and the Greyhound bus terminal. Several historic neighborhoods on the east side of the Willamette also offer great housing, shopping, eating, and access via public transportation.

Typical of Northwest cities, Portland has seen, along with progressively more sophisticated arts and business communities, an influx of talented chefs specializing in the new pan-Asian, or fusion, cuisine. Regional ingredients such as salmon and crab are prepared with Asian touches, such as ginger and lemongrass, noodles and rice. Ever-present coffee bars and microbreweries (the McMenamin brothers have built an empire here) keep people warm on drizzly days in fall, winter, and spring.

Portland businesses benefit from the city's mid-Pacific coast location, between San Francisco and Seattle, Los Angeles and Vancouver. The enormous Oregon Convention Center, across the river from downtown, has 150,000 square feet of open exhibit space and many reception, banquet, and meeting rooms. Such facilities also exist at Montgomery Park (Northwest Portland), the World Trade Center (downtown), and several smaller, historic spaces such as the Pittock Mansion (Northwest Portland) and Portland's White House (Northeast Portland), a bed-and-breakfast with a 1,650-square-foot ballroom. If companies aren't already expanding to Portland, they're being founded here. Nike has stuck by its hometown, and the city has no shortage of Internet start-up companies.

Portland's location makes it a natural jumping-off point for camping, skiing, mountain climbing, hiking, and flyfishing (*see* Fish and Fishing). Just 30 miles east of Portland, the dramatic landscape of the Columbia Gorge includes Multnomah Falls, the second-highest waterfall in the country (*see* Waterfalls). Hood River, 45 minutes west of Portland, is a mecca for boardsailing. Most of Oregon's hundred or so wineries are clustered west and southwest of Portland in the upper Willamette Valley, home of the famous Oregon pinot noirs.

Organizations of Interest

Portland Metropolitan Chamber of Commerce, 221 NW 2nd Ave., Portland 97209, (503) 228-9411.

Portland Oregon Visitors Association, 26 SW Salmon, Portland 97204, (503) 222-2223.

Ports

Oregon has 23 public ports located along the Columbia River and the Pacific Coast. Deep-draft ports promote Oregon's export economy and secure for Oregon an important role as a Pacific Rim trading partner. Shallow-draft ports extending farther up rivers are important for hauling bulk cargoes, such as agricultural commodities, for fishing, and for recreation. Port districts are public agencies run by elected or appointed commissioners. In addition to waterborne trade, port districts operate marinas, airports, railroads, and industrial sites.

The major ports in the state for waterborne commerce are Astoria at the mouth of the Columbia River, Coos Bay on the Pacific Coast, and the Port of Portland on the Columbia River.

Astoria is located 12 miles inland from the mouth of the Columbia. Commercial cargoes include forest products and noncontainerized cargoes. The port also provides berths and pier space for dockside repair of large vessels. Recreational activities are increasingly important for the port. The battleship *Missouri* attracted 57,000 visitors in 1998. A total of 125,000 visitors used the port that year for recreational activities. In addition, large oceangoing cruise ships called at Astoria six times in 1998.

Coos Bay is the largest natural harbor between San Francisco and Puget Sound. It is Oregon's second-busiest port. More than 4.5 million tons of forest products and other cargoes move through the port each year. An average of 250 deep-draft vessels and 120 cargo barges call at the port each year.

Newport on the central coast is a fishing and general cargo port.

Portland, located about a hundred river miles inland from the Pacific Ocean on a 40-foot-deep navigation channel, provides competitive cargo and passenger access to regional, national, and international markets. It is the largest wheat-exporting center in the nation, the second-largest grain-exporting center, and ninth in total tonnage (10.7 million short tons of cargo handled in 1997). The Port of Portland is the linchpin of the Columbia-Snake Rivers system, which extends another 374 miles from Portland all the way to Lewiston, Idaho. Portland handles agricultural commodities, minerals, automobiles, containerized (bulk) cargoes, and break-bulk (noncontainerized, nonbulk) cargoes. The following volumes were handled in 1999:

The shipyard on Swan Island, Willamette River.
From *Portland from the Air* by Sallie Tisdale (essay) and Russ Heinl (photos).

Port Activity

Containers	293,262 containers (15th-largest container port in U.S.)
Automobiles	308,813 autos (5th-largest auto port in U.S.)
Grain	3.6 million short tons (2nd-largest grain port in U.S.)
Minerals	3.9 million short tons
Breakbulk Cargo	752,914 short tons

Source: Port of Portland

About 60,000 workers in Portland depend directly on the port for their employment; that means about one in eight jobs in the Portland area depend on world trade that is influenced by the marine port. Marine-related activities produced more than $440 million in total income in 1997 and generated more than $700 million in revenues for regional businesses. The total value of waterborne trade (imports and exports) is about $9.5 billion.

Oregon Ports

Alsea, Port of, P.O. Box 1060, Waldport 97394, (541) 563-3872.

Arlington, Port of, P.O. Box 279, Arlington 97812, (541) 454-2868.

Astoria, Port of, 1 Portway St., Astoria 97103, (503) 325-4521.

Bandon, Port of, P.O. Box 206, Bandon 97411, (541) 347-3206.

Brookings Harbor, Port of, P.O. Box 848, Brookings 97415, (541) 469-2218.

Cascade Locks, Port of, P.O. Box 307, Cascade Locks 97014, (541) 374-8619.

Coos Bay, Oregon International Port of,

As the Crow Flies

Distances Between Portland, Oregon, and . . .

Buenos Aires, Argentina, 6,802 miles (10,946 km, 5,911 nautical miles)

Cairo, Egypt, 6,982 miles (11,236 km, 6,067 nautical miles)

Cape Town, South Africa, 10,240 miles (16,480 km, 8,899 nautical miles)

Havana, Cuba, 2,730 miles (4,393 km, 2,372 nautical miles)

Hong Kong, 6,561 miles (10,559 km, 5,702 nautical miles)

Honolulu, Hawaii, 2,594 miles (4,174 km, 2,254 nautical miles)

Jakarta, Indonesia, 8,427 miles (13,562 km, 7,323 nautical miles)

London, England, 4,927 miles (7,929 km, 4,281 nautical miles)

Los Angeles, California, 820 miles (1,319 km, 712 nautical miles)

New York, New York, 2,449 miles (3,941 km, 2,128 nautical miles)

Sydney, Australia, 7,659 miles (12,326 km, 6,656 nautical miles)

Tokyo, Japan, 4,853 miles (7,810 km, 4,217 nautical miles) ✶

P.O. Box 1215, Coos Bay 97420, (541) 267-7678.

Coquille River, Port of, P.O. Box 640, Myrtle Point 97458, (503) 378-1018.

Garibaldi, Port of, P.O. Box 10, Garibaldi 97118, (503) 322-3292.

Gold Beach, Port of, P.O. Box 1126, Gold Beach 97444, (541) 247-6269.

Hood River, Port of, P.O. Box 239, Hood River 97031, (541) 386-1645.

Morrow, Port of, P.O. Box 200, Boardman 97818, (541) 481-7678.

Nehalem, Port of, P.O. Box 238, Wheeler 97147, (541) 368-7212.

Newport, Port of, 600 SE Bay Blvd., Newport 97364, (503) 265-7758.

Portland, Port of, P.O. Box 3529, Portland 97208, (503) 231-5000.

Port Orford, Port of, P.O. Box 490, Port Orford 97465, (541) 332-7121.

St. Helens, Port of, P.O. Box 598, St. Helens 97051, (503) 397-2888.

Siuslaw, Port of, P.O. Box 1220, Florence 97439, (541) 997-3426.

The Dalles, Port of, 3636 Klindt Dr., The Dalles 97058, (541) 298-4148.

Tillamook Bay, Port of, 4000 Blimp Blvd., Tillamook 97141, (503) 842-2413.

Toledo, Port of, 625 NW Bay Boulevard, Toledo 97391, (541) 336-5207.

Umatilla, Port of, P.O. Box 879, Umatilla 97882, (541) 922-3224.

Umpqua, Port of, P.O. Box 388, Reedsport 97467, (541) 271-2232.

Organizations of Interest

Oregon Ports Association, 1288 Court St NE, Salem 97301, (503) 585-1250, fax: (503) 364-9919.

Prisons

Oregon houses nearly 8,000 offenders in 13 state prisons. Some inmates are housed in out-of-state rental beds to prevent overcrowding. Due to a forecast that predicts the prison population will more than double by 2006, the state has embarked on an ambitious program to expand several existing prisons and construct up to seven new ones by the year 2005.

Community-corrections programs are responsible for supervision of over 28,000 offenders in the community who are on probation, parole, or post-prison supervision after completion of a prison sentence. Oregon counties manage their own offenders who are subject to jail, parole, post-prison supervision, and/or probation. Oregon has one of the lowest recidivism rates in the nation: More than two-thirds of its former offenders remain out of prison for more than three years.

The death penalty in Oregon has become law, then been repealed several times. Voters twice repealed capital punishment, and the Oregon Supreme Court struck down one death penalty law. In the state's history, 59 people have been put to death, first by hanging, later by gas, and now by lethal injection. Since 1904,

115 people were sentenced to death in Oregon, and 59 of them were executed, the most recent in 1996. Their ages ranged from 17 to 67. There are currently 23 inmates on death row.

Prisons

Columbia River Correctional Institution, 9111 NE Sunderland Ave., Portland 97211-1708, (503) 280-6646.

Eastern Oregon Correctional Institution, 2500 Westgate, Pendleton 97801-9699, (541) 276-0700.

Mill Creek Correctional Facility, 5465

Inmate Population by Status as of July 1, 1997

	Probation		Prison		Parole	
Sex	Count	Percent	Count	Percent	Count	Percent
Women	4,467	23.8	425	5.5	1,210	11.1
Men	14,284	76.2	7,527	94.5	9,737	88.9
Total	18,751	100.0	7,952	100.0	10,947	100.0
Race						
Asian	170	0.9	75	1.0	93	0.8
Black	1,063	5.7	961	12.5	1,357	12.4
Hispanic	1,108	5.9	813	10.6	991	9.1
Native American	213	1.1	163	2.1	186	1.7
White	16,197	86.4	5,670	73.8	8,326	76.1
Age						
30 & under	8,936	47.7	3,083	40.1	4,043	36.9
31-45	8,028	42.8	3,463	45.1	5,607	51.2
Over 45	1,785	9.5	1,136	14.8	1,297	11.8
Crime Type						
Person	3,336	17.8	5,664	74.4	3,783	38.6
Property	5,843	31.2	971	12.8	2,978	30.4
Statute	9,572	51.0	979	12.9	3,029	30.9
Offense Group						
Assault	1,014	5.4	756	9.9	838	8.6
Homicide	71	0.4	1,272	16.7	292	3.0
Rape	261	1.4	896	11.8	427	4.4
Kidnapping	37	0.2	187	2.5	80	0.8
Robbery	321	1.7	988	13.0	893	9.1
Sodomy	196	1.0	730	9.6	323	3.3
Sex abuse	737	3.9	525	6.9	540	5.5
Arson	76	0.4	83	1.1	62	0.6
Burglary	1,457	7.8	626	8.2	1,418	14.5
Forgery	465	2.5	34	0.4	216	2.2
Theft	2,380	12.7	174	2.3	749	7.7
Vehicle Theft	853	4.5	125	1.6	524	5.4
Driving	1,564	8.3	81	1.1	558	5.7
Drugs	7,305	39.0	727	9.5	2,194	22.4
Escape	30	0.2	28	0.4	51	0.5
Other	1,984	10.6	382	5.0	625	6.4

Source: Oregon Department of Corrections

Turner Rd., Salem 97301-9400.

Oregon Corrections Intake Center, 2206-B Kaen Rd., Oregon City 97045-4090, (503) 655-8420.

Oregon State Correctional Institution, 3405 Deer Park Dr. SE, Salem 97310-9385, (503) 373-0101.

Oregon State Penitentiary, 2605 State St., Salem 97310-0505, (503) 378-2453.

Oregon Women's Correctional Center, 2809 State St., Salem 97310-0500, (503) 378-2441.

Powder River Correctional Facility, 3600 13th St., Baker City 97814-1346, (541) 523-6680.

Santiam Correctional Institution, 4005 Aumsville Hwy. SE, Salem 97301-9112, (503) 378-8235.

Shutter Creek Correctional Institution, 2000 Shutters Landing Rd., North Bend 97459-0303, (541) 756-6666.

Snake River Correctional Institution, 777 Stanton Blvd., Ontario 97914-0595, (541) 881-5000.

South Fork Forest Camp, 48300 Wilson River Hwy., Tillamook 97141, (503) 842-2811.

Two Rivers Correctional Institution, 82911 Beach Access Rd., P.O. Box 1470, Umatilla 97882, (541) 922-2001.

Radio and Television Stations

Oregon has a full range of radio and television stations—all types of music, talk, news, and specialized programs are represented.

Radio Stations

City	Call Letters	Channel	Affiliation
Albany	KEED	1600 AM	Christian
Albany	KGAL	1580 AM	News, Talk
Albany	KHPE	107.9 FM	Contemporary Christian
Albany	KRKT	99.9 FM	Country
Albany	KRKT	990 AM	Classic Country
Albany	KSHO	920 AM	Adult Standards
Ashland	KSMF	89.1 FM	National Public Radio

Radio Stations *(continued)*

City	Call Letters	Channel	Affiliation
Ashland	KSOR	90.1 FM	National Public Radio
Ashland	KSRG	88.3 FM	National Public Radio
Astoria	KAST	92.9 FM	Adult Contemporary
Astoria	KAST	1370 AM	News, Talk
Astoria	KCYS	98.1 FM	Hot Country
Astoria	KKEE	94.3 FM	Oldies
Astoria	KMUN	91.9 FM	National Public Radio
Astoria	KVAS	1230 AM	Country
Bend	KBND	1110 FM	News, Talk
Bend	KICE	100.7 FM	Progressive Country
Bend	KLRR	107.5 FM	Adult Contemporary, AAA
Bend	KNLR	97.5 FM	Contemporary Christian
Bend	KOAB	91.3 FM	National Public Radio
Bend	KQAK	105.7 FM	Oldies
Bend	KTWS	98.3 FM	Classic Rock
Brookings	KURY	95.3 FM	Variety
Brookings	KURY	910 AM	News, Talk
Burns	KQHC	92.7 FM	Goodtime Oldies
Burns	KZZR	1230 AM	Country
Central Point	KOPE	103.5 FM	News, Talk
Coos Bay	KACW	107.3 FM	Hot Adult Contemporary
Coos Bay	KBBR	1340 AM	News, Talk
Coos Bay	KDCQ	93.5 FM	Coos Bay
Coos Bay	KHSN	230 AM	Adult Standards
Coos Bay	KOOS	94.9 FM	Country
Coos Bay	KSBA	88.5 FM	National Public Radio

Radio Stations *(continued)*

City	Call Letters	Channel	Affiliation
Coos Bay	KYSG	106.5 FM	Positive Radio
Coos Bay	KYTT	98.7 FM	Contemporary Christian
Coquille	KSHR	97.3 FM	Hot Country
Coquille	KWRO	630 AM	News, Talk
Corvallis	KBVR	88.7 FM	Oregon State University
Corvallis	KEJO	1240 AM	Adult Pop Standards
Corvallis	KFLY	101.5 FM	Adult Contemporary
Corvallis	KOAC	550 AM	National Public Radio
Cottage Grove	KNND	1400 AM	Country Coast to Coast
Dallas	KWIP	880 AM	Hispanic Music
Enterprise	KWVR	92.1 FM	Country
Enterprise	KWVR	1340 AM	News, Talk, Sports
Eugene	KDUK	104.7 FM	Contemporary Hits
Eugene	KEHK	102.3 FM	All Rock 'n' All Hits
Eugene	KKNU	93.1 FM	Contemporary Country
Eugene	KKNX	840 AM	Oldies
Eugene	KKTT	97.9 FM	Contemporary Country
Eugene	KKXO	1450 FM	Adult Standards
Eugene	KLCC	89.7 FM	National Public Radio
Eugene	KMGE	94.5 FM	Adult Contemporary
Eugene	KPNW	1120 AM	News, Talk, Sports
Eugene	KUGN	590 AM	News, Talk
Eugene	KZEL	96.1 FM	Classic Rock
Eugene	KNRQ	1320 AM, 95.3 FM	Alternative
Florence	KCTS	1250 AM, 106.9 FM	Soft AC, Country
Gold Beach	KGBR	92.7 FM	Adult Contemporary, Country
Grants Pass	KAGI	930 AM	National Public Radio
Grants Pass	KAJO	1270 AM	News, Adult MOR
Grants Pass	KLDR	98.3 FM	Adult Contemporary, Current

Radio Stations *(continued)*

City	Call Letters	Channel	Affiliation
Gresham	KMHD	89.1 FM	National Public Radio
Gresham	KMUZ	1230 AM	Spanish
Hermiston	KOHU	1360 AM	Country
Hermiston	KQFM	99.3 FM	Oldies
Hillsboro	KUIK	1360 AM	Talk, Sports
Hood River	KCGB	105.5 FM	Hot Adult Contemporary
Hood River	KIHR	1340 AM	Country, Talk
John Day	KJDY	1400 AM, 94.5 FM	Country
Klamath Falls	KFLS	96.5 FM	Country
Klamath Falls	KFLS	1450 AM	Oldies
Klamath Falls	KKRB	106.9 FM	Adult Contemporary
Klamath Falls	KSKF	90.9 FM	National Public Radio
La Grande	KLBM	1450 FM	La Grande
La Grande	KWRL	99.9 FM	Adult Contemporary
Lakeview	KQIK	93.5 FM	Country
Lakeview	KQIK 1	230 AM	Country, Oldies
Lebanon	KXPC	103.7	FM Country
Lincoln City	KBCH	1400 FM	Nostalgic
McMinnville	KLYC	1260 AM	Adult Contemporary, Oldies
Medford	KAKT	105.1 FM	Country
Medford	KBOY	95.7 FM	Classic Rock
Medford	KCNA	102.7 FM	Medford
Medford	KDOV	91.7 FM	News, Talk—Christian
Medford	KKJJ	107.5 FM	Medford
Medford	KTMT	93.7 FM	Contemporary Hits
Medford	KTMT	880 AM	Sports
Milton-Freewater	KTEL	1490 AM	Classic Country
Myrtle Point	KTBR	94.1 FM	Talk, Entertainment
Newport	KCRF	96.7 FM & 98.3 FM	Oldies
Newport	KLCO	90.5 FM	National Public Radio
Newport	KNPT	1310 AM	News, Talk
Newport	KSND	95.1 FM	Adult Contemporary
Pendleton	KRBM	90.9 FM	National Public Radio

(continued on next page)

Radio Stations *(continued)*

City	Call Letters	Channel	Affiliation
Pendleton	KTIX	1240 AM	News, Talk
Pendleton	KUMA	107.7 FM	Adult Contemporary
Pendleton	KUMA	1290 AM	Adult Standards
Pendleton	KWHT	103.5 FM	Country
Portland	KBBT	107.5 FM	Alternative Rock
Portland	KBNP	1410 AM	Business, News, Talk
Portland	KBPS	1450 AM	National Public Radio
Portland	KEWS	620 AM	Talk
Portland	KEX	1190 AM	Full Service, Adult Contemporary
Portland	KFXX	910 AM	Sports Talk
Portland	KGON	92.3 FM	Classic Rock
Portland	KKCW	103.3 FM	Adult Contemporary
Portland	KKJZ	106.7 FM	NAC
Portland	KKRH	105.1 FM	Hot Adult Contemporary
Portland	KKRZ	100.3 FM	Contemporary Hits
Portland	KKSL	1290 AM	Portland
Portland	KKSN	97.1 FM	Oldies
Portland	KKSN	1520 AM	Adult Standards
Portland	KNRK	94.7 FM	Alternative Rock
Portland	KOPB	91.5 FM	National Public Radio
Portland	KOTK	1080 AM	Talk
Portland	KPAM	860 AM	Christian Hit Radio
Portland	KUFO	101.1 FM	Active Rock
Portland	KUPL	98.5 FM	Contemporary Country
Portland	KUPL	970 AM	Straight Country
Portland	KWJJ	99.5 FM	Contemporary Country
Portland	KXL	95.5 FM	Adult Contemporary
Portland	KXL	750 AM	News, Talk
Portland	KXYQ	1010 AM	Talk
Prineville	KIJK	95.1 FM	Hot Country
Prineville	KRCO	690 AM	Country
Prineville	KWEG	96.5 FM	Adult Contemporary
Reedsport	KLLU	1030 AM	Modern, Classic Country
Reedsport	KRBZ	99.5 FM	70s
Rogue River	KRRM	94.7 FM	Classical Country

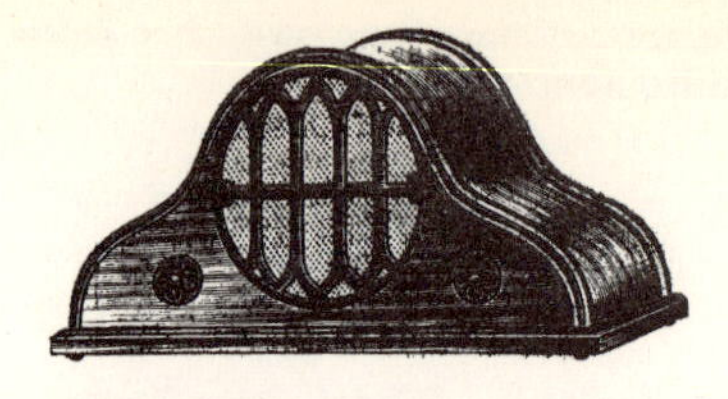

Radio Stations *(continued)*

City	Call Letters	Channel	Affiliation
Roseburg	KKMX	104.3 FM	Adult Contemporary
Roseburg	KQEN	1240 AM	Adult Hits, Sports, Talk
Roseburg	KRNR	1490 AM	Country
Roseburg	KRSB	103.1 FM	Contemporary Country
Roseburg	KSRS	91.5 FM	National Public Radio
Roseburg	KTBR	950 AM	Talk, Entertainment
Salem	KBZY	1490 AM	Adult Contemporary
Salem	KCCS	1220 AM	Christian Worship Music
Springfield	KORE	1050 AM	Christian and Talk
St. Helens	KOHI	1600 AM	Country, Talk
Sweet Home	KFIR	720 AM	Modern, Classic Country
The Dalles	KACI	1300 AM, 97.7 FM	Good Times Oldies
The Dalles	KMCQ	104.5 FM	Adult Contemporary,
The Dalles	KODL	1440 AM	Country
Tillamook	KMBD	1590 AM	News, Talk
Tillamook	KTIL	104.1 FM	Adult Contemporary
Waldport	KORC	820 AM	Adult Standards
Woodburn	KCKX	1460 AM	Real Country
Woodburn	KWBY	940 AM	Spanish

Television Stations

City	Channel	Call Letters	Affiliation
Bend	21	KTVZ	NBC
Bend	39	KFXO-LP	Fox
Brookings	49	KBSC	Warner Brothers
Coos Bay	11	KCBY	CBS
Coos Bay	23	KMTZ	NBC
Coos Bay	49	K49DM	PAX

Television Stations *(continued)*

City	Channel	Call Letters	Affiliation
Corvallis	7	KOAC	PBS
Eugene	9	KEZI	ABC
Eugene	13	KVAL	CBS
Eugene	16	KMTR	NBC
Eugene	25	KEVU	UPN
Eugene	28	KEPB	PBS
Eugene	34	KLSR	Fox
Eugene	41	K41DF	Spanish
Eugene	53	KAMK-LP	PAX
Klamath Falls	2	KOTI	NBC
Klamath Falls	22	KFTS	PBS
Klamath Falls	31	KDKF	KDKF
La Grande	13	KTVR	PBS
Medford	5	KOBI	NBC
Medford	8	KSYS	PBS
Medford	10	KTVL	CBS
Medford	12	KDRV	ABC
Medford	26	KMVU	Fox
Pendleton	11	KFFX	Fox
Portland	2	KATU	ABC
Portland	4	KMST	A1
Portland	6	KOIN	CBS
Portland	8	KGW	NBC
Portland	10	KOPB	PBS
Portland	12	KPTV	UPN
Portland	24	KNMT	Independent (TBN-religious)
Portland	32	KWBP	Warner Bros.
Portland	49	KPDX	Fox
Portland	54	KPXG	PAX
Portland	56	K56EI	Spanish
Portland	58	K58CO	Worship-religious
Portland	62	K62DV	HSN—shopping
Reedville	4	KENY	A1
Roseburg	4	KPIC	CBS
Roseburg	36	KTVC	PAX
Roseburg	46	KMTX	NBC
Salem	22	KPXG	PAX
Salem	32	KWPB	Warner Brothers
Salem	61	K61CC	Worship-religious
The Dalles	14	KRHP	Worship-religious

Organizations of Interest

Oregon Association of Broadcasters, P.O. Box 449, 111 W 7th St., Eugene 97440, (541) 343-2101.

Oregon Cable Telecommunications Association, 960 Liberty St. SE, No. 200, Salem 97302, (503) 362-8838.

Oregon Public Broadcasting, 7140 SW Macadam, Portland 97219, (503) 293-1904, www.opb.org.

Railroads

(*SEE ALSO* TRANSPORTATION) At present, 21 railroads operate 2,600 route miles in Oregon. In 1996, rail freight exceeded 55 million tons. Farm products were the single largest commodity group shipped by rail, exceeding 5 million tons annually. Lumber and wood products were the next largest commodity to move by rail. Amtrak intercity passenger service hit peak ridership of 488,000 passengers in 1997. The passenger line from Eugene to Portland is part of a federally designated Pacific Northwest high-speed rail corridor that extends to Vancouver, Canada. Also, intercity trains travel south to San Diego, California, and east to Chicago via Seattle and Spokane.

In addition to the passenger and freight services on the main lines, railroad buffs can visit over a dozen excursion railways and railroad museums in Oregon.

Chinese House Railroad Museum, 20 S Bonanza, Echo 97826.

Crooked River Railroad Co., P.O. Box 387, Redmond 97756, (541) 548-8630. This is an 1800s western-theme dinner train, located 3 miles north of Bend. The operators stage train robberies and murder mysteries. Reservations needed.

Depot Park and DeWitt Museum, Bridge and Main Sts., Prairie City 97869,

Train of the Future

A new generation of speedy, tilting Talgo-brand trains was inaugurated by Amtrak in 1998 in the Cascadia Corridor, extending 466 miles from Vancouver, British Columbia, to Eugene. The Spanish-developed rail cars feature coach and "business class" seating, large windows, movies and plug-in music, outlets for laptop computers, and information from satellites about current locations and estimated arrival times.

These new trains represent a milestone in passenger rail's recovery in the Pacific Northwest. Trains in the Cascadia Corridor are drawing more riders every year as Amtrak and state governments invest in better equipment, faster travel times, and improved service. This year more than 550,000 people will ride trains or Amtrak buses in the corridor, including about 100,000 from Portland to Eugene, more than double the passenger count of five years ago.

(541) 820-3598. This historic depot museum was once the western terminus of the Sumpter Valley Railroad.

Depot Rail Museum, 473 E Historic Columbia River Hwy., Troutdale 97060, (503) 667-8268.

Mount Hood Scenic Railroad, 110 Railroad Ave., Hood River 97031, (503) 386-3556. This excursion railroad links the Columbia River Gorge with the foothills of snowy Mount Hood. For rail buffs, the Mount Hood Railroad offers one of the few rail switchbacks in the United States. A variety of excursions are run over 44 miles of tracks. Beginning in mid-April, excursion trains pass through the blossom-filled orchard of Hood River apple country. Summer scenery is spectacular, as are fall color excursions. Trains run periodically until December.

Northwest Rail Museum, P.O. Box 19342, Portland 97280, (503) 244-4449.

Oregon Electric Railway Historical Society, Oregon Electric Railway Museum, P.O. Box 702, Forest Grove, OR 97116.

Oregon Electric Railway Museum, P.O. Box 308, Lake Oswego 97034, (503) 222-2226. This trolley museum is part of the Western Antique Powerland Museum in Brooks, Oregon, 25 miles west of exit 263 on I-5 (about 10 miles north of Salem).

Over the Hill Live Steamers, 36951 South Chiloquin Rd., Chiloquin 97624, (541) 783-2670. This is a scale-sized live steam railroad operating on 13,000 feet of 7.5-inch-gauge track. Rides are given on Sundays from 11:00 A.M. to 3:00 P.M., from Memorial Day through October.

Railroad Park, Table Rock Rd. and Berrydale Ave, Medford 97501. The city of Medford exists today because of the railroad that reached the Rogue Valley in the 1800s. Railroad Park recalls the significance and romance of the train. Rides are available on the second and fourth Sundays from 11:00 A.M. to 3:00 P.M.

SamTrak-East Portland Traction Company, P.O. Box 22548, Portland 97269, (503) 653-2380. Diesel-electric excursions.

Sumpter Valley Railway Company, P.O. Box 389, Baker City 97814, (541) 894-2268. The Sumpter Valley Railway is a 3-foot, narrow-gauge steam railroad that operates summer weekends and holidays on a restored, scenic section of track between McEwen and Sumpter in Northeast Oregon's Blue Mountain region.

Sunset Station Lodge, P.O. Box 109, Rockaway Beach 97136, (503) 355-2000. This is an inn with a railroad theme. The central building is a historic railroad depot. Décor in rooms includes historic train-related art. One block from the sea.

Train Mountain Railroad Museum, 36941 S Chiloquin Rd., Chiloquin 97624-9728, (541) 783-3030. 1/8"-scale railroad.

Washington Park and Oregon Zoo Railway, 4001 SW Canyon Rd., Portland 97221, (503) 226-1561. The 30-inch-gauge steam railroad circumnavigates the zoological park between Oregon Museum of Science and Industry, Oaks Amusement Park, and Sellwood. The one-hour, 8-mile scenic ride passes along the Willamette

River and through Oaks Bottom Wildlife Refuge.

Willamette Shore Trolley, P.O. Box 308, Lake Oswego 97034, (503) 222-2226. Runs from 311 State St. in downtown Lake Oswego to River Place in downtown Portland and offers beautiful views of the Willamette River, a 1,400-foot tunnel, and a 686-foot trestle.

Regional Governments

Regional governments are multijurisdictional associations of local governments working together on issues such as solid-waste management and land-use planning that cross local and even state jurisdictional boundaries. One of the largest, Metro, covers approximately 460 square miles and 24 cities, including Portland, and is the nation's only elected regional government and the only one organized under a home-rule charter. The following are regional government entities in Oregon:

Central Oregon Intergovernmental Council, 2363 SW Glacier Pl., Redmond 97756; (541) 548-8163.

Idaho-Oregon Planning and Development Assn., Inc. and Community Development Corporation (CDC), 10624 W Executive Dr., Boise, ID 83713, (208) 322-7033.

Lane Council of Governments, 125 E 8th Ave., Eugene 97401, (541) 682-4283.

Metro, 600 NE Grand Ave., Portland 97232-2736, (503) 797-1700, www.multnomah.lib.or.us/metro.

Mid-Columbia Council of Governments, 1113 Kelly Ave., The Dalles 97058, (541) 298-4101.

Mid-Willamette Valley Council of Governments, 105 High St. SE, Salem 97301, (503) 588-6177.

North Coast Senior Services, P.O. Box 698, Wheeler 97147, (503) 368-4200.

Oregon Cascades West Council of Governments, P.O. Box 685, Albany 97321, (541) 967-8720.

Rogue Valley Council of Governments, P.O. Box 3275, Central Point 97502, (541) 664-6674.

Umpqua Regional Council of Governments, Douglas County Courthouse, 1036 SE Douglas Ave., #8, Roseburg 97470, (541) 440-4231.

Rivers

(*See also* Columbia River and Columbia River Gorge; Hells Canyon and the Snake River; Waterfalls; Whitewater Kayaking and River Running; Wild and Scenic Rivers; Willamette River and Valley; Windsurfing) Oregon possesses 111,619 miles of rivers and streams, providing hydroelectric power, irrigation, fish migration and farming, navigation along the Columbia, and recreational opportunity. Oregon's rivers flow into several general hydrologic systems: (1) rivers that drain from the Coast Range directly into the Pacific Ocean, (2) rivers that drain into landlocked lakes of the Great Basin in Southern Oregon, and (3) all the rest that flow to the Pacific via the Columbia or its tributaries.

Columbia. The Columbia, Oregon's largest river, forms the boundary with Washington from the Pacific Ocean to just east of McNary Dam. It is also the state's link with the sea, providing a major waterway for maritime trade.

Deschutes. With its ruggedly beautiful scenery, the Deschutes features formidable whitewater and plentiful steelhead and rainbow trout.

John Day. Much of the John Day is known for its abundant bass and steelhead, deep and colorful canyons, and geologic formations. The Service Creek to Tumwater Falls segment of the John Day contains important archaeological and historical sites. The North Fork also offers challenging whitewater rafting and the chance to view remains of early mining activities.

Klamath. The Bureau of Land Management has given the Klamath River Canyon its highest scenic classification. The river's flow from the high-desert interior through coastal rain forest creates a wide diversity of habitats supporting an abundance of wildlife. The Klamath supports a genetically unique population of rainbow trout and several endangered species, including Lost River and short-nose suckers. At least 40 prehistoric sites can be found in the canyon, which was once populated by several Native American tribes.

McKenzie. From Clear Creek to Scott Creek, the McKenzie is a challenge to whitewater rafters and those in drift boats. Also a popular site for fly-fishing, its water is especially clear and cold.

Rogue. Emerging from the western slope of the Cascade Mountains, the Rogue is renowned for whitewater boating and sport fishing. The Upper Rogue River's diverse landscape includes pumice flats, deep gorges and chutes, and unique ecological systems.

Blossom Bar on the Rogue River. Photo by Susan Dupere.

Snake (*see* also Hells Canyon and the Snake River). The Snake River is the major tributary of the Columbia, supplying water for irrigation and power in Oregon. Rising in Yellowstone National Park, it arcs through Idaho, then forms part of the Oregon-Idaho border, where the Snake has carved Hells Canyon, the deepest, most rugged river gorge in the United States. Hells Canyon is over 40 miles long and, at one point, more than 8,000 feet deep.

Willamette. The Willamette River, the longest river entirely within Oregon, has its headwaters in the high Cascades, north of Crater Lake. The Willamette Valley has been the most populated drainage basin in the state since the beginning of white settlement, its fertile land sustaining fruit orchards, dairy farms, and lumber mills. The river's banks touch Eugene, Corvallis, Albany, and Salem, before entering the Columbia River near Portland.

Roads and Highways

(*See also* Transportation; Vehicle Registration and Driver's Licenses) In 1917, the Oregon legislature designated 4,317 miles of mostly unpaved county roads as the state highway system. Today, Oregon has over 96,000 miles of public roads, 7,500 miles of them owned and operated by the State of Oregon Department of Transportation (the state actually owns over 11,000 miles of roads, but about 3,700 are located in state parks and forests that are managed by other state governmental agencies) and 728 miles of interstate highways.

Oregonians and visitors drove more than 51 million miles on the state highway system every day in 1996. Only 29 percent of Oregonians commute to and from work by some means other than a single-occupancy vehicle, and during peak hours about 60 percent of Oregon's urban highway miles are heavily congested. In metropolitan areas, the number of vehicle miles traveled per capita annually is 8,085. On an average weekday, approximately 19,000 trucks enter Oregon carrying 250,000 tons of goods, most entering from Washington (38 percent) and California (25 percent). Of the approximately 6,150 miles of non-interstate rural state highways, 78 percent are considered to be generally suitable for bicycling (i.e., roads with shoulders at least four feet wide or with traffic volumes lower than 1,000 vehicles per day). Of the 632 miles (1,017 kilometers) of urban state highways, 32 percent have bikeways on both sides of the road.

Roads cross the state's mountain ranges through a number of mountain passes. Weather conditions, especially during winter, can be treacherous, so it is a good idea for drivers to be aware of road and weather conditions. Mountain-pass road conditions are monitored and reported daily on the **Oregon State Department of Transportation** website at www.odot.state.or.us/travel and via radio and television weather and driving reports. Under severe snow conditions, snow tires and chains may be required to travel across the mountain passes. Some passes are closed for the better part of the winter; others may close for brief periods of time during especially heavy snowfall.

Major Mountain Passes

Blue Box Summit, 4,025 feet, Cascade Mountains, Oregon 26.

Cascade Summit, 5,920 feet, Cascade Mountains, Oregon 138.

Deadmans Pass, 4,193 feet, Blue Mountains, I-84.

Dixie Pass, 5,279 feet, Oregon 26.

Hayden Mountain Summit, 4,625 feet, Oregon 66.

McKenzie Pass, 5,325 feet, Cascade Mountains, Oregon 242.

Quartz Mountain Pass, 5,306 feet, Oregon 140.

Santiam Pass, 4,817 feet, Cascade Mountains, U.S. 20.

Siskiyou Summit, 4,310 feet, Siskiyou Mountains, I-5.

Willamette Pass, 5,128 feet, Cascade Mountains, Oregon 58.

Road Reports by Phone

Inside Oregon, (800) 977-6368.

Oregon Department of Transportation, Transportation Building, 355 Capitol St. NE, Salem 97310, (888) ASK-ODOT.

Outside Oregon, (503) 588-2941.

Rocks and Gems

Most of the semiprecious stones found in Oregon are from the quartz family of minerals (jasper, bloodstone, and geodes filled with quartz crystals), as well as green garnet, green jasper (known as "Oregon Jade"), pink rhodonite, and fire opals. In the Klamath Mountains, serpentine rock may contain impressive aggregates of red garnets and jade. Tumbled and cut, all make colorful and unusual jewelry.

Oregon ranks high among states in the production of semiprecious gems. The U.S. Bureau of Mines has set the annual value of Oregon gem production at $750,000, but the figure is probably much higher since rockhounds often buy, sell, and trade on an individual basis. Rockhounding has become so popular that several organizations in the central part of the state (especially the Prineville and Crook County Chambers of Commerce) have created service groups for this recreational pursuit.

Also popular with craftspeople and collectors is petrified (silicified) wood, ranging in size from small limbs to logs several feet in diameter. Some of the best examples have been found in buried stumps, petrified as the wood turned to stone over millions of years. The Clarno area of Wasco and Wheeler Counties has revealed many high-quality specimens.

Small diamonds have sometimes been found in Oregon in gold placer concentrates. Uncut diamonds look much like agates, and many gold panners have probably discarded valuable gems. A number of geologists believe diamonds can be found in the Blue Mountains of northeastern Oregon and in the serpentine, dunite, and peridotite of southwestern Oregon.

Agates. Oregon is one of four Northwest states with the most agates. Agate pebbles abound on many beaches, their rough exterior concealing beautiful bands and designs.

Opals. While opal deposits are prevalent in Oregon, there is more quantity to be found than quality. An amorphous silica with a high water content characterizes opals, and even most gem-quality opals will be prone to drying out, thus losing their shimmery loveliness, or being too breakable to form into jewelry. This is the reason high-grade opals are so expensive. Oregon contains three opal mines: two in Lake County near La Pine and another in Morrow County at Opal Butte. The latter produces valuable stones, such as rare fire and blue opals. Discovery of gems at Opal Butte started an opal rush in the 1890s, but limited supplies of quality gems forced these new commercial mines to close. Rockhounds picked over the site until 1986, when the West Coast Gemstones Company proposed a new operation to the owners of the land and Opal Butte closed to the public. Fortunately the site is now open for a limited season.

Serpentine. Though serpentine is normally found below the ocean floor, occasionally slabs were folded into mountains during collisions between ocean and continental plates 150 million years ago. When freshly broken, the soft, green rock is known as soapstone. The nation's most impressive example of an exposed serpentine slab stands nearly on end in Central Oregon's Canyon Mountains. Colorful, sculptured examples of serpentine may be found outside the town of Gold Beach.

Sunstones. Sunstones are rare crystals of the mineral feldspar and have been designated as the official state gemstone. As large as 3 inches across, some sunstones shimmer with embedded flecks of copper, while others evidence colors such as pale yellow, soft pink, crimson, deep blue, or intense green. High-grade specimens are so valuable that most deposits have been claimed and are strictly closed to the public. The retail value of cut sunstones ranges from $15 to over $100 per carat, while red, blue, and green samples, or large or clear stones, bring even higher prices. The U.S. Bureau of Land Management has designated one long-popular site, 25 miles north of Plush, a free, public collecting area. For information call BLM's Lakeview office, (541) 947-2177.

Thundereggs. Oregonians' significant attachment to the thunderegg as a symbol of the state's cultural heritage and unique geology reaches back to ancient Native American legend. The rock takes its name from the Thunder Spirits who lived on the peaks of Mount Hood and Mount Jefferson, gods who, when they fought, stole the massive eggs of the mythical thunderbird's nest to propel at one another. Millions of thundereggs are indeed scattered at the base of these mountains. Although the thunderegg is Oregon's official state rock, it is actually not a rock at all. Most are large agates in nodules, though they can be found as geodes in rhyolite, welded tuff, or perlitic rocks. Thundereggs range in weight from under an ounce to more than a ton. Most eggs found are about 2 to 6 inches in diameter.

Thundereggs may be identified by their lumpy or ribbed exterior, usually rust-colored, which covers an inner layer of iron or manganese, often thinly coated with opal or chalcedony. Within that layer lies more chalcedony or opal, though some eggs are hollow or filled with carnelian, cinnabar, jasper, or various zeolites. In some eggs the layering fans from one edge because the egg was rotated by earth movement while the filling was being deposited. Thundereggs are sold widely at airport and hotel gift shops and at rock and gem shows. Popular offerings are intricately banded slices of the rock, as well as jewelry and bolo ties made using pieces.

Collecting thundereggs may be done at many sites; some sites are free and others

Jeweled Beach

Children and adults alike delight in hunting for agates on Oregon's beaches. Plentiful in many areas such as Agate Beach, north of Newport, the beautiful translucent stones appear like rare gems at the tide line, or cover a beach as if a treasure chest had been upended there. Agates come from mineral deposits left in holes in volcanic rocks and freed when the surrounding rock erodes. They can be icy white, pale yellow, golden, orange, or shot through with a variety of colors. Wave action and sand polish the pebbles to a glossy sheen, and few are the visitors to an agate-studded beach who can resist picking up a pocketful.—Magnificent Places: Oregon Coast, text by Jack and Jan McGowan, photographs by Rick Schafer.

charge admission. Visitors to free sites need their own tools and should expect to do much of the digging themselves; fee sites rent tools and have usually made the rocks more accessible.

Organizations and Events of Interest

Bureau of Land Management, 1300 S G. St., Lakeview 97630, (541)) 947-2177.

Oregon Department of Geology and Mineral Industries, 800 NE Oregon St., Portland 97232, (503) 731-4100.

West Coast Gemstones, Inc., P.O. Box 133, College Place, WA 99324, fax: (509) 527-1233.

Annual Gem Show, Oregon City, November, (503) 631-3128.

Oregon Agate and Mineral Society, 8138 SE Stark, Portland 97215, no phone, meetings at 8:00 P.M. on first and third Fridays.

Rock Swap and Campout, Keno, July, (541) 882-8276.

Rodeos

Oregon is not only cowboy country, it is the home of one of the top 10 rodeos in the world, the Pendleton Round-Up, where folks say "Let 'er Buck" every September. The Pendleton Round-Up may be the granddaddy of all Oregon rodeos, but it is far from the only place where you can feel manure under your boots and see the best of the local and national cowboys ridin', ropin', and bronc bustin'. Major rodeos include events sanctioned by the Professional Rodeo Cowboys Association (PRCA), which means that competitors are accumulating points for national standings in specific rodeo events and for the overall national champion cowboy competition. Following is a sampling of rodeo, Oregon style.

Organizations and Events of Interest

Cowboys Then and Now, 729 NE Oregon St., Portland 97232, (503) 731-3200. The Cattleman's Heritage Foundation, with funding from the state's Beef Council, presents the story of the cowboy and the cow industry in Oregon at this nonprofit museum. Features include a century-old chuck wagon and a tack room with saddles donated by real, honest-to-goodness cowboys.

Benton County Fair and Rodeo, Corvallis, August, (541) 757-1521.

Big Loop Rodeo, Jordan Valley, May, (541) 575-1900.

Bronc Riding Blowout, Baker City, July, (800) 523-4011.

Bull Riding Blowout, Baker City, July, (800) 523-1235.

Catherine Creek Rodeo Buck-Turn-and-Burn Bull Rama, Union, July, (541) 573-2636.

Chief Joseph Days, Joseph, July, (800) 585-4121.

Clackamas County Fair and Rodeo, Canby, August, (503) 266-1136.

Coos County Fair and Rodeo, Myrtle Point, August, (541) 572-2002.

Cottage Grove Amateur Rodeo, Cottage Grove, July, (541) 343-4298.

Crooked River Round-Up Rodeo, Prineville, July, (541) 447-6575.

Eastern Oregon Livestock Show (PRCA rodeo) Union, June, (541) 963-8551.

Elgin Stampede PRCA Rodeo, Elgin, July, (541) 437-9522.

Eugene Pro Rodeo, Eugene, July, (541) 747-1120.

Flying U Rodeo, Prineville, April, (541) 447-6575.

Haines Stampede and Rodeo, Haines, July, (800) 523-1235.

High School Rodeo, John Day, May, (541) 575-1900.

June Dairy Festival Parade and Rodeo, Tillamook, June (503) 842-7525.

Klamath County Fair and Jefferson Stampede Rodeo, Klamath Falls, August, (541) 883-3796.

Molalla Buckaroo Rodeo, Molalla, July, (503) 829-8388.

Morrow County Fair and Oregon Trail Pro Rodeo, Heppner, August, (541) 676-9474

Nyssa Nite Rodeo, Nyssa, June, (541) 372-3405.

Oregon High School Rodeo Finals, Prineville, June, (541) 447-6575.

Pendleton Round-Up, Pendleton, September, (800) 45-RODEO.

The Pendleton Round-Up, circa 1955. The annual event was founded in 1910. From *Oregon, My Oregon* by Ray Atkeson.

Most of Salem's business is government business, with a low-key commercial sector and little industrial output. An important boost to the local economy comes in early September when the Oregon State Fair, the largest state fair in the Northwest, takes over the city. Fine dining is available at two or three venues, and bed-and-breakfast inns enhance the city's lodging offerings.

Willamette University, the oldest university in the West, is a major presence in Salem. Its historic and modern buildings coexist pleasantly, while Mill Creek and a small but valuable botanical garden contribute to the peaceful landscape.

For the most part, Salem looks after its history. The historic Mission Mill Village gives visitors a sense of the area's early years, with its 4.5-acre spread of restored buildings, including a woolen mill, a parsonage, a Presbyterian church, and several homes. The mill itself, which drew water from Mill Creek, is now a museum. The Jason Lee House, built in 1841 on the property is the oldest remaining frame house in the Northwest.

While cars and buses are Salem's major modes of transport, and modern bridges span the Willamette River, residents and visitors to the area can still enjoy the Wheatland and Buena Vista cable-operated ferries. At Bush House, a Victorian home built by newspaper publisher Asahel Bush, the adjacent conservatory and rose gardens are well-maintained and an art gallery occupies the original barn.

Built in 1938 after the original burned, the Oregon State Capitol is a tribute to the state's history. Impressive Works Progress Administration (WPA) murals line the entry, while other murals and friezes present scenes from Oregon history. Art-

Philomath Frolic and Rodeo, Philomath, July, (541) 929-2611.

Salem Rodeo, Salem, May, (503) 364-3288.

Santiam Canyon Stampede/Rodeo, Sublimity, July-August, (503) 589-2999.

Sisters Rodeo and Parade, Sisters, June, (541) 549-0121.

Sportsman Holiday and Rodeo, Sweet Home, July, (541) 367-6186.

St. Paul Rodeo, St. Paul, July, (503) 633-2011.

Sutherlin Stampede Rodeo, August, Sutherlin, (800) 371-5829.

Umpqua Valley Round-Up, Roseburg, June, (541) 672-5777.

U.S. Team Roping Championships, Prineville, June, (541) 447-6575.

Washington County Fair and Rodeo, Hillsboro, July, (503) 648-1416.

Salem

Oregon's state capital, Salem, is located in the Willamette Valley, a broad, fertile stretch of land between the Cascade and Coast Ranges. With more than 107,000 residents, Salem is Oregon's third-largest city, behind Portland and Eugene. All border I-5, the major highway running from Canada to San Diego.

Fighting for the Capital

Oregon had been established as a territory for only a month before Democrats and Whigs started a political tug-of-war for power, using the location of the state capital as a proxy. Democrats lost the 1848 national election—but not before President James Polk had appointed General Joseph Lane as territorial governor. Lane resisted the Whig control of Oregon City as long as he could, finally resigning when President Zachary Taylor, a Whig, appointed a new governor, John Gaines, in 1850.

Democratic elected officials, with control of the legislature, felt they had the support of the people and couldn't bear a Whig governor on top of a Whig-dominated judiciary. The "Salem Clique," as they were called afterward, met secretly in December to plot their future. They resolved to move the capital from Oregon City to Salem, and the bill passed easily in the Democratic legislature. Early in 1852, the move was complete, but the Whigs weren't finished yet, appropriating the issue as a legal one.

The Oregon Supreme Court agreed with the governor—2 Whigs to 1 Democrat—that Oregon City was indeed the state capital, and the Salem Clique swung back by convincing the Democratic U.S. Congress to take up its cause.

Whigs still ran things in Oregon City, though, and the Whig territorial treasurer refused to pay the salaries of the officials who met in Salem. The federal Department of the Treasury gave this stalemate to the U.S. Supreme Court to solve. By the time the Supreme Court justices ruled, upholding the lower-court decision, Congressional Democrats had passed a law establishing Salem as the capital of Oregon Territory and sent it to the latest Whig president, Millard Fillmore. Fillmore had other priorities for Congress, though, and chose not to waste political capital on the location of Oregon's capital. On December 3, 1854, the full legislature convened in Salem.

Oregonians weren't finished with the issue, though, and a suspicious fire destroyed Salem's new capitol building. The legislature, meeting in neutral Corvallis, decided to let the people decide. After all of the Democrats' posturing as the voice of the electorate, the people voted for Eugene City. Disgruntled officials asserted that many ballots had arrived late, and a new election was set. Salem came in third place again, prompting the legislature to void the ballot measure entirely on the grounds that its wording had been "confusing." Two referendums later, 14 years after the Salem Clique first sneaked out of Oregon City, voters finally approved Salem as its "new" capital.

deco details, marble walls, and an observation deck are topped by "The Golden Pioneer" figure atop the building's dome.

Nearby attractions may be more interesting than Salem itself. A hundred-year-old Benedictine abbey rests on Mount Angel, a butte sacred to local Native Americans. The abbey's library, designed by Finnish architect Alvar Aalto, houses a worthy collection of ancient manuscripts. East of Salem 25 miles, the broad waterfalls of Silver Falls State Park rival those of the Columbia Gorge.

Salmon (SEE ALSO ENDANGERED SPECIES; FISH AND FISHING) Pacific salmon are born in fresh water, migrate to the ocean, and return as adults to the streams where they were born to spawn and die. Prior to European settlement, the waters of Oregon teemed with salmon, and the largest of these, the chinook, was designated the state fish. More than a century of heavy fishing, damming of rivers, timbering, and other habitat alterations have taken their toll. Today's salmon populations are much reduced, and some individual runs of salmon on specific streams have been designated as endangered or threatened species. Four species of salmon are found in Oregon waters; a fifth North Pacific species, pink salmon, is only occasionally found in Oregon's coastal waters.

Chum or dog salmon *(Oncorhynchus keta).* Average weight 9 pounds but can weigh more than 30 pounds.

Top Catch—Oregon's Trophy Salmon

Species	Weight	Caught from	By	Year
Chinook	83 lbs., 0 oz.	Umpqua River	Ernie St. Claire	1910
Chum	23 lbs., 0 oz.	Kilchis River	Roger Nelson	1990
Coho	25 lbs., 5.25 oz.	Siltcoos Lake	Ed Martin	1966
Kokanee	4 lbs., 14.7 oz.	Wallowa Lake	Don Exon	1998

Source: Oregon Department of Fish and Wildlife

Coho or silver salmon (*Oncorhynchus kisutch).* Runs 6 to 12 pounds. Spawns November to January but begins entering rivers in August.

King or chinook salmon (*Oncorynchus tshawytscha).* Weighing 30 to 40 pounds, sometimes up to 100 pounds. Spawns May to January.

Sockeye or red salmon (*Oncorynchus nerka).* Length to 33 inches, can weigh up to 15 pounds, most are 3.5 to 8 pounds.

Endangered and Threatened Salmonid Populations Found in Oregon Waters

Endangered
Oregon Coast coho
Snake River fall chinook
Snake River sockeye
Snake River spring/summer chinook

Threatened
Umpqua River sea-run cutthroat trout
Upper Columbia River steelhead

Proposed Threatened
Columbia River chum
Lower Columbia River chinook
Lower Columbia River steelhead
Middle Columbia River steelhead
Snake River Basin steelhead
Southern Oregon and California coastal chinook
Southern Oregon/Northern California coho
Upper Willamette steelhead

Candidate
Klamath Mountain Province steelhead
Oregon Coast steelhead
Southwest Washington/Lower Columbia River coho
All Oregon sea-run cutthroat populations
All other Oregon steelhead populations

Scenic Drives

While there are beautiful drives throughout Oregon, a number of routes have been designated by either state or federal agencies as "scenic byways." Those designated as "National Scenic Byway" or "All-American Road" are given such status for their outstanding archaeological, cultural, historical, natural, recreational, and scenic qualities. Oregon's National Scenic Byways are the Oregon Cascade Lakes Highway, Highway 101-Pacific Coast Scenic Byway—Oregon Section, McKenzie Pass and Santiam Pass, and Oregon's Outback Scenic Byway.

Cascade Mountains

Cascade Lakes Highway Scenic Byway. Loop drive through Cascades from Bend. This 87-mile route begins west from Bend as Century Drive, which becomes the Cascade Lakes Highway (Oregon 46), south to Oregon 42, east to U.S. 97, and north on U.S. 97 back to Bend. The loop winds through Central Oregon's mountains and forest and passes numerous lakes, including Todd Lake, Sparks Lake, Cultus Lake, and Crane Prairie Reservoir. The drive traverses Deschutes National Forest, which offers fishing, hiking, and rafting, and Mount Bachelor, which offers some of the best skiing in the West. Like the McKenzie and Santiam Pass route, this highway has outstanding views of Mount Bachelor and the Three Sisters.

McKenzie-Santiam Pass Scenic Byway. Loop through the Cascades on U.S. 20 and Oregon 242 and 126. This national scenic byway proceeds from the junction of Oregon 126 and 142 near Belknap Springs along Oregon 126 north to U.S. 20, then east to Sisters, turning back west on Oregon 242 to Oregon 126. This drive passes in view of some of the most spectacular volcanoes in the Oregon Cascades. The Three Sisters and Broken Top tower above the byway, their beauty further enhanced by waterfalls, lava fields, and scenic lakes.

Robert Aufderheide Memorial Drive. Loop drive through Willamette National Forest. It follows Oregon 19 north from Westfir to the junction with Oregon 126 near Rainbow. Named after Robert Aufderheide, a supervisor of the Willamette National Forest (1954–1959), this loop follows the Willamette River North and Middle Forks and the McKenzie River through scenic forests.

The King of Roads

By the early 1900s, as communities increased along the river edges, a highway through the Gorge seemed necessary. By 1916 it was a reality. Heralded as a great engineering feat, the highway hairpinned through some of the Gorge's most spectacular scenery, displaying dry masonry walls and viaducts fashioned by Italian stonemasons, rubble parapets with arched openings, and windowed tunnels blasted through solid rock. The Northwest's first paved road was so beautiful the Illustrated Long News *reported: "It is the king of roads." Although only one-third of the highway's original 73 miles remain drivable, the "king of roads" still winds through what many called the grand dame of gorges.—*
Portrait of Oregon, text by Sandra L. Keith, photographs by Rick Schafer.

Central Oregon

Oregon's Outback Scenic Byway. Lakeview to La Pine on Oregon 395 and U.S. 97. This 145-mile National Scenic Byway takes travelers from the Cascades' green eastern slopes through the wide-open spaces of Oregon's arid "outback." The drive passes spectacular natural features, such as Fort Rock and Abert Rim, and crosses expanses of desert and through Picture Rock Pass, where the region's earliest inhabitants etched their history in the surrounding rock.

Columbia River Gorge

Historic Columbia River Highway Scenic Byway. Troutdale to The Dalles, paralleling the Columbia River. Located within the Columbia River Gorge National Scenic Area, this highway is listed on the National Register of Historic Places. It follows the Columbia River south of I-84 in two segments from Troutdale, just east of Portland, to The Dalles. The first segment begins near exit 18 off I-84, climbing along the lower slope of the Cascades and moving east to Portland Women's Forum State Park, where the old Chanticleer Inn once stood. The inn was where the highway's planners first met. A mile farther east is Crown Point, where the dazzling view extends for miles up- and downriver. A wealth of waterfalls—including much-photographed Multnomah Falls—wildflowers, and mossy forest are all part of this first segment, which ends at Dodson. Farther east along I-84, the scenic route begins again from exit 76 to Mosier, the Rowena Plateau, Rowena Crest Overlook, The Nature Conservancy's Tom McCall Preserve, and on to The Dalles, its eastern end.

Northeastern Oregon

Blue Mountain Scenic Byway. Ukiah, Heppner, Lexington, Ione, and Cecil to I-84 on Oregon 53. This byway offers an alternative route off I-84 and features a national historic district, Oregon Trail sites, the Wild and Scenic John Day River, the North Fork John Day Wilderness, and remnants of historic mining and early settlements.

Elkhorn Scenic Byway. Loop from Baker City to Haines, Grande Ronde Lake, Anthony Lakes, Granite, Sumpter, Phillips Lake, and return to Baker City on Oregon 30. This 106-mile loop winds through the Elkhorn Mountains in the northeast corner of the state. Travelers can see remnants of

Interstate 84 hugs the Columbia River east of Portland. From *Portland from the Air* by Sallie Tisdale (essay) and Russ Heinl (photos).

Journey Through Time Scenic Byway. Biggs to Baker City via Wasco, Moro, Shaniko, Antelope, Fossil, Dayville, John Day, and Sumpter on U.S. 97 and Oregon 218 and 7. This 280-mile byway passes parts of the Barlow Road near Biggs to the Oregon Trail at Baker City. Take U.S. 97 south from Biggs to Antelope, head east on Oregon 218 to Fossil and John Day, then continue on Oregon 7 to Baker City. Along the way are the painted hills and palisades of John Day Fossil Beds National Monument (*see* National Parks, Monuments, and Recreation Areas), numerous historic sites, including Kam Wah Chung & Company Museum in John Day (*see* Museums), gold-rush mining settlements, the Sumpter Valley Railway, and the Oregon Trail.

mining and pioneer history in Baker County and the scenic vistas of the Elkhorn Mountains. The drive can be closed in places during winter due to snow.

Hells Canyon Scenic Byway. Joseph to Hells Canyon. The byway winds south and east following the 50-mile route of Forest Road 39 through Wallowa-Whitman National Forest, including a section of Hells Canyon National Recreation Area. The route begins 5 miles south of Oregon 350 (about 8 miles east of Joseph on Little Sheep Creek) and wanders from grassy fields to old-growth forests and rivers. The dramatic topography ranges from the deepest river gorge in North America—Hells Canyon—to the high peaks of the Wallowa Mountains. Vistas are fantastic year-round. Numerous recreation sites are available. The route terminates at the junction with Oregon 86, 10 miles east of Halfway. When the Wallowa Mountain Loop Road is combined with Oregon 82, 86, 350, and I-84, an expanded route of about 230 miles is created through many towns, including Baker City, La Grande, Elgin, Wallowa, Lostine, Enterprise, Joseph, Halfway, and Richland.

Pacific Coast

Pacific Coast Scenic Byway, Oregon section of U.S. 101, Astoria to the California border on U.S. 101. From the mouth of the Columbia River, this byway parallels Oregon's spectacular coastline for more than 200 miles, through rain forest and along sandy beaches and dunes, rugged shoreline cliffs, and verdant farmland. Travelers will pass by dozens of state parks, Oregon Dunes National Recreation Area, picturesque towns, and most of Oregon's lighthouses.

Southern Oregon

The Rogue-Umpqua Scenic Byway. Roseburg to Gold Hill on Oregon 138, 230, and 234. Known as the "highway of waterfalls," the Rogue-Umpqua Scenic Byway ascends deep into the Cascades. About 18 miles east of Roseburg the North Umpqua meets head-on with the Little River at Colliding Rivers, then proceeds along the North Umpqua, providing whitewater thrills and superb steelhead runs as it tumbles through Umpqua National Forest, passing over a half-dozen waterfalls. At Lemolo Lake, Oregon 138 heads south to Diamond Lake at the base of Mount Thielsen. At the south end of Diamond Lake, the scenic byway turns right onto Oregon 230 and offers a clear look at the peaks and ridges above Crater Lake. From there, Oregon 230 follows the Rogue River and merges with Oregon 62 near the town of Union Creek. The scenic byway heads west on Oregon 234 past Table Rocks and meets the Rogue River again in Gold Hill, the byway's southern portal.

Volcanic Legacy Scenic Byway. Diamond Lake Junction to the California border on U.S. 97 and Oregon 138, 62, and 140. This Southern Oregon byway offers views of Crater Lake National Park (*see* National Parks, Monuments, and Recreation Areas), the volcanic landscape created by the eruption of Mount Mazama (*see* Volcanoes and Volcanism), the high-desert and wetland habitats of the Klamath Basin, and scenic farmlands. The byway begins on U.S. 97 at Diamond Lake Junction, halfway between Bend and Klamath Falls. It follows the 33-mile rim drive around Crater Lake, then follows Oregon 62, Oregon 140, and U.S. 97 south of Klamath Falls to the California border. The Francis S. Landrum Historic Wayside at the route's end commemorates the Applegate Emigrant Trail.

Organizations of Interest

Federal Highway Works Administration, Oregon Division, 530 Center St. NE, #100, Salem 97301, (503) 399-2053.

Oregon State Department of Transportation, State Byway Coordinator, 555 13th St. NE, Salem 97310, (503) 986-4261, www.odot.state.or.us/index.htm.

Seals and Sea Lions

The Oregon Coast may be as well-known for its pinnipeds as it is for its large sea stacks. Three species of pinnipeds are found along the rocks and beaches: harbor seals, California sea lions, and Steller sea lions. The Oregon Department of Fish and Wildlife has been keeping track of these creatures since the 1970s, and its surveys indicate that the animals are doing well here. The population of Steller sea lions, a threatened species, is stable; the harbor seal population has grown to about 10,000, and California sea lions have numbered 5,000 to 7,000 during peak times (as of 1996 survey). The best place to see sea lions is at Sea Lion Caves (*see* Caves), about 11 miles north of Florence.

> **Master Divers**
>
> *Searching for squid and fish, the Steller sea lion can dive 600 feet deep, swimming up to 17 miles an hour with a breaststroke, instead of using fishlike movements.*—Ann Saling, *The Great Northwest Nature Factbook.*

Harbor seals. From *Going Wild in Washington and Oregon* by Susan Ewing (text) and Gretchen Daiber (illustrations).

Shipwrecks

Beset by extensive shoals and sandbars at the mouths of rivers, rimmed with spectacular rocks, and catching the full brunt of breakers that build up a head of steam across the entire Pacific Ocean, many ships have ended their last voyage on the Oregon Coast. One of the earliest and most enduring wrecks is the *Brother Jonathan,* a side-wheel coastal steamer that struck a rock north of Crescent City, California, and sank on the California-Oregon border on July 30, 1865. More than 190 miners, prostitutes, sailors, and

The New Carissa *defied measures to sink it offshore from Coos Bay in 1999.* Photo courtesy U.S. Coast Guard.

politicians died in the shipwreck. Among the drowned were the newly appointed governor of Washington Territory and the commander of United States forces in the West during the Civil War.

Underwater explorers located the wreck of the *Brother Jonathan* in 1993, using advanced underwater search technology. Since then, treasure salvagers have recovered large quantities of $5, $10 and $20 gold pieces, worth an estimated $5 to $10 million today. Efforts continue, as of this writing, to locate the ship's safe, which may contain an army payroll and more gold.

Nine Japanese submarines patrolled the eastern Pacific during World War II, including the Pacific Coast. In the early days of the war, there were persistent reports of submarine sightings off the Oregon Coast and elsewhere, and there have been occasional reports of one or more sunken submarines, including abandoned mini-submarines, but none of these reports has ever been confirmed.

The Columbia River bar is known as the graveyard of the Pacific. Strong and variable currents cause the sands at the mouth of the river to shift constantly. The *Peter Iredale* sank just south of the Columbia's mouth in 1960. While no lives were lost, memories of the ship endure because what remains of the vessel can still be seen stuck in the sand at Fort Stevens State Park, just off the northern end of U.S. 101. While jetties, dredges, and navigation improvements have made "crossing the bar" much safer than in the old days, the passage across the bar is still treacherous, especially in bad weather and with limited visibility.

A specialized salvage tug, the *Salvage Chief*, stationed nearby in Astoria, has remained on call for nearly 50 years and regularly comes to the aid of vessels that encounter distress while crossing the bar. Tourists can view the venerable *Salvage Chief* at the Port of Astoria.

In February 1999, the *Salvage Chief* would have pulled the 44,527-ton wood-chip carrier *New Carissa* off the beach north of Coos Bay, except that the same storm that pushed the *New Carissa* aground also kept the *Salvage Chief* from crossing the bar and venturing down the coast to her aid. The *New Carissa* arrived at Coos Bay on February 4, 1999, to pick up a load of wood chips. She anchored outside the harbor to await a pilot and to ride out a storm that was kicking up 20- to 30-foot waves. The storm caused her to drag her anchors. This wasn't detected until it was too late, and the ship ran aground in the shifting coastal storms, broadside to the full force of the pounding Pacific waves. Despite the best efforts of salvagers—first to save the ship, then to limit oil pollution—she broke up on the beach. The bow section was eventually towed to sea and sunk in deep water. The stern section remains on the beach as of this writing, though salvagers planned either to refloat the stern or break it up onsite and cart it away. The *New Carissa,* the most significant modern shipwreck on the Oregon Coast, is a reminder of the hazards and the risks of the sea and this rugged coast, despite the most modern advances in shipping and navigation.

Skiing and Snowboarding

Skiing in July? If you can't afford a ticket to Chile, head for Oregon's Mount Bachelor or Timberline at Mount Hood, which boasts that it has the longest ski season in North America. Oregon certainly has some of the best skiing in the country in the Cascades, including great powder. Northwesterners have long considered Mount Bachelor as the place to go for the region's best powder—a treat for Northwest skiers who are accustomed to the wet "Cascade cement." While downhill skiing remains popular, snowboarding and cross-country skiing rival downhill for outdoor-recreation dollars. For cross-country skiers, in addition to groomed trails at Nordic ski areas and most downhill resorts, many miles of Forest Service roads and thousands of acres of public land provide endless routes for recreation. Logging roads are excellent for cross-country skiing because they are usually closed to vehicles during the winter.

The downhill ski areas are located in the Cascades from Mount Hood to Mount Ashland, and smaller ones are located farther east. Mount Hood, the most heavily trafficked area, has plenty of options, with a number of ski resorts scattered over its summit, including the highest, Timberline, with its classic 1930s lodge and "Magic Mile," an easy-cruising run above timberline. Plenty of smaller, uncrowded, and inexpensive sites are located throughout the state as well.

Ski Areas

Anthony Lakes, La Grande, (541) 856-3277, ski@anthonylakes.com. Area: 360 acres. Elevation: 8,000 to 7,100 feet. Terrain: 33 percent novice, 34 percent intermediate, 33 percent expert. Downhill skiing and snowboarding, 13 kilometers of cross-country trails.

Cooper Spur, Mount Hood, (541) 352-7803, (541) 352-7803. Elevation: 8,000 to 7,500 feet. Terrain: 50 percent novice, 40 percent intermediate, 10 percent expert. Two surface lifts, downhill skiing, snowboarding, 10 kilometers of groomed cross-country trails.

Ferguson Ridge, Enterprise, (541) 432-4170. Area: 600 feet of vertical drop. Elevation: 7,000 to 6,000 feet. Terrain: Beginning and intermediate. Seven downhill trails, two lifts. Cross-country nearby.

Hoodoo Ski Bowl, Sisters, (541) 822-3799. Snow conditions: (541) 822-3337. Elevation: 7,000 to 6,000 feet. Terrain: 30 percent novice, 40 percent intermediate, 30 percent expert. Four lifts, downhill skiing, snowboarding, seven kilometers of cross-country trails, plus nearby Forest Service trails.

Mount Ashland, Ashland, (541) 482-2897. Snow conditions: (541) 482-2754. Elevation: 7,500 to 6,350 feet. Terrain: 15 percent novice, 35 percent intermediate, 50 percent expert. Downhill skiing and snowboarding, four chairs, 23 trails. Night skiing Thursday through Saturday.

Mount Bachelor, Bend, (541) 382-2442, (800) 829-2442. Snow conditions: (541) 382-7888. www.mtbachelor.com. Area: 3,600 acres. Elevation: 9,065 to 5,800 feet. Terrain: 15 percent novice, 25 percent intermediate, 35 percent advanced/intermediate, 25 percent expert. Seventy downhill runs, 13 lifts, 56 kilometers of groomed cross-country trails.

Mount Bailey Snowcats, Diamond Lakes Resort, Diamond Lake, (541) 793-3333, (800) 733-7593. SkiGus@mountbailey.com. Elevation: 8,363 to 5,400 feet. Terrain: 50 percent intermediate, 50 percent difficult. Two Snow-Cats, with capacity for 12 skiers per day; snowboarders advised to carry ski poles to get across flat spots.

Mount Hood Meadows, Mount Hood, (503) 337-2222. Snow conditions: (503) 227-SNOW. www.skihood.com. Elevation: 7,300 to 4,523 feet. Terrain: 15 percent beginner, 50 percent intermediate, 35 percent advanced. Ten chairlifts, pony lift, rope tow, 15 kilometers of groomed cross-country trails.

Mount Hood Skibowl, Mount Hood, (503) 272-3206. Snow conditions: (503) 222-BOWL. www.skibowl.com. Elevation: 5,066 to 3,600 feet. Four chairlifts, five rope tows.

Spout Springs, Weston, (541) 566-2164. Area: 550 feet of vertical drop. Eleven trails, four lifts, 21 kilometers of groomed cross-country trails.

Timberline, Mount Hood, (503) 272-3311. Snow conditions: (503) 222-2211. www.timberlinelodge.com. Area: More than 1,000 acres. Elevation: 8,500 to 6,000 feet. Five chairlifts.

Warner Canyon, Lakeview, (541) 947-5001. Area: 730 feet of vertical drop. One lift, 14 trails, 2.4 kilometers of cross-country trails.

Willamette Pass, Cascade Summit, (800) 444-5030. Snow conditions: (541) 345-SNOW. www.willamettepass.com. Area: 210 acres, with 1,531 feet of vertical drop. Elevation: 6,683 to 5,120 feet. Five chairlifts.

Wing Ridge Telemark Tours, Joseph, (541) 426-4322, (800) 646-9050, wingski@wingski.com. Backcountry tours over 30 square miles in the Big Sheep and Aneroid Lake drainages, with over 2,000 feet of vertical drop.

> ### Central Oregon Skiing
> *Central Oregon's great outdoors has everything from 500,000-year-old lava land to the latest in high-tech ski resorts. Seven hundred thousand skiers a year flock to Mount Bachelor, where they ski from November until early summer on 54 summit-to-base runs (served by nine lifts). It's a popular spot for both cross-country and alpine skiing; it's also where the U.S. ski team trains.—Janet Thomas, At Home in Hostel Territory.*

Mount Hood has been a favorite skiing destination for decades. From *Ski and Snow Country* by Ray Atkeson (photos) and Warren Miller (text).

Sno-Parks

Plowed lots are maintained during the winter on state, federal, and private lands throughout the Northwest specifically for nonmotorized vehicles and snowmobiles. Recreationists pay for the plowing, signing, and maintenance of the facilities through a permit program. To be legally parked in a designated Sno-Park lot, a vehicle must have a permit (passes are required from Nov. 15 through April 30), Oregon-issued permits are good for lots in Washington and Idaho. Permits can be purchased at U.S. Forest Service district offices and at most outdoor-recreation retail shops.

Organizations and Events of Interest

Oregon Ski Industries Association, (503) 598-4742.

Special Service Districts

A special service district is an independent governmental entity run by an elected governing body that provides a specific service in an area that either lies beyond municipal boundaries or crosses boundaries. Special districts are financed through property taxes or service fees. Oregon has about 30 different types of special service districts that provide such functions as water control, irrigation, ports, air-quality control, fire protection and response, hospitals, mass transit; parks and recreation, weed control, emergency communications, diking, and soil and water conservation districts.

District Type and Number

Ambulance, 3
Cemetery, 29
Councils of governments, 2
County services, 7
Domestic water supply, 98
Drainage, 16
Education Service, 9
Emergency communications, 8
Health and hospitals, 2
Irrigation, 65
Libraries, 13
Parks and recreation, 42
People's Utility Districts, 4
Ports, 21
Roads, 41
Rural fire protection, 222
Sanitation, 42
Soil and water conservation, 34
Television translators, 2
Transit, 8
Vector control, 14
Water control, 20
Water-improvement, 9
Water services, 16

Organizations of Interest

Special Districts Association of Oregon, 727 Center St. NE, No. 208, Salem 97301, (503) 371-8667, (800) 285-5461, www.sdao.com.

Speed Limits

Oregon's "basic rule" says you must drive at a speed that is reasonable and prudent at all times. It applies on all streets and highways, even where there are maximum speed limits posted, and takes into consideration such factors as road surface and width, intersection hazards, weather, visibility, and any other conditions that might affect safety. Driving at speeds that are unsafe for existing conditions, even if that speed is slower than what is legal or posted, is a violation.

Certain agencies in Portland and Beaverton use automated photo-radar equipment that photographs speeders, and the district court will find and ticket you if you get your picture taken. Also, if you drive slower than normal traffic, you must use the right lane or drive as close as possible to the right curb or edge of the road to allow traffic to pass. If you are passing slow traffic, you must obey the speed law.

In addition to the basic rule, Oregon has the following maximum speed limits:

City Streets (in any city or on roads within an urban growth boundary in heavily populated counties, such as Multnomah, Washington, Clackamas, Lane, Marion, Jackson, and Linn)
5 miles per hour in alleys
20 miles per hour in business districts, when passing school grounds or crosswalks when children can reasonably be expected to be present and signs or signals are posted
25 miles per hour in residential districts and in public parks

Interstates and Highways
25 miles per hour maximum on all ocean shores, where vehicles are permitted
55 miles per hour for all trucks and passenger transport vehicles on all highways, including interstate highways
55 miles per hour in urban areas
65 miles per hour in rural areas on I-5 and I-84

Sports Teams

Oregon cities and towns field highly competitive professional and semipro sports teams. The best known is the basketball powerhouse Portland Trail Blazers, a team that has had a winning season in all but two years since 1980.

Baseball

A number of Oregon minor league baseball teams participate in the Northwest League. These include:

Salem-Keizer Volcanoes, P.O. Box 20936, Keizer 97307, (503) 390-2225, www.volcanoesbaseball.com. Games broadcast on KYKN 1430 AM.

Southern Oregon Timberjacks, P.O. Box 1457, Medford 97501, (541) 770-5364, www.tjacks.com. Games broadcast on KRRM-FM 94.7.

Portland Rockies, P.O. Box 998, Portland 97207, (503) 223-2837, www.portlandrockies.com. Games broadcast on KKSN 1520 AM.

Eugene Emeralds Baseball Club, 2077 Willamette St., Eugene 97405, (541) 342-5367, fax: (541) 342-6089.

Basketball

The Portland Trail Blazers were established in 1970 as an expansion team of the National Basketball Association. Since 1989, the Trail Blazers have been owned by Microsoft cofounder Paul Allen. After several early, team-building years, the Trail Blazers caught fire with legendary center Bill Walton and captured the NBA championship in 1977. The Trail Blazers have continued to be successful. They have rarely missed the playoffs in the 1980s and 1990s and have reached the NBA finals twice, in 1990 and 1992. They reached the Western Conference finals again in 2000.

Tickets: Portland Trail Blazers, P.O. Box 4448, Portland 97208, (503) 231-8000

The Trail Blazers thrill home court fans at Portland's Rose Garden. Photo by Ernie Sapigao.

Home Court: The Rose Garden, 1 Center Court, Portland.

Portland Trail Blazers Team History

Season	Games Wins-Losses
1999-00	59-23
1998-99	35-15
1997-98	46-36
1996-97	49-33
1995-96	44-38
1994-95	44-38
1993-94	47-35
1992-93	51-31
1991-92	57-25
1990-91	63-19
1989-90	59-23
1988-89	39-43
1987-88	53-29
1986-87	49-33
1985-86	40-42
1984-85	42-40
1983-84	48-34
1982-83	46-36
1981-82	42-40
1980-81	45-37
1979-80	38-44
1978-79	45-37
1977-78	58-24
1976-77	49-33
1975-76	37-45
1974-75	38-44
1973-74	27-55
1972-73	21-61
1971-72	18-64
1970-71	29-53

Hockey

Portland was the first U.S. city to have a pro hockey team and the first U.S. city to compete for the Stanley Cup, hockey's top prize. Portland's modern hockey era began in 1960, with the construction of Memorial Coliseum. Two pro teams have played at the Coliseum, the Buckaroos (1960-1975) and the Winterhawks (since 1976) of the World Hockey League (WHL). For the 1998-99 season, the Winterhawks' record was 25 wins, 36 losses, and 13 ties. The team placed fifth in the Western Division, losing in the first round of playoffs to the Tri-CityAmericans. Following are some of the outstanding years of the Winterhawks:

Winterhawks History

1997-98	WHL regular season champions; playoff champions; Memorial Cup
1996-97	First in Western Division
1982-83	Memorial Cup
1981-82	Playoff champion
1979-80	Regular season championship

Soccer

Oregon boasts two professional soccer teams. The Portland Pythons belong to an indoor soccer league, the Premier Soccer Alliance, which is aligned with the United Kingdom's World Indoor Soccer League. The Portland Pythons' first full professional season was completed in 1999. The Cascade Surge, based in Salem, is aligned with the Premier Development Soccer League, part of the United Soccer Leagues. This league is the starting point for players working toward major-league soccer. The league is open to amateur players, including college players.

Organizations of Interest

Cascade Surge, McCulloch Stadium, Willamette University, Mission and Winter Sts., P.O. Box 2689, Salem 97308-2689, (503) 362-7308, www.cascadesurge. com.

Portland Pythons, 12064 SW Garden Place, Tigard 97223, (503) 684-5425, www.portlandpythons.com.

Places of Interest

Oregon Sports Hall of Fame Museum, 900 SW 5th Ave, Portland, (503) 227-7466.

State Parks and Recreation Areas

(*See Also* National Forests; National Parks, Monuments, and Recreation Areas) The Oregon Parks System began in 1913, when Gov. Oswald West took to the state legislature his goal of preserving ocean beaches. The beach along Crescent Beach (now part of Ecola State Park), Arch Cape, Cannon Beach, and Nehalem Bay became a public highway. In the years that followed, the Highway Commission purchased property and solicited land donations. After World War II, people who had endured anxiety, rationing, and, finally, victory were ready to enjoy themselves. From 1949 to 1952, recreation boomed. Protected coastal areas were expanded and 27 campgrounds were established. In the late 1980s, the legislature created the Oregon State Parks and Recreation Department to check the conflicts of interest inherent in land control by the Transportation Department. In 1996, 40 million people visited 240 state parks for the day, and 2 million stayed overnight.

For more information on all state parks and park activities, such as when fishing is permitted or when to avoid crowds, call the State Parks Information Center. Half of Oregon's state-park campgrounds allow you to reserve a campsite up to 11 months in advance. The other half are first-come, first-served, with check-in at 2:30 P.M. each day.

State Parks Information Center, (800) 551-6949, reservations: (800) 452-5687. Both lines are open from 8:00 A.M. to 5:00 P.M., Monday through Friday. The reservations line is operational 8:00 A.M. to 9:00 P.M. from June to September.

Central and Eastern Oregon

Clyde Holliday State Recreation Site, (800) 932-4453, borders the John Day River, where steelhead can be seen swimming upriver to spawn. Cottonwood trees afford beauty and shade, while appearances by Rocky Mountain elk and mule deer enhance the feeling of quiet seclusion.

Deschutes River State Recreation Area, (800) 551-6949, is located where the Deschutes and Columbia Rivers merge, making it a popular day-use and overnight site for fishing, boating, camping, and horseback riding. From late February through June, wildflowers bloom along the

(Continued on page 178)

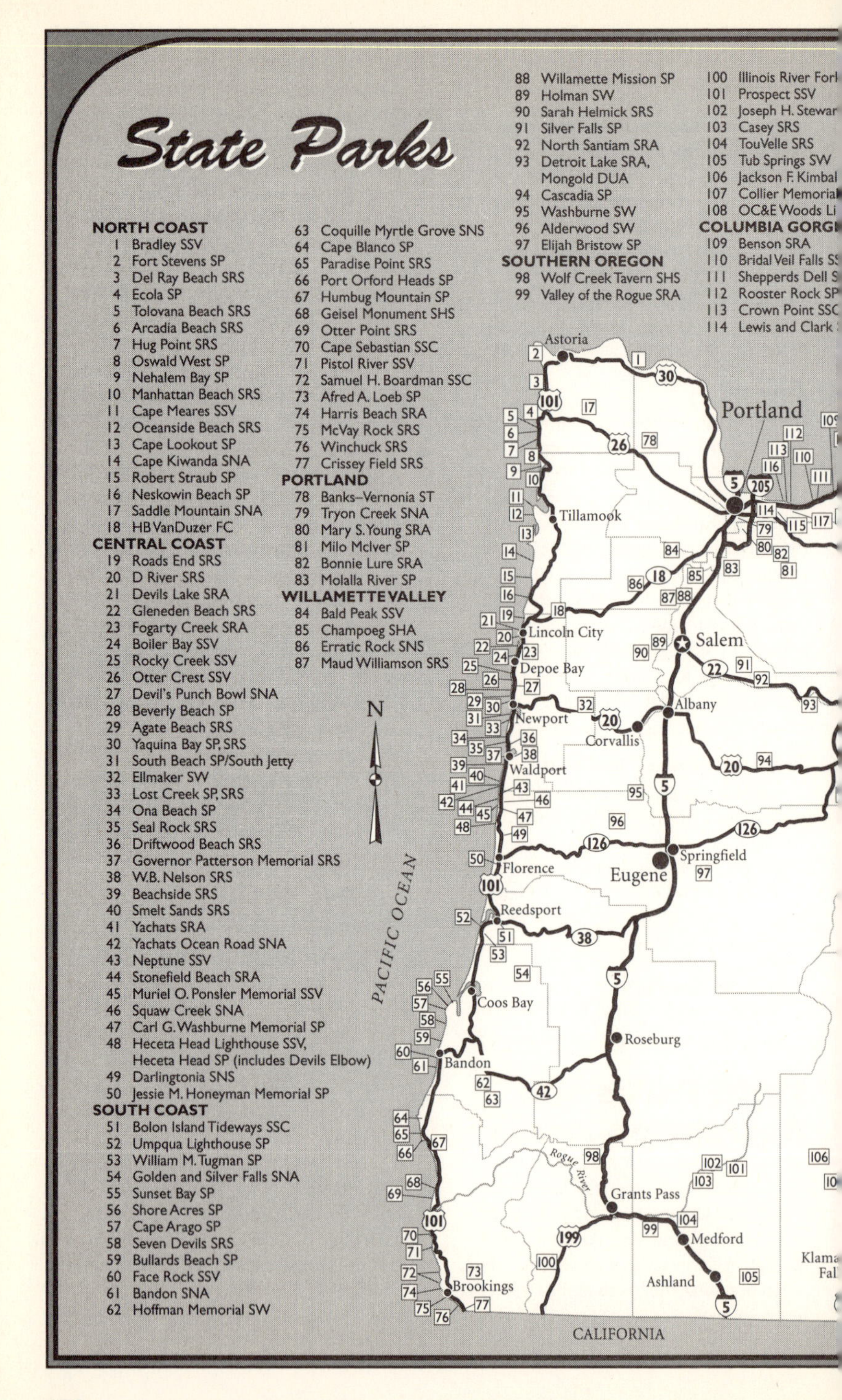
State Parks
NORTH COAST
1 Bradley SSV
2 Fort Stevens SP
3 Del Ray Beach SRS
4 Ecola SP
5 Tolovana Beach SRS
6 Arcadia Beach SRS
7 Hug Point SRS
8 Oswald West SP
9 Nehalem Bay SP
10 Manhattan Beach SRS
11 Cape Meares SSV
12 Oceanside Beach SRS
13 Cape Lookout SP
14 Cape Kiwanda SNA
15 Robert Straub SP
16 Neskowin Beach SP
17 Saddle Mountain SNA
18 HB VanDuzer FC
CENTRAL COAST
19 Roads End SRS
20 D River SRS
21 Devils Lake SRA
22 Gleneden Beach SRS
23 Fogarty Creek SRA
24 Boiler Bay SSV
25 Rocky Creek SSV
26 Otter Crest SSV
27 Devil's Punch Bowl SNA
28 Beverly Beach SP
29 Agate Beach SRS
30 Yaquina Bay SP, SRS
31 South Beach SP/South Jetty
32 Ellmaker SW
33 Lost Creek SP, SRS
34 Ona Beach SP
35 Seal Rock SRS
36 Driftwood Beach SRS
37 Governor Patterson Memorial SRS
38 W.B. Nelson SRS
39 Beachside SRS
40 Smelt Sands SRS
41 Yachats SRA
42 Yachats Ocean Road SNA
43 Neptune SSV
44 Stonefield Beach SRA
45 Muriel O. Ponsler Memorial SSV
46 Squaw Creek SNA
47 Carl G. Washburne Memorial SP
48 Heceta Head Lighthouse SSV, Heceta Head SP (includes Devils Elbow)
49 Darlingtonia SNS
50 Jessie M. Honeyman Memorial SP
SOUTH COAST
51 Bolon Island Tideways SSC
52 Umpqua Lighthouse SP
53 William M. Tugman SP
54 Golden and Silver Falls SNA
55 Sunset Bay SP
56 Shore Acres SP
57 Cape Arago SP
58 Seven Devils SRS
59 Bullards Beach SP
60 Face Rock SSV
61 Bandon SNA
62 Hoffman Memorial SW
63 Coquille Myrtle Grove SNS
64 Cape Blanco SP
65 Paradise Point SRS
66 Port Orford Heads SP
67 Humbug Mountain SP
68 Geisel Monument SHS
69 Otter Point SRS
70 Cape Sebastian SSC
71 Pistol River SSV
72 Samuel H. Boardman SSC
73 Afred A. Loeb SP
74 Harris Beach SRA
75 McVay Rock SRS
76 Winchuck SRS
77 Crissey Field SRS
PORTLAND
78 Banks–Vernonia ST
79 Tryon Creek SNA
80 Mary S. Young SRA
81 Milo McIver SP
82 Bonnie Lure SRA
83 Molalla River SP
WILLAMETTE VALLEY
84 Bald Peak SSV
85 Champoeg SHA
86 Erratic Rock SNS
87 Maud Williamson SRS
88 Willamette Mission SP
89 Holman SW
90 Sarah Helmick SRS
91 Silver Falls SP
92 North Santiam SRA
93 Detroit Lake SRA, Mongold DUA
94 Cascadia SP
95 Washburne SW
96 Alderwood SW
97 Elijah Bristow SP
SOUTHERN OREGON
98 Wolf Creek Tavern SHS
99 Valley of the Rogue SRA
100 Illinois River For
101 Prospect SSV
102 Joseph H. Stewar
103 Casey SRS
104 TouVelle SRS
105 Tub Springs SW
106 Jackson F. Kimbal
107 Collier Memoria
108 OC&E Woods Li
COLUMBIA GORG
109 Benson SRA
110 Bridal Veil Falls S
111 Shepperds Dell S
112 Rooster Rock SP
113 Crown Point SSC
114 Lewis and Clark
N
PACIFIC OCEAN
Astoria
Portland
Tillamook
Lincoln City
Depoe Bay
Salem
Newport
Corvallis
Albany
Waldport
Florence
Eugene
Springfield
Reedsport
Coos Bay
Roseburg
Bandon
Rogue River
Grants Pass
Medford
Ashland
Brookings
CALIFORNIA

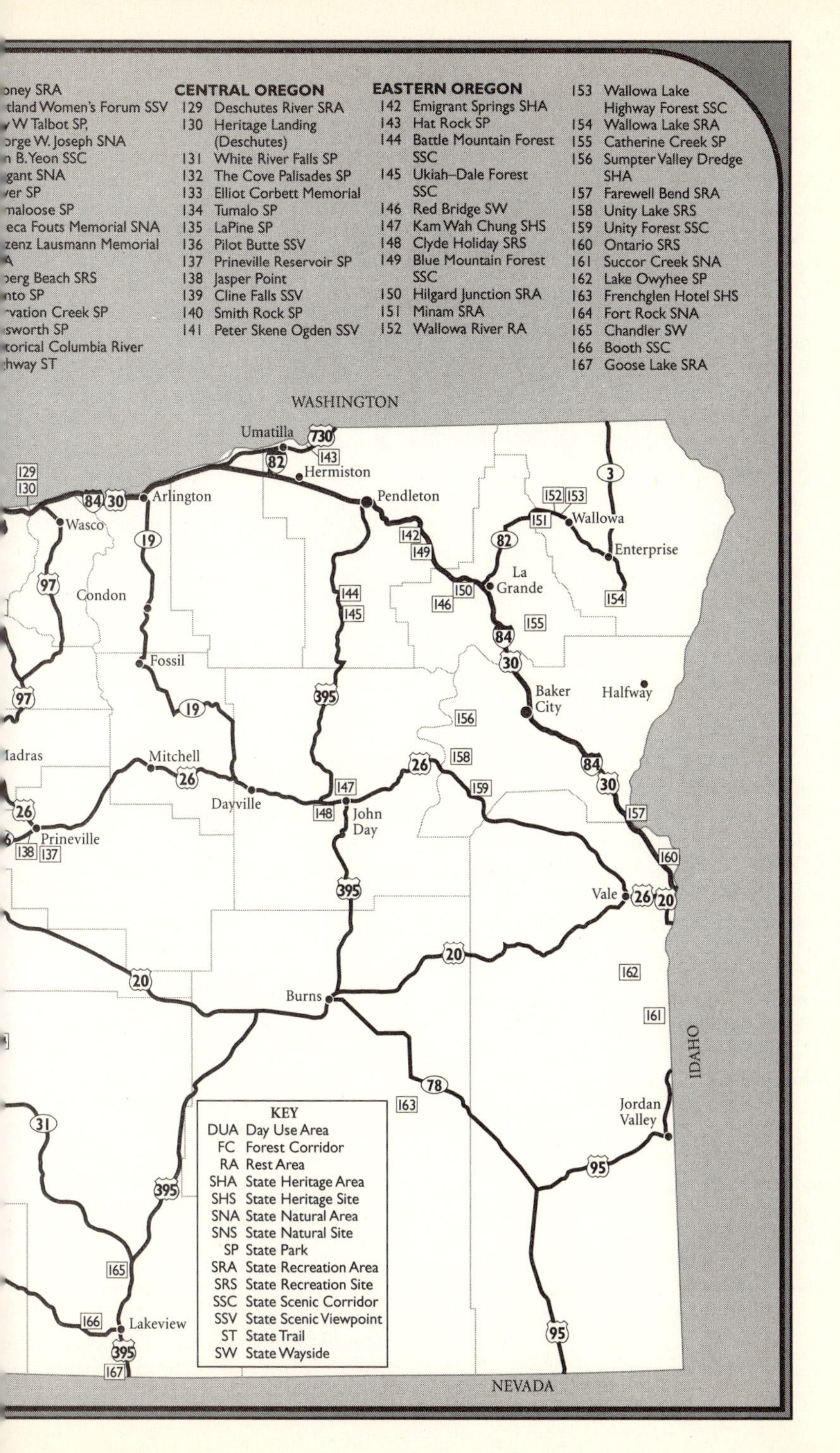

CENTRAL OREGON
129 Deschutes River SRA
130 Heritage Landing (Deschutes)
131 White River Falls SP
132 The Cove Palisades SP
133 Elliot Corbett Memorial
134 Tumalo SP
135 LaPine SP
136 Pilot Butte SSV
137 Prineville Reservoir SP
138 Jasper Point
139 Cline Falls SSV
140 Smith Rock SP
141 Peter Skene Ogden SSV
EASTERN OREGON
142 Emigrant Springs SHA
143 Hat Rock SP
144 Battle Mountain Forest SSC
145 Ukiah–Dale Forest SSC
146 Red Bridge SW
147 Kam Wah Chung SHS
148 Clyde Holiday SRS
149 Blue Mountain Forest SSC
150 Hilgard Junction SRA
151 Minam SRA
152 Wallowa River RA
153 Wallowa Lake Highway Forest SSC
154 Wallowa Lake SRA
155 Catherine Creek SP
156 Sumpter Valley Dredge SHA
157 Farewell Bend SRA
158 Unity Lake SRS
159 Unity Forest SSC
160 Ontario SRS
161 Succor Creek SNA
162 Lake Owyhee SP
163 Frenchglen Hotel SHS
164 Fort Rock SNA
165 Chandler SW
166 Booth SSC
167 Goose Lake SRA
WASHINGTON
Umatilla
Hermiston
Pendleton
Arlington
Wasco
Condon
Fossil
Wallowa
Enterprise
La Grande
Baker City
Halfway
Mitchell
Dayville
John Day
Prineville
Vale
Burns
Jordan Valley
Lakeview
IDAHO
NEVADA
KEY
DUA Day Use Area
FC Forest Corridor
RA Rest Area
SHA State Heritage Area
SHS State Heritage Site
SNA State Natural Area
SNS State Natural Site
SP State Park
SRA State Recreation Area
SRS State Recreation Site
SSC State Scenic Corridor
SSV State Scenic Viewpoint
ST State Trail
SW State Wayside

canyon walls. On hotter days, the riverside Atiyeh Trail provides comfortable hiking in the shade of birch and alder trees, a favorite nesting spot for orioles.

Emigrant Springs State Heritage Area, (541) 983-2277, near the summit of the Blue Mountains, offers visitors a chance to camp (including horse camping) and explore a main stop of pioneers coming over this most difficult part of the Oregon Trail. The large park encompasses both old-growth forest, abundant flora and wildlife, and modern amenities such as a full-sized basketball court, an amphitheater for evening programs, and heated cabins. Emigrant Springs makes a great base camp for exploring other nearby remnants of the Oregon Trail, such as the underground tour in Pendleton, a depiction of what life was like for Chinese immigrants of the 1800s.

Fort Rock State Natural Area, (800) 551-6949, is a near-circle of monolithic walls jutting out of the flat, high desert just off Oregon 31 between Bend and Lakeview. Early Native Americans canoed to and from this site, which was an island with a volcano set in a prehistoric shallow sea. They left behind some of the earliest artifacts of human activity found in Oregon.

Hat Rock State Park, (800) 551-6949, named for its outcroppings of basalt, stands 9 miles east of Umatilla on the Columbia River. This was the first landmark noted by Lewis and Clark on their way down the Columbia. Sagebrush hills surround acres of grass and groves of cottonwood trees. Located on the south shore of Lake Wallula, the park offers fishing, waterskiing, jetboating, swimming, and a separate pond stocked with rainbow trout.

Sumpter Valley Dredge State Heritage Area, (541) 894-2486, off Oregon 7 at the base of the towering Elkhorn Mountains, still bears the scars of the gold rush. As the Powder River rushes down from the Elkhorns through the park, tailings line the river's banks for miles before it flows into Phillips Reservoir.

Wallowa Lake State Recreation Area, (541) 432-4185, a gateway to Hells Canyon National Recreation Area, provides the chance to fish, canoe, even ride bumper boats. Wildlife can be spotted along the hiking trails, and the campground is surrounded on three sides by 9,000-foot snowcapped mountains. Joseph, a nearby artist's community is known for tours of top-quality bronze foundries and showrooms

White River Falls State Park, (800) 551-6949, plunging 90 feet over a basalt shelf, is found just east of the Tygh Valley along Oregon 216. The park offers picnicking, fishing, and hiking, including a challenging 0.25-mile trail into the canyon to the site of one of the area's first hydroelectric power plants.

Coast Range and Willamette Valley

Cascadia State Park, (503) 854-3406, is a large park with just two dozen campsites (open March to October), giving the visitor a sense of seclusion and serenity. Picnic grounds on the west side are open year-round. Soda Creek Falls can be reached via a 0.75-mile trail, while another trail winds through old-growth Douglas fir along the South Santiam River, a good site for fishing and swimming. Visitors can still see ruts from the Santiam Wagon Road, a military route from the 1800s.

Erratic Rock State Natural Site, (800) 551-6949, six miles east of Sheridan off Oregon 18, is a unique geologic specimen, a 40-ton rock deposited by prehistoric flooding. The expanse of the Willamette Valley's vineyards makes for a great view while you hike the trail to the rock.

Molalla River State Park, (800) 551-6949, located near Canby where the Willamette, Molalla, and Pudding Rivers converge, provides a floodplain habitat for waterfowl, wading birds (there is a large blue heron rookery), deer, reptiles, and amphibians. Picnic or run the dog in one of the several large, grassy field areas or set off fishing from the boat ramp.

Columbia Gorge

Bridal Veil Falls State Scenic Viewpoint, (800) 551-6949, is located on U.S. 30 (Historic Columbia River Highway) near milepost 28. Situated in what was once a major logging zone, this park's main attractions are its two hiking trails, though restrooms and picnic areas for short stops are easily accessed from the parking lot. The park's wheelchair-accessible Upper Trail meanders along the precipices of the Columbia Gorge, with wild native plants such as lupine, trillium, and bleeding heart marked by signs. A 120-foot basalt tower, called the Pillars of Hercules, can be viewed from this path. The Lower Trail is steep, with many switchbacks and some poison ivy on its mile-long round-trip course to the base of the falls.

Crown Point State Scenic Corridor, (503) 695-2261, reached from the Historic Columbia River Highway or exit 22 on U.S. 30 near Corbett, is known as the site of historic Vista House. Built in 1916, at the same time as the old highway, it was one of the first resort-style stopping places in the state, providing refreshments and views of the Gorge's splendor. Open from March through October, the renovated octagonal building has an interpretive display of the Gorge's historic and geologic points of interest.

Portland's Women's Forum State Scenic Viewpoint, (800) 551-6949, near Crown Point and Vista House, has one of the best views of the Gorge.

Oregon Coast

Cape Lookout State Park, (503) 842-4981, can be reached by traveling 1.5 hours west from Portland through Wilson Pass. This route across the Coast Range features waterfalls, panoramic views, and fishing areas. Cape Lookout is on a sandspit between Netarts Bay and the Pacific Ocean. Beachcombers may find glass floats or spot a whale, while a lush old-growth forest encompasses eight miles of hiking trails. One shorter trail has signs marking native trees and other plants, while the second trail begins with a description of the local salmon restoration project. Cape Lookout is part of the Three Capes Scenic Route, along with Cape Kiwanda and Cape Meares.

Fort Stevens, (503) 861-1671, south of Astoria, is one of the largest state-park campgrounds in the United States, offering beach access, swimming, a historic shipwreck, and a military fort dating back to the Civil War. Hiking and biking trails range through both forests and sand dunes.

Honeyman State Park, (541) 997-3641, the second-largest overnight campground in the state, is located three miles south of Florence on U.S. 101. Two freshwater lakes offer boating and swimming, or you can hike two miles of sand dunes between the lake and the ocean. From October 1 through April 30 each year, access to Oregon Dunes National Recreation Area is provided from the K and L campsites. Reservations are recommended for the winter holidays.

Nehalem Bay State Park, (503) 368-5154, though not the most remote park, provides a serene site for kayaking, swimming, and fishing in Nehalem Bay, beach dunes with a view of Neahkanie Mountain, prolific wildlife, and the chance to catch your own crab to cook over the camp stove. Restaurants and shops in the neighboring towns of Manzanita and Nehalem offer a break from tent life.

Umpqua Lighthouse State Park, (541) 271-4118, (541) 271-4631, is barely a mile from Winchester Bay's Salmon Harbor. Surrounded by dunes as high as 500 feet, freshwater Lake Marie is the hub of camping and day use. Open for angling and nonmotorized boating, the park also has a small sandy beach for swimming. Tours of the 65-foot lighthouse and adjacent museum are offered May 1 to September 30.

Southern Oregon

OC&E Woods Line State Trail, (800) 551-6949, a 110.4-mile rail-to-trail conversion, is Oregon's longest linear park.

Decades ago, the Oregon, California and Eastern Railroad thrived, carrying timber and cattle and crossing the A Canal in Klamath Falls on a steel bridge built in 1898. The trail, open to anything without a motor, begins in Klamath Falls and continues east to Bly, then north to bucolic Sycan Marsh. The trail is paved between the Klamath Falls trailhead and Oregon 39 (the steel bridge is part of this section). Unpaved from the highway, the trail winds through ranchlands, rivers, and forested buttes, popular with mountain bikers and anglers.

Tub Springs State Wayside, (800) 551-6949, is on the Applegate Trail amid towering firs, where travelers in the mid-1800s could rest before heading across the mountain pass into Ashland. You can drink from the recently renovated tubs installed in the 1930s to provide fresh water.

Wolf Creek Inn State Heritage Site, (541) 866-2474 (reservations), is a remnant of the late 1800s, when the Applegate Trail provided an alternative for pioneers to the last section of the Oregon Trail. Listed on the National Register of Historic Places, the inn still offers meals and lodging. Interpretive panels in front of the tavern describe the hardships of life on the Applegate Trail.

Organizations of Interest

Reservations Northwest, (800) 452-5687, fax: (503) 378-6308, park.info@state.or.us.

Salem Headquarters, (503) 378-6305, fax: (503) 378-6447.

State Parks Information Center, (800) 551-6949, fax: (503) 872-5289.

State Symbols

State Animal. Named as the state animal in 1969 by the state legislature, the beaver *(Castor canadensis)* was nearly trapped to extinction by early settlers but has been reestablished in watercourses throughout the state. The beaver's dam-building activities are important to natural water flow and erosion control. Oregon's nickname is the "Beaver State," and this furry, toothy creature is the symbol of Oregon State University's athletic teams.

The meadowlark, Oregon's state bird. Illustration by Joyce Bergen. From *The Great Northwest Nature Factbook* by Ann Saling.

State Bird. The meadowlark *(Sturnella neglecta)* was the preferred choice for state bird by schoolchildren, who picked it in 1927 in a poll sponsored by the Oregon Audubon Society. A native songbird, the western meadowlark has brown with buff and black plumage, bright yellow on its underside, and a black crescent on its breast. Its outer tail feathers are mainly white and are easily visible when it flies.

State Dance. The square dance was designated the official state dance in 1977. The pioneer origins of square dancing reflect Oregon's pioneer heritage.

State Fish. Largest of the Pacific salmons, the chinook salmon *(Oncorhynchus tshawytscha)*—or king salmon—was designated the state fish in 1961.

State Flag. Adopted in 1925, the navy blue and gold state flag features the state shield surrounded by 33 stars, with "STATE OF OREGON" lettered above it and "1859" (the year Oregon became a state) below it. The flag's reverse side has a beaver, the only state flag with a different pattern on its reverse side.

State Flower. Oregon grape *(Berberis aquifolium)* was selected as the state flower in 1899. This native Pacific Coast evergreen plant has waxy green leaves that resemble holly leaves, small yellow flowers in early summer, and a dark blue berry in the fall.

State Gemstone. The sunstone was designated as the state gemstone in 1987. It is a large, brightly colored transparent gem prized by collectors.

Oregon, My Oregon

Land of the Empire Builders,
Land of the Golden West;
Conquered and held by free men,
Fairest and the best.
Onward and upward ever,
Forward and on, and on;
Hail to thee, Land of Heroes,
My Oregon.

Land of the rose and sunshine,
Land of the summer's breeze;
Laden with health and vigor,
Fresh from the Western seas.
Blest by the blood of martyrs,
Land of the setting sun;
Hail to thee, Land of Promise,
My Oregon.

—State song by J.A. Buchanan and Henry B. Murtagh

State Insect. Oregon's official insect, the Oregon swallowtail butterfly *(Papilio oregonius),* was designated in 1979. This beautiful native yellow butterfly is found in the sagebrush canyons of the Columbia River and its tributaries, including the Snake.

State Nut. Of the entire U.S. commercial crop of hazelnuts, 99 percent are grown in Oregon. The Oregon hazelnut *(Corylus avellana),* unlike wild varieties, grows on single-trunked trees up to 30 or 40 feet tall. It was designated the state nut in 1989.

State Rock. The thunderegg, a geode, was the first choice of rockhounds to be the official state rock. The thunderegg officially became the state rock in 1965.

State Seal. The state seal consists of an escutcheon, or shield, supported by 33 stars and divided by a ribbon called an "ordinary," inscribed with "THE UNION." Above the ordinary are mountains and forests, an elk, a covered wagon and ox team, the Pacific Ocean with setting sun, and a departing British man-of-war and arriving American merchant ship (signifying the waning of British and rise of American power in the territory). Below the ordinary is a quartering with a sheaf of wheat, a plow, and a pickax. The crest is the bald eagle. Around the perimeter of the seal is the legend "STATE OF OREGON 1859."

State Seashell. Named in 1848 after the Oregon Territory, the Oregon hairy triton *(Fusitriton oregonensis)* is one of the largest snails found in the state, reaching lengths up to 5 inches. It was designated the state seashell in 1991.

State Song. J. A. Buchanan of Astoria and Henry B. Murtagh of Portland wrote "Oregon, My Oregon" in 1920. The song was the winner of a statewide competition sponsored by the Society of Oregon Composers. It became the official state song in 1927.

State Tree. Named for famed Scottish botanist David Douglas, the Douglas fir *(Pseudotsuga menziesii)* was designated state tree in 1939. These trees can grow to 325 feet in height and 15 feet in diameter, though a 200-foot-tall, 6-foot-diameter tree is more usual.

Taxes

In 1997, Oregon ranked 31st nationally in the total amount of taxes citizens pay, and Oregonians pay an average of $1,525 per person in state and local taxes. The state's total tax revenues for 1997 were $4.9 billion. State income taxes comprise the greatest share of Oregon's tax base. The next largest source, 30 percent, is property taxes. Combined income and property taxes account for over 70 percent of total Oregon state and local tax revenue.

Statewide Taxes

Personal Income Tax. Income taxes are assessed on individuals, estates, and trusts, part-year residents, and nonresidents with income from Oregon. For 1997, the income tax rates (applied to taxable income) were as follows: ***Single return:*** 5 percent on the first $2,250; 7 percent on the next $3,450; and 9 percent on everything over $5,700. ***Joint Return:*** 5 percent on the first $4,500; 7 percent on the next $6,900; and 9 percent on everything over $11,400.

Business Taxes: Corporations doing business in Oregon pay excise taxes (the minimum excise tax is $10). Corporations not doing business, but that have income from Oregon, pay income tax (6.6 percent of net income).

Inheritance Tax: If a federal estate tax return is required, an inheritance tax return must also be filed in Oregon (within nine months after death).

Property Tax: This tax applies to owners of real and business personal property and is based on the assessed value of taxable property. County assessors set permanent rates for all taxing districts, effective as of 1997-98. However, the tax rates cannot exceed $15 per $1,000 of real market value.

Sin Taxes: (1) Owners of gaming machines, such as video poker and Keno, pay an amusement-device tax. (2) Manufacturers and/or import wholesalers of malt beverages and wines pay a privilege tax. (3) Manufacturers, wholesalers, and retailers of distilled spirits, malt beverages, and wines pay license fees. (4) Employees who serve alcoholic beverages pay for service permits. (5) Licensed cigarette and tobacco distributors pay a tax by use of stamps or meter impressions.

Timber Taxes: (1) Timber owners pay a severance tax on the value of harvested timber. (2) A forest-products harvest tax is paid on timber cut from any land in Oregon.

Unemployment Insurance: As of 1997, new employers were assigned a fixed rate of 3 percent. Existing employers paid tax rates ranging from 1 percent to 5.4 percent. The tax was paid on the first $20,000 of wages paid to each employee. The rate schedule depends in effect on the balance in a trust fund as of August 31 of each year and the amount of revenue needed to maintain the balance at a level adequate to pay benefits.

Utilities and Railroad Taxes: (1) Railroads and investor-owned utilities operating within the state pay an annual fee. (2) For-hire and private motor carriers operating into, within, and through the state pay weight-mile taxes. The rate is limited to .25 percent of gross operating revenues of investor-owned utilities and .35 percent of gross operating revenues of railroads. Motor carriers pay applications, plate fees, and per-mile rates based on vehicle weight.

Vehicles and Fuel: Fees for testing and licensing of drivers, vehicle titles and registration, and fuel importation and purchase include the following: (1) Vehicle registration fees are $30 (custom plates are $80); vehicle title fees are $10; driver's license (good for four years) is $26.25 (standard) and $51.25 (commercial). (2) Various fees are assessed for commercial license tests; motorcycle endorsements, vehicle identification number, emissions inspections, disability placards, and other items. (3) The gasoline tax is 24 cents per gallon. (4) Petroleum suppliers and importers pay a petroleum load fee.

Miscellaneous: (1) An emergency communications tax for 911 phone services is paid by individuals through telephone companies providing local exchange access services in Oregon ($.75 per line per month). (2) Possessors of non-petroleum hazardous substances pay a hazardous substance fee. (3) Operators of dry-cleaning facilities pay a dry-cleaning tax.

Local Government Taxes

A payroll tax for mass-transit systems is paid by employers in the Tri-Met (Portland area) and Lane Transit (Eugene) districts. (2) Self-employment tax for mass-transit systems is paid by sole proprietors and partnerships with business earnings in these districts. (3) In Multnomah County, businesses pay an income tax. (4) Many local governments in Oregon collect other taxes, such as hotel-motel taxes.

State Government Tax Collections in 1997 (millions of dollars)

Alcohol and tobacco	166
Corporation license	5
Corporation net income	384
Death and gift	34
Hunting and fishing	26
Individual income	3,273
Insurance premiums	76
Motor fuels	421
Motor vehicles and operators	352
Occupancy and business	115
Public utilities	9
Severance	53

Source: U.S. Bureau of the Census

Licenses, Permits, and Fees

In addition to taxes, the state takes in revenue from fees for licensing occupations, uses, and privileges, such as fishing and hunting licenses.

Organizations of Interest

Oregon Department of Revenue, P.O. Box 14600, Salem 97309-5049, tax help: (503) 378-4988, TTY: (800) 886-7204, TTY in Salem only: (503) 945-8617, Spanish language line: (503) 945-8618, www.dor.state.or.us.

The Dalles The Dalles is where some Oregon Trail pioneers loaded their wagons onto rafts or barges and floated down the Columbia to the mouth of the Willamette River, then upriver to Oregon City. The historic significance of The Dalles (named for the French word that means "trough" and pertaining to the "trough" of the Columbia) refers not only to Lewis and Clark, the Oregon Trail, and The Dalles Dam. For centuries this area was a hub of fishing and trading activity among Native Americans. After guiding the first explorers and assisting with river crossings during the Oregon Trail years, the Indians' fishing and hunting were increasingly restricted by the new presence of the U.S. government. Between 1853 and 1855, 11 treaties took away most of the tribal land in Western Oregon and the Columbia Plateau. Tribes that had not been completely wiped out by disease were moved onto reservations, including the Warm Springs Reservation south of The Dalles.

The Columbia River forms most of the border between Washington and Oregon, and The Dalles, which the Indians called *Winquatt* ("place encircled by rock cliffs"), marked the intersection of the early coastal and valley tribes. Cedar-planked longhouses 200 feet in length dotted the shores when Lewis and Clark came through in 1805, and the area was well-known for its plentiful fish. Salmon were valuable currency in an extensive trade network that ran up the coast to Vancouver Island, and inland as far as Minnesota.

A thoughtful distillation of this history can be found at The Dalles's main attraction, the $21.6 million Columbia Gorge Discovery Center. One of the most impressive exhibits is a 33-foot moving model in which Columbia River dams are lifted out to animate Celilo Falls, the giant cataracts that were drowned by the construction of The Dalles Dam. Just across the river in Washington, within Horsethief Lake State Park, Native American petroglyphs are preserved on canyon walls, accessible via park ranger-guided tours.

The city maintains historic houses representing Colonial, Gothic Revival, Italianate, and American Renaissance architecture, and provides maps through **The Dalles Convention and Visitor Bureau,** (800) 255-3385. The privately owned Williams House Inn, worth a visit, is an 1899 Queen Anne house listed on the National Register of Historic Places and surrounded by a 3-acre arboretum.

Wasco County's seasonal cherry harvest is the nation's largest. The Dalles's cherry canneries start buzzing in spring, employing migrant pickers who patronize small businesses. The annual Cherry Festival takes place in mid-April.

The Dalles is a hub year-round for traffic along I-84, Oregon's major east-west highway, and the town's convention amenities invite organizations and business conferences from around the region.

Tides The range of tidal movement is affected by a number of factors, including

Picturing Wind and Waves

Throughout the year, Oregon's cliffs and rocks withstand the turbulence of the North Pacific high tides. The most dramatic high tide shows are staged in the fall and winter, when gale force winds lift the waves as high as 60 feet and then drop them with a thunderous roar. It's not uncommon to witness waves leaping over U.S. 101.

—Bryan F. Peterson, *Photographing Oregon with Professional Results.*

Exploring the surf. From *Wind on the Waves* by Kim R. Stafford (text), Ray Atkeson and Rick Schafer (photos).

the shape and slope of the shoreline, the cycles of the moon, and storm conditions. Tides can vary widely, from a range of only a few feet to tens of feet between high and low tides, thus it is not possible to specify an average range for all of Oregon's marine shoreline. The most extreme tides—the highest high and the lowest low—occur during the new and full moons; the least variation from low to high waters coincides with the quarter moons. Generally, the highest tides occur during winter months. Consult tide tables published for specific areas, which are available at most sporting goods stores and bookstores, as well as the Internet, for specific information.

Following are some approximate ranges and highs and lows for Oregon tide stations.

Astoria: Tidal range is generally about 7 to 10.5 feet, with maximum high tides measured at well over 12 feet and lowest tides at 2 feet below mean low water (–2 feet).

Charleston, Coos Bay: Tidal range is about 5 to 7 feet, with the highest tides up to about 10.5 feet and the lowest tides at about –2.5 feet.

Port Orford: Tidal range is about 6 to 8 feet, with the highest tides about 10 feet and the lowest over –2 feet.

South Beach, Yaquina River: Tidal range is generally about 7 to 9 feet, with the highest tides measuring over 11.5 feet and lowest at just over –2.5 feet.

Organizations of Interest

The National Oceanic and Atmospheric Administration, www.opsd.nos.noaa.gov. This organization's National Ocean Survey collects and archives tidal data and makes it available on the Internet.

Transportation

(SEE ALSO AIRPORTS; PORTS; RAILROADS; ROADS AND HIGHWAYS) Oregon has a very efficient, multimodal system for moving goods and people throughout the state and connecting the state to the rest of the United States and the world, including the Pacific Rim. Agriculture, wood products, fishing, high tech, tourism—all sectors of the state's economy depend on the efficient movement of goods and services.

Air Travel

More than 400 airports operate in Oregon. The state operates 30 general aviation airports that serve recreational, agricultural, and forestry purposes, and nine cities have scheduled airline service: Astoria, Eugene, Klamath Falls, Medford, Newport, North Bend, Pendleton, Portland, and Redmond. Portland International Airport (PDX), operated by the Port of Portland, is the largest commercial airport in the state and operates as the hub for flights elsewhere. Nearly 3.1 million passengers passed through Oregon's airports in 1996. Spending by these air travelers and associated economic impacts totaled $5.6 billion. Spending related to tenant companies at airports is estimated at $5.9 billion. Aviation supported a total of 24,700 jobs in the state.

Public Transit

By the year 2020, Oregon's population is expected to grow by over a million people—700,000 of them in the Willamette Valley. Public transit will become increasingly important as the metropolitan areas grows. Statewide, the present public-transit systems provide more than 86 million rides each year. The metropolitan transit systems operating are the Portland metropolitan area's Tri-Met, Corvallis Transit System, Lane County Transit, Salem Area Transit, and Albany Transit, plus 25 small city and rural systems. Public-transit service providers operate light-rail and urban bus systems as well as door-to-door, dial-a-ride, and other specialized services, especially in smaller communities. Despite the range of public-transit services presently available and planned, in 1996 about 68 percent of working Oregonians commuted alone by automobile.

State-sponsored carpool programs and park-and-ride services presently operate in Albany, Bend, Corvallis, Eugene, Medford, Portland, and Salem. These programs provide commuters with choices and ultimately will reduce the strain and public cost of operating the road system.

Railroads

Rail transportation in Oregon includes passenger service provided by AMTRAK; common carrier; line-haul freight services provided by Union Pacific, Burlington Northern, and several feeder lines; and a number of historical lines now operated as tourist excursions. AMTRAK trains connect Portland and other cities north to Washington, south to California, and east to Boise, Idaho. The major freight lines also follow these routes.

Roads and Highways

The State Department of Transportation maintains about 7,500 miles of highways, with more than 16,000 lane-miles of pavement. The total road mileage in the state, including city, county, state, and other publicly owned roads, is 84,920 miles. Trucks carry 64 percent by value and 76 percent by weight of all Oregon freight that is shipped elsewhere in the United States. Seattle-Portland truck tonnages are the greatest of any major metropolitan origin-destination pairs in the West.

Waterborne Commerce

Waterborne commerce continues to be Oregon's major international trading link. Oregon's 23 ports on the Columbia River system and the Pacific Coast support maritime commerce, operate airports, and promote economic development. The Columbia-Snake river system is the second-largest grain-exporting system in the world. A 40-foot dredged channel serves the Port of Portland, located 110 river miles from the Pacific Coast. Portland moved the second-largest amount of goods by volume on the entire Pacific Coast in 1997.

Oregon's ports have diversified in recent years in ways that help the economies of their regions. Tourism and recreation services especially comprise a growing priority for ports. The Port of Hood River, for example, has developed a nationally important facility for windsurfers.

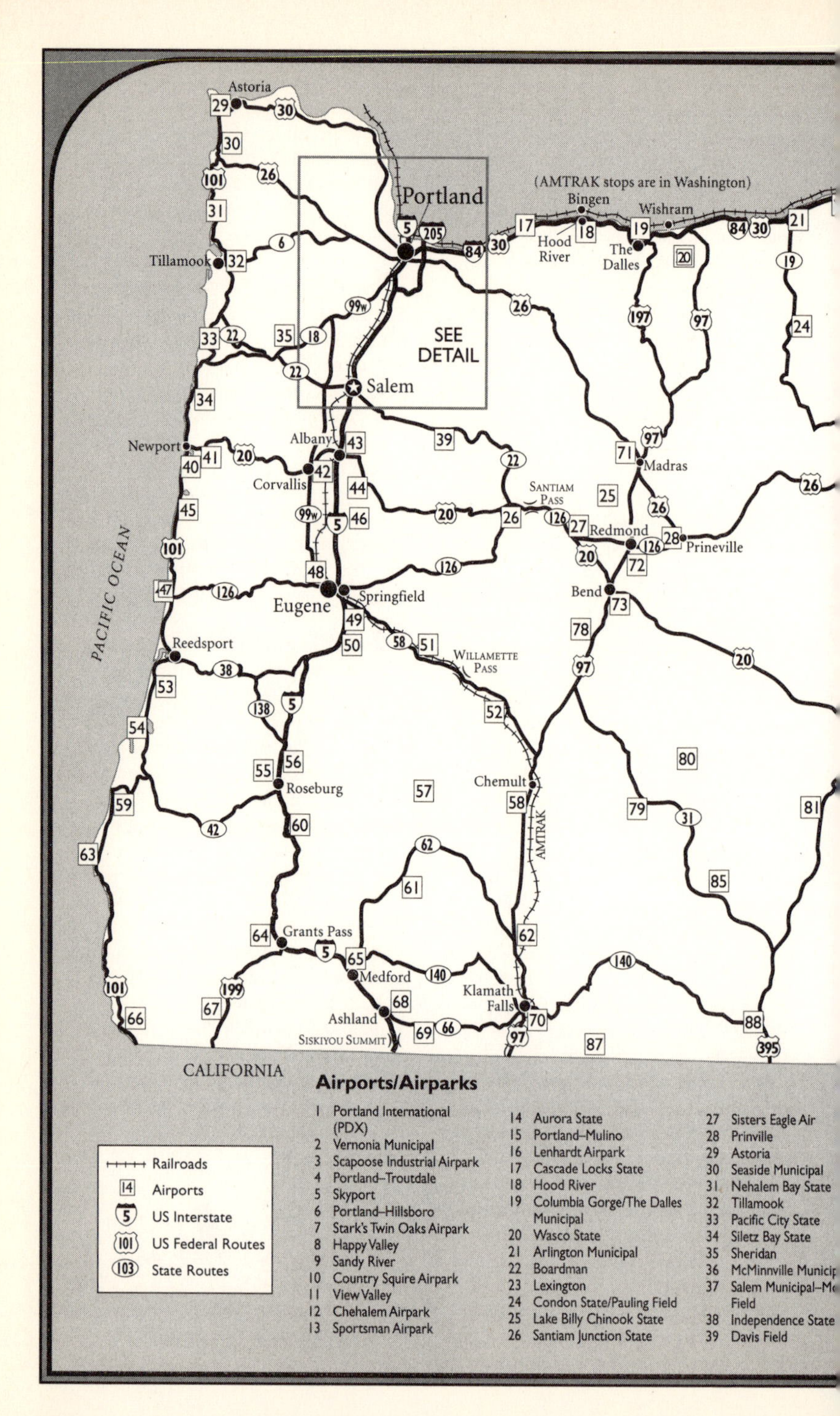

Astoria
Portland
SEE DETAIL
Salem
(AMTRAK stops are in Washington)
Bingen
Wishram
Hood River
The Dalles
Tillamook
Newport
Albany
Corvallis
Madras
SANTIAM PASS
Redmond
Prineville
Bend
Eugene
Springfield
Reedsport
WILLAMETTE PASS
PACIFIC OCEAN
Chemult
AMTRAK
Roseburg
Grants Pass
Medford
Klamath Falls
Ashland
SISKIYOU SUMMIT
CALIFORNIA
Railroads
Airports
US Interstate
US Federal Routes
State Routes
Airports/Airparks
1 Portland International (PDX)
2 Vernonia Municipal
3 Scapoose Industrial Airpark
4 Portland–Troutdale
5 Skyport
6 Portland–Hillsboro
7 Stark's Twin Oaks Airpark
8 Happy Valley
9 Sandy River
10 Country Squire Airpark
11 View Valley
12 Chehalem Airpark
13 Sportsman Airpark
14 Aurora State
15 Portland–Mulino
16 Lenhardt Airpark
17 Cascade Locks State
18 Hood River
19 Columbia Gorge/The Dalles Municipal
20 Wasco State
21 Arlington Municipal
22 Boardman
23 Lexington
24 Condon State/Pauling Field
25 Lake Billy Chinook State
26 Santiam Junction State
27 Sisters Eagle Air
28 Prinville
29 Astoria
30 Seaside Municipal
31 Nehalem Bay State
32 Tillamook
33 Pacific City State
34 Siletz Bay State
35 Sheridan
36 McMinnville Municip
37 Salem Municipal–M Field
38 Independence State
39 Davis Field

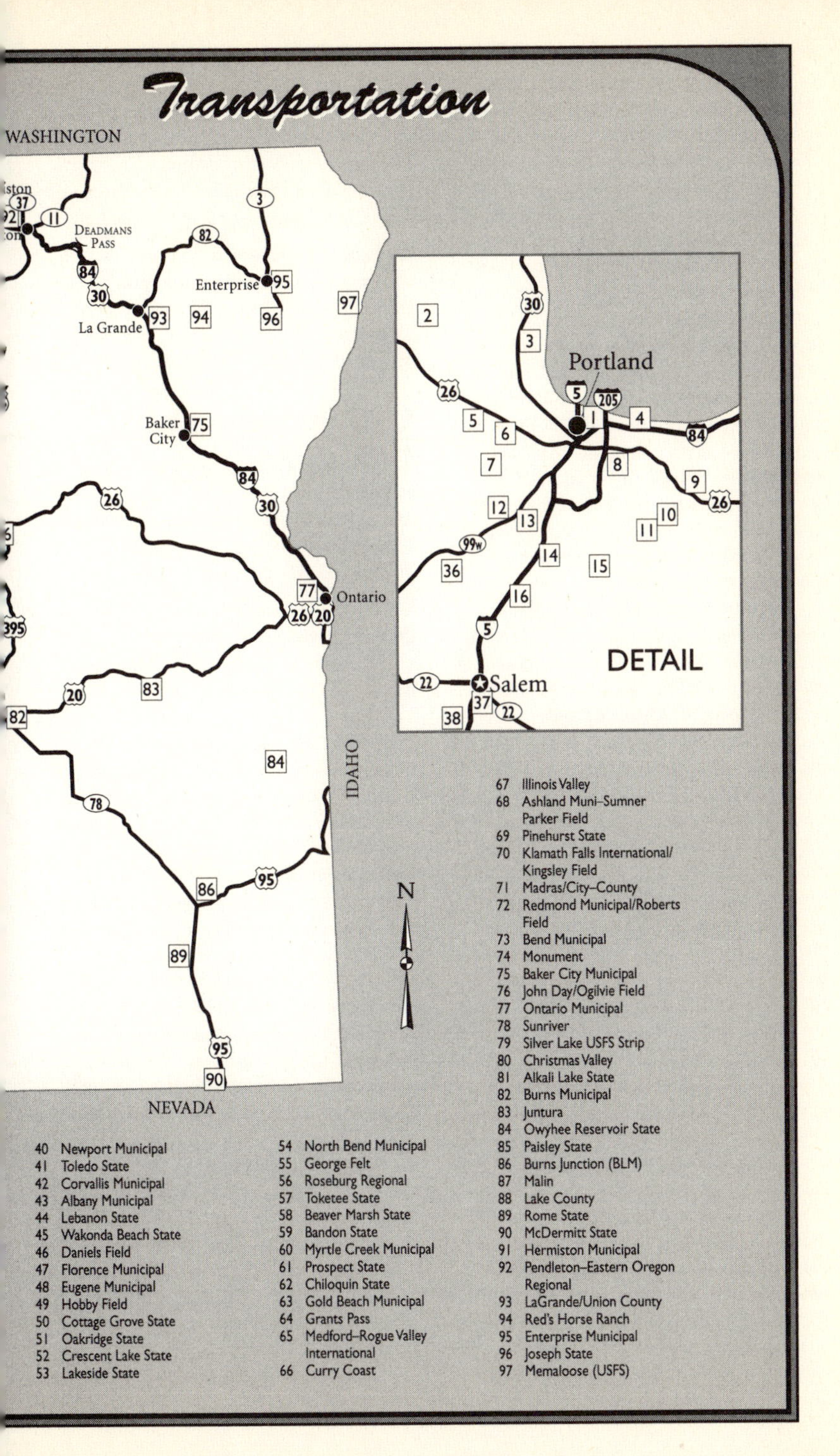
Transportation
WASHINGTON
DEADMANS PASS
Enterprise
La Grande
Baker City
Ontario
IDAHO
NEVADA
Portland
Salem
DETAIL
N
40 Newport Municipal
41 Toledo State
42 Corvallis Municipal
43 Albany Municipal
44 Lebanon State
45 Wakonda Beach State
46 Daniels Field
47 Florence Municipal
48 Eugene Municipal
49 Hobby Field
50 Cottage Grove State
51 Oakridge State
52 Crescent Lake State
53 Lakeside State
54 North Bend Municipal
55 George Felt
56 Roseburg Regional
57 Toketee State
58 Beaver Marsh State
59 Bandon State
60 Myrtle Creek Municipal
61 Prospect State
62 Chiloquin State
63 Gold Beach Municipal
64 Grants Pass
65 Medford–Rogue Valley International
66 Curry Coast
67 Illinois Valley
68 Ashland Muni–Sumner Parker Field
69 Pinehurst State
70 Klamath Falls International/ Kingsley Field
71 Madras/City–County
72 Redmond Municipal/Roberts Field
73 Bend Municipal
74 Monument
75 Baker City Municipal
76 John Day/Ogilvie Field
77 Ontario Municipal
78 Sunriver
79 Silver Lake USFS Strip
80 Christmas Valley
81 Alkali Lake State
82 Burns Municipal
83 Juntura
84 Owyhee Reservoir State
85 Paisley State
86 Burns Junction (BLM)
87 Malin
88 Lake County
89 Rome State
90 McDermitt State
91 Hermiston Municipal
92 Pendleton–Eastern Oregon Regional
93 LaGrande/Union County
94 Red's Horse Ranch
95 Enterprise Municipal
96 Joseph State
97 Memaloose (USFS)

Travel and Tourism

SEE ALSO MUSEUMS; FAIRS AND FESTIVALS; NATIONAL PARKS: PERFORMING ARTS. Travel and tourism are important components of Oregon's diverse economy. In 1996, about 27.7 million travelers visited Oregon; about 10.7 million were out-of-state travelers. Travel spending in Oregon has increased about 5.4 percent per year since 1991 and reached $5.2 billion in 1998. During 1998, visitor spending in Oregon directly supported about 74,000 jobs with a payroll of $1.1 billion. Visitors spent $2.1 billion on accommodations and $1.2 billion on food and beverages. About one-third of these expenditures were made in the greater Portland area. Visitors from out of state spent about $84 per person per day in 1996; in-state travelers spent $52 per person per day. International visitors spent about $98 per person per day.

Magnificent natural scenery and environment comprise the major stimulus for tourism in Oregon. The $8.8 billion economic impact of tourism is generated largely by people sightseeing and vacationing in or near the state's mountains, meadows, mountain lakes, rivers, deserts, and coast. The major natural tourism destinations include the Basin and Range Province with its magnificent fault-block mountains, such as Steens and Hart Mountains, and stunning assemblages of migrating birds; exotics features such as Hells Canyon of the Snake River; fossil beds in the John Day country; volcanic features such as Fort Rock near Bend, Mount Hood, and Crater Lake north of Klamath Falls; the Columbia River basalt flows and Columbia River Gorge, including Multnomah Falls and other scenic wonders; the stunning Coast and Cascade Ranges, their trails and lakes, and their salmon runs and other fisheries, which are magnets for anglers.

Human-made attractions are also important tourism destinations. Portland, the City of Roses, is an important destination. Ashland, on the I-5 corridor at the southern end of the state, is home to a world-famous Shakespeare Festival and has more bed-and-breakfasts per capita than any other city. Other major attractions include beach towns from Astoria to Brookings; the Oregon Coast Aquarium in Newport; windsurfing in the Columbia River Gorge near Hood River; downhill skiing at Mount Hood and Mount Bachelor; river rafting on rivers all over the state; and the End of the Oregon Trail Interpretive Center in Oregon City.

Organizations of Interest

Oregon Tourism Commission, Department of Economic Development, 775 Summer St. NE, Salem 97310, (503) 986-0120, www.traveloregon.com.

Universities and Colleges

Oregon has an extensive system of postsecondary institutions, including the state university system, which includes seven state universities, 32 private universities and colleges, and 17 community colleges.

Organizations of Interest

Department of Higher Education, P.O. Box 3175, Eugene 97403, (541) 346-5700.

Community Colleges

Oregon's 17 community college are not a part of the Oregon state university system but are locally controlled, state-supported institutions. These two-year colleges have a total enrollment of nearly 80,000 students. They provide the following legislatively mandated services: transfer education (the first two years of a four-year college education), professional technical education and job-related training (one-year certificate or two-year degree program), and developmental education programs for adult learners (high-school equivalency certificate or adult high-school diploma).

Blue Mountain Community College, 2410 NW Carden Ave., P.O. Box 100, Pendleton 97801-0100, (541) 276-1260, www.bmcc.cc.or.us. Enrollment: 2,847.

Central Oregon Community College, 2600 NW College Way, Bend 97701-5998, (541) 383-7700, www.cocc.edu. Enrollment: 3,305.

Chemeketa Community College, 4000 Lancaster Dr. NE, P.O. Box 14007, Salem

Johnson Hall, University of Oregon at Eugene. From *Oregon III* by Ray Atkeson.

97309-7070, (503) 399-5000, www.chemek.cc.or.us. Enrollment: 11,507.

Clackamas Community College, 19600 S Molalla Ave., Oregon City 97045-9049, (503) 657-6958 x2401, www.clackamas.cc.or.us. Enrollment: 6,613.

Clatsop Community College, 1653 Jerome Ave., Astoria 97103-3698, (503) 325-0910, www.clatsopcollege.com. Enrollment: 1,359.

Columbia Gorge Community College, 400 E Scenic Dr., The Dalles 97058-2282, (541) 296-6182, www.cgcc.cc.or.us. Enrollment: 811.

Klamath Community College, 241 Williams Ave., Klamath Falls 97601-2704, (541) 882-3521, www.kcc.cc.or.us. Enrollment: 223.

Lane Community College, 4000 E 30th Ave., Eugene 97405-0640, (541) 747-4501, www.lanecc.edu. Enrollment: 12,149.

Linn-Benton Community College, 6500 SW Pacific Blvd., Albany 97321-3774, (541) 917-4999, www.lbcc.cc.or.us. Enrollment: 6,061.

Mount Hood Community College, 26000 SE Stark St., Gresham 97030-3300, (503) 491-6422, www.mhcc.cc.or.us. Enrollment: 7,595.

Oregon Coast Community College Service District, 332 SW Coast Hwy., Newport 97365-4928, (541) 265-2283, www.occc.cc.or.us. Enrollment: 461.

Portland Community College, P.O. Box 19000, Portland 97280-0990, (503) 244-6111, www.pcc.edu. Enrollment: 19,826.

Rogue Community College, 3345 Redwood Hwy., Grants Pass 97527-9298, (541) 471-3500, www.rogue.cc.or.us. Enrollment: 3,432.

Southwestern Oregon Community College, 1988 Newmark, Coos Bay 97420-2912, (541) 888-2525, www.southwestern.cc.or.us. Enrollment: 3,060.

Tillamook Bay Community College Service District, 6385 Tillamook Ave., Bay City 97107-9641, (503) 842-8222, www.tbcc.cc.or.us. Enrollment: 444.

Treasure Valley Community College, 650 College Blvd., Ontario 97914-3498, (541) 889-6493, www.tvcc.cc.or.us. Enrollment: 2,159.

Umpqua Community College, P.O. Box 967, Roseburg 97470-0226, (541) 440-4600, www.umpqua.cc.or.us. Enrollment: 3,093.

Organizations of Interest

Community Colleges Commissioner, Office of Community College Services, 255 Capitol St. NE, Salem, 97310-1341, (503) 378-8648, www.occs.state.or.us.

Private Universities and Colleges

Oregon's private colleges and universities provide higher education to 30 percent of the state's four-year college students, over 25,000 students. During the 1996-97 school year, Oregon's independent higher-education institutions produced more than 6,000 graduates; 29 percent of all bachelor's degrees awarded in the state; 34 percent of all master's degrees; and 67 percent of all first professional degrees.

The Art Institutes International at Portland, 2000 SW 5th Ave., Portland 97205, (503) 228-6528. Enrollment: 148.

Cascade College, 9101 E Burnside St., Portland 97216, (503) 255-7060. Enrollment: 292.

Concordia University, 2811 NE Holman, Portland 97211, (503) 288-9371. Enrollment: 977.

Dove Bible Institute, 845 Alder Creek Dr., Medford 97504, (541) 776-9942. Enrollment: 28.

Eugene Bible College, 2155 Bailey Hill Rd., Eugene 97405, (541) 485-1780. Enrollment: 219.

George Fox University, 414 N Meridian, Newberg 97132, (503) 538-8383. Enrollment: 2,235.

ITT Technical Institute, 6035 NE 78th Ct., Portland 97218, (503) 255-6500. Enrollment: 567.

Lewis and Clark College, 0615 SW Palatine Hill Rd., Portland 97219, (503) 768-7000. Enrollment: 3,053.

Linfield College, 900 SE Baker St., McMinnville 97128, (503) 434-2200. Enrollment: 2,763.

Linfield College, School of Nursing, 2255 NW Northrup St., Portland 97210,

(503) 413-7161. Enrollment: 350.

Marylhurst University, P.O. Box 261, Marylhurst 97036, (503) 636-8141. Enrollment: 1,147.

Mount Angel Seminary, St. Benedict 97373, (503) 845-3951. Enrollment: 179.

Multnomah Bible College, 8435 NE Glisan St., Portland 97220, (503) 255-0332. Enrollment: 750.

National College of Naturopathic Medicine, 049 SW Porter St., Portland 97201, (503) 499-4343. Enrollment: 380.

Northwest Christian College, 828 11th Ave. E, Eugene 97401, (541) 343-1641. Enrollment: 438.

Oregon College of Art and Craft, 8245 SW Barnes Rd., Portland 97225, (503) 297-5544. Enrollment: 397.

Oregon College of Oriental Medicine, 10525 SE Cherry Blossom Dr., Portland 97216, (503) 253-3443. Enrollment: 168.

Oregon Graduate Institute, P.O. Box 91000, Portland 97291-1000, (503) 748-1121. Enrollment: 622.

Pacific Northwest College of Art, 1241 NW Johnson St., Portland 97209, (503) 226-4391. Enrollment: 243.

Pacific University, 2043 College Way, Forest Grove 97116, (503) 357-6151. Enrollment: 1,854.

Pioneer Pacific College, 25195 SW Parkway Ave., Wilsonville 97070, (503) 682-3903. Enrollment: 198.

Process Work Center of Portland, 2049 NW Hoyt St., Portland 97209, (503) 223-8188. Enrollment: 10.

Reed College, 3203 SE Woodstock

Blvd., Portland 97202, (503) 771-1112. Enrollment: 1,338.

Salem Bible College, 4500 Lancaster Dr. NE, Salem 97305, (503) 304-0092. Enrollment: 21.

University of Phoenix, 13190 SW 68th Pkwy., Tigard 97223, (503) 670-0590. Enrollment: 1,200.

University of Portland, 5000 N Willamette Blvd., Portland 97203, (503) 283-7911. Enrollment: 2,721.

Walla Walla College School of Nursing, Portland Campus, 10355 SE Market, Portland 97216, (503) 251-6115. Enrollment: 103.

Warner Pacific College, 2219 SE 68th Ave., Portland 97215, (503) 775-4366. Enrollment: 639.

Western Baptist College, 5000 Deer Park Dr. SE, Salem 97301, (503) 581-8600. Enrollment: 701.

Western Business College, 425 SW Washington, Portland 97204, (503) 222-3225. Enrollment: 518.

Western Seminary, 5511 SE Hawthorne Blvd., Portland 97215, (503) 233-8561. Enrollment: 652.

Western States Chiropractic College, 2900 NE 132nd Ave., Portland 97230, (503) 256-3180. Enrollment: 475.

Willamette University, 900 State St., Salem 97301, (503) 370-6300. Enrollment: 2,502.

Organizations of Interest

Oregon Independent Colleges Association, 7150 SW Hampton St., No. 101, Portland 97223, (503) 639-4541, www.osshe.edu/one/4yrinsti.htm.

Public Universities

The Oregon University System (OUS) comprises seven colleges and universities under the control of the governor-appointed State Board of Higher Education. The chancellor is the system's chief executive officer. Each Oregon county has access to public higher-education services offered by OUS institutions and their 28 affiliated education centers. Total unduplicated headcount for the 1997-98 academic year was 92,692, which includes regular classes and continuing-education courses. Noncredit enrollment for the 1997-98 academic year totaled 129,862. The state system is governed by an 11-member **State Board of Higher Education,** P.O. Box 3175, Eugene 97403, (541) 346-5700.

Eastern Oregon University, 1410 "L" Ave., La Grande 97850-2899, (541) 962-3300, (800) 452-8639, www.eou.edu. Enrollment: 3,893. Degree programs: All undergraduate students at Eastern Oregon University, regardless of their residence, pay the same tuition. Even international students who come to Eastern pay the same tuition as their Oregon peers. Tuition and fees total $3,233 annually, which is 66 percent below the national average to attend a public, residential, four-year college in the United States, and an amazing 85 percent below the national average to attend a private, residential, four-year college, according to the *Chronicle of Higher Education.* Eastern is clearly one of the most outstanding tuition values in the United States and is the only four-year university in Eastern Oregon.

Oregon Health Sciences University, 3181 SW Sam Jackson Park Rd., Portland 97201-3098, (503) 494-8311, www.ohsu.edu. Enrollment: 1,505. Degree programs: Oregon Health Sciences University (OHSU) is the state's only academic institution dedicated to the education of health professionals and biomedical researchers. OHSU includes the Schools of Dentistry, Medicine, and Nursing; OHSU Hospital; Doernbecher Children's Hospital; dozens of primary care and specialty clinics; three research institutes; and several outreach and public service units. With more than 9,300 employees, OHSU is Portland's largest employer and the fifth-largest in Oregon.

Oregon Institute of Technology, 3201 Campus Dr., Klamath Falls 97601-8801, (541) 885-1000, oit@oit.edu, www.oit.edu. Enrollment: 3,102. Degree programs: Oregon Institute of Technology (OIT), which provides a computer-intensive, industry-responsive curriculum, is the only accredited public institute of technology in the Pacific Northwest. The institute offers

Willamette University

As emigrants streamed over the Oregon Trail, the fertile, temperate Willamette Valley quickly became the most popular place to settle. In 1853, the territorial legislature chartered Willamette University, making it one of the oldest universities in the West. The preparatory department, the first department to organize, reflected the East Coast's emphasis on traditional subjects. The trustees' report in that first year listed these offerings: "Reading, Writing, Geography (with map drawing), Orthography, Punctuation, Arithmetic (mental and written), History, Grammar, Natural Philosophy, Chemistry, Astronomy, Logic, Rhetoric, Botany, Moral Science, Algebra (Davies Elementary and Davies Bourdon), Geometry (Elementary and Davies Legendre), Trigonometry, Surveying, Drawing, Needlework, Music (Vocal and Instrumental), Latin, and Elocution. The members of the School, both male and female are required to furnish a composition or declamation weekly: the advanced students being required to read their own compositions in presence of the other members of the school."

bachelor's-degree programs in engineering and health technologies, management and applied sciences, and a master's of science in engineering technology program. OIT is the only campus in the nation that is totally heated and cooled geothermally. While the college is based in Klamath Falls, OIT also serves the Portland area, the heart of Oregon's high-tech community, through two additional locations, one in Clackamas County and another in Washington County. In 1997, OIT began offering on-site programs in Bend.

Oregon State University, Corvallis 97331, (541) 737-0123, osu.orst.edu. Enrollment: over 14,618. Degree programs: Undergraduate and graduate degrees in more than 220 distinct academic programs in the areas of agricultural sciences, business, engineering, forestry, health and human performance, home economics and education, liberal arts, oceanography and atmospheric sciences, pharmacy, science, and veterinary medicine.

Portland State University, 630 SW Mill St., P.O. Box 751, Portland 97207-0751, (503) 725-3000, (800) 547-8887, www.pdx.edu. Enrollment: 32,992. Degree programs: Undergraduate degrees, certificate programs, and graduate degrees through the doctoral level. Academic units include the College of Liberal Arts and Sciences, the College of Urban and Public Affairs, the Graduate School of Education, the Graduate School of Social Work, and the Schools of Business Administration, Engineering and Applied Science, Fine and Performing Arts, and Extended Studies.

Southern Oregon University, 1250 Siskiyou Blvd., Ashland 97520, (541) 552-6111, admissions@sou.edu, www.sou.edu. Enrollment: 7,822. Degree programs: Through 22 departments in the schools of Arts and Letters; Business; Sciences; and Social Science, Education, and Health and Physical Education. There are 37 baccalaureate degree offerings, 7 master's degree programs, and 17 professional or preprofessional options. Southern Oregon University is a designated center of excellence for the fine and performing arts, with arts and cultural events abounding on campus and in Ashland. The Schneider Museum of Art, galleries, and performing arts groups on campus complement the local theater companies, art galleries, and nationally acclaimed Oregon Shakespeare Festival. Classes are offered in Medford and Ashland, as well as via distance-learning programs throughout the state.

University of Oregon, Eugene 97403, (541) 346-3036, www.uoregon.edu. Enrollment: 22,125. Degree programs: Baccalaureate through doctoral degrees in liberal arts, sciences, and professional programs—architecture and allied arts, business, education, journalism, communication, law, and music.

Western Oregon University, Monmouth 97361, (503) 838-8000, www.wou.edu. Enrollment: 6,635. Degree programs: Western Oregon University (WOU)—the oldest university in the Oregon university system—was founded in 1856 by pioneers who crossed the Oregon Trail. WOU offers almost 40 bachelor's and 3 master's degrees through its two schools—the School of Liberal Arts and Sciences and the School of Education, as well as a nationally accredited teacher-education program.

Vehicle Registration and Driver's Licenses

Oregon has nearly 2.5 million licensed drivers and 4 million registered vehicles. Each year, Driver and Motor Vehicle Services (DMV) issues more than 150,000 new driver's licenses and renews a half million more.

To license a vehicle in Oregon, one must meet certain requirements. Because Oregon is a mandatory insurance state, proof of insurance must be shown, including name of insurer and policy number. Driving without liability insurance on a highway or public road can result in fines, suspension of driving privileges, and possible vehicle towing. New registrants will likely need to arrange a vehicle-identification (VIN) inspection. In the Portland metropolitan or Medford areas, emissions testing is required, unless the car is really old. The Oregon Department of Environmental Quality website at www.deq.state.or.us/aq/vip/vip.htm offers information about vehicle testing.

Only residents who live in Oregon can register their vehicles in the state and may be required to prove it because Oregon's relatively low vehicle-registration fees tempt people from states with value-based fees to illegally register their vehicles in Oregon. Recreational vehicles are especially "big ticket" items because many states charge a registration fee or tax on RVs based on the vehicle's value, which can be upward of $100,000 or more. In California, a motor home with that kind of valuation can cost more than $10,000 to register for the first year, compared to $224 to register for two years in Oregon. Making a false application is a Class A misdemeanor. If caught, Oregon will cancel your registration and notify the state where you live. You may also be subject to fines and civil or criminal penalties.

Basic Annual Registration Fees

All-terrain vehicle	$10
Heavy trailer	30
Light trailer	9
Motorcycle/moped	30
Passenger vehicle	30
Snowmobile	10

Applicants for disabled parking privileges must have a physician certify need. A permanent placard may be issued if your physician certifies that your disability lasts longer than four years.

A number of specialized plates are available to Oregon vehicle owners, including personalized plates and plates that display one's state college alma mater or veteran status. Some of the proceeds from specialized plates support designated programs, such as university scholarships and litter control along Oregon's highways.

Organizations of Interest

Driver and Motor Vehicle Services (DMV), 1905 Lana Avenue, NE, Salem, OR 97314-1020, (503)-945-5000. Check local listings for DMV locations around the state.

The Auto Arrives

The first automobile arrived in Oregon in 1899. By 1905, Oregon began to register vehicles and in the 1930s began testing and licensing drivers.

Vital Statistics

According to the U.S. Census Bureau, 42,811 live births were recorded in 1995, as were 29,000 deaths, 25,600 marriages (or 8.2 per 1,000 population), and

15,000 divorces (4.8 per 1,000 population). Among the leading causes of death per 100,000 residents were heart disease (240.1), cancer (214.7), cerebrovascular diseases (77.7), chronic obstructive pulmonary disease (45.4), and accidents (43.5). Infant mortality in 1995 was 6.1 per 1,000 live births.

The Oregon State Vital Records Office maintains all records of births, deaths, marriages, and divorces. Certified copies of birth or death certificates or records of marriage or divorce can be ordered from the department for a small fee. The department has records dating from 1903 for births and deaths, marriage records from 1906, and divorce records from 1925. Birth records (including indexes) have a 100-year access restriction; death records have a 50-year access restriction.

Some county offices maintain vital records, and others do not. Some earlier records for the City of Portland and individual counties are available from the Oregon State Archives. Marriage and divorce records not available at the state office may be available from the county clerk in the county where the license was issued. County clerks also have some records from before 1906. Fees vary.

Organizations of Interest

Oregon State Archives, 800 Summer Street NE, Salem, OR 97310.

Oregon State Vital Records Office, Oregon Health Division, Center of Health Statistics, 800 NE Oregon St., #205, Portland 97232, (503) 731-4108, recording: (503) 731-4095, fax: (503) 234-8417.

Volcanoes and Volcanism

(*See also* Earthquakes; Mount Hood; National Parks, Monuments, and Recreation Areas; Scenic Drives) You don't have to look hard anywhere in Oregon to see evidence of its volcanic history, from tall volcanic peaks to broad lava flows that look like barren moonscapes. Oregon's volcanic nature is the result of offshore processes. The floor of the Pacific Ocean sinks beneath the west coast of North America from southern British Columbia to northern California. As the sinking lithospheric slab reaches a depth of about 60 miles, red-hot steam rises and melts the overlying, already hot mantle, forming basalt or andesite magma. The volcanoes occur along a line that marks where the sinking slab beneath gets hot enough to trigger rising steam and lava.

Convergence between the North American and Juan de Fuca plates continues at about 4 centimeters per year in the direction of north-50-degrees-east, a slowing of 2 to 3 centimeters per year since 7 million years ago. According to most interpretations, volcanism in the Cascades has been an on-again-off-again activity, with the most recent episodes beginning about 5 million years ago and resulting in

Blast of the Past

Mount Mazama may have been Oregon's highest volcano 6,700 years ago, almost 12,000 feet high before its summit collapsed in some of the most violent eruptions of any recent Cascade volcano. After thousands of years of violent eruptions, Mount Mazama's final crater opened with an enormous eruption that piled ash 70 feet thick at the volcano's base and filled canyons to the top with 250 feet of pumice and ash. Airborne ash blanketed thousands of square miles in the Northwest, reaching as far as central Montana and Saskatchewan. Avalanches of pumice, moving at 100 miles an hour, gushed down the mountainside. Some flows cooled at the volcano's base, others moved out across the countryside, one kept going for 40 miles along the Rogue River Valley, and another swept across Diamond Lake, leaving 30-foot-thick pumice piles. Pumice and volcanic ash from Mount Mazama eventually covered 350,000 square miles, and the crater's collapse left a 6-mile-wide, 4,000-foot-deep caldera that now holds Crater Lake.

Fort Rock, the remains of an ancient volcano, rises from the desert floor northwest of Lakeview. From *Oregon III* by Ray Atkeson.

more than 3,000 vents. One of the most violent eruptions in the Oregon Cascades was that of Mount Mazama, now known as Crater Lake. It was once Oregon's highest volcano, almost 12,000 feet in elevation before its summit collapsed in an eruption some 6,700 years ago. Mount Mazama ejected the largest amount of pumice of any volcano known. The caldera, which is now filled by Crater Lake, was produced by an eruption that destroyed a volcano the size of Mount St. Helens and sent volcanic ash as far east as Nebraska.

Despite the examples of Mount Mazama and the violent eruption of Mount St. Helens in neighboring Washington State in 1980, the eruptions of Cascade Range basaltic volcanoes typically were not highly explosive. Oozing lava flows have produced the most voluminous eruptive material. More than 2,500 square miles of ancient lava flows underlie the vast, agricultural Columbia Plateau that dips down into northeastern Oregon from Washington. One of the most extensive lava flows is right in the Portland metropolitan area. Called the Boring Lava, because it originated near the town of Boring, it includes at least 32 and possibly 50 cinder cones and small shield volcanoes. This gives Portland the distinction of having the largest number of volcanoes in or near its city limits of any city in the United States. Among the city's extinct volcanoes are Rocky Butte, Powell Butte, and Mount Tabor. Along the foothills of the Cascade Mountains east of the Sandy River and southeast of Oregon City, several vents furnished enough lava to form a lava plain. The lavas southeast of Oregon City displaced the ancestral Willamette River to the west, where it cut its present gorge.

Organizations of Interest

Cascades Volcano Observatory, Vancouver, Washington, vulcan.wr.usgs.gov/home.html. Though located in Washington, this facility is a good source of information about all the Cascade volcanoes. The observatory assesses potential hazards of Oregon's volcanoes and warns of potential eruptions, landslides, and debris flows. You can monitor the state's volcanic activity on the observatory's website.

Major Volcanoes

	Elevation
Belknap	6,874 feet
Broken Top	9,152 feet
Crater Lake/Mount Mazama (Hillman Peak)	8,156 feet
Diamond Peak	8,750 feet
Lava Butte	4,970 feet
Mount Bachelor	9,065 feet
Mount Bailey	8,363 feet
Mount Hood	11,235 feet
Mount Jefferson	10,495 feet
Mount McLoughlin	9,496 feet
Mount Thielsen	9,182 feet
Mount Washington	7,796 feet
Newberry Caldera at Paulina Peak	7,985 feet
Three-Fingered Jack	7,841 feet
Three Sisters:	
North Sister	10,085 feet
Middle Sister	10,047 feet
South Sister	10,358 feet

Major Lava Fields

Belknap Crater lava field, Linn County
Brown Mountain Lava Field, Klamath County
Devil's Garden and Lava Butte, Lake County
Diamond Craters Outstanding Natural Area, Harney County
Jordan Craters and Saddle Butte Lava Field, Malheur County
Lava Lands Visitor Center, Deschutes County
Newberry Crater, Newberry Crater National Volcanic Monument

Voting and Elections

Residents of Oregon who are U.S. citizens and 18 years of age or older are eligible to vote. Voters may register up to the 21st day before an election. Voter registration forms are located at county election offices and at many schools, banks, and other public buildings. They are also available from the state Elections Division and its website at www.sos.state.or.us. You must notify your county election office in writing if your address or name changes or if you want to change your political party affiliation. The easiest way to do this is by sending a new voter registration card to your county.

Oregon has a slightly higher percentage of the voting population registered to vote (72.7 percent) than does the United States as a whole (62.0 percent). Likewise, the percentage of the voting-age population that votes in the state (60.9 percent) is slightly higher than the national rate (44.6 percent). Voters with a major political-party affiliation tend to vote more frequently than voters of minor parties or independents. Older voters tend to vote more than younger voters. In the May 19, 1998, primary election, while overall turnout was 33 percent, only 12 percent of voters aged 18 to 34 voted, but 65 percent of voters aged 65 to 79 cast a ballot.

When registering to vote, Oregon residents have the option to identify with a political party (Democratic, Libertarian, Natural Law, Pacific, Reform, Republican, Socialist, and U.S. Taxpayers) or as nonaffiliated or "independent." Members of the Democratic and Republican parties in Oregon vote in their parties' primaries. The minor parties hold conventions to determine which of their candidates will stand at the general election.

Elections

All elections in Oregon are held on one of four dates (except in case of emergency): the second Tuesday in March, the third Tuesday in May, the third Tuesday in September, and the first Tuesday after the first Monday in November. Primary and general elections are held in May and November of even-numbered years. Special elections may be conducted in May and November of odd-numbered years. Local elections are usually held on the March and September dates. Oregon's presidential primary is held in March of presidential election years.

The Elections Division of the Oregon Secretary of State's office publishes and mails a voter information pamphlet for each primary and general election and most special elections about the candidates and measures that will be on the ballot. The pamphlet is distributed to every household in Oregon. Most counties also publish pamphlets with information about local candidates and measures.

For each ballot measure, the voters pamphlet contains the measure number, title, full text, impartial explanatory and financial impact statements, and arguments both for and against the measure. Supporters and opponents of each measure can pay $300 to file a 300-word argument that will appear in the statewide pamphlet. Oregon allows an unlimited number of arguments to be filed for each measure.

All elections in Oregon are held by mail. Oregon has conducted local elections by mail since 1981, and the first statewide mail election was held in 1993. For the vote-by-mail system, a ballot is automatically mailed to each registered voter. The marked ballot must be returned to the county clerk in the preaddressed return envelope or at a designated drop site. Ballots are not counted until election day. Ballots can legally be mailed any time between 20 and 14 days before the election. For state elections, the window is expanded to 20 to 18 days to have more consistency as to when voters will receive their ballots. The voted ballot must be received in the county elections office or at a designated drop site by 8:00 P.M. on election night.

Registered voters may also vote by absentee ballot in the primary and general elections. In the 1998 primary election, nearly two-thirds of all votes were cast by absentee ballot. In November 1999 voters approved extending vote-by-mail to the primary and general elections.

Organizations of Interest

Secretary of State, Elections Division, 141 State Capitol, Salem 97310-0722, (503) 986-1518, www.sos.state.or.us.

Voter Turnout

General Election Voters

Year	Registered Voters	Number Voting	Turnout
1998	1,965,981	1,160,400	59.0 %
1996	1,962,155	1,399,180	71.3 %
1994	1,832,774	1,254,265	68.4 %
1992	1,775,416	1,498,959	84.4 %
1990	1,476,500	1,133,125	74.5 %

Source: *Oregon Blue Book*

Primary Election Voters

Year	Registered Voters	Number Voting	Turnout
1998	1,906,677	655,340	34.9 %
1996	1,851,499	698,990	37.75 %
1994	1,730,562	661,717	38.24 %
1992	1,543,315	758,459	49.14 %
1990	1,437,462	660.990	45.98 %

Source: *Oregon Blue Book*

Running for Office

To run for elected office in Oregon, a candidate for state office must file with the Elections Division of the Secretary of State's office. To run for the U.S. House of Representatives, U.S. Senate, or the U.S. presidency, a candidate must file with the Federal Elections Commission. Candidates for local office must file with city or county election offices. Candidates must also file campaign finance reports that document the sources and distribution of contributions. Candidates running for state office must file at least two pre-election reports and one post-election report for both primary and general elections.

Initiatives and Referendums

Oregon allows initiatives and referendums to be placed on the ballot. For an initiative to qualify for the ballot, the person filing it (called the Chief Petitioner) must prepare a petition, file it, obtain a ballot title, prepare a cover and signature sheet, circulate the petition, file for signature verification with

Hikers refresh themselves at Tunnel Falls in the Columbia Gorge. Photo by Susan Dupere.

the state Elections Division, and file campaign and expenditure information. To qualify for the ballot, 6 percent of registered voters must sign the initiative petition. A referendum can be placed on the ballot either by referral from the state legislature or voter petition (this requires 4 percent of voters to sign).

Waterfalls The Northwest has prime conditions for creating spectacular waterfalls: lots of rivers, steep terrain, and rain. Oregon has more than 400 identified waterfalls—too many to list here. Waterfalls at lower elevations are at their best in the winter and early spring when rivers are engorged with rain, while high-elevation falls are most impressive in early summer, when streams are filled with snowmelt.

> **Multnomah Falls**
>
> *Multnomah Falls, at 620 feet high, is the fourth-highest waterfall in the United States and the Northwest's highest. After a week of below-freezing temperatures and a high wind-chill factor, Multnomah Falls freezes almost solid with stalactite-like icicles.*

The Columbia Gorge is perhaps the best place to find a lot of waterfalls in a relatively small area, 77 of them, including spectacular 620-foot Multnomah Falls, which is viewable from I-84; Bridal Veil Falls (two tiers, upper falls: 60 to 100 feet, lower falls: 40 to 60 feet); Latourell and Upper Latourell Falls (249 and 75 to 100 feet, respectively); two-tiered Sheppards Dell Falls (the lower falls is 40 to 60 feet, the upper section is 35 to 50 feet) in Sheppards Dell State Park; and Coopey Falls along Coopey Creek (150 to175 feet horsetail falls).

The Cascades south of the Columbia Gorge to Mount Washington contain some 106 cataracts throughout the region. Oregon 214 goes through Silver Falls State Park 14 miles southeast of Silverton and 25 miles east of Salem. Silver Creek Canyon has 10 major waterfalls, all within moderate walking distance of the main highway. South Falls is the highest of the park's falls at 177 feet.

Other areas of Oregon have a wealth of waterfalls. In the Coast Range, 267-foot Munson Creek Falls is the highest. It is located about halfway between Tillamook and Beaver off U.S. 101, just a short hike from Munson Creek Falls County Park. Farther south, three impressive waterfalls are nestled deep within the Mapleton Ranger District of Siuslaw National Forest, each accessible from Kentucky Falls Trail: Upper Kentucky Falls (80 to 100 feet along Kentucky Creek), Lower Kentucky Falls, and North Fork Smith Falls. In Siskiyou National Forest, Coquille River Falls crashes 40 to 60 feet along the Coquille River. The Rogue River also has numerous falls and rapids along its length.

Weather and Climate

(See table on page 200)

Oregon is wet and mild in the west, snowy in the Cascades, and, in the east, hot in summer and cold in winter. The highest temperature ever recorded in the state is 119°F, the lowest -54°F. Yet these extremes are rarely encountered anywhere in the state, or in any given year. In half of the years on record, no temperature in the state has exceeded 110°F, nor fallen below -27°F. In the Willamette Valley, home to most Oregonians, the mean temperature in January, the coldest month, is 38°F; in July, the warmest month, the mean is 66°F.

The average annual rainfall varies from less than eight inches in drier plateau regions to as much as 200 inches along the upper west slopes of the Coast Range. The state demonstrates a definite winter rainfall pattern. West of the Cascades about half the rain falls from December through February; very little falls during the summer.

The heaviest snowfalls occur in the high Cascade passes. Average annual snow totals can reach 300 to 550 inches. A maximum annual snowfall of 833.5 inches (1951–52) and a snow accumulation (depth) of 252 inches have been recorded at Crater Lake National Park.

Storms occur infrequently in Oregon. Hailstorms occur very infrequently in the summer. When they do, they are very local but can cause considerable local crop damage. Thunderstorms occur four or five days a year in the valleys and up to 15 times per year in the eastern part of the state. Hurricane-force winds occasionally strike the Oregon Coast, especially in winter. Sometimes these storms move inland and up the Columbia Gorge.

Winter storms can produce flooding episodes in the Willamette Valley and along coastal streams. Significant flooding events are known to occur on average every four years in the Willamette Valley and every twoyears on coastal streams. The effects of floods have been controlled to a considerable extent by construction of dams and other flood control structures and through better community planning.

In such a resource-rich state, the climate controls the economy to a very considerable extent. The mild temperatures and abundant rainfall in the Coast Range and on the western slopes of the Cascades make this one of the best tree-growing regions in the nation. The long growing season in the river valleys is important for fruit production and truck farming. Abundant winter precipitation also recharges water supplies for irrigation, which is important for agriculture throughout the year.

The drier regions of the state are used for wheat growing and for rangeland and livestock production. See page 200 for a synopsis of climatological records for a 30-year period.

Wetlands

About 2 percent of Oregon is wetland terrain. Though small in total area, these 1.4 million acres are especially important habitats because they reduce flooding, improve water quality, and provide wildlife habitat. About 30 percent of Oregon's terrestrial vertebrates (164 species) use freshwater marshes, and the estuaries (mouths of rivers) are used by more than a hundred bird species. Over the years, nearly 38 percent of the state's wetlands have been filled in or converted to other uses.

In the Coast Range, wetland habitats are associated primarily with river estuaries.

1950-1983 Climate Records

Town	Altitude (ft.)	Temperature: Record High °F/(m/y)	Temperature: Record Low °F/(m/y)	Rain: Daily High in. (m/y)	Snow: Monthly High in. (m/y)	Snow: Daily High in. (m/y)
Ashland	1,780	105 (8/78)	-4 (12/72)	3.00 (12/64)	20.5 (1/69)	
Astoria	6	103 (7/61)	6 (12/72)	5.12 (1/82)	26.3 (1/69)	10.8 (1/71)
Baker	3,368	106 (8/61)	-39 (12/78)	1.96 (6/58)	19.2 (1/51)	
Bandon	80	91 (10/78)	12 (12/72)	4.99 (12/61)	18.0 (1/69)	
Bend	3,599	102 (8/72)	-24 (12/72	2.64 (11/60)	51.9 (11/73)	
Brookings	80	103 (9/73)	18 (12/72)	6.88 (12/54)	6.0 (1/72)	
Burns	4,141	100 (7/80)	-27 (1/82)	3.87 (10/82)	26.8 (12/83)	7.0 (11/83)
Clatskanie	92	102 (7/58)	5 (12/72)	3.10 (11/60)	33.0 (1/54)	
Corvallis	225	105 (8/72)	-7 (12/72)	4.28 (1/65)	24.0 (1/69)	
Cottage Grove	650	105 (8/78)	-5 (12/72)	4.80 (11/61)	46.8 (1/69)	
Dallas	325	106 (7/56)	-2 (12/72)	4.32 (12/64)	32.0 (1/69)	
Drain	292	107 (8/78)	0 (1/62)	4.44 (11/61)	30.0 (1/69)	
Elgin	2,655	110 (8/61)	-27 (12/64)	1.93 (11/63)	49.5 (12/71)	
Enterprise	3,790	105 (8/61)	-30 (12/64)	1.49 (4/78)	23.9 (1/57)	
Estacada	410	107 (7/56)	7 (1/57)	3.80 (1/72)	25.0 (1/72)	
Eugene	359	108 (8/81)	-12 (12.72)	5.15 (2/81)	47.1 (1/69)	22.9 (1/69)
Forest Grove	180	109 (7/56)	-4 (12/72)	3.04 (12/55)	27.0 (1/54)	
Grants Pass	925	108 (8/71)	-1 (12/72)	4.30 (2/56)	19.7 (1/69)	
Heppner	1,950	107 (8/61)	-15 (12/72)	2.05 (10/57)	29.1 (1/69)	
Hermiston	624	113 (8/61)	31 (1/57)	3.36 (10/57)	22.6 (1/69)	
Hood River	500	108 (8/77)	-18 (1/57)	3.05 (12/64)	84.5 (1/80)	
Klamath Falls	4,098	104 (8/72)	-17 (12/72)	2.58 (12.64)	37.6 (12/52)	
La Grande	2,755	109 (8/61)	-22 (12/64)	2.22 (12/56)	29.5 (12/71)	
Lakeview	4,774	100 (7/75)	-20 (12/72)	2.27 (12/64)	49.2 (1/64)	
Madras	2,230	106 (8/72)	-34 (1/57)	2.14 (12/64)	22.5 (1/69)	
McMinnville	148	106 (8/72)	-5 (12/72)	2.90 (2/68)	23.6 (3/51)	
Medford	1,298	115 (7/46)	-6 (12/72)	3.75 (12/64)	22.6 (1/30)	9.3 (1/71)
Milton-Freewater	839	111 (8/61)	-24 (12/68)	1.82 (1/56)	29.7 (1/69)	
Newport	154	100 (7/61)	1 (12/72)	4.60 (1/65)	11.0 (12/72)	
Ontario	2,145	113 (8/61)	-25 (1/62)	1.59 (9/59)	25.0 (1/79)	
Oregon City	167	107 (7/56)	6 (12/64)	3.35 (11/60)	18.9 (1/69)	
Pendleton	1,482	113 (8/61)	-22 (1/57)	1.88 (10.82)	41.6 (1/50)	13.3 (1/50)
Portland	21	107 (8/81)	-3 (2/50)	2.62 (11/73)	41.4 (1/50)	10.6 (1/50)
Prineville	2,840	105 (8/72)	-34 (12/72)	1.51 (8/76)	21.2 (1/60)	
Reedsport	60	97 (9/73)	11 (12/72)	5.68 (12/75)	32.0 (1/69)	
Riddle	663	110 (8/77)	-3 (1/62)	3.41 (12/65)	22.8 (1/69)	
Salem	196	108 (8/81)	-12 (12/72)	3.16 (2/49)	32.8 (1/50)	10.8 (1/43)
Seaside	10	105 (7/61)	5 (12/72)	4.19 (11/60)	20.0 (1/69)	
Sexton Summit	3,836	100 (7/46)	-2 (1/62)	5.98 (1/74)	106.7 (1/69)	34.1 (1/69)
Stayton	465	106 (8/78)	-7 (12/72)	4.47 (10/55)	15.0 (1/69)	
Union	2,765	108 (8/61)	-24 (12/64)	1.90 (5/52)	26.3 (12/71)	
Vale	2,240	110 (8/61)	-28 (1/62)	1.92 (8/79)	16.0 (1/75)	

Source: National Oceanic and Atmospheric Administration

> ***Great Blue Heron***
>
> *The great blue heron is a permanent resident of coastal areas and on lakes and rivers west of the Cascades. A subspecies lives inland. The Portland area has so many that the city has honored the blue heron as its official city bird. In nesting season, nearly 1,000 herons live in river basins and wetlands within 3 to 5 miles of downtown Portland.*—Ann Saling, *The Great Northwest Nature Factbook.*

They abound in young salmon, crab, and other marine species, as well as marine mammals, waterfowl, and shorebirds. All of Oregon's salmon runs depend on the coastal estuaries during critical life stages.

The freshwater, riverine wetlands of the Willamette Valley have suffered from urban and agricultural development. Seasonal wetlands have been drained, and other areas have been altered for flood control.

The high-elevation wetlands on the eastern flank of the Cascades support large bird populations. Many of these wetlands are in their natural state, though the lakes and marshes of the Upper Klamath Basin have been altered and greatly diminished in their capacity.

The shallow lakes in the Basin and Range areas of southeastern Oregon are some of the largest wetland systems in the West. Seasonal lakes in this region are important stops along the Pacific Flyway. The marshes in and around Malheur Lake (50,000 acres during high water) support the largest inland colonial nesting colonies of waterbirds in the state. The Malheur area, the Warner Valley, and Summer and Abert Lakes attract huge numbers and over a hundred species of migrating birds.

Many of the wetlands in the Blue Mountains have been drained and converted to agricultural lands. Similarly, few natural wetlands remain in the Columbia Basin.

Whitewater Kayaking and River Running

(*SEE ALSO* RIVERS; WILD AND SCENIC RIVERS) Oregon's rivers are a paddler's paradise. Whether kayaker, canoeist, or rafter, there is something for everyone, from high desert to steep creeks to coastal estuaries. Some runs are remote; others are easily accessible from urban areas. River running in Oregon is a year-round activity, depending where you choose to go. Water levels stay up with fall and winter rains, spring snowmelt, and summer dam releases.

Rivers are graded according to their difficulty. The grade reflects the gradient of the river, the hazards, and the ease or difficulty of access or rescue. Readers interested in running any of the rivers described below should first consult a specialized river-running guidebook—several good ones are available in any good Oregon bookstore—and possibly also consult a guide or excursion service. Following are comments on several rivers renowned for their scenery and for the river running experience that they offer.

Alsea River. The Alsea runs from the crest of the Coast Range to the Pacific at Waldport. The upper Alsea offers exciting runs, while the lower Alsea, below the joining of the North and South Forks, is a favored fishing stream with easy access from Oregon 34.

Clackamas River. Located close to Portland, the Clackamas is one of the most frequently run rivers in the state and has claimed a disproportionate share of lives—109 between 1970 and 1980, a national record. Clackamas scenery is spectacular, with whitewater dominating the upper reaches and nice drifting available in the lower reaches. Despite its proximity to Portland and heavy use, the river is large enough to offer scenery and isolation year-round.

Deschutes River. The Deschutes and its tributaries drain the east side of the Cascades. The Deschutes is Oregon's second-longest river and flows through downtown Bend. The upper Deschutes has

Whitewater rodeo on the Clackamas River. Photo by Susan Dupere.

both light and heavy water flows. Below Lake Billy Chinook, the water level is controlled by dams, which makes for fine river running throughout summer.

John Day River. The John Day runs 280 miles from the Blue Mountains in northeast Oregon to its confluence with the Columbia River west of Arlington. The John Day is the longest undammed river remaining in the Pacific Northwest.

McKenzie River. Running the McKenzie is very popular, perhaps because of the river's proximity to Eugene. The McKenzie drains a volcanic basin, where the river has cut through successive layers of consolidated volcanic ash (tuff) and lava flows. The scenery includes thick forests, volcanic formations, and farmlands in its lower reaches.

Rogue River. The incomparable Rogue and its tributaries originate near Crater Lake. The river flows about 180 miles into the Pacific at Gold Beach. About 84 miles of the river have been designated as part of the national Wild and Scenic Rivers System. The 35-mile section below Grave Creek is world renowned for river running. The lowest reach of the river is crowded with excursion vessels in summer.

Sandy River. The Sandy River and its tributaries drain the western slopes of Mount Hood and discharge into the Columbia Gorge. Because of the high elevations drained, the short distances involved, and the steep gradient, the Sandy River system tends to have good water throughout summer.

Umpqua River. The main Umpqua runs northwest from Roseburg to the Pacific Ocean. There is fine whitewater above Roseburg and more recreational boating below.

Willamette River. The Willamette is Oregon's aqueous artery. More than half of all Oregonians live in its valley. Those who recreate on the water are very fortunate indeed! Much of the river scenery is protected by a greenway program. The cities and towns have numerous riverside parks that provide access and recreation opportunities. The upper and middle sections of the river are a drifter's paradise, especially in summer. The Upper Willamette above Eugene is, in general, whitewater territory for experienced river runners. The middle and lower sections of the river are ideal for extended paddling trips and, in summer, float trips. Oregon's

State Parks and Recreation Department publishes the "Willamette River Recreation Guide," which provides a useful orientation to recreation on the Willamette.

Organizations of Interest

Grande Ronde Whitewater Boaters Club, 1610 Cedar, La Grande 97850.

Lower Columbia Canoe Club, 1714 SE 52nd Ave., Portland 97215.

McKenzie River Paddlers, 38305 Jasper-Lowell Rd., Fall Creek 97438.

Northwest Rafters Association, P.O. Box 19008, Portland 97219.

Oregon Kayak Club, P.O. Box 692, Portland 97207.

Santiam Whitewater Association, 32560 SW Arbor Lake Drive, Wilsonville 97070.

Southern Oregon Association of Kayakers, P.O. Box 462, Jacksonville 97530.

Willamette Kayak and Canoe Club, P.O. Box 1062, Corvallis 97339.

Wild and Scenic Rivers

The landmark federal Omnibus Oregon National Wild and Scenic Rivers Act of 1988 placed 40 Oregon river segments totalling over 1,500 miles under federal protection, the largest river protection system in the Lower 48. "Wild and scenic" refers to portions of rivers designated by Congress to "possess outstandingly remarkable scenic, recreational, geologic, fish and wildlife, historic, cultural or other similar values." Designation creates corridors about 0.25 mile on each side to protect the rivers, and the rivers are protected from federally supported dam building as well. In addition to federal protection, under the Oregon Scenic Waterways Program the state may designate a river as a "scenic waterway." Parts of 19 Oregon rivers are designated scenic waterways, as well as Waldo Lake. All except the Nestucca River section and Waldo Lake are also protected as National Wild and Scenic Rivers.

Big Marsh Creek
Chetco River
Clackamas River
Crescent Creek
Crooked River
Crooked River (North Fork)
Deschutes River
Donner und Blitzen River
Eagle Creek
Elkhorn Creek
Elk River
Grande Ronde River
Illinois River
Imnaha River
John Day River
John Day River (North Fork)
John Day River (South Fork)
Joseph Creek
Klamath River
Little Deschutes River
Lostine River
Malheur River
McKenzie River
Metolius River
Minam River
North Powder River
North Umpqua River
Owyhee River
Owyhee River (North Fork)
Powder River
Quartzville Creek
Roaring River
Rogue River
Rogue River (Upper)
Salmon River
Sandy River
Smith River
Sprague River (North Fork)
Squaw Creek
Sycan River
Wallowa River
Wenaha River
West Little Owyhee River
White River
Willamette River (North Fork of the Middle Fork)

Wild Horses and Burros

Wild horses and burros are descended from animals that either escaped from, or were released by, early Spanish explorers, then miners and Native American tribes. Over 2,000 unbranded, unclaimed, free-roaming horses and burros live on Oregon public lands. Because these animals have virtually no predators, their numbers grow at a rapid rate, creating overgrazed soil prone to erosion and habitat destroyed for other wildlife. To address the issue, the Bureau of Land Management (BLM) removes some wild horses and burros every three years, rotating between 21 Herd Management Areas (HMAs), which range in size from 40,000 to 500,000 acres.

Since 1973, the BLM has submitted the captured animals for adoption through its Adopt-a-Horse-or-Burro Program. Each year, between 6,000 and 8,000 horses and 500 to 1,000 burros are offered to qualified caregivers, who are supervised for one year before the title is formally transferred. Homes are found for about 350 animals each year; animals that are considered unadoptable are returned to the range. Horses are available for adoption from state prison systems, where, in cooperation with the BLM, the horses are halter- and saddle-trained.

More information on adoption opportunities is available on the Internet at www.or.blm.gov/Burns/burns_wild_horses_and_burros.htm, or through the **Burns District Office, Bureau of Land Management,** (541) 573-4400.

Wilderness

(SEE ALSO NATIONAL FORESTS) Wilderness areas, managed by the U.S. Forest Service and national forest staffs, are lands set aside by Congress as those places "untrammeled by man, where man himself is a visitor who does not remain." Generally this means that there are no commercial enterprises; no permanent roads; no use of motor vehicles, motorized equipment, or motorboats; no landing of aircraft; no other form of mechanical transport; and no structure or installation. So if it's nature you yearn for, head for Oregon's wilderness areas. There are over 2 million acres of designated wilderness, almost all of which lie within the boundaries of national forests. Three wilderness areas extend from Oregon into other states: the Hells Canyon Wilderness is in Oregon and Idaho, the Red Buttes Wilderness is in Oregon and California, and the Wenaha-Tucannon Wilderness is in Oregon and Washington.

Badger Creek Wilderness, 24,000 acres. Mount Hood National Forest, Barlow Ranger District, (541) 467-2291.

Black Canyon Wilderness, 13,400 acres. Ochoco National Forest, Paulina Ranger District, (541) 477-3713.

Boulder Creek Wilderness, 19,100 acres. Umpqua National Forest, Diamond Lake Ranger District, (541) 498-2531.

Bridge Creek Wilderness, 5,400 acres. Ochoco National Forest, Big Summit Ranger District, (541) 416-6645.

Bull of the Woods Wilderness, 34,900 acres. Mount Hood National Forest (27,427 acres), Estacada, Ranger District, (503) 630-6861. Willamette National Forest (7,473 acres), Detroit Ranger District, (541) 854-3366.

Columbia Wilderness, 39,000 acres. Mount Hood, Hood River Ranger District, (541) 352-6002.

Cummins Creek Wilderness, 9,173 acres. Siuslaw National Forest, Waldport Ranger District, (541) 563-3211.

Diamond Peak Wilderness, 54,185 acres. Deschutes National Forest (34,413 acres), Crescent Ranger District, (541) 433-2234. Willamette National Forest (19,772 acres), Rigdon Ranger District, (541) 782-2283.

Drift Creek Wilderness, 5,798 acres. Siuslaw National Forest, Waldport Ranger District, (541) 563-3211.

Eagle Cap Wilderness, 358,541 acres. Wallowa-Whitman National Forest, Eagle Cap Ranger District, (541) 426-4978.

Gearhart Mountain Wilderness, 22,809 acres. Fremont National Forest, Bly Ranger District, (541) 353-2427.

Grassy Knob Wilderness, 17,200 acres. Siskiyou National Forest, Powers Ranger District, (541) 439-3011.

Hells Canyon Wilderness, 13,095 acres (Oregon portion).Wallowa-Whitman National Forest, Hells Canyon Ranger District, (541) 426-4978.

Kalmiopsis Wilderness, 179,655 acres. Siskiyou National Forest, Chetco Ranger District, (541) 469-2196.

The Kalmiopsis Wilderness

The Kalmiopsis Wilderness was named after a rare rhododendron relative that grows wild only in this region (it has its own botanical genus and dates back 150 million years). This 78,850-acre wilderness was proclaimed a national monument in 1909 and was closed to logging and all vehicles in 1946. It's a vast and silent landscape of ravines, rock gardens, lakes, rivers, and wildflowers—a place to get happily lost in for days.—Janet Thomas, *At Home in Hostel Territory.*

Menagerie Wilderness, 4,800 acres. Willamette National Forest, Sweet Home Ranger District, (541) 367-5168.

Middle Santiam Wilderness, 7,500 acres. Willamette National Forest, Sweet Home Ranger District, (541) 367-5168.

Mill Creek Wilderness, 17,400 acres. Ochoco National Forest, Prineville Ranger District, (541) 416-6500.

Monument Rock Wilderness, 19,650 acres. Malheur National Forest (12,620 acres), Prairie City Ranger District, (541) 820-3311.Wallowa-Whitman National Forest (7,030 acres), Unity Ranger District, (541) 446-3351.

Mount Hood Wilderness, 46,560 acres. Hood River Ranger District, (541) 352-6002. Mount Hood National Forest, Zigzag Ranger District, (503) 622-7674.

Mount Jefferson Wilderness, 107,008 acres. Deschutes National Forest (32,734 acres), Sisters Ranger District, (541) 352-2111. Mount Hood National Forest (5,021 acres), Clackamas Ranger District, (503) 630-4256. Willamette National Forest (69,253 acres), Detroit Ranger District, (541) 854-3366.

Mount Thielsen Wilderness, 54,267 acres. Deschutes National Forest (7,107 acres), Crescent Ranger District, (541) 433-2234. Umpqua National Forest (21,593 acres), Diamond Lake Ranger District, (541) 498-2531.Winema National Forest (25,567 acres), Chemult Ranger District, (541) 365-7001.

Mountain Lakes Wilderness, 23,071 acres. Winema National Forest, Klamath Ranger District, (541) 885-3400.

Mount Washington Wilderness, 52,778 acres. Deschutes National Forest (38,622 acres), Sisters Ranger District, (541) 549-2111. Willamette National Forest (14,116 acres), McKenzie Ranger District, (541) 822-3381.

North Fork John Day Wilderness, 121,352 acres. Umatilla National Forest (107,058 acres), North Fork John Day Ranger District, (541) 427-3231. Wallowa-Whitman National Forest (14, 294 acres), Baker Ranger District, (541) 523-4476.

North Fork Umatilla Wilderness, 20,435 acres. Umatilla National Forest, Walla Walla Ranger District, (509) 522-6290.

Red Buttes Wilderness, 3,750 acres (Oregon portion). Rogue River National Forest (350 acres), Applegate Ranger District, (541) 899-1812. Siskiyou National Forest (3,400), Applegate Ranger District, (541) 899-1812.

Rock Creek Wilderness, 7,486 acres. Siuslaw National Forest, Waldport Ranger District, (541) 563-3211.

Rogue-Umpqua Divide Wilderness, 33,200 acres. Rogue River National Forest (6,850 acres), Prospect Ranger District, (541) 560-3400. Umpqua National Forest (26,350 acres), Tiller Ranger District, (541) 825-3201.

Salmon-Huckleberry Wilderness, 44,560 acres. Mount Hood National Forest, Zigzag Ranger District, (503) 622-7674.

Sky Lakes Wilderness, 116,300 acres. Rogue River National Forest (75,695 acres), Butte Falls Ranger District, (541) 865-2700. Winema National Forest (40,605 acres), Klamath Ranger District, (541) 885-3400.

Strawberry Mountain Wilderness, 68,700 acres. Malheur National Forest, Prairie City Ranger District, (541) 820-3311.

Three Sisters Wilderness, 286,708 acres. Deschutes National Forest (94,370 acres), Bend Ranger District, (541) 388-5664, and Sisters Ranger District, (541) 549-2111.

Willamette National Forest (192,338 acres), McKenzie Ranger District, (541) 822-3381.

Waldo Lake Wilderness, 39,200 acres. Willamette National Forest, Oakridge Ranger District, (541) 782-2291.

Wenaha-Tucannon Wilderness, 66,375 acres (Oregon portion). Umatilla National Forest, Pomeroy Ranger District, (509) 843-1891, and Walla Walla Ranger District, (509) 522-6290.

Wild Rogue Wilderness, 25,658 acres. Siskiyou National Forest, Gold Beach Ranger District, (541) 247-3600.

Willamette River and Valley

The Willamette River is the longest river entirely within Oregon, 309 miles long, and the Willamette River Valley has been the state's most densely populated region since the beginning of white settlement. The Willamette and its 11 major tributaries (McKenzie, Long Tom, Calapooia, Marys, North Santiam, Luckiamute, Yamhill, Pudding, Molalla, Tualatin, and Clackamas Rivers) cover a watershed drainage area of 11,500 square miles, from the Columbia River to the Calapooya Mountains, and from the Cascade Range to the Coast Range. The Willamette River mainstem begins where the Willamette's Coast and Middle Forks merge, near Eugene. In volume of flow, it is the tenth largest river in the United States. The Willamette system has 13 major dams, though none is on the main stem. There is a locks for vessels at Willamette Falls. The main stem of the Willamette flows north for 187 river miles from Eugene and empties into the Columbia River at Portland's northern boundary.

The Willamette Valley is the most heavily populated region in Oregon and includes the metropolitan areas of Portland, Salem, and Eugene. Approximately 75 percent of Oregonians live in the Willamette Valley, and about two-thirds of the state's population lives within 20 miles of the river. The valley was the destination of choice for most of the pioneers who braved the Oregon Trail. The rich land was the state's earliest agricultural area and is still its richest. By value, nearly half of the state's annual agricultural bounty is grown in the valley.

The density of population and heavy land use have resulted in a cosmopolitan area abutted by acres of farmland and vineyards, but the cost has been the health of the river and native habitat. One environmental group estimates that less than one-tenth of 1 percent of the original native habitat in the Willamette Valley below 1,000 feet in elevation is intact. Toxic materials found in the river include a stew of industrial chemicals, heavy metals, pesticides, and sewage. Many native fish and wildlife populations have dropped dangerously low in number, some to the verge of extinction. Resident fish have been found to contain mercury, DDT, PCBs, and dioxin, and fish deformities are common in some stretches of the river.

Despite its ills, the Willamette was designated one of 14 American Heritage Rivers in 1997. The designation recognizes outstanding stretches of U.S. rivers as part of a program to support community-based efforts to restore and protect their environmental, economic, cultural, and historic values.

Willamette Falls

"At the time of our visit to the falls of the Willamette . . . the salmon leap the falls; and it would be inconceivable, if not actually witnessed, how they can force themselves up, and after a leap of ten to twelve feet retain strength enough to stem the force of the water above. . . . I never saw so many fish collected together before."—Captain Charles Wilkes of the U.S. Exploring Expedition, 1841.

Windsurfing

Columbia River Gorge

The Columbia River Gorge is to windsurfers what Yosemite is to rock climbers and Utah is to skiers. It is a mecca, a shrine, the ultimate challenge. With its dependable winds, easy access, and great

Windsurfing on the Columbia River. Photo by Susan Dupere.

local infrastructure, the Columbia River Gorge is one of the best locations in the world for windsurfers. The town of Hood River is the center of the sport, with nearly every equipment manufacturer represented, and old fruit warehouses now house custom board- and sail-making lofts.

The sport of windsurfing dates back to the 1970s. The Columbia River Gorge has been its epicenter almost from the beginning because of its steady, strong winds and sheltered waters. The difference in climate between the west and east ends of the Columbia Gorge account for the steady winds. Each day, the sun heats the dry air on the east side of the gorge. This creates a pressure differential between east and west, which produces steady winds, often more than 30 miles per hour.

Another important feature of the Gorge is the strong current of the mighty Columbia River. When the downstream current meets the opposing upstream-flowing wind, large swells result. These two forces cancel out each other. The expert windsurfer is able to balance current and wind and never has to sail upriver to return to the starting point. Sailing the waves of the Gorge is like skiing over moguls; it is especially exciting—but not for the novice.

Gorge sailing kicks in each year in March and continues through September. Wind and waves being what they are, the Gorge sailor must travel each day to the ideal location, generally only a few miles up or down the river. Access is easy, as roads parallel both sides of the river.

Oregon Coast

Other than the Gorge, the Oregon Coast, accessible from U.S. 101, offers the most challenging, accessible, and enjoyable expert windsurfing. Open-ocean sailing involves jumping waves while heading, and surfing on the return.

While the water is always cold, weather and sea conditions are best for windsurfing between May and September, when the wind blows steadily from the northwest and the surf averages 3 to 6 feet. The best locations for ocean windsurfing are generally just to the south of jutting headlands. When the northwest winds encounter these headlands, the headlands generally refract the winds so that they pick up speed as they bend around the headland. The other attribute to look for is a gently sloping sandy beach for easy access and good surf.

Events of Interest

Gorge Games, Hood River, July, (541) 386-7774.

Wine

Long growing seasons and gentle ripening are the keys to great wine. Oregon's fertile river valleys and adjacent uplands, around the 45th parallel, are blessed with just the right conditions for great grape growing. Wine has been made in these regions for a century or more, but the modern Oregon wine industry dates from the 1960s. About 125 commercial wineries are now operational in Oregon (second in the United States to California), and more than 9,000 acres of premium varietal wine grapes are grown, mainly cabernet sauvignon, chardonnay, gewurztraminer, merlot, pinot blanc, pinot gris, pinot noir, riesling, sauvignon blanc, and zinfandel. More than 14,000 tons of wine grapes were harvested in 1998. This crop was valued at $17.3 million.

Columbia River and Walla Walla Region

The Columbia River and Walla Walla wine regions (shared with Washington State) have long, hot summer days and crisp, cool autumn nights. Rainfall is low. Wines are very flavorful and intense. Warm weather wines such as zinfandel, cabernet sauvignon, merlot, riesling, semillon, sauvignon blanc, and chardonnay are produced in this region.

Flerchinger Vineyards, Hood River, (541) 386-2882.

Hood River Vineyards, Hood River, (541) 386-3772.

Seven Hills Vineyard, Milton-Freewater, (541) 938-7710.

North Willamette Valley

Most of Oregon's wineries are in the North Willamette Valley, which runs from the Columbia River through the Portland metropolitan area to just below Salem, the state capital. This region has a very mild climate. Growing areas include Yamhill County, Washington County, the Red Hills of Dundee, and the Eola Hills northwest of Salem. Literally dozens of wineries are within an hour's drive east and west of Portland. Tasting rooms feature pinot noir, chardonnay, pinot gris, riesling, gewurztraminer, pinot blanc, cabernet sauvignon, merlot, and other varieties.

Acme Wineworks (Thomas Winery), Carlton, (503) 852-6969.

Adelsheim Vineyard, Newberg, (503) 538-3652.

Amity Vineyards, Amity, (503) 835-2362.

Antica Terra, Portland, (503) 221-7614.

Archery Summit, Dayton, (503) 864-4300.

Argyle/Dundee Wine Company, Dundee, (503) 538-8520.

Autumn Wind Vineyard, Newberg, (503) 538-6931.

Beaux Freres, Newberg, (503) 537-1137.

Belle Pente Vineyards, Carlton, (503) 852-6389.

Bethel Heights Vineyards, Salem, (503) 581-2262.

Brick House Vineyards, Newberg, (503) 538-5136.

Cameron Winery, Dundee, (503) 538-0336.

Champoeg Vineyard, Aurora, (503) 678-2144.

Chateau Benoit Winery, Carlton, (503) 864-2291.

Chateau Bianca Winery, Dallas, (503) 623-6181.

Chehalem/Ridgecrest, Nehalem, (503) 538-4700.

Cooper Mountain Vineyards, Beaverton, (503) 649-0027.

Cristom Vineyards, Salem, (503) 375-3068.

Cuneo Cellars, Amity, (503) 835-2782.

Domaine Drouhin Oregon, Dundee, (503) 864-2700.

Domaine Serene Vineyards, Carlton, (503) 852-7777.

Duck Pond Cellars, Dundee, (503) 538-3199.

Edgefield Winery, Troutdale, (503) 665-2992.

Elk Cove Vineyards, Gaston, (503) 985-7760.

Eola Hills Wine Cellars, Rickreall, (503) 623-2405.

Erath Vineyards Winery, Dundee, (503) 538-3318.

Evesham Wood Winery, Salem, (503) 371-8478.

The Eyrie Vineyards, McMinnville, (503) 472-6315.

Flynn Vineyards, Rickreall, (503) 623-8683.

Golden Valley Winery, McMinnville, (503) 472-2739.

Helvetia Winery and Vineyards, Hillsboro, (503) 647-5169.

Honeywood Winery, Salem, (503) 362-4111.

Ken Wright Cellars, Carlton, (503) 852-7070.

Kramer Vineyards, Gaston, (503) 662-4545.

Kristin Hill Winery, Amity, (503) 835-0850.

La Merleausine, Cave Junction, (503) 662-3280.

Lange Winery, Dundee, (503) 538-6476.

A balloonist soars above lush, productive vineyards. From *Oregon Wine Country* by Robert M. Reynolds (photos) and Judy Peterson-Nedry (text).

Laurel Ridge Winery, Forest Grove, (503) 359-5436.

Marquam Hill Vineyards, Molalla, (503) 829-6677.

McKinlay Vineyard, Newberg, (503) 625-2534.

Medici Vineyards, Newberg, (503) 538-9668.

Momokawa Sake, Ltd., Forest Grove, (503) 357-7056.

Montinore Vineyards, Forest Grove, (503) 359-5012.

Morgan Lake Cellars, Dallas, (503) 623-6420.

Nehalem Bay Wine Co., Nehalem, (503) 368-5300.

Nicolas Rolin Vineyards, Portland, (503) 282-7542.

Oak Grove Orchards Winery, Rickreall, (503) 364-7052.

Oak Knoll Winery, Hillsboro, (503) 648-8198.

Orchard Heights Winery, Salem, (503) 363-0375.

Panther Creek Cellars, McMinnville, (503) 472-8080.

Ponzi Vineyards, Beaverton, (503) 628-1227.

Raptor Ridge, Scholls, (503) 887-5595.

Redhawk Vineyard, Salem, (503) 362-1596.

Rex Hill Vineyard, Newberg, (503) 538-0666.

St. Innocent Winery, Salem, (503) 378-1526.

St. Josef's Wine Cellar, Canby, (503) 651-3190.

Shafer Vineyard Cellars, Forest Grove, (503) 367-6604.

Shallon Winery, Astoria, (503) 325-5978.

Sokol Blosser Winery, Dundee, (503) 864-2282.

Stangeland Vineyards, Salem, (503) 581-0355.

Starr and Brown Winery, Portland, (503) 289-5974.

Tempest Vineyards, Amity, (503) 835-2600.

Torii Mor Winery, McMinnville, (503) 434-1439.

Tualatin Vineyards, Forest Grove, (503) 357-5005.

Wasson Brothers Winery, Sandy, (503) 668-3124.

Westry Wines, Portland, (503) 434-6357.

Wild Winds Winery, Salem, (503) 391-9991.

WillaKenzie Estate, Yamhill, (503) 662-3280.

Willamette Valley Vineyards, Turner, (800) 344-9463.

Wine Country Farm Cellars, Dayton, (503) 864-3446.

Witness Tree Vineyard, Salem, (503) 585-7874.

Yamhill Valley Vineyards, McMinnville, (503) 843-3100.

South Willamette Valley

The South Willamette Valley, from Salem to just below Eugene, produces warmer climate varieties such as marechal foch, merlot, and cabernet franc. Vineyards are found on thick beds of bluish-gray sandstone, which produces firm, compact soils.

Airlie Winery, Monmouth, (503) 838-6013.

Alpine Vineyards, Monroe, (541) 424-5851.

Bellfountain Cellars, Corvallis, (503) 929-3162.

Benton Lane Winery, Monroe, (541) 765-2060.

Broadley Vineyards, Monroe, (541) 847-5934.

Chateau Lorane, Lorane, (541) 942-8028..

High Pass Winery, Junction City, (541) 998-1447.

Hinman Vineyards/Silvan Ridge, Eugene, (541) 345-1945, (800) 736-3709.

Holley Blue Vineyard, Corvallis, (541) 757-7777.

Houston Vineyards, Eugene, (541) 747-4681.

King Estate Winery, Eugene, (541) 942-9874.

LaVelle Vineyards, Elmira, (541) 935-9406.

RainSong Vineyards Winery, Cheshire, (541) 998-1786.

Secret House Vineyards Winery, Veneta, (541) 935-3774.

Serendipity Cellars, Monmouth, (541) 938-7710.

Springhill Cellars, Albany, (541) 928-1009.

Tyee Wine Cellars, Corvallis, (541) 753-8754.

Rogue Valley

The sunny Rogue Valley in Southern Oregon is the highest, warmest, and driest wine region in the state. It is also the oldest wine-growing region, for it was here that the potential of Oregon's valleys for viticulture was first recognized in the late 1800s.

Academy Wines, Jacksonville, (541) 846-6817.

Ashland Vineyards, Ashland, (541) 488-0088.

Bear Creek Vineyards, Cave Junction, (541) 592-3727.

Bridgeview Vineyards, Cave Junction, (541) 592-4688.

Foris Vineyards, Cave Junction, (541) 592-3752.

Troon Vineyard, Grants Pass, (541) 846-6562.

Valley View Winery, Jacksonville, (541) 899-8468.

Weisinger's of Ashland, Albany, (541) 488-5989.

Umpqua Valley

The Umpqua Valley around the city of Roseburg, actually a lace of small hillsides and drainages, produces some of the finest vintages in the state.

Abacela Vineyards, Roseburg, (541) 679-6642.

Callahan Ridge Winery, Roseburg, (541) 673-7901.

DeNino Umpqua River Estate, Roseburg, (541) 673-1975.

Girardet Wine Cellars, Roseburg, (541) 679-7252.

Henry Estate Winery, Umpqua, (541) 459-5120.

Hillcrest Vineyard, Roseburg, (541) 673-3709.

La Garza Cellars, Roseburg, (541) 679-9654.

Other

Mountain View, Bend, (541) 388-8339.

Flying Dutchman, Otter Rock and Newport, (541) 765-2060.

Wine and Wine-related Festivals

Ag Fest, April, State Fairgrounds, Salem.

Astoria Crab Seafood and Wine Classic, April, Astoria.

Gold Beach Wine and Food Festival, February, Gold Beach.

Greatest of the Grape, March, Canyonville.

McMinnville Wine and Food Classic, March, McMinnville.

Newport Seafood and Wine Festival, February, Newport.

Oregon Horticultural Show, January, Portland.

Oregon Wine and Food Festival, February, Salem.

Oregon Wine Month, February, statewide.

OSU Winegrape Research Day, February, Corvallis.

Pear and Wine Festival, May, Hood River.

Savor the Flavor, February, Hillsboro.

Tastevin Tour, Polk County Wineries, May, Salem.

Umpqua Valley Wine, Art and Jazz Festival, September, Oakland.

Vintage Release Festival Willamette Valley Vineyards, March, Turner.

Organizations of Interest

Oregon Wine Advisory Board, 1200 NW Naito Parkway, #400, Portland 97209, (800) 242-2363, owab@teleport.com.

Zip Codes

To find a zip code for a specific address, use the zip code finder at the U.S. Postal Service website at www.usps.gov/ncsc/lookups.

Acorn Park 97402
Adams 97810
Adel 97620
Adrian 97901
Agate Beach 97365
Agness 97406
Albany 97321
Allegany 97407
Aloha 97007
Alsea 97324
Alvadore 97409
Amity 97101
Antelope 97001
Arcadia 97913
Arch Cape 97102
Arlington 97812
Arock 97902
Ashland 97520
Ashwood 97711
Astoria 97103
Athena 97813
Aumsville 97325
Aurora 97002
Azalea 97410
Baker City 97814
Bandon 97411
Banks 97106, 97109, 97125,
Bates 97817
Bay City 97107
Beatty 97621
Beaver 97108
Beavercreek 97004
Beaverton 97005, 97006, 97007, 97008, 97075, 97076, 97077, 97078
Bend 97701, 97702, 97707, 97708, 97709
Beulah 97911
Biggs 97065
Birkenfeld 97016
Blachly 97412
Blodgett 97326
Blue River 97413
Bly 97622
Boardman 97818
Bonanza 97623
Boring 97009
Bridal Veil 97010
Bridgeport 97819
Brighton 97136
Brightwood 97011
Broadbent 97414
Brogan 97903
Brookings 97415
Brooks 97305
Brothers 97712
Brownsville 97327
Burlington 97231
Burns 97710, 97720
Burns Junction 97910
Butte Falls 97522
Butteville 97002
Buxton 97109
Cairo 97914
Camas Valley 97416
Camp Sherman 97730
Canby 97013
Cannon Beach 97110
Canyon City 97820
Canyonville 97417
Cape Meares 97141
Carlton 97111
Cascade Locks 97014
Cascade Summit 97425
Cascadia 97329

Cave Junction 97523
Cayuse 97821
Cedar Hills 97225
Cedar Mill 97229, 97291
Celilo 97058
Central Point 97502
Charbonneau 97070
Charleston 97420
Chemult 97731
Cheshire 97419
Chiloquin 97624, 97639, 97604
Christmas Valley 97641
Clackamas 97015
Clarno 97001
Clatskanie 97016
Claude 97914
Cloverdale 97112
Coburg 97408
College Crest 97401
Colton 97017
Columbia City 97018
Condon 97823
Coos Bay 97420
Coquille 97423
Corbett 97019
Cornelius 97113
Corners 97068
Corvallis 97330, 97331, 97333, 97339
Cottage Grove 97424
Cove 97824
Crabtree 97335
Crane 97732
Crater Lake 97604
Crawfordsville 97336
Crescent 97733
Crescent Lake 97425
Creswell 97426
Crooked River 97760
Crow 97401
Culp Creek 97427
Culver 97734
Curtin 97428
Dairy 97625
Dale 97880
Dallas 97338
Damascus 97009
Danner 97910
Days Creek 97429
Dayton 97114
Dayville 97825
Deadwood 97430
Deer Island 97054
Depoe Bay 97341
Detroit 97342
Dexter 97431
Diamond 97722
Diamond Lake 97731
Dillard 97432
Donald 97020
Dorena 97434
Dover 97022
Drain 97435
Drewsey 97904
Dufur 97021
Dundee 97115
Durham 97224
Durkee 97905
Eagle Creek 97022
Eagle Crest 97756
Eagle Point 97524
East Lake 97739
Echo 97826
Eddyville 97343
Elgin 97827
Elkton 97436
Elmira 97437
Enterprise 97828
Estacada 97023
Eugene 97401, 97402, 97403, 97404, 97405, 97408, 97412, 97440, 97455
Fairview 97024
Fall Creek 97438
Falls City 97344
Fields 97710
Fir Grove 97401
Florence 97439
Forest Grove 97116
Forest Heights 97229
Fort Klamath 97626
Fort Rock 97735
Fort Stevens 97121
Fossil 97830
Foster 97345

Fox 97831
Frenchglen 97736
Friend 97021
Gales Creek 97117
Galice 97532
Gardiner 97441
Garibaldi 97118
Gaston 97119
Gates 97346
Gervais 97026
Gladstone 97027
Glendale 97442
Gleneden Beach 97388
Glenwood 97116
Glide 97443
Gold Beach 97444
Gold Hill 97525
Government Camp 97028
Grand Island 97114
Grand Ronde 97347
Grants Pass 97526, 97527, 97528, 97543
Grass Valley 97029
Greenleaf 97430
Gresham 97030, 97080
Haines 97833
Halfway 97834
Halsey 97348
Hammond 97121
Happy Valley 97015, 97236, 97266
Harper 97906
Harrisburg 97446
Hebo 97122
Helix 97835
Helvetia 97124
Heppner 97836
Hereford 97837
Hermiston 97838
Hillsboro 97123, 97124
Hines 97738
Hood River 97031, 97041
Hubbard 97032
Huntington 97907
Idanha 97350
Idleyld Park 97447
Imbler 97841
Imnaha 97842
Independence 97351
Interlachen 97024
Ione 97843
Ironside 97908
Irrigon 97844
Irving 97401
Island City 97850
Jacksonville 97530
Jamieson 97909
Jasper 97438
Jefferson 97352
Jennings Lodge 97267
John Day 97845
Johnson City 97267
Jonesboro 97911
Jordan Valley 97910
Joseph 97846
Junction City 97448
Juntura 97911
Kah-Nee-Ta 97761
Keizer 97307, 97303
Keno 97627
Kent 97033
Kerby 97531
Kernville 97367
Kimberly 97848
King City 97224
Kinzua 97830
Klamath Falls 97601, 97602, 97603
Lafayette 97127
La Grande 97850
Lake Grove 97034, 97035
Lake Oswego 97034, 97035
Lakeside 97449
Lakeview 97630
Langlois 97450
La Pine 97739
Lawen 97740
Leaburg 97489
Lebanon 97355
Lees Camp 97141
Lexington 97839
Liberal 97038
Lincoln City 97367
Logsden 97357
Long Creek 97856
Lorane 97451
Lostine 97857
Lowell 97452
Lyons 97358
Madras 97741
Malin 97632
Manning 97125
Manzanita 97130
Mapleton 97453
Marcola 97454
Marion 97359
Marylhurst 97036

Maupin 97037
Mayville 97830
Maywood Park 97220
McKenzie Bridge 97413
McMinnville 97128
McNary 97880
Meacham 97859
Medford 97501, 97504
Mehama 97384
Merlin 97532
Merrill 97633
Metolius 97741
Midland 97634
Mikkalo 97861
Mill City 97360
Milton-Freewater 97862
Milwaukie 97222, 97267, 97269
Mist 97016
Mitchell 97750
Mohler 97131
Molalla 97038
Monitor 97071
Monmouth 97361
Monroe 97456
Monument 97864
Moro 97039
Mosier 97040
Mountain Park 97035
Mount Angel 97362
Mount Hood 97041
Mount Vernon 97865
Mulino 97042
Multnomah 97219
Murphy 97533
Murphys Camp 97473
Myrtle Creek 97457
Myrtle Point 97458
Neahkahnie 97131
Nehalem 97131
Neotsu 97364
Neskowin 97149
Netarts 97143
Newberg 97132
New Pine Creek 97635
Newport 97365-97366
North Bend 97459
North Plains 97133
North Powder 97867
North Santiam 97325
Norway 97460, 97458
Noti 97461
Nyssa 97913
Oak Grove 97222, 97267, 97268
Oakland 97462
Oakridge 97463
O'Brien 97534
Oceanside 97134
Odell 97044
Ontario 97914
Ophir 97464
Oregon City 97045
Orenco 97123, 97124
Otis 97368
Otter Crest 97365
Otter Rock 97369
Owyhee Corners 97913
Oxbow 97840
Pacific City 97135
Paisley 97636
Parkrose 97220, 97230
Paulina 97751
Pendleton 97801
Philomath 97370
Phoenix 97535
Pilot Rock 97868
Pine Grove 97037
Pistol River 97444
Pleasant Hill 97405, 97455
Plush 97637
Portland 97201-25, 97227-33, 97236, 97238, 97240, 97242, 97251, 97253-56, 97258-59, 97266-69, 97271-72, 97280-83, 97286, 97290-94, 97296, 97298-99
Port Orford 97465
Post 97752
Powell Butte 97753
Powers 97466
Prairie City 97869
Princeton 97721
Prineville 97754
Progress 97005
Prospect 97536
Rainier 97048
Redland 97045
Redmond 97756
Reedsport 97467
Remote 97468
Rhododendron 97049
Richland 97870
Rickreall 97371
Riddle 97469
Riley 97758
Ritter 97872
Riverside 97917

Rockaway Beach 97136
Rock Creek 97229
Rockwood 97233
Rogue Elk 97451
Rogue River 97537
Rome 97910
Roseburg 97470
Rose Lodge 97372
Rowena 97058
Rufus 97050
Saginaw 97472
Saint Benedict 97373
Saint Helens 97051
Saint Louis 97026
Saint Paul 97137
Salem 97301-06, 97308-14
Sandy 97055
Santa Clara 97404
Scappoose 97056
Scholls 97123
Scio 97374
Scottsburg 97473
Scotts Mills 97375
Seal Rock 97376
Selma 97538
Seneca 97873
Shady Cove 97539
Shaniko 97057
Shedd 97377
Sheridan 97378
Sherwood 97140
Siletz 97380
Silver Lake 97638
Silverton 97381
Sisters 97759
Sixes 97476
South Beach 97366
Sprague River 97639
Spray 97874
Springdale 97060
Springfield 97477, 97478
Stanfield 97875
Stayton 97383
Sublimity 97385
Summer Lake 97640
Summerville 97876
Sumpter 97877
Sunriver 97707
Sutherlin 97479
Sweet Home 97386
Swisshome 97480
Talent 97540
Tangent 97389
Tenmile 97481
Terrebonne 97760
The Dalles 97058
Thurston 97482
Tidewater 97390
Tigard 97223, 97224, 97281
Tillamook 97141
Tiller 97484
Timber 97144
Timberline Lodge 97028
Toledo 97391
Tollgate 97759
Tongue Point 97103
Trail 97541
Triangle Lake 97412
Troutdale 97060
Tualatin 97062
Turner 97359, 97392
Twin Rocks 97136
Tygh Valley 97063
Ukiah 97880
Umatilla 97882
Umpqua 97486
Union 97883
Unity 97884
University 97403
Vale 97918
Vaughn 97487
Veneta 97487
Verboort 97116
Vernonia 97064
Vida 97488
Walden 97424
Waldport 97394
Walker 97426
Wallowa 97885
Walterville 97489
Walton 97490
Wamic 97063
Wankers 97068
Warm Springs 97761

Warren 97053
Wasco 97065
Wedderburn 97491
Welches 97067
Wemme 97067
Westfall 97920
Westfir 97492
Westlake 97493
West Linn 97068
Weston 97886
Westport 97016
West Salem 97304
West Slope 97225
West Union 97124
Wheeler 97147
White City 97503
Wilbur 97494
Wilderville 97543
Willamette 97068
Willamina 97396
Williams 97544
Willowcreek 97918
Wilsonville 97070
Winchester 97495
Winston 97496
Wolf Creek 97497
Woodburn 97071
Wood Village 97060
Yachats 97498
Yamhill 97148
Yoncalla 97499
Zigzag 97049

Zoos and Aquariums

(*SEE ALSO* SEALS AND SEA LIONS) There are several places to view exotic wildlife and sea life in Oregon. The Oregon Zoo in Portland's Washington Park, Wildlife Safari in Southern Oregon, the Oregon Coast Aquarium in Newport, and the tiny Depoe Bay Aquarium in Depoe Bay.

Nestled on 65 acres in Southwest Portland, the Oregon Zoo's exhibits allow visitors to view animals in their natural

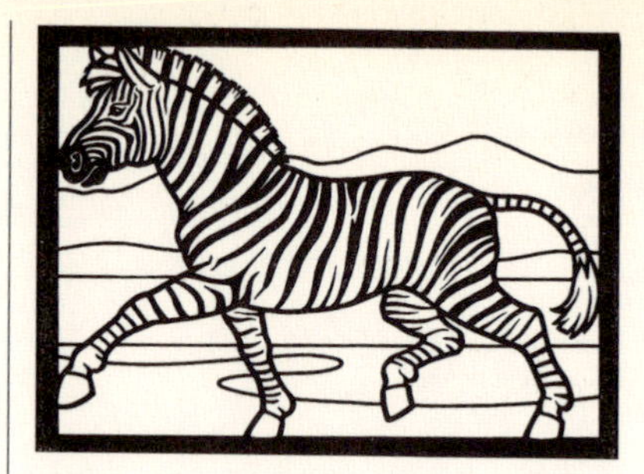

habitats, such as the Alaska tundra, the African savannah, or a rain forest. During the summer and during the December holiday season zoo-goers can ride the zoo train, a 4-mile ride through the lush, wooded hillsides of Washington Park. The 600 acres of Wildlife Safari in Winston, Oregon, just south of Roseburg, provide an open wildlife area visitors can drive through to view exotic wildlife.

The Oregon Coast Aquarium in Newport and the nearby Mark O. Hatfield Marine Science Center have exhibits of sea life, including coastal wetlands habitat, sandy and rocky shore animals, and playful sea otters, seals, and sea lions. The Hatfield Marine Science Center (HMSC), a field station of Oregon State University, has a touch pool and octopus tank, along with interactive exhibits.

Depoe Bay Aquarium, Depoe Bay 97341, (541) 765-2259.

Oregon Coast Aquarium, Inc., 2820 SE Ferry Slip Rd., Newport 97365, (541) 867-3474, www.aquarium.org.

Oregon State University Hatfield Marine Science Center, 2030 S Marine Science Dr., Newport 97365, (541) 867-0100, www.hmsc.orst.edu

Oregon Zoo, 4001 SW Canyon Rd., Portland 97221, (503) 226-1561, www.zooregon.org.

Wildlife Safari, P.O. Box 1600, Winston 97496-0231, (541) 679-6761, (800) 355-4848, www.wildlifesafari.org.

News Highlights, 1998–99

The following is a collection of news events from mid-1998 to late 1999. The Oregon Almanac *wishes to credit stories from* The Oregonian, *the Associated Press, the (Eugene)* Register-Guard, *and the (Medford)* Mail-Tribune, *as the primary sources of information for News Highlights.*

The Economy: The Story Was Asia. Hundreds of Oregon workers lost their jobs in 1998 because of Asia's economic crisis. Thousands more were laid off. A year after Asian stocks and currencies started sliding, Northwest workers were losing jobs due to the crisis. Oregon companies began to cite Asia's problems as a cause of their own difficulties.

As the Asian crisis worsened, job growth slowed along with corporate income-tax payments. Some of Oregon's large high-technology companies reported lower earnings. Northwest exports to Asia, whose growth led the nation at times during the past decade, declined. Asians bought fewer Northwest products, which, priced in dollars, became more expensive as Far East currencies weakened.

Reduced demand in Asia for timber and electronics depressed worldwide sales, with negative economic repercussions for Northwest sawmills and high-technology companies. While some Asian economies began to recover from their bout with the Asian economic "flu," throughout 1999 Oregon continued to feel the impact on its agriculture and timber industries.

School Violence Strikes Oregon High School. Fifteen-year-old freshman Kipland P. "Kip" Kinkel, suspended from Thurston High School in Springfield for bringing a gun to school, returned on the morning of May 21, 1998, and opened fire on his fellow students. The hail of more than 50 bullets from the 22-caliber rifle wounded 23 and killed 1. The victims were all in the cafeteria having breakfast before the start of the regular school day. Seventeen-year-old varsity wrestler Jake Ryker put an end to the carnage by wrestling Kinkel to the ground and disarming him. Ryker was one of the wounded. Later in the day, police found that Kinkel had slain his parents, both popular local teachers, before leaving for school.

Students offered a conflicted portrait of Kip Kinkel. Some described him as the "class clown"; others said he had a dark side and an obsession with bombs and violence. Kinkel listened to the music of Satanist rocker Marilyn Manson. He bought a 9-mm Glock pistol with money he earned doing chores around the house. Kinkel wore a trench coat to school on the day of the rampage. In September 1999, Kinkel pleaded guilty to four counts of murder and 26 counts of attempted murder.

What About the Weather? Weather woes plagued the state throughout 1998 and 1999. Melting snow in the mountains also caused havoc around Prineville. Parts of Crook County were declared a disaster area after several days of flooding that began May 29, 1998. About 400 homes were evacuated during the flood, which began after unusually heavy rainfall in the area. About a hundred homes were severely damaged. Several city bridges, streets, and parks also sustained damage.

A nasty storm socked the Oregon Coast on Nov. 23, 1998, and raged inland, tearing down trees and knocking out power as it rolled northeast into the Willamette Valley. More than 100,000 Portland General Electric customers lost power. It was the most widespread power failure since the great windstorm of December 1995, when 300,000 homes lost electricity. And it was just the beginning.

Punishing coastal storms in March 1999 caused significant erosion in some beachfront communities. Home and business owners requested state permission to armor the shoreline with walls of riprap (massive rock boulders). Allowing property owners to build walls of boulders on the beach is controversial in Oregon, where the public's right to enjoy the beaches is jealously guarded. Any intrusion on the beaches by private property owners requires state permission. Only owners of properties in place before 1977, when state land-use laws were adopted, are routinely allowed to use boulders for protection. Following the March storms, the state issued just over a dozen emergency permits in popular vacation spots such as Rockaway Beach and Neskowin.

Winter hung on into April along the coast, where it snowed during the first week of April 1999. An avalanche on a popular climbing route on Mount Hood killed one man and tossed three companions at least a hundred yards through jagged rocks and icy snow. Record snowpack in the mountains threatened to raise summer lake levels in Eastern Oregon, especially Malheur, Harney, and Mud Lakes. Ranchers were concerned about being flooded out.

Tragedy occurred on Jan. 29, 1993 with the collapse of the Sunset Tunnel on Sunset Highway (U.S. 26). A state employee who was on site to supervise repair work was killed when the tunnel collapsed from a water leak. The tunnel opened in August 1941 and was the only wood-braced tunnel still in regular use on Oregon highways. Before the roof fell in, Sunset Tunnel had been pounded by days of steady rainfall and muddy streams were flowing from both sides of the tunnel.

Death of a War Hero. Death Row for a Criminal. Major General Marion Carl, 82, of Roseburg was one of the nation's most highly decorated aviators and the Marine Corps' first flying ace. In June 1998, after he had gone to bed, 19-year-old Jesse Fanus barged into Carl's house, pointed a pump-action shotgun at the general's wife, 74-year-old Edna Carl, who was watching TV, and demanded all her money and the keys to her car. Awakened by the disturbance, Marion Carl came out of the bedroom to find the intruder pointing the shotgun at his wife. He lunged at Fanus, who turned on him and leveled a shot directly at his head, mortally wounding him. On May 5, 1999, Jesse Fanus was found guilty and sentenced to death. He is the youngest resident of Oregon's death row.

Assisted Suicide. In August 1998, the Oregon Health Division reported that during the first 10 months following passage of Oregon's first-in-the-nation assisted suicide law, 10 terminally ill patients requested suicide medication under the law. Eight of the 10 patients used the medication to end their lives; the other two died naturally. The average age of the patients was 71. Nine had cancer; one suffered from heart disease. Some patients used the suicide medication on the same day that the prescription was written; others waited as long as 16 days before ending their lives.

Nine physicians wrote the prescriptions, refuting the concern that one or two doctors in the state would emerge as the prescription-writing "doctors of death." Also, it appears likely that assisted suicide will be chosen only by a few terminally ill patients. In 1996, for example, about 5,000 people died from cancer in Oregon; yet in the first 10 months after assisted suicide became legal, only nine cancer patients chose to end their own lives.

Competition for Prized Mushrooms. The matsutake mushroom can bring as much as $900 per pound from Japanese gourmet diners, and the Cascades have been a prime source of the coveted mushrooms. In 1997, an average day saw 1,600 pickers along the Cascade crest bringing in 20 pounds apiece of mushrooms bringing $10 to $13 a pound. A total of 3,733 pickers bought permits from the Winema and Deschutes National Forests. The pickings were not so good in 1998, though; forest rangers estimate no more than 400 pickers brought in a meager two pounds a day that sold for about $4.26 a pound. Only 1,216 permits were sold. In an effort to increase their harvest, pickers extended their activities into Crater Lake National Park in the fall of 1998, where mushroom picking for profit is illegal. A 1996 General Accounting Office study of the state of the national parks found that mushroom poaching was the most serious threat to the ecology of Crater Lake National Park. Mushroom harvesting without a permit is a misdemeanor punishable by a fine of $500.

Fall 1998 Election Results. Sen. Ron Wyden handily won his first senatorial reelection bid in balloting in November 1998. Wyden entered the U.S. Senate in 1996 after winning a special election that followed Robert Packwood's resignation. Peter DeFazio (4th District-Southern Oregon) and Earl Blumenauer (3rd District-East Portland) were returned to office in easy victories. Two new faces in Congress are Darlene Hooley (5th District-mid-Willamette Valley) and Greg Walden (2nd District).

Of the many ballot measures put before voters, it can be said that generally the best financed campaigns won. Major new ballot initiatives that won voter approval included Measure 60, which extends the vote-by-mail system to all elections, and Measure 66, which earmarks 15 percent of Oregon State Lottery profits to parks and salmon-restoration projects. Also approved were measures to legalize marijuana for medical use and to open adoption records to adult children. Measures that were defeated included efforts to recriminalize marijuana, to ban clear-cutting of forests, and to prohibit public-employee unions from using payroll deductions for collecting political-action funds.

Strange Deaths on Oregon Beaches. Beginning in November 1998, and throughout the following year, sea lions, seals, and even Pacific gray whales seemed to die in increased numbers. Some people believed a shortage of food caused by abnormal ocean currents-the legacy of El Niño-was the primary cause. Others suspected poisoning by domoic acid, a natural substance associated with harmful algae blooms. A third possibility was a bacterial infection known as leptospirosis, which usually targets humans and domestic animals. While the causes may forever be unproved, the incidents of stranded, dying, and dead marine mammals on Oregon's shores served as a grim reminder of the fragility of life and the necessity of protecting Oregon's ocean and coast from degradation and harm.

Abortion Protest Verdict. On Feb. 2, 1999, a federal jury in Portland ordered a coalition of abortion protesters to pay $109 million in damages for putting the names and addresses of four doctors on two "wanted"-style posters and a website called "The Nuremberg Files." The jury found that the posters and the website constituted illegal threats of violence under federal clinic-protection and anti-racketeering statutes. First Amendment scholars said the unanimous verdict had important free-speech ramifications and could affect the tactics of protesters.

The Ship that Would Not Die. On Feb. 4, 1999, a 639-foot wood-chip carrier, the *New Carissa*, went aground on the Coos Bay North Spit. She carried 400,000 gallons of bunker and diesel fuel. The ship had anchored outside the bar because the weather was too rough to board a pilot. After the anchors began to drag, the ship attempted to maneuver away from the lee shore, but the weather got the better of her and drove her hard aground in the sand, about two miles north of the harbor entrance.

Initial salvage efforts were hampered by bad weather, and after several days of brutal pounding by the surf, the ship began leaking fuel. With the assistance of the U.S. Navy, the hull was set on fire. The fire burned about half the fuel but also weakened the ship and she broke in half. About 70,000 gallons of fuel leaked in the Coos Bay area before the 400-foot bow section was pulled off the beach. The bow then broke loose from a tug and the ship washed ashore again near Waldport, where about 2,000 more gallons leaked. The bow, with 130,000 gallons of bunker fuel remaining aboard, was once again towed out to sea, where it was bombed and finally sank on March 11.

Meanwhile, back on the beach, workers removed about 14,000 gallons of oil from the 220-foot stern section, which remained firmly planted where it originally grounded.

Salvage crews armed with acetylene torches eventually reduced the rusting stern section to scrap iron and carted it off.

Landmark Tobacco Verdict. In March 1999, a Multnomah County jury ordered Philip Morris Inc. to pay a record-setting $81 million in damages to the estate of a Portland school janitor who died of lung cancer after smoking Marlboro cigarettes for 42 years. Jurors were angered by Philip Morris documents showing that company officials knew for decades that cigarettes are addictive and can cause cancer. The decision was the nation's largest such verdict; however, on May 13, 1999, the judge later reduced the amount of the award to $32 million. Tobacco industry analysts were concerned that the Portland verdict might foreshadow a flood of similar successful suits against tobacco companies.

Medical Marijuana. Oregon became the first state to take an active part in regulating marijuana for medical use, issuing registration cards to anyone who has cancer, glaucoma, HIV disease, severe wasting, pain, nausea, seizures, or muscle spasms, and to people whose doctors agree that marijuana might alleviate symptoms. Jeanelle Bluhm, who has multiple sclerosis, received the first such license on May 21, 1999, to relieve painful muscle spasms brought on by multiple sclerosis. She told a reporter from *The Oregonian* that she plans to home-can some tomatoes and put up some marijuana in sandwich bags.

Paiute Leader Returns 121 Years Later. Chief Egan and his brother-in-law were killed in an ambush in the last major war between Northwest tribes and the U.S. government, in 1878. They were beheaded. Army surgeons sent their skulls to Washington, D.C., where they remained in government museums. In 1989 and 1990, Congress passed legislation requiring that human remains, burial items, and other cultural items be repatriated. The descendants of Chief Egan got their turn finally, in May 1999. Thirty of the chief's descendants gathered on the Burns Paiute Reservation to welcome home the remains of their great chief. They recalled how, after the Bannock War, the Paiutes were scattered to reservations in Nevada, Idaho, and Oregon-a culture and a people fractured. They praised their chief for once again bringing their people together for a ceremony linked to a shared past and a shared future. The remains, in two small cedar boxes, were placed inside a large tepee. Outside, a fire burned all night, signaling that a chief had died.

Out Dam Spots. Following the listing of some salmon runs for federal protection under the Endangered Species Act, Portland General Electric announced in May 1999 that it would aid the fish and improve Portland's water supply by eliminating the Little Sandy and Marmot Dams. Located on streams that feed into Roslyn Lake, the dams were built early in the 20th century to direct water into a small powerhouse. Removal of the Little Sandy Dam would open up the Little Sandy River basin for salmon and steelhead, allowing water to flow into a 12-mile stretch-now virtually dry-from the dam to where the Little Sandy meets the Bull Run River. Removing Marmot Dam would open 10 miles of the Sandy River to salmon and steelhead. The removal of the dams signals a mounting willingness to alter Oregon's infrastructure to restore habitat for the benefit of fish. A study by the Oregon Natural Resources Council, a Portland-based conservation group, concluded that breaching the dams would result in a net economic benefit to the region of $86.7 million.

Brightest Kid in U.S. Twelve-year-old Vino Vasudevan is the eighth-grader who scored a perfect 1,600 on the Scholastic Aptitude Tests (SATs) in a national search for gifted children by researchers at Johns Hopkins University. Of the 600,000 gifted seventh- and eighth-graders the program has tracked through two decades, Vino, from Lake Oswego, is the first to earn perfect scores on both the math and verbal portions of the aptitude tests. Winners were honored on June 12, 1999 at Johns Hopkins.

Adios, Keiko. Keiko the killer whale, made famous in the movie *Free Willy*, was returned to the waters of his birth off the coast of Iceland. Keiko was captured in 1979 for live display, and after a brief sojourn in an amusement park in Canada, he was moved to Mexico City, where he languished for years under poor environmental conditions. Cellular telephone pioneer Craig McCaw of Seattle established the Free Willy Foundation and arranged for Keiko's relocation to a specially built pool at the Oregon Coast Aquarium in Newport. With round-the-clock care and attention, Keiko regained his health and became the most popular tourist attraction on the Oregon Coast. On Sept. 9, 1998, however, it was time to say bye-bye to Keiko as he took off for Iceland aboard a specially equipped Air Force C-17 cargo plane. Keiko now lives in a net pen in a fjord off the island of Westmann, Iceland. Plans are to release him to the wild when he is able to fend for himself. To follow Keiko's progress to freedom, check out www.keiko.org.

Nuclear Reactor Steams Up the Columbia. On the weekend of Aug. 7-8, 1999, Oregonians who happened to be anywhere near the Columbia River saw a most unusual site-a 1,000-ton shrink-wrapped nuclear reactor being towed upriver on a barge. The reactor, from the Trojan Nuclear Plant, was on its way to its final resting place in a 45-foot-deep trench on the Hanford Nuclear Reservation in Washington State. The decommissioned reactor, considered low-level nuclear waste, was filled with 200 tons of concrete, encased in thick steel, and plastic-wrapped to protect against radiation leakage. The Trojan plant, located near Rainier, operated from 1976 to 1993. Its owner, Portland General Electric, shut it down 20 years ahead of schedule amid operating problems and anti-nuclear protests. The plant's highly radioactive fuel rods are still on the Trojan site, where they will be stored until they can be transferred to a national high-level nuclear repository. That repository is still in the planning stages and is years away from opening.

Adoptees Finally Get Access to Birth Records. Oregon's controversial law allowing adoptees access to their birth records finally went into effect on May 31, 2000, more than two years after it was enacted. The law, passed as Measure 58 in November 1998, had been slogging its way through the courts since December 1998. A group of birth mothers challenged the new law, arguing that it violated an implied contract that they would be protected and that they would never be contacted by the children they relinquished.

On May 30, 2000, U.S. Supreme Court Justice Sandra Day O'Connor rejected a request to delay the law from going into effect. The U.S. Supreme Court refused to review a similar Tennessee law in 1997. The next day, the first day the Oregon Health Division began processing birth certificate requests, more than a dozen adoptees showed up to file their request in person, adding to the 2,334 applications the agency had already received.

Adoptees can find the application for their original birth certificates on the Oregon Health Division web site at www.ohd.hr.state.or.us/chs/certif/preadopt.htm. On the same site, birth mothers can download a "contact preference form," which allows them to state whether they wish to be contacted, contacted only through an intermediary, or not contacted at all. If they choose not to be contacted, they must file a detailed family medical history.

Alaska, Alabama, Delaware, Kansas, and Tennessee also allow adult adoptees access to original birth certificates.

Blaze of Glory. On Sunday, June 4, 2000, the Portland Trail Blazers succumbed to the Los Angeles Lakers in the seventh game of the last round of the NBA semifinals. The Blazers had staged a formidable comeback, after being down three games to one in the series. And while it was LA that prevailed, the Blazers made them wait until the last eight minutes of the last game to do so. The Lakers rallied in the fourth quarter, scoring 15 consecutive points and wiping out a 15-point Portland lead. The final hard-fought score was 89-84.

Further Reading

Abbott, Carl, Sy Adler, and Deborah Howe, editors. *Planning the Oregon Way: A Twenty-Year Evaluation.* Corvallis: Oregon State University Press, 1994.

Alt, David D. and Donald W. Hyndman. *Roadside Geology of Oregon.* Missoula, Mont.: Mountain Press Publishing Company, 1978.

Amato, Ann. *Ancient Forests and Western Man: A Pictorial History of the West Coast.* Portland, Ore.: Frank Amato Publications, 1993.

Anderson, Chris. *Edge Effects: Notes from an Oregon Forest (The American Land and Life).* Iowa City: University of Iowa Press, 1997.

Arno, Steven and Romona Hammerly. *Northwest Trees.* Seattle, Wash.: The Mountaineers, 1984.

Atkeson, Ray, *Oregon, My Oregon.* Portland, Ore.: Graphic Arts Center Publishing Company, 1998.

———, with Richard Ross. *Oregon III.* Portland, Ore.: Graphic Arts Center Publishing Company, 1987.

———, with Rick Schafer and Kim Stafford. *Wind on the Waves.* Portland, Ore.: Graphic Arts Center Publishing Company, 1992.

———. with Warren Miller. *Ski and Snow Country: The Golden Years of Skiing in the West, 1930s-1950s.* Portland, Ore.: Graphic Arts Center Publishing Company, 2000.

Bagley, Clarence. *The Acquisition and Pioneering of Old Oregon.* Fairfield, Wash.: Ye Galleon Press, 1983.

Bancroft, Hubert Howe. *History of Oregon. (The Works of Hubert Howe Bancroft—Vol. XXIX-XXX).* San Francisco, Calif.: History Co., 1886-88.

Bannan, Jan. *Oregon State Parks: A Complete Recreation Guide.* Seattle, Wash.: The Mountaineers, 1994.

Barnes, Christine. *Central Oregon: View from the Middle.* Helena, Mont.: American & World Geographic Publishers, 1996.

Baskas, Harriet. *Atomic Marbles & Branding Irons: A Guide to Museums, Collections, and Roadside Curiosities in Washington and Oregon.* Seattle, Wash.: Sasquatch Books, 1993.

———. *Museums of the Northwest: Discover the Best Collections in Washington, Oregon, and Lower British Columbia.* Seattle, Wash.: Sasquatch Books, 1999.

Blair, Karen J. *Women in Pacific Northwest History: An Anthology.* Seattle: University of Washington Press, 1988.

Boag, Peter G. *Environment and Experience: Settlement Culture in Nineteenth-Century Oregon.* Berkeley: University of California Press, 1992.

Booth, Brian, editor. *Wildmen, Wobblies & Whistle Punks: Stewart Holbrook's Lowbrow Northwest.* Corvallis: Oregon State University Press, 1992.

Butruille, Susan G., and Kathleen Petersen. *Women's Voices from the Oregon Trail: The Times that Tried Women's Souls and a Guide to Women's History Along the Oregon Trail.* Boise, Idaho: Tamarack Books, 1994.

Canniff, Kiki. *The Best Free Historic Attractions in Oregon and Washington.* Willamina, Ore.: Kip2s Enterprises, 1995.

———. *Northwest Golfer: A Guide to Every Golf Course Where the Public Is Welcome in Oregon & Washington.* Portland, Ore.: Frank Amato Publications, 1996.

Coffman, Lloyd W. *Blazing a Wagon Trail to Oregon: A Weekly Chronicle of the Great Migration of 1843.* Enterprise, Ore.: Echo Books, 1993.

Cox, Thomas R. 1988. *The Park Builders: A History of the State Parks in the Pacific Northwest.* Seattle: University of Washington Press, 1993.

Cressman, Luther Sheeleigh. *The Sandal and the Cave: The Indians of Oregon.* Corvallis: Oregon State University Press, 1981.

Csuti, Blair A., editor. *Atlas of Oregon Wildlife: Distribution, Habitat, and Natural History.* Corvallis: Oregon State University Press, 1997.

Dietrich, William. *The Final Forest.* New York: Simon & Schuster, 1992.

———. *Northwest Passage: The Great Columbia River.* New York: Simon & Schuster, 1995.

Dodds, Gordon B. *Oregon: A Bicentennial History.* New York: Norton, 1977.

Duncan, David James. *The River Why.* San Francisco: Sierra Clubs Books, 1983.

Durbin, Kathie. *Tree Huggers: Victory, Defeat & Renewal in the Northwest Ancient Forest Campaign.* Seattle, Wash.: The Mountaineers, 1996.

Egan, Timothy. *The Good Rain: Across Time and Terrain in the Pacific Northwest.* New York: Vintage Books, 1990.

Ewing, Susan. *Going Wild in Washington and Oregon: Seasonal Excursions to Wildlife and Habitats.* Seattle, Wash.: Alaska Northwest Books, 1993.

Foley, Tom, and Tish Steinfeld. *How to Rent a Fire Lookout in the Pacific Northwest.* Berkeley, Calif.: Wilderness Press, 1996.

Franklin, Jerry F., and C. T. Dyrness. *Natural Vegetation of Oregon and Washington.* Corvallis: Oregon State University Press, 1988.

Friedman, Ralph. *Tracking Down Oregon.* Caldwell, Idaho: The Caxton Printers, Ltd., 1978.

Gerspacher, Lucy, photography by Jim Piper, *Hazelnuts & More.* Portland, Ore.: Graphic Arts Center Publishing Company, 1995.

Gulick, Bill. *Roadside History of Oregon.* Missoula, Mont.: Mountain Press Publishing Co., 1991.

Harris, Stephen L. *Fire & Ice: The Cascade Volcanoes,* revised edition. Seattle, Wash.: Pacific Search Press, 1980.

Hastings, Lansford W. *The Emigrants' Guide to Oregon and California, Containing Scenes and Incidents of a Party of Oregon Emigrants; A Description of Oregon.* Bedford, Mass.: Applewood Books, 1994.

Heinl, Russ, with Sallie Tisdale. *Portland from the Air.* Portland, Ore.: Graphic Arts Center Publishing Company, 2000.

Hult, Ruby E. *Lost Mines and Treasures of the Pacific Northwest.* Portland, Ore.: Binfords & Mort, 1960.

Ikenberry, Donna Lynn. *Oregon's Outback: An Auto Tour Guide to Southeast Oregon.* Portland, Ore.: Frank Amato Publications, 1996.

———. *Discovering Oregon's Wilderness Areas.* Portland, Ore.: Frank Amato Publications, 1998.

Ingles, Lloyd G. *Mammals of the Pacific States: California, Oregon, Washington.* Palo Alto, Calif.: Stanford University Press, 1965.

Ingrid Wendt, editor. *From Here We Speak: An Anthology of Oregon Poetry* (*Oregon Literature Series,* vol. 4). Corvallis: Oregon State University Press, 1994.

Irving, Stephanie. *Best Places Destinations: Oregon Coast.* Seattle, Wash.: Sasquatch Books, 1999.

Irving, Washington. *Astoria,* Clatsop edition. Portland, Ore.: Binfords & Mort, 1967.

Johnson, Charles Grier Jr. *Common Plants of the Inland Pacific Northwest.* Portland, Ore.: USDA Forest Service, Pacific Northwest Region, 1998.

Keller, Robb. *Paddling Oregon.* Helena, Mont.: Falcon Publishing Company, 1998.

Kesey, Ken. *Sometimes a Great Notion.* 1964. Reprint, New York: Penguin Books. 1988.

Keyser, James D. *Indian Rock Art of the Columbia Plateau.* Seattle: University of Washington Press, 1992.

Kirk, Ruth, ed. *The Enduring Forests: Northern California, Oregon, Washington, British Columbia, and Southeast Alaska.* Seattle: The Mountaineers, 1996.

Laskin, David. *Rains All the Time: A Connoisseur's History of Weather in the Pacific Northwest.* Seattle, Wash.: Sasquatch Books, 1997.

Leonard, William P., Herbert A. Brown, Lawrence L. C. Jones, Kelly R. McAllister, and Robert M. Storm. *Amphibians of Washington and Oregon.* Seattle, Wash.: Seattle Audubon Society, 1993.

Lewty, Peter J. *To the Columbia Gateway: The Oregon Railway and the Northern Pacific, 1879-1884.* Pullman: Washington State University Press, 1987.

Littlefield, Carroll D. *Birds of Malheur National Wildlife Refuge Oregon.* Corvallis: Oregon State University Press, 1990.

Mathews, Daniel. *Cascade-Olympic Natural History: A Trailside Reference.* Portland, Ore.: Raven Editions and Portland Audubon Society, 1988.

McKay, Floyd J. *An Editor for Oregon: Charles A. Sprague and the Politics of Change.* Corvallis: Oregon State University Press, 1998.

Meier, Gary. *Oregon Outlaws: Tales of Old-Time Desperadoes.* Boise, Id.: Tamarack Books, 1995.

Molina, Randy, Thomas O'Dell, Daniel Luoma, Michael Amaranthus, Michael Castellano, and Kenelm Russell. *Biology, Ecology, and Social Aspects of Wild Edible Mushrooms in the Forests of the Pacific Northwest: A Preface to Managing Commercial Harvest.* Portland, Ore.: U.S. Department of Agriculture, Forest Service, Pacific Northwest Research Station, 1993.

Nicholas, Jonathan, and C. Bruce Forster. *Portland.* Portland, Ore.: Graphic Arts Center Publishing Company, 1993.

O'Donnell, Terence. *That Balance So Rare: The Story of Oregon.* Portland, Ore.: Oregon Historical Society, 1988.

———. *An Arrow in the Earth: General Joel Palmer and the Indians of Oregon.* Portland, Ore.: Oregon Historical Society, 1991.

Oregon Story: 1850-2000, The. Written by the staff of *The Oregonian.* Portland, Ore.: Graphic Arts Center Publishing Company, 2000.

Pandell, Karen, and Chris Stall. *Animal Tracks of the Pacific Northwest.* Seattle, Wash.: The Mountaineers, 1981.

Peterson, Bryan F. *Photographing Oregon with Professional Results.* Portland, Ore.: Graphic Arts Center Publishing Company, 1984.

Pintarich, Paul. *The Boys Up North: Dick Erath and the Early Oregon Winemakers,* Portland, Ore.: Wyatt Group, 1997.

Plumb, Gregory A. *A Waterfall Lover's Guide to the Pacific Northwest.* Seattle, Wash.: The Mountaineers, 1989.

Ramsey, Jarold, ed. *Coyote Was Going There: Indian Literature of the Oregon Country.* Seattle: University of Washington Press, 1977.

Reynolds, Robert M., with Judy Peterson-Nedry. *Oregon Wine Country.* Portland, Ore.: Graphic Arts Center Publishing Company, 1998.

———, with Joan Campf. *Oregon's National Forests.* Portland, Ore.: Graphic Arts Center Publishing Company, 1990.

Rollins, Philip Ashton, ed. *The Discovery of the Oregon Trail: Robert Stuart's Narratives of His Overland Trip Eastward from Astoria in 1812-13.* Lincoln: University of Nebraska Press, 1995.

Ronda, James P. *Astoria & Empire.* Lincoln: University of Nebraska Press, 1993.

Saling, Ann. The *Great Northwest Nature Factbook: A Guide to the Region's Remarkable Animals, Plants & Natural Features,* revised edition. Portland, Ore.: Westwinds Press, 1999.

Schafer, Rick, with Sandra L. Keith. *Portrait of Oregon.* Portland, Ore.: Graphic Arts Center Publishing Company, 1994.

———, with Jack and Jan McGowan. *Magnificent Places: Oregon Coast.* Portland, Ore: Graphic Arts Center Publishing Company, 1996.

———, with Paul Linnman. Foreword by Peter Jacobsen. *Oregon Golf: The Oregon Coast, Southern Oregon, Portland & Environs, Central Oregon.* Portland, Ore.: Graphic Arts Center Publishing Company, 1999.

Sheehan, Madelynne Diness. *Fishing in Oregon.* Portland, Ore.: Flying Pencil Publications, 1995.

Smith, Dwight, James B. Norman, Pieter T. Dykman, and James Norman. *Historic Highway Bridges of Oregon.* Portland, Ore.: Oregon Historical Society, 1989.

Snively, Gloria. *Exploring the Seashore in British Columbia, Washington and Oregon.* Vancouver and London: Gordon Soules Book Publishers, 1978.

Stienstra, Tom. *Pacific Northwest Camping: The Complete Guide to More than 45,000 Campsites in Washington and Oregon.* San Francisco, Calif.: Foghorn Press, 1996.

Sullivan, William. *Exploring Oregon's Wild Areas: A Guide for Hikers, Backpackers, Climbers, X-C Skiers, & Paddlers,* 2nd edition, revised. Seattle, Wash.: The Mountaineers, 1997.

Taylor, George H., and Chris Hannon. *The Climate of Oregon: From Rain Forest to Desert.* Corvallis: Oregon State University Press, 1999.

Terrill, Steve. *Oregon Wildflowers.* Englewood, Colo.: Westcliffe Publishing, 1995.

Thoele, Mike. *Footprints Across Oregon.* Portland, Ore.: Graphic Arts Center Publishing Company, 1989.

Thomas, Janet. *At Home in Hostel Territory: A Guide to Friendly Lodges from Seward to Santa Cruz.* Seattle, Wash.: Alaska Northwest Books, 1994.

Tisdale, Sallie. *Stepping Westward: The Long Search for Home in the Pacific Northwest.* New York: Henry Holt, 1991.

Walth, Brent. *Fire at Eden's Gate: Tom McCall and the Oregon Story.* Portland: Oregon Historical Society, 1994.

Weis, Norman D. *Ghost Towns of the Northwest.* Caldwell, Idaho: The Caxton Printers, Ltd., 1993.

Willamette Kayak and Canoe Club, *Soggy Sneakers: A Guide to Oregon Rivers.* Seattle, Wash.: The Mountaineers, 1994.

Woog, Adam. *Sexless Oysters and Self-Tipping Hats: 100 Years of Invention in the Pacific Northwest.* Seattle, Wash.: Sasquatch Books, 1991.

Wuerthner, George. *Oregon Mountain Ranges.* Helena, Mont.: American Geographic, 1987.

Appendix: Oregon State Constitution Preamble and Declaration of Rights

PREAMBLE

We the people of the State of Oregon to the end that Justice be established, order maintained, and liberty perpetuated, do ordain this Constitution.

ARTICLE I BILL OF RIGHTS

SECTION 1. NATURAL RIGHTS INHERENT IN PEOPLE. We declare that all men, when they form a social compact are equal in right: that all power is inherent in the people, and all free governments are founded on their authority, and instituted for their peace, safety, and happiness; and they have at all times a right to alter, reform, or abolish the government in such manner as they may think proper.

SECTION 2. FREEDOM OF WORSHIP. All men shall be secure in the Natural right, to worship Almighty God according to the dictates of their own consciences.

SECTION 3. FREEDOM OF RELIGIOUS OPINION. No law shall in any case whatever control the free exercise, and enjoyment of religeous (sic) opinions, or interfere with the rights of conscience.

SECTION 4. NO RELIGIOUS QUALIFICATION FOR OFFICE. No religious test shall be required as a qualification for any office of trust or profit.

SECTION 5. NO MONEY TO BE APPROPRIATED FOR RELIGION. No money shall be drawn from the Treasury for the benefit of any religeous (sic), or theological institution, nor shall any money be appropriated for the payment of any religeous (sic) services in either house of the Legislative Assembly.

SECTION 6. NO RELIGIOUS TEST FOR WITNESSES OR JURORS. No person shall be rendered incompetent as a witness, or juror in consequence of his opinions on matters of religeon (sic); nor be questioned in any Court of Justice touching his religeous (sic) belief to affect the weight of his testimony.

SECTION 7. MANNER OF ADMINISTERING OATH OR AFFIRMATION. The mode of administering an oath, or affirmation shall be such as may be most consistent with, and binding upon the conscience of the person to whom such oath or affirmation may be administered.

SECTION 8. FREEDOM OF SPEECH AND PRESS. No law shall be passed restraining the free expression of opinion, or restricting the right to speak, write, or print freely on any subject whatever; but every person shall be responsible for the abuse of this right.

SECTION 9. UNREASONABLE SEARCHES OR SEIZURES. No law shall violate the right of the people to be secure in their persons, houses, papers, and effects, against unreasonable search, or seizure; and no warrant shall issue but upon probable cause, supported by oath, or affirmation, and particularly describing the place to be searched, and the person or thing to be seized.

SECTION 10. ADMINISTRATION OF JUSTICE. No court shall be secret, but justice shall be administered, openly and without purchase, completely and without delay, and every man shall have remedy by due course of law for injury done him in his person, property, or reputation.

SECTION 11. RIGHTS OF ACCUSED IN CRIMINAL PROSECUTION. In all criminal prosecutions, the accused shall have the right to public trial by an impartial jury in the county in which the offense shall have been committed; to be heard by himself and counsel; to demand the nature and cause of the accusation against him, and to have a copy thereof; to meet the witnesses face to face, and to have compulsory process for obtaining witnesses in his favor; provided, however, that any accused person, in other than capital cases, and with the consent of the trial judge, may elect to waive trial by jury and consent to be tried by the judge of the court alone, such election to be in writing; provided, however, that in the circuit court ten members of the jury may render a verdict of guilty or not guilty, save and except a verdict of guilty of first degree murder, which shall be found only by a unanimous verdict, and not otherwise; provided further, that the existing laws and constitutional provisions relative to criminal prosecutions shall be continued and remain in effect as to all prosecutions for crimes committed before the taking effect of this amendment. [Constitution of 1859; Amendment proposed by S.J.R. 4, 1931, and adopted by the people Nov. 8, 1932; Amendment proposed by S.J.R. 4, 1933 (2d s.s.), and adopted by the people May 18, 1934]

Note: The leadline to SECTION 11 was a part of the measure submitted to the people by S.J.R. 4, 1933 (2d s.s.).

SECTION 12. DOUBLE JEOPARDY; COMPULSORY SELF-INCRIMINATION. No person shall be put in jeopardy twice for the same offence (sic), nor be compelled in any criminal prosecution to testify against himself.

SECTION 13. TREATMENT OF ARRESTED OR CONFINED PERSONS. No person arrested, or confined in jail, shall be treated with unnecessary rigor.

SECTION 14. BAILABLE OFFENSES. Offences (sic), except murder, and treason, shall be bailable by sufficient sureties. Murder or treason, shall not be bailable, when the proof is evident, or the presumption strong.

SECTION 15. FOUNDATION PRINCIPLES OF CRIMINAL LAW. Laws for the punishment of crime shall be founded on these principles: protection of society, personal responsibility, accountability for one's actions and reformation. [Constitution of 1859; Amendment proposed by S.J.R. 32, 1995, and adopted by the people Nov. 5, 1996]

SECTION 16. EXCESSIVE BAIL AND FINES; CRUEL AND UNUSUAL PUNISHMENTS; POWER OF JURY IN CRIMINAL CASE. Excessive bail shall not be required, nor excessive fines imposed. Cruel and unusual punishments shall not be inflicted, but all penalties shall be proportioned to the offense. In all criminal cases whatever, the jury shall have the right to determine the law, and the facts under the direction of the Court as to the law, and the right of new trial, as in civil cases.

SECTION 17. JURY TRIAL IN CIVIL CASES. In all civil cases the right of Trial by Jury shall remain inviolate.

SECTION 18. PRIVATE PROPERTY OR SERVICES TAKEN FOR PUBLIC USE. Private property shall not be taken for public use, nor the particular services of any man be demanded, without just compensation; nor except in the case of the state, without such compensation first assessed and tendered; provided, that the use of all roads, ways and waterways necessary to promote the transportation of the raw products of mine or farm or forest or water for beneficial use or drainage is necessary to the development and welfare of the state and is declared a public use. [Constitution of 1859; Amendment proposed by S.J.R. 17, 1919, and adopted by the people May 21, 1920; Amendment proposed by S.J.R. 8, 1923, and adopted by the people Nov. 4, 1924]

SECTION 19. IMPRISONMENT FOR DEBT. There shall be no imprisonment for debt, except in case of fraud or absconding debtors.

SECTION 20. EQUALITY OF PRIVILEGES AND IMMUNITIES OF CITIZENS. No law shall be passed granting to any citizen or class of citizens privileges, or immunities, which, upon the same terms, shall not equally belong to all citizens.

SECTION 21. EX-POST FACTO LAWS; LAWS IMPAIRING CONTRACTS; LAWS DEPENDING ON AUTHORIZATION IN ORDER TO TAKE EFFECT; LAWS SUBMITTED TO ELECTORS. No ex-post facto law, or law impairing the obligation of contracts shall ever be passed, nor shall any law be passed, the taking effect of which shall be made to depend upon any authority, except as provided in this Constitution; provided, that laws locating the Capital of the State, locating County Seats, and submitting town, and corporate acts, and other local, and Special laws may take effect, or not, upon a vote of the electors interested.

SECTION 22. SUSPENSION OF OPERATION OF LAWS. The operation of the laws shall never be suspended, except by the Authority of the Legislative Assembly.

SECTION 23. HABEAS CORPUS. The privilege of the writ of habeas corpus shall not be suspended unless in case of rebellion, or invasion the public safety require it.

SECTION 24. TREASON. Treason against the State shall consist only in levying war against it, or adhering to its enemies, giving them aid or comfort. No person shall be convicted of treason unless on the testimony of two witnesses to the same overt act, or confession in open Court.

SECTION 25. CORRUPTION OF BLOOD OR FORFEITURE OF ESTATE. No conviction shall work corruption of blood, or forfeiture of estate.

SECTION 26. ASSEMBLAGES OF PEOPLE; INSTRUCTION OF REPRESENTATIVES; APPLICATION TO LEGISLATURE. No law shall be passed restraining any of the inhabitants of the State from assembling together in a peaceable manner to consult for their common good; nor from instructing their Representatives; nor from applying to the Legislature for redress of greviances (sic).

SECTION 27. RIGHT TO BEAR ARMS; MILITARY SUBORDINATE TO CIVIL POWER. The people shall have the right to bear arms for the defence (sic) of themselves, and the State, but the Military shall be kept in strict subordination to the civil power[.]

SECTION 28. QUARTERING SOLDIERS. No soldier shall, in time of peace, be quartered in any house, without the consent of the owner, nor in time of war, except in the manner prescribed by law.

SECTION 29. TITLES OF NOBILITY; HEREDITARY DISTINCTIONS. No law shall be passed granting any title of Nobility, or conferring hereditary distinctions.

SECTION 30. EMIGRATION. No law shall be passed prohibiting emigration from the State.

SECTION 31. RIGHTS OF ALIENS; IMMIGRATION TO STATE. [Constitution of 1859; repeal proposed by H.J.R. 16, 1969, and adopted by the people May 26, 1970]

SECTION 32. TAXES AND DUTIES; UNIFORMITY OF TAXATION. No tax or duty shall be imposed without the consent of the people or their representatives in the Legislative Assembly; and all taxation shall be uniform on the same class of subjects within the territorial limits of the authority levying the tax. [Constitution of 1859; Amendment proposed by H.J.R. 16, 1917, and adopted by the people June 4, 1917]

SECTION 33. ENUMERATION OF RIGHTS NOT EXCLUSIVE. This enumeration of rights, and privileges shall not be construed to impair or deny others retained by the people.

SECTION 34. SLAVERY OR INVOLUNTARY SERVITUDE. There shall be neither slavery, nor involuntary servitude in the State, otherwise than as a punishment for crime, whereof the party shall have been duly convicted. [Added to Bill of Rights as unnumbered Section by vote of the people at time of adoption of the Oregon Constitution in accordance with Section 4 of Article XVIII thereof]

SECTION 35. FREE NEGROES AND MULATTOES. [Added to Bill of Rights as unnumbered Section by vote of the people at time of adoption of the Oregon Constitution in accordance with Section of Article XVIII thereof; Repeal proposed by H.J.R. 8, 1925, and adopted by the people Nov. 2, 1926]

SECTION 36. LIQUOR PROHIBITION. [Created through initiative petition filed July 1, 1914, and adopted by the people Nov. 3, 1914; Repeal proposed by initiative petition filed March 20, 1933, and adopted by the people July 21, 1933]

SECTION 36. CAPITAL PUNISHMENT ABOLISHED. [Created through initiative petition filed July 2, 1914, and adopted by the people Nov. 3, 1914; Repeal proposed by S.J.R. 8, 1920 (s.s.), and adopted by the people May 21, 1920, as Const. Art. I, §.38]

Note: At the general election in 1914 two sections, each designated as Section 36, were created and added to the Constitution by separate initiative petitions. One of these sections was the prohibition section and the other abolished capital punishment.

SECTION 36a. PROHIBITION OF IMPORTATION OF LIQUORS. [Created through initiative petition filed July 6, 1916, and adopted by the people Nov. 7, 1916; Repeal proposed by initiative petition filed March 20, 1933, and adopted by the people July 21, 1933]

SECTION 37. PENALTY FOR MURDER IN FIRST DEGREE. [Created through S.J.R. 8, 1920, and adopted by the people May 21, 1920; Repeal proposed by S.J.R. 3, 1963, and adopted by the people Nov. 3, 1964]

SECTION 38. LAWS ABROGATED BY AMENDMENT ABOLISHING DEATH PENALTY REVIVED. [Created through S.J.R. 8, 1920, and adopted by the people May 21, 1920; Repeal proposed by S.J.R. 3, 1963, and adopted by the people Nov. 3, 1964]

SECTION 39. SALE OF LIQUOR BY INDIVIDUAL GLASS. The State shall have power to license private clubs, fraternal organizations, veterans' organizations, railroad corporations operating interstate trains and commercial establishments where food is cooked and served, for the purpose of selling alcoholic liquor by the individual glass at retail, for consumption on the premises, including mixed drinks and cocktails, compounded or mixed on the premises only. The Legislative Assembly shall provide in such detail as it shall deem advisable for carrying out and administering the provisions of this amendment and shall provide adequate safeguards to carry out the original intent and purpose of the Oregon Liquor Control Act, including the promotion of temperance in the use and consumption of alcoholic beverages, encourage the use and consumption of lighter beverages and aid in the establishment of Oregon industry. This power is subject to the following:

(1) The provisions of this amendment shall take effect and be in operation sixty (60) days after the approval and adoption by the people of Oregon; provided, however, the right of a local option election exists in the counties and in any incorporated city or town containing a population of at least five hundred (500). The Legislative Assembly shall prescribe a means and a procedure by which the voters of any county or incorporated city or town as limited above in any county, may through a local option election determine whether to prohibit or permit such power, and such procedure shall specifically include that whenever fifteen per cent (15%) of the registered voters of any county in the state or of any incorporated city or town as limited above, in any county in the state, shall file a petition requesting an election in this matter, the question shall be voted upon at the next regular November biennial election, provided said petition is filed not less than sixty (60) days before the day of election.

(2) Legislation relating to this matter shall operate uniformly throughout the state and all individuals shall be treated equally; and all provisions shall be liberally construed for the accomplishment of these purposes. [Created through initiative petition filed July 2, 1952, and adopted by the people Nov. 4, 1952]

SECTION 40. PENALTY FOR AGGRAVATED MURDER. Notwithstanding Sections15 and 16 of this Article, the penalty for aggravated murder as defined by law shall be death upon unanimous affirmative jury findings as provided by law and otherwise shall be life imprisonment with minimum sentence as provided by law. [Created through initiative petition filed July 6, 1983, and adopted by the people Nov. 6, 1984]

SECTION 41. WORK AND TRAINING FOR CORRECTIONS INSTITUTION INMATES; WORK PROGRAMS; WORK PROGRAMS; LIMITATIONS; DUTIES OF CORRECTIONS DIRECTOR.

(1) Whereas the people of the state of Oregon find and declare that inmates who are confined in corrections institutions should work as hard as the taxpayers who provide for their upkeep; and whereas the people also find and declare that inmates confined within corrections institutions must be fully engaged in productive activity if they are to successfully re-enter society with practical skills and a viable work ethic; now, therefore, the people declare:

(2) All inmates of state corrections institutions shall be actively engaged full-time in work or on-the-job training. The work or on-the-job training programs shall be established and overseen by the corrections director, who shall ensure that such programs are cost-effective and are designed to develop inmate motivation, work capabilities and cooperation. Such programs may include boot camp prison programs. Education may be provided to inmates as part of work or on-the-job training so long as each inmate is engaged at least half-time in hands-on training or work activity.

(3) Each inmate shall begin full-time work or on-the-job training immediately upon admission to a corrections institution, allowing for a short time for administrative intake and processing. The specific quantity of hours per day to be spent in work or on-the-job training shall be determined by the corrections director, but the overall time spent in work or training shall be full-time. However, no inmate has a legally enforceable right to a job or to otherwise participate in work, on-the-job training or educational programs or to compensation for work or labor performed while an inmate of any state, county or city corrections facility or institution. The corrections director may reduce or exempt participation in work or training programs by those inmates deemed by corrections officials as physically or mentally disabled, or as too dangerous to society to engage in such programs.

(4) There shall be sufficient work and training programs to ensure that every eligible inmate is productively involved in one or more programs. Where an inmate is drug and alcohol addicted so as to prevent the inmate from effectively participating in work or training programs, corrections officials shall provide appropriate drug or alcohol treatment.

(5) The intent of the people is that taxpayer-supported institutions and programs shall be free to benefit from inmate work. Prison work programs shall be designed and carried out so as to achieve savings in government operations, so as to achieve a net profit in private sector activities or so as to benefit the community.

(6) The provisions of this Section are mandatory for all state corrections institutions. The provisions of this Section are permissive for county or city corrections facilities. No law, ordinance or charter shall prevent or restrict a county or city governing body from implementing all or part of the provisions of this Section. Compensation, if any, shall be determined and established by the governing body of the county or city which chooses to engage in prison work programs, and the governing body may choose to adopt any power or exemption allowed in this Section.

(7) The corrections director shall contact public and private enterprises in this state and seek proposals to use inmate work. The corrections director may: (a) install and equip plants in any state corrections institution, or any other location, for the employment or training of any of the inmates therein; or (b) purchase, acquire, install, maintain and operate materials, machinery and appliances necessary to the conduct and operation of

such plants. The corrections director shall use every effort to enter into contracts or agreements with private business concerns or government agencies to accomplish the production or marketing of products or services produced or performed by inmates. The corrections director may carry out the director's powers and duties under this Section by delegation to others.

(8) Compensation, if any, for inmates who engage in prison work programs shall be determined and established by the corrections director. Such compensation shall not be subject to existing public or private sector minimum or prevailing wage laws, except where required to comply with federal law. Inmate compensation from enterprises entering into agreements with the state shall be exempt from unemployment compensation taxes to the extent allowed under federal law. Inmate injury or disease attributable to any inmate work shall be covered by a corrections system inmate injury fund rather than the workers compensation law. Except as otherwise required by federal law to permit transportation in interstate commerce of goods, wares or merchandise manufactured, produced or mined, wholly or in part by inmates or except as otherwise required by state law, any compensation earned through prison work programs shall only be used for the following purposes: (a) reimbursement for all or a portion of the costs of the inmate's rehabilitation, housing, health care, and living costs; (b) restitution or compensation to the victims of the particular inmate's crime; (c) restitution or compensation to the victims of crime generally through a fund designed for that purpose; (d) financial support for immediate family of the inmate outside the corrections institution; and (e) payment of fines, court costs, and applicable taxes.

(9) All income generated from prison work programs shall be kept separate from general fund accounts and shall only be used for implementing, maintaining and developing prison work programs. Prison industry work programs shall be exempt from statutory competitive bid and purchase requirements. Expenditures for prison work programs shall be exempt from the legislative appropriations process to the extent the programs rely on income sources other than state taxes and fees. Where state taxes or fees are the source of capital or operating expenditures, the appropriations shall be made by the legislative assembly. The state programs shall be run in a businesslike fashion and shall be subject to regulation by the corrections director. Expenditures from income generated by state prison work programs must be approved by the corrections director. Agreements with private enterprise as to state prison work programs must be approved by the corrections director. The corrections director shall make all state records available for public scrutiny and the records shall be subject to audit by the Secretary of State.

(10) Prison work products or services shall be available to any public agency and to any private enterprise of any state, any nation or any American Indian or Alaskan Native tribe without restriction imposed by any state or local law, ordinance or regulation as to competition with other public or private sector enterprises. The products and services of corrections work programs shall be provided on such terms as are set by the corrections director. To the extent determined possible by the corrections director, the corrections director shall avoid establishing or expanding for-profit prison work programs that produce goods or services offered for sale in the private sector if the establishment or expansion would displace or significantly reduce preexisting private enterprise. To the extent determined possible by the corrections director, the corrections director shall avoid establishing or expanding prison work programs if the establishment or expansion would displace or significantly reduce government or nonprofit programs that employ persons with developmental disabilities. However, the decision to establish, maintain, expand, reduce or terminate any prison work program remains in the sole discretion of the corrections director.

(11) Inmate work shall be used as much as possible to help operate the corrections institutions themselves, to support other government operations and to support community charitable organizations. This work includes, but is not limited to, institutional food production; maintenance and repair of buildings, grounds, and equipment; office support services, including printing; prison clothing production and maintenance; prison medical services; training other inmates; agricultural and forestry work, especially in parks and public forest lands; and environmental clean-up projects. Every state agency shall cooperate with the corrections director in establishing inmate work programs.

(12) As used throughout this Section, unless the context requires otherwise: "full-time" means the equivalent of at least forty hours per seven day week, specifically including time spent by inmates as required by the Department of Corrections, while the inmate is participating in work or on-the-job training, to provide for the safety and security of the public, correctional staff and inmates; "corrections director" means the person in charge of the state corrections system.

(13) This Section is self-implementing and supersedes all existing inconsistent statutes. This Section shall become effective April 1, 1995. If any part of this Section or its application to any person or circumstance is held to be invalid for any reason, then the remaining parts or applications to any persons or circumstances shall not be affected but shall remain in full force and effect. [Created through initiative petition filed Jan. 12, 1994, and adopted by the people Nov. 8, 1994; Amendment proposed by H.J.R. 2, 1997, and adopted by the people May 20, 1997; Amendment proposed by H.J.R. 82, 1999, and adopted by the people Nov. 2, 1999]

Note: Added to Article I as unnumbered section by initiative petition (Measure No. 17, 1994) adopted by the people Nov. 8, 1994.

Note: An initiative petition (Measure No. 40, 1996) proposed adding an unnumbered section relating to crime victims' rights to Article I. That Section, appearing as Section 42 of Article I in previous editions of this Constitution, was declared void for not being enacted in compliance with Section I, Article XVII of this Constitution. See Armatta v. Kitzhaber, 327 Or. 250, 959 P.2d 49 (1998).

SECTION 42. RIGHTS OF VICTIM IN CRIMINAL PROSECUTIONS AND JUVENILE COURT DELIQUENCY PROCEEDINGS.

(1) To preserve and protect the right of crime victims to justice, to ensure crime victims a meaningful role in the criminal and juvenile justice systems, to accord crime victims due dignity and respect and to ensure that criminal and juvenile court delinquency proceedings are conducted to seek the truth as to the defendant's innocence or guilt, and also to ensure that a fair balance is struck between the rights of crime victims and the rights of criminal defendants in the course and conduct of criminal and juvenile court delinquency proceedings, the following rights are hereby granted to victims in all prosecutions for crimes and in juvenile court delinquency proceedings: (a) The right to be present at and, upon specific request, to be informed in advance of any critical stage of the proceedings held in open court when the defendant will be present, and to be heard at the pretrial release hearing and the sentencing or juvenile court delinquency disposition; (b) The right, upon request, to obtain information about the conviction, sentence, imprisonment, criminal history and future release from physical custody of the criminal defendant or convicted criminal and equivalent information regarding the alleged youth offender or youth offender; (c) The right to refuse an interview, deposition or other discovery request by the criminal defendant or other person acting on behalf of the criminal defendant provided, however, that nothing in this paragraph shall restrict any other constitutional right of the defendant to discovery against the state; (d) The right to receive prompt restitution from the convicted criminal who caused the victim's loss or injury; (e) The right to have a copy of a transcript of any court proceeding

in open court, if one is otherwise prepared; (f) The right to be consulted, upon request, regarding plea negotiations involving any violent felony; and (g) The right to be informed of these rights as soon as practicable.

(2) This Section applies to all criminal and juvenile court delinquency proceedings pending or commenced on or after the effective date of this Section. Nothing in this Section reduces a criminal defendant's rights under the Constitution of the United States. Except as otherwise specifically provided, this Section supersedes any conflicting Section of this Constitution. Nothing in this Section is intended to create any cause of action for compensation or damages nor may this Section be used to invalidate an accusatory instrument, ruling of a court, conviction or adjudication or otherwise suspend or terminate any criminal or juvenile delinquency proceedings at any point after the case is commenced or on appeal.

(3) As used in this Section: (a) "Convicted criminal" includes a youth offender in juvenile court delinquency proceedings. (b) "Criminal defendant" includes an alleged youth offender in juvenile court delinquency proceedings. (c) "Victim" means any person determined by the prosecuting attorney to have suffered direct financial, psychological or physical harm as a result of a crime and, in the case of a victim who is a minor, the legal guardian of the minor. In the event that no person has been determined to be a victim of the crime, the people of Oregon, represented by the prosecuting attorney, are considered to be the victims. In no event is it intended that the criminal defendant be considered the victim. (d) "Violent felony" means a felony in which there was actual or threatened serious physical injury to a victim or a felony sexual offense. [Created through H.J.R. 87, 1999, and adopted by the people Nov. 2, 1999]

Note: The effective date of House Joint Resolutions 87, 89, 90 and 94, compiled as Sections 42, 43, 44 and 45, Article I, is Dec. 2, 1999.

Note: Sections 42, 43, 44 and 45, were added to Article I as unnumbered sections by the amendments proposed by House Joint Resolutions 87, 89, 90 and 94, 1999, and adopted by the people Nov. 2, 1999.

SECTION 43. RIGHTS OF VICTIM AND PUBLIC TO PROTECTION FROM ACCUSED PERSON DURING CRIMINAL PROCEEDINGS; DENIAL OF PRETRIAL RELEASE.

(1) To ensure that a fair balance is struck between the rights of crime victims and the rights of criminal defendants in the course and conduct of criminal proceedings, the following rights are hereby granted to victims in all prosecutions for crimes: (a) The right to be reasonably protected from the criminal defendant or the convicted criminal throughout the criminal justice process and from the alleged youth offender or youth offender throughout the juvenile delinquency proceedings. (b) The right to have decisions by the court regarding the pretrial release of a criminal defendant based upon the principle of reasonable protection of the victim and the public, as well as the likelihood that the criminal defendant will appear for trial. Murder, aggravated murder and treason shall not be bailable when the proof is evident or the presumption strong that the person is guilty. Other violent felonies shall not be bailable when a court has determined there is probable cause to believe the criminal defendant committed the crime, and the court finds, by clear and convincing evidence, that there is danger of physical injury or sexual victimization to the victim or members of the public by the criminal defendant while on release.

(2) This Section applies to proceedings pending or commenced on or after the effective date of this Section. Nothing in this Section abridges any right of the criminal defendant guaranteed by the Constitution of the United States, including the rights to be represented by counsel, have counsel appointed if indigent, testify, present witnesses, cross-examine witnesses or present information at the release hearing. Nothing in this Section creates any cause of action for compensation or damages nor may

this Section be used to invalidate an accusatory instrument, ruling of a court, conviction or adjudication or otherwise suspend or terminate any criminal or juvenile delinquency proceeding at any point after the case is commenced or on appeal. Except as otherwise specifically provided, this Section supersedes any conflicting Section of this Constitution.

(3) As used in this Section: (a) "Victim" means any person determined by the prosecuting attorney to have suffered direct financial, psychological or physical harm as a result of a crime and, in the case of a victim who is a minor, the legal guardian of the minor. In the event no person has been determined to be a victim of the crime, the people of Oregon, represented by the prosecuting attorney, are considered to be the victims. In no event is it intended that the criminal defendant be considered the victim. (b) "Violent felony" means a felony in which there was actual or threatened serious physical injury to a victim or a felony sexual offense.

(4) The prosecuting attorney is the party authorized to assert the rights of the victim and the public established by this Section. [Created through H.J.R. 90, 1999, and adopted by the people Nov. 2, 1999]

Note: See notes under Section 42 of this Article.

SECTION 44. TERM OF IMPRISONMENT IMPOSED BY COURT TO BE FULLY SERVED; EXCEPTIONS.

(1)(a) A term of imprisonment imposed by a judge in open court may not be set aside or otherwise not carried out, except as authorized by the sentencing court or through the subsequent exercise of: (A) The power of the Governor to grant reprieves, commutations and pardons; or (B) Judicial authority to grant appellate or post-conviction relief. (b) No law shall limit a court's authority to sentence a criminal defendant consecutively for crimes against different victims.

(2) This Section applies to all offenses committed on or after the effective date of this Section. Nothing in this Section reduces a criminal defendant's rights under the Constitution of the United States. Except as otherwise specifically provided, this Section supersedes any conflicting Section of this Constitution. Nothing in this Section creates any cause of action for compensation or damages nor may this Section be used to invalidate an accusatory instrument, ruling of a court, conviction or adjudication or otherwise suspend or terminate any criminal or juvenile delinquency proceedings at any point after the case is commenced or on appeal.

(3) As used in this Section, "victim" means any person determined by the prosecuting attorney to have suffered direct financial, psychological or physical harm as a result of a crime and, in the case of a victim who is a minor, the legal guardian of the minor. In the event no person has been determined to be a victim of the crime, the people of Oregon, represented by the prosecuting attorney, are considered to be the victims. In no event is it intended that the criminal defendant be considered the victim. [Created through H.J.R. 94, 1999, and adopted by the people Nov. 2, 1999]

Note: See notes under Section 42 of this Article.

SECTION 45. PERSON CONVICTED OF CERTAIN CRIMES NOT ELIGIBLE TO SERVE AS JUROR ON GRAND JURY OR TRIAL JURY IN CRIMINAL CASE.

(1) In all grand juries and in all prosecutions for crimes tried to a jury, the jury shall be composed of persons who have not been convicted: (a) Of a felony or served a felony sentence within the 15 years immediately preceding the date the persons are required to report for jury duty; or (b) Of a misdemeanor involving violence or dishonesty or served a sentence for a misdemeanor involving violence or dishonesty within the five years immediately preceding the date the persons are required to report for jury duty.

(2) This Section applies to all criminal proceedings pending or commenced on or after the effective date of this Section, except a criminal proceeding in which a jury has been impaneled and sworn on the effective date of this Section. Nothing in this Section reduces a criminal defendant's rights under the Constitution of the United States. Except as otherwise specifically provided, this Section supersedes any conflicting Section of this Constitution. Nothing in this Section is intended to create any cause of action for compensation or damages nor may this Section be used to disqualify a jury, invalidate an accusatory instrument, ruling of a court, conviction or adjudication or otherwise suspend or terminate any criminal proceeding at any point after a jury is impaneled and sworn or on appeal. [Created through H.J.R. 89, 1999, and adopted by the people Nov. 2, 1999]

Note: See notes under Section 42 of this Article.

Index

accidents, hunting, 86
agates, 161, 162
agriculture, 10-14; crops and products, 11-12; regions, 10
airports/aviation, 14-15, 184-85; busiest, 7
Alvord Desert, 7, 45
American Indians, 15-17; federally recognized, 15-16; Nez Perce National Historical Park, 125; petroglyphs and pictographs, 142-43; tribal courts, 90
amphibians, 17-18; endangered and threatened, 47-48
animal(s): amphibians and reptiles, 17-18; endangered and threatened, 47-48; hunting, 85-86; mammals, 105-6; pronghorns, 106; seals and sea lions, 169; state, 7, 180; wild horses and burros, 203-4. *See also* wildlife refuges; zoos
aquariums, 216. *See also* fish
archives, 18
area: land, 7; largest city, 7; largest and smallest counties, 35; water, 7
area codes, 19
Army Corps of Engineers, 108
art museums, 113-14
arts, 19-20; performing, 139-42. *See also* festivals and events
Astoria, 20-21, 150
automobile, first in Oregon, 193
avalanches, 21

Bach Festival, 140
Basin and Range Province, 21
basketball, 173-74, 175
bays, 29. *See also* estuaries
beaches, 29-30. *See also* dunes
beer: microbreweries, 107-8
Bend, 21-22
biking, 135-36
bird(s), 22-24; endangered and threatened, 47-48; great blue heron, 201; hunting, 86; meadowlark, 23; state, 7, 180
Bonneville Power Administration, 24
bridges, covered, 40-41
Britt Festival, 140
Buckaroos, 175
budget, state, 71
burros, wild, 203-4

calendar of annual events, 54-56. *See also* festivals and events
camping, 136-37
canyon(s), deepest, 7; Hells Canyon, 73, 124, 168
capes and headlands, 30
capital, state, 7; establishment of, 165. *See also* Salem
Cascade Mountains, 111; scenic drives, 166-67
caves, 24-25; Oregon Caves National Monument, 125
Celilo Falls, 16, 31
charities/charitable funds, 25-26
children's museums, 114
cities and towns, 26-29; largest in area, 7; largest and smallest in population, 27; mileage between, 109; populations of, 27-28; record temperatures, 200; zip codes, 211-16. *See also* Astoria; Eugene; Klamath Falls; Medford; Portland; Salem; The Dalles; Vanport
climate, 199; record temperatures, 200
climbing, 137-38
coast, 29-30; length of coastline, 7; safety tips, 30; scenic drives, 168; state parks, 179; windsurfing, 207. *See also* estuaries; lighthouses
Coast Guard, 110
colleges, 188-93; community, 188-90
Columbia Plateau, 30
Columbia River and Columbia River Gorge, 31-32; scenic drives, 167; state parks, 179; windsurfing, 206-7; wineries, 208
commercial fishing, 57
commodities commissions, 13
community colleges, 188-90
congressional delegation, 32-34; U.S. Representatives, 33-34; U.S. Senate, 32. *See also* elected officials
congressional districts, 33
constitution. *See* laws
consular corps, 34
Coos Bay, 49, 150-51
counties, 34-40; largest and smallest by area, 35; largest and smallest by population, 35; map, 36; profiles of, 35-40
county fairs, 14
county seats, 36
courts: circuit court districts, 89; federal,

89-90; local, 88; state, 88-89; tribal, 90
covered bridges, 40-41
Crater Lake, 92, 123; depth, 7
crops and products, 11-12; animal products, 12; berries, 11; field crop production, 11; fruits and nuts, 12; horticulture, 12; seed crops, 11; vegetables, 12

"D" River, 7
Dalles, The. *See* The Dalles
dams, 41-44
dance, state, 180
deepest: canyon, 7; lake, 7
desert, 45
desert and rangeland plants, 147
distances: between cities in Oregon, 109; between Portland and U.S. and international cities, 152
districts: circuit court, 89; congressional, 33; legislative, 94; special service, 173-74
Donation Land Law, 134
driver's licenses, 193
dunes, 45, 62; Oregon Dunes National Recreation Area, 125-26; tallest, 7. *See also* beaches

earthquakes, 45-46
economy. *See* agriculture; exports; trade; tourism
elected officials, 46-47. *See also* congressional delegation; elections; government; legislature
elections, 196-98. *See also* congressional delegation; elected officials
endangered species: animals, 47-48; plants, 48-49; salmon, 166
estuaries, 49-50. *See also* bays; coast
Eugene, 50; performing arts, 141
events. *See* festivals and events
explorers, 50-52. *See also* history; Lewis and Clark
exports, 86-87. *See also* trade

fairs, 52-57; county, 14. *See also* festivals and events
Favell Museum of Western Art and Artifacts, 7
festivals and events, 52-57; performing arts, 139-41; rodeos, 163-64; wine, 210-11. Festivals and events are also included in text for individual cities and topics
fire lookouts, 56-57
fire(s), 64; Tillamook Burn, 64; worst, 7
fish, 57-58; aquariums, 216; endangered and threatened, 47-48; largest salmon, 166; salmon, 165-66; 7, 180; sturgeon, 57
fish hatcheries, 58-61
fishing, 57-58
flag, state, 180
flower(s): endangered and threatened, 48-49; state, 7, 180; wildflowers, 147-48
forest products industry, 62-65
forests, 61-62; national, 117-22. *See also* wilderness
fossils, 65-66; John Day Fossil Beds National Monument, 124

game, hunting, 85-86
gem(s), 161-63; state, 7, 180
geography, 143-46
gold, 66-67
golf, 67-68
government: regional, 159; state, 68-71. *See also* congressional delegation; elected officials; judicial system; legislature
governor(s), 71-72; current, 7
grassland, national, 122; map, 120-21
great blue heron, 201

hang gliding, 138
Harney County, area, 7
hatcheries, fish: national, 61; state, 58-61
hazelnuts, 7, 13. *See also* crops and products
Hells Canyon, 7, 73, 124; scenic drives, 168
high technology, 73-74
highest: mountains, 112; point, 7
highways, 160-61, 185. *See also* scenic drives
hiking, 136-37
historical societies, 18
history, 74-82; American Indians, 15-17; Donation Land Law, 134; establishment of state capital, 165; explorers, 50-52; gold, 66-67; Lewis and Clark, 97-98; museums, 114-15; Oregon Trail, 133-35. *See also* archives; historical societies; museums; National Register of Historic Places; news highlights from 1998-99
hockey, 174, 175
Hood River, 82
horses, wild, 203-4
hot springs, 82-85
Hull-Oakes Lumber Company, 64
hunting, 85-86

income, per capita, 7
Indians. *See* American Indians
initiatives and referendums, 197-98
insect(s): endangered and threatened, 47-48; state, 7, 181
international trade, 86-87

judicial system, 88-90; cases filed annually, 88; federal courts, 89-90; local courts, 88; state courts, 88-89; tribal courts, 90

Kalmiopsis Wilderness, 205
kayaking, whitewater, 201-3
Klamath Basin, 130
Klamath Falls, 90-91
Klamath Lake, 7

lakes, 91-93; Crater Lake, 92, 123; deepest, 7, 92; highest, 92; largest, 7, 91-92
land area, 7
land claims, 134
landmarks, natural, 122-23. *See also* National Register of Historic Places
largest: cities, 27; lake, 7, 91-92; salmon, 166
lava fields, major, 196
laws, 93; Donation Land Law, 134; speed limits, 173
legislative districts, 94
legislature, 93-97. *See also* elected officials; government
length: of coastline, 7; of OC&E Woods Line State Park, 7; of Willamette River, 7
Lewis and Clark, 51-52, 97-98; national sites commemorating, 124. *See also* explorers
libraries, 98-102; academic, 100; archives, 18; Oregon Documents Depository Program, 99; public, 100; special-interest, 100-2; state, 98-99
licenses, 183; driver's, 193; fishing, 57; hunting, 86
lighthouses, 102-3
lost treasure, 104-5
lowest point, 7
lumber, 64. *See also* forest products industry; timber; trees

mammals, 105-6. *See also* animals
maps: area codes, 19; circuit court districts, 89; congressional districts, 33; counties and county seats, 36; geographic features, 144-45; Indian reservations, 17; national forests, parks, wilderness areas, and wildlife refuges, 120-21; Oregon, 8-9; state legislative districts, 94; state parks, 176-77; transportation, 186-87
marine pilots, 106
McCall, Tom
meadowlark, 23
Medford, 106-7
microbreweries, 107-8
mileage chart, 109. *See also* distances
military, 108-10; Army Corps of Engineers, 108; Coast Guard, 110; museums and parks, 110; Umatilla Chemical Depot, 108-9
minerals: gold, 66-67; rocks and gems, 161-63. *See also* mines
mines, lost, 104
minimum wage, 110
miscellaneous facts, 7
motto, state, 7
Mount Bachelor, 172
Mount Hood, 112-13
Mount Mazama, 194
mountains, 111-12; Cascade Mountains, 166-67; highest, 112; Mount Bachelor, 172; Mount Hood, 112-13; Mount Mazama, 194; mountain passes, 161; ski areas, 171-72
Multnomah County, population, 7
Multnomah Falls, 198; height, 7
museums, 113-16; art, 113-14; children's, 114; history, 114-15; military, 110; natural history and science, 115-16. *Museums are also included in text for individual cities and topics*
mushrooms, 116-17
music festivals, 53, 56, 140

national archives, 18
national forests, 117-22; map, 120-21. *See also* forests; wilderness
national grassland, 122; map, 120-21
national monuments, 123-26; map, 120-21
national natural landmarks, 122-23
national parks, 123-26; map, 120-21. *See also* national forests; wilderness
national recreation areas, 123-26
National Register of Historic Places, 126-28
national wildlife refuges, 128-30
Native Americans. *See* American Indians
natural history museums, 115-16
Newberry Crater, 130-31. *See also* volcanoes
news highlights from 1998-99, 217-21

newspapers, 131-33; largest, 7
nickname, state, 7
nut, state, 7, 181

obsidian, 131. *See also* rocks and gemstones
OC&E Woods Line State Park, 7, 179-80
Oregon: map, 8-9; miscellaneous facts and records, 7. *See also* state
Oregon Documents Depository Program, 99-100
Oregon Shakespeare Festival, 140
Oregon Trail, 133-35; wagon prints, 134
organizations. Organizations are included in sections on individual topics

PAC-10, 138-39
park(s): longest linear, 7; military, 110; national, 123-26; state, 175-80. *See also* national forests; wilderness
Pendleton, 139
performing arts, 139-42
periodicals, 131-33
petroglyphs and pictographs, 142-43
pilots, marine, 106
plants, 146-48; desert and rangeland, 147; endangered and threatened, 48-49; poisonous, 147; trees and shrubs, 147. *See also* flowers; mushrooms
poisonous plants, 147. *See also* mushrooms
population, 148; density, 7; of largest and smallest cities, 27-28; of largest and smallest counties, 35; of individual cities and towns, 27-28; prison, 153; racial makeup, 148; vital statistics, 193-94
Portland, 148-50, 151; area, 7; distances to U.S. and international cities, 152; performing arts, 141-42; population, 7; sports teams, 173-75
Portland Buckaroos, 175
Portland Pythons, 174-75
Portland Trail Blazers, 173-74, 175
Portland Winterhawks, 174
ports, 150-52, 185; activity, 151
power: Bonneville Power Administration, 24; dams, 41-44
prisons, 152-54; inmate demographics, 153
pronghorns, 106
public transit, 185
Pulitzer Prize winners, 131
Pythons, 174-75

radio stations, 154-56
rafting, whitewater, 201-3
railroads, 157-59, 185
rainfall: highest daily per town, 200; least, 7; Steens Mountain, 21. *See also* weather
records:miscellaneous, 7; rainfall, 7, 200; temperatures, 7, 200
recreation, 135-38; biking, 135-36; camping and hiking, 136-37; climbing, 137-38; hang gliding, 138; windsurfing, 206-7
recreation areas, state, 175-80
referendums, 197-98
regional governments, 159
regulations: fishing, 58; hunting, 86
representatives: state, 96-97; U.S., 33-34
reptiles, 17-18; endangered and threatened, 47-48
reservations, 16
reservoirs, 91-93
rivers, 159-60; dams on, 41-44; Hood River, 82; longest and shortest, 7; Snake River, 73; whitewater kayaking and river running, 201-3; wild and scenic, 203; Willamette River, 7, 206
roads and highways, 160-61, 185; Columbia River Gorge, 167; scenic drives, 166-69; speed limits, 173
rocks and gems, 161-63; state, 7, 180, 181
rodeos, 163-64

Salem, 164-65; performing arts, 141
salmon, 165-66. *See also* fish; fish hatcheries
scenic drives, 166-69. *See also* roads and highways
science museums, 115-16
seal, state, 181
seals and sea lions, 169. *See also* aquariums
seashell, state, 7, 181
senators: state, 95; U.S., 32
shellfish, 57. *See also* fish
shipwrecks, 169-71
shrubs, 147
skiing, 171-72
smallest cities, 27
Snake River, 73
snakes, 17-18
Sno-Parks, 172
snowboarding, 171-72
snowfall. *See* weather and climate
soccer, 174-75
song, state, 7, 181
special service districts, 173-74

speed limits, 173
sport fishing, 57-58
sports teams: PAC-10, 138-39; professional, 173-75
state: agencies and departments, 68-71; animal, 7, 180; archives, 18; bird, 7, 180; capital, 7, 165; dance, 180; fish, 7, 180; flag, 180; flower, 7, 180; gemstone, 7, 180; government, 68-71; House of Representatives, 95-97; insect, 7, 181; libraries, 98-99; motto, 7; nickname, 7; nut, 7, 181; officials, 46-47; parks, 175-80; recreation areas, 175-80; rock, 7, 181; seal, 181; seashell, 7, 181; Senate, 93-95; song, 7, 181; symbols, 180-81; taxes, 181-83; tree, 7, 181
Steens Mountain, 21
stream miles, 7
sturgeon, 57
sunstone, 162, 180
symbols, state, 7, 180-81

taxes, 181-83; licenses, permits, and fees, 183; local government, 182-83; statewide, 181-82
television stations, 156-57
temperatures, 200; highest and lowest, 7, 200. *See also* weather and climate
The Dalles, 16, 183
theater. *See* performing arts
thundereggs, 162-63
tides, 183-84
Tillamook Burn, 7, 64
Tillamook Naval Air Station Museum, 7
timber, harvests, 7, 63. *See also* forest products industry; trees
tourism, 188
trade: international, 86-87; waterborne commerce, 185; wheat-exporting status, 7. *See also* exports
Trail Blazers, 173-74, 175
trains, 157-59; Talgo, 158
transportation, 184-87, air travel, 184-85; map, 186-87; public transit, 185; railroads, 185; roads and highways, 185; waterborne commerce, 185
travel and tourism, 188
treasure, lost, 104-5
tree(s), 147; ancient stumps, 62; commercial species, 61-62; harvested, 7, 63; state, 7, 181. *See also* forests; forest products industry; lumber; timber
tribes: federally recognized, 15-16; tribal courts, 90. *See also* American Indians

Umatilla Chemical Depot, 108-9
universities and colleges, 188-93; community colleges, 188-90; libraries, 100; PAC-10, 138-39; private, 190-91; public, 191-93; Willamette University, 192
Upper Klamath Lake, 7
urbanization, 148

Vanport, 27
vehicle registration, 193
vital statistics, 193-94
volcanoes, 194-96; major, 196; Mount Mazama, 194; Newberry Crater, 130-31; scenic drives, 169
voting and elections, 196-98; voter turnout, 197

wages, 110
wagon prints, 134
water area, 7
waterfalls, 31, 198-99; highest, 7; Multnomah Falls, 198; Willamette Falls, 206
weather and climate, 199; temperatures, 200
western fence lizard, 17
wetlands, 199, 201
whales, endangered and threatened, 47-48
whitewater kayaking and river running, 201-3
wild and scenic rivers, 203. *See also* rivers
wilderness, 204-6; Kalmiopsis Wilderness, 205; map, 120-21. *See also* national forests; national parks
wildflowers, 147-48; endangered and threatened, 48-49. *See also* plants
wildlife refuges, 128-30; map, 120-21. *See also* animals
Willamette Falls, 206
Willamette River, 206; length, 7
Willamette University, 192
Willamette Valley, 206; state parks, 178-79; wineries, 208-10
windsurfing, 206-7
wine, 207-11; festivals, 210-11; wineries, 208-10
Winterhawks, 174

zip codes, 211-16
zoos, 216